THE HISTORY OF
THE KINGS OF BRITAIN

broadview editions
series editor: L.W. Conolly

THE HISTORY OF
THE KINGS OF BRITAIN

Geoffrey of Monmouth

edited and translated by Michael A. Faletra

broadview editions

Library and Archives Canada Cataloguing in Publication

Geoffrey, of Monmouth, Bishop of St. Asaph, 1100?–1154

The history of the kings of Britain / Geoffrey of Monmouth ; edited and translated by Michael A. Faletra.

Includes bibliographical references and index.

ISBN 978-1-55111-639-6

1. Great Britain—History—To 1066. 2. Great Britain—Kings and rulers. 3. Celts—Folklore. I. Faletra, Michael A., 1972– II. Title.

DA140.G4 2007   942.01   C2007-905247-9

Broadview Editions

The Broadview Editions series represents the ever-changing canon of literature by bringing together texts long regarded as classics with valuable lesser-known works.

Advisory editor for this volume: Colleen Franklin

Broadview Press is an independent, international publishing house, incorporated in 1985. Broadview believes in shared ownership, both with its employees and with the general public; since the year 2000 Broadview shares have traded publicly on the Toronto Venture Exchange under the symbol BDP.

We welcome comments and suggestions regarding any aspect of our publications–please feel free to contact us at the addresses below or at broadview@broadviewpress.com / www.broadviewpress.com

North America
PO Box 1243, Peterborough, Ontario, Canada K9J 7H5
Tel: (705) 743-8990; Fax: (705) 743-8353
email: customerservice@broadviewpress.com
2215 Kenmore Ave. Buffalo, NY, USA 14207

UK, Ireland, and continental Europe
NBN International
Estover Road
Plymouth PL6 7PY UK
Tel: 44 (0) 1752 202 300
Fax: 44 (0) 1752 202 330
email: enquiries@nbninternational.com

Australia and New Zealand
UNIREPS, University of New South Wales
Sydney, NSW, 2052
Australia
Tel: 61 2 9664 0999; Fax: 61 2 9664 5420
email: info.press@unsw.edu.au

The interior of this book is printed on 100% recycled paper.

PERMANENT   100%

PRINTED IN CANADA

Contents

Acknowledgements

The years spent working on this edition were certainly not passed in isolation. Though Geoffrey of Monmouth has been dead for over eight hundred years, he loomed constantly in my thoughts and often constituted an almost tangible presence as I construed his Latin into English. I can only hope I have not met with his complete disapproval. In a more direct way, the staff at Broadview Press have facilitated this project in countless ways, large and small, and I especially want to thank Julia Gaunce and Marjorie Mather, as well as all the press's anonymous reviewers who have greeted this project with care and interest. I am also grateful to Reed College for endowing me with the Ruby Grant that got this translation off the ground, and to the University of Vermont for providing the professional development funding to see it through. Gail Sherman, Jeff Westover, Lisabeth Buchelt, Jolanta Komornicka—good comrades and fine critics all—did me an inestimable service by reading drafts of the manuscript. I have also benefited from the advice, interest and support of numerous colleagues, especially Jacques Bailly, Karen Bondaruk, Laurie Broughton, Anne Clark, Mary Crane, Diana Cruz, Wally Englert, Maureen Harkin, Val Rohy, Dick Schrader, Robert Stanton, Lisa Steinman, David Townsend, Mark Usher, and Chris Vaccaro. And I am especially grateful to my parents, Charlie and Peggy Faletra, for everything they have done. But my greatest debt by far is to my wife, Annie Lighthart, who has been a perpetual support to me through these long months, reading countless drafts, weathering my irascibility, and giving me the priceless gift of time. Through her patience and diligence she has proven more than ever to be my best reader and my best friend. To her, and to our son Sam, this book is lovingly dedicated.

Introduction

If the Middle Ages had a bestseller, surely Geoffrey of Monmouth's *History of the Kings of Britain* (*Historia Regum Britannie*) was it. While more canonical medieval texts like *Beowulf* and *Sir Gawain and the Green Knight* are extant in only a single manuscript apiece, *The History of the Kings of Britain* survives in 215 manuscripts dating from the twelfth to the sixteenth centuries, a number that confirms its status as one of the most popular non-religious texts in medieval Europe. From its first appearance around 1138, the book's narration of the deeds of the ancient Britons, the Celtic people who inhabited Britain before the advent of the Anglo-Saxons, has appealed to kings and bishops, poets and courtiers, knights and scholars. Written for Anglo-Norman patrons amid the gathering winds of an imminent English civil war, *The History* traces the continuity of the British kingship from its origins in ancient Troy to its eventual failure in the face of Saxon invasions. Although his subject matter was insular in nature, Geoffrey's work proved compelling enough to be found in most of the courts and monastic houses throughout Europe, and was translated or adapted into Old French, Middle English, Old Icelandic, and other languages; it even made it as far east as Poland. As one of the first texts to appear at the dawn of the print era, it was later available to influence such English writers as Edmund Spenser, Michael Drayton, Thomas Heywood, John Milton, John Dryden, and Lord Tennyson. Raphael Holinshed's *Chronicles*, the major historical source for Shakespeare's plays, also derives its early history of Britain from Geoffrey of Monmouth. In fact, Geoffrey narrates some of the oldest existing accounts of King Lear, Cymbeline, and even Old King Cole. Most importantly, he provides the first complete narrative of the reign of King Arthur, precipitating a literary vogue that would flourish throughout the remainder of the Middle Ages and survive into the twenty-first century.

Despite its immense and persistent popularity, controversy has followed Geoffrey's book almost since its inception. Twelfth-century man of letters Gerald of Wales joked that readers of the book would summon demons to their obviously erroneous souls, while William of Newburgh, a contemporary historian, deemed Geoffrey's book an insidious collection of lies and damned lies, especially those parts of it that dealt with the spurious King Arthur. Even many of the writers who translated *The History* into other languages routinely omitted and rewrote sections of

Geoffrey's allegedly authoritative account of the pre-Saxon British past. Indeed, when one subjects the book to the kind of scrutiny employed by modern historians, it is easy to see why it generated so much hostility. Geoffrey's accounts of the insular past frequently contradict earlier and more respected historians, and many of the episodes he narrates are fanciful at best and strain historical credibility, even by medieval standards. The prophecy given to Brutus by the goddess Diana in Book One, for instance, is more redolent of classical pagan epic than scrupulous Christian chronicle, as is the gripping tale of how King Arthur slays a giant atop Mont-St.-Michel, which reads more like a romance than a history. Geoffrey himself does little to assuage the skeptical reader: he claims that his source is an ancient book in the British language—something none of his Norman audiences could possibly read, if the book even existed in the first place—and thus allows himself the historiographic space to tell the often glorious history of the Britons as he sees fit. Whether consciously or not, Geoffrey offers his readers far more in the way of fiction than historical fact, and it is perhaps as a work of literary achievement that the text can best be analyzed. However, despite—or perhaps because of—the text's tenuous claims to veracity and its questionable historical method, *The History of the Kings of Britain* nonetheless weaves an engaging narrative that has captivated readers for almost nine hundred years.

Geoffrey of Monmouth in Twelfth-Century Britain

Twelfth-century Norman Britain was a polyethnic state. Officially, the French-speaking Normans, themselves the descendants of Scandinavian Vikings, had conquered the Germanic Anglo-Saxon people at the momentous Battle of Hastings on October 14, 1066. The land over which they took control, however, was far from ethnically homogeneous, nor did it immediately become Francophone territory.[1] The Anglo-Saxons whom the Normans displaced had in the fifth and sixth centuries themselves displaced an earlier group, a Celtic people known as the ancient Britons. The descendants of those Britons who were not slain or assimilated retreated to the western parts of Britain, where they became the Welsh and Cornish, retaining their Celtic culture and languages into the twelfth century and beyond. There were other ethnic groups to be found in

---

[1] Referencing Geoffrey of Monmouth, Jeffrey J. Cohen provides a fascinating study of how such ethnic tensions played out on a local level in "The Flow of Blood in Medieval Norwich," *Speculum* 79 (2004): 26–65.

Norman Britain as well: in the far north were the Picts and Scots, in the midlands of England there were still many Scandinavians, descendants of the Danish Vikings whom Alfred the Great had settled there in the ninth century. In the wake of the Conquest, the Normans had brought over from the Continent either as allies or mercenaries small but significant populations of Jews, Flemings, and Bretons. Finally, though the Normans had dispatched the English soundly at Hastings, their territorial ambitions were not limited to England alone, and they had begun to colonize and conquer Wales from as early as 1081. It is useful to view Geoffrey of Monmouth's *History of the Kings of Britain* against the backdrop of this political and ethnic complexity, for the work explicitly discusses the relationships between peoples—especially the Britons and Anglo-Saxons—and their respective claims to political dominance over the island.

Geoffrey himself was born probably around 1090–1105, the generation after the Norman Conquest, in the town of Monmouth, which was situated on the borderlands of the Welsh territories that the Normans were now intent on annexing. The Normans established many of their allies from Brittany in Monmouthshire around this time, and it is likely that Geoffrey's father, Arthur, was one of these Breton settlers, possibly even a kinsman of Wihenoc, the new Breton lord of Monmouth. Culturally and linguistically, the Bretons and Welsh were closely related, both, in fact, descendants of the Celtic Britons. The Breton and Welsh languages, moreover, were sufficiently similar (though not completely mutually comprehensible) to allow some limited types of communication between them. From childhood, then, Geoffrey benefited from the cultural situation in Monmouth; he was probably at least bilingual in Breton and Norman French, and he doubtless was exposed to many local Welsh customs and legends as well. However, despite the fact that some scholars think that Geoffrey's Breton ancestry and championing of the ancient Britons (especially King Arthur) make him a pro-Welsh writer, one should remember that Geoffrey's patrons were never Welshmen but always members of the Anglo-Norman elite.[1] Geoffrey's appointment to

---

[1] For three variant views, see the discussions in J.S.P. Tatlock, *The Legendary History of Britain: Geoffrey of Monmouth's Historia Regum Britanniae and Its Early Vernacular Versions* (Berkeley: U of California P, 1950); E.M.R. Ditmas, "Geoffrey of Monmouth and the Breton Families in Cornwall," *Welsh History Review* 6 (1973): 452–61; and John Gillingham, "The Context and Purposes of Geoffrey of Monmouth's *History of the Kings of Britain*," *Anglo-Norman Studies* 13 (1990): 99–118. Finally, Michelle Warren's *History on the Edge: Excalibur and the Borders of Britain, 1100–1300* (Minneapolis: U of Minnesota P, 2000) explores the implications of Geoffrey's book as an instance of "border writing."

the tempestuous bishopric of St. Asaph's in Wales in 1152, confirms this, since it was a position unlikely to be granted to one whose loyalty to the Norman overlords of Britain was ever in question.

As a Breton, it is possible that Geoffrey may, however, have felt that he occupied a precarious position in the context of Anglo-Norman colonial ambitions in Wales, retaining a certain degree of sympathy for his fellow Celts in the face of Norman encroachments on their territory. We can discern from *The History of the Kings of Britain* itself that Geoffrey certainly admired the achievements of the British ancestors of the Welsh. More than any other writer, medieval or modern, he provides for the Britons the outline of an illustrious past, a history peopled with wise kings and bold warriors. It is a testament to Geoffrey's achievement that the Welsh themselves translated his Latin *chef d'œuvre* back into Welsh, and the resulting Welsh *Bruts* (as these translations were called) effectively became one of the cornerstones of subsequent Welsh historical traditions. On the other hand, *The History of the Kings of Britain* concludes with the ancient Britons decisively defeated by the Anglo-Saxons, their remnant degenerating into an inferior people. As Geoffrey explains: "Through their habitual barbarity, they were no longer called Britons but 'Welsh,'" and he repeats the standard Anglo-Saxon derivation of the word "Welsh" as meaning "foreigner, slave." Although Geoffrey's *History* apparently plays to both sides, its last laugh is certainly against the Welsh.

An examination of the scant documentary evidence we possess of Geoffrey reveals little definitive evidence as to the precise purposes behind his *magnum opus*, but we can confirm that from at least the 1120s, Geoffrey had moved away from the borderland town of his birth and was moving comfortably in elite Anglo-Norman circles. After spending at least some of his youth in Monmouth or the vicinity, he eventually took up residence in the town of Oxford, where his name appears in seven charters dating from 1129 to 1151. Based on the context of these charters, it is reasonable to suppose that Geoffrey may have belonged to the College of St. George, a religious foundation of Augustinian secular canons; such a position would certainly be compatible with his penchant for scholarship.[1] Although the university that would later grace Oxford had not yet been founded, the town was already an administrative center as well as a nexus for some of the new scholastic thought that was emerging from the Continent. Indeed, Michael

---

[1] Michael Curley, *Geoffrey of Monmouth* (New York: Twayne, 1994), 2.

Curley has identified the men in Geoffrey's circle in Oxford as "some of the most influential and learned men of twelfth-century England."[1] Among Geoffrey's acquaintances there we can include Alexander, the Bishop of Lincoln, to whom in 1135 Geoffrey dedicated *The Prophecies of Merlin*, which originally was published independently of *The History* proper; Robert de Chesney, the man who succeeded Alexander in 1148 and to whom Geoffrey dedicated his last work, *The Life of Merlin*; Ralph of Monmouth, a canon of the cathedral school at Lincoln; and probably Robert de Warelwast, the Bishop of Exeter, who was known to patronize antiquarian interests. Geoffrey may also have personally known the Welshman Caradoc of Llancarvan, whose *Life of Gildas* evinces an interest in the insular past similar to Geoffrey's.[2] However, none of these men was more influential on Geoffrey's career than Walter, the Archdeacon of Oxford and Provost of St. George's College. It was Walter who allegedly gave to Geoffrey "a certain very ancient book in the British language" (*quondam Britannici sermonis librum vetustissimam*), the putative source of *The History of the Kings of Britain* and a subject of endless debate among students of Geoffrey's work (see the discussion below). Walter of Oxford and Geoffrey seem to have been close associates and probably friends, sharing a common interest in the British past.

Our last glimpses of Geoffrey in the existing charters suggest that this very interest in the British past may have had certain material benefits: Geoffrey became the bishop-elect of the new See of St. Asaph's in North Wales, a bishopric created by the Normans as a means of consolidating their power in that region. Basil Clarke surmises that Geoffrey's appointment to this post was overtly political, for he was consecrated as bishop on 24 February 1152, a mere eight days after being first ordained a priest.[3] The rapidity of his ordination and advancement suggests that Geoffrey was evidently a trusted man in the eyes of the Anglo-Norman authorities and that his elevation to the bishopric was an indirect reward for services rendered. Around this same time, Geoffrey composed his final work, *The Life of Merlin* (*Vita Merlini*),[4]

---

[1] Curley 3.

[2] Curley 4. Geoffrey in fact gives Caradoc as a reference to readers who wish to learn about British history subsequent to the close of *The History of the Kings of Britain*. It seems less likely, in my opinion, that Geoffrey had the personal acquaintance of either William of Malmesbury or Henry of Huntington, two contemporary historians whom he references far less warmly at the conclusion of *The History*.

[3] Basil Clarke, ed., *The Life of Merlin: Geoffrey of Monmouth's Vita Merlini* (Cardiff: U of Wales P, 1973), 34.

[4] *The Life of Merlin* is included in Appendix B of this volume.

which draws upon a much deeper knowledge of Welsh traditions than anything in *The History*, especially in its presentation of additional prophecies by the title character. In this work, Merlin laments the wars that are tearing the country apart and anticipates a time of peace and prosperity. A stable Norman regime, Geoffrey implies, achieves precisely this. What the evidence from Geoffrey's biography makes abundantly clear, then, is that Geoffrey of Monmouth felt comfortable among both his fellow *literati* as well as the Anglo-Norman elite, who seem to have received his works with attention and approval.

Although Geoffrey may thus have enjoyed the privileges of healthy patronage later in his life, the complexities of power struggles in Britain may have early on inspired in him a studied ambivalence in regard to Anglo-Norman politics. This would have been of particular advantage in the turbulent 1130s, the very decade in which he was composing *The History of the Kings of Britain*. His masterpiece emerges on the literary scene in Britain at the moment of its greatest social turmoil since the Conquest. The death of King Henry I in 1135, a ruler who was greatly feared and respected, had led to a dispute over the succession. Henry himself had named his daughter Matilda, his only surviving legitimate child, as heir to the throne; naming a female heir was, of course, unprecedented. Taking advantage of discontent among the barons over this unusual situation, Henry's nephew Stephen seized the opportunity and, sailing over from the Continent, declared himself king. The Anglo-Norman aristocracy was divided in its loyalties, and by the year 1141 a civil war had broken out between King Stephen's faction and the supporters of Matilda. Geoffrey, from everything we can tell, was in the process of composing *The History of the Kings of Britain* at precisely this period, 1135–1138. While an all-out civil war had not yet broken out by the time he completed his work, it must have loomed large in the public consciousness. In a certain sense, it is fruitful to read Geoffrey's history as an attempt at reconciliation, a warning against weakening the kingdom through internal dissension. Numerous episodes of fraternal discord and internecine warfare throughout *The History* drive this point home, perhaps none more poignantly than the story of King Leir and his daughters. Unlike in Shakespeare's later version of this story (for which Geoffrey's *History* was an indirect source), the faithful Cordelia triumphs over her sisters and then rules wisely for many years, a positive example, perhaps, of the virtues of legitimate inheritance over more tenuous claims to the throne.

Although it is difficult to ascertain where Geoffrey's own political sympathies lie, the majority of those manuscripts of *The History* that still include an opening epistle are dedicated to Robert Earl of Gloucester, the illegitimate son of Henry I and half-brother of Matilda. This dedication, as well as, in some manuscripts, an additional "double dedication" to Waleran Beaumont, the Count of Mellent, suggests that Geoffrey's patrons were of the camp loyal to Matilda and supporters of her claim to the throne. The story of Leir and Cordelia would carry a special urgency in this context, as the female Cordelia's right to rule is trumpeted there. However, the political tide in the 1130s shifted often, and we cannot ultimately claim that Geoffrey's dedications reflect anything more than the savvy marketing of an aspiring writer.[1] One single manuscript—the very one, in fact, of which the present edition is a direct translation—includes a dedication to King Stephen himself. It does not resolve the matter to realize that the last time Geoffrey's name appears as a witness is as bishop-elect on the 1153 Treaty of Westminster, the document that ratified the peace between King Stephen and Henry Plantagenet, Matilda's son, who would the next year succeed to the throne as Henry II.[2] When Geoffrey of Monmouth died in 1155, he had lived long enough to see this new and ambitious king ascend to the throne and offer Britain the potential for peace and unity that, as author of a work that so often warns against the dangers of kingdoms divided, Geoffrey probably long felt it needed.

The Sources and Composition of *The History of the Kings of Britain*

To defer credit for one's scholarly work upon some earlier authority was a trope in the Middle Ages, a development, perhaps, of the humility topos. Indeed, medieval readers would be suspicious of any work of literature or history that did not cite some legitimate (and preferably recognizable) authority. This practice led to some writers actually inventing fictitious authorities for their works. Wolfram von

---

[1] Laurie Finke and Martin Shichtman's observations about Anglo-Norman patronage and Geoffrey's history as "symbolic capital" are particularly apt. See Laurie A. Finke and Martin B. Shichtman, *King Arthur and the Myth of History* (Gainesville: UP of Florida, 2004), esp. 46–70.

[2] Michael Curley provides an excellent overview of all the relevant biographical information in *Geoffrey of Monmouth* (New York: Twayne, 1994), 1–10. Another useful review of the documentary evidence can be found in J.E. Lloyd, "Geoffrey of Monmouth," *English Historical Review* 57 (1942): 460–68.

Eschenbach, for example, claims that his highly original Grail romance *Parzival* was a translation of an earlier romance by one "Kyot the Provençal." Geoffrey Chaucer similarly claims that his *Troilus and Criseyde* is a translation into English of the Troy story as told by Dares and Dictys, though we know that he in fact based his version largely on Boccaccio's *Teseida*. Geoffrey of Monmouth's claim, then, that *The History of the Kings of Britain* is a *translation* of the "certain very ancient book in the British language" given to him by his associate Walter of Oxford should therefore be subject to considerable scrutiny.[1]

When one looks closely at Geoffrey's *History*, it becomes clear that the work is not a translation at all but a finely-woven composite of a number of texts of varying historical value. In retrospect, Geoffrey's claim to be *translating* Walter's British book seems a convenient fiction. It is more likely either that Walter's book contained not the continuous narrative that Geoffrey presents but a collection of miscellaneous historical materials, or that Geoffrey simply invented the book altogether in order to bolster his text's authority as a legitimate witness to the past. In any case, four major objections render Geoffrey's claim untenable as it stands. First, if Walter's book ever did exist, it is highly improbable that so few close parallels would appear anywhere else in any antecedent written Welsh traditions, given the scope and depth of the material this purported British book contained. One need only compare a few pages of the Welsh *Mabinogion* (roughly contemporary with *The History*) or the oldest Welsh triads to see that the historical material presented by Geoffrey has little in common with the bardic, heroic, gnomic, and semi-mythological literature that was actually being composed in Wales in the sixth through twelfth centuries. Secondly, there is a good deal of circumstantial evidence to suggest that Geoffrey's Welsh was not very good. Though he seems at least to have had a grasp of basic vocabulary, *The History* contains too many faulty etymologies and too many misspelled Welsh names for us to trust Geoffrey's claim to fluency in that language (or an earlier version of it).[2] A third point against Geoffrey's claim to have translated an ancient British book is that, in the century or so that followed the publication of *The History*,

---

[1] See, however, the thoughtful argument of Geoffrey Ashe, "'A Certain Very Ancient Book': Traces of an Arthurian Source in Geoffrey of Monmouth's *History*," *Speculum* 56 (1981): 301–23.

[2] Some see Geoffrey's translation of Welsh place-names as proof enough that he was fluent in the language. See, for example, T.D. Crawford, "On the Linguistic Competence of Geoffrey of Monmouth," *Medium Aevum* 51 (1982): 152–62.

Geoffrey's work was itself retranslated into Welsh. There are, in fact, dozens of Welsh renderings of *The History*. While these Welsh *Bruts* have not yet been sufficiently catalogued and classified, what scholarship has been published confirms the fact that Geoffrey's *History* quickly became historical fact for the medieval Welsh, displacing older traditions. Surely, if the contents of Walter's ancient book were legitimate, and therefore already in circulation, there would be no need for the Welsh *Bruts* to rely on Geoffrey's questionable history.

The final and most persuasive argument against Geoffrey's claim to be translating Walter's book rests in precise verbal parallels with three well-known Anglo-Latin texts. Specifically, certain passages in *The History* draw upon the sixth-century polemicist Gildas as well as the eighth-century Anglo-Saxon historian Bede and the ninth-century Welsh historian known as Pseudo-Nennius (hereafter simply Nennius) in ways that are too striking to be coincidental. In fact, Geoffrey borrows episodes wholesale from these three writers and quotes Gildas and Bede almost verbatim at certain points.[1] Surely, if he were working with a genuine "ancient British book," his re-translation of the book from Welsh or Breton and then back into Latin would certainly not conform word-for-word to passages from these earlier Anglo-Latin and Cambro-Latin historians. A close analysis of *The History*, moreover, reveals that Geoffrey not only directly quotes these earlier writers but that he breaks up their narratives and, to use a modern analogy, "cuts and pastes" bits and pieces of them throughout his own work, often in ways that destroy or obscure the context and meaning of the original. Therefore, in addition to the fact that Geoffrey's ancient British book is largely an invention, it seems that his *History* does not even conform with any reasonable accuracy to established and authoritative historical accounts.

If needed, we could easily dismiss Geoffrey's *History* as a hoax or forgery. Not only did his source not exist (at least not in the form he implies), but almost everything Geoffrey says about the pre-Saxon period has been soundly discredited. However, it seems unlikely that Geoffrey was a prankster of the lowest sort, and it is therefore reasonable to try to evaluate his work by standards different from those of modern historians. For example, we might interpret his statement regarding his source more liberally, seeing his claim to be *translating* the ancient book as a

---

[1]   See especially Neil Wright, "Geoffrey of Monmouth and Gildas" in *Arthurian Literature* 2 (1982): 1–40, and "Geoffrey of Monmouth and Bede," *Arthurian Literature* 6 (1986): 27–59.

loose and misleading way of saying that he had access to a book or books potentially containing old documents or histories in Old Welsh (or some other "British" language, such as Cornish or Breton). Indeed, unless we wish to conjecture that Walter of Oxford was in on a hoax, we can assume that he did give Geoffrey some kind of collection of antiquarian documents or short tales in Welsh. Many scholars suppose such a miscellany, if it existed at all, to have contained a collection of regnal lists, old charters, short legends or saints' lives, rather than a single narrative history like Geoffrey's.[1] Whether the book existed at all, and whether it was even his main source, Geoffrey certainly made a creative use of whatever materials regarding the insular past that were available to him. As mentioned above, these would have included Gildas, Bede, and Nennius. The number of *The History's* other likely sources is enormous, revealing Geoffrey's broad reading and again making it improbable that a single ancient British book was his only source. These likely sources include a set of royal Welsh genealogies, similar to the ones contained in a number of Old and Middle Welsh manuscripts; the tenth-century *Welsh Annals* (*Annales Cambriae*); Caradoc of Llancarvan's *Life of Gildas* and other saints' lives, such as the legend of St. Ursula; William of Malmesbury's *Deeds of English Bishops* and *The Deeds of the Kings of the English*; the Old French *Gormont et Isembard*, an eleventh-century *chanson de geste*; and at least one Welsh, Cornish, or Anglo-Latin political prophecy attributed to the legendary Merlin. Finally, *The History of the Kings of Britain* is strewn with occasional references, quotations, or verbal echoes drawn from Geoffrey's reading of such classical authors as Caesar, Martial, Juvenal, Cicero, Apuleius, and Statius—all of whose works would have been part of a typical liberal arts education in the twelfth century.[2] Virgil's *Aeneid* and Livy's *Ab Urbe Condita* provide less tangible but deeper and more pervasive classical influences.

If Geoffrey's *History* is, in fact, more a tightly woven collection of folklore, epic, and fragments of earlier histories than modern scholars might deem a genuine account of the past, how can we begin to evaluate his narration of British history? Examination of Geoffrey's loose

---

[1] Of particular interest in this regard is the theory proposed by Christopher Brooke that the *Book of Llandaff*, a miscellany of Welsh charters, etc., may have been composed by Geoffrey. See C. Brooke, "The Archbishops of St David's, Llandaff, and Caerleon-on-Usk," in *Studies in the Early British Church*, ed. Nora K. Chadwick (Cambridge: Cambridge UP, 1958), 201–42.

[2] Geoffrey's reading of later Latin writers such as Augustine, Orosius, Boethius, and Landulphus Sagax also cannot be discounted.

adaptation of his three major verifiable historical sources—Gildas, Bede, and Nennius—brings into particular relief many of the innovative emphases of *The History of the Kings of Britain* and helps us toward a better understanding of Geoffrey's work. Pseudo-Nennius, who was probably a ninth-century Welshman, seems to have influenced Geoffrey in the most overt way, providing the basic framework (and perhaps even the inspiration) for Geoffrey's entire work: Nennius's *History of the Britons* (*Historia Brittonum*) narrates the foundation of Britain by a Trojan exile named Britto (whom Geoffrey replaces with the more classical-sounding Brutus) and sketches the history through the Roman occupation and Saxon invasions before concluding with brief accounts of Arthur and certain early English and Welsh kings. As we read *The History of the Kings of Britain*, we can see Geoffrey at work reworking and expanding much of this Nennian material, especially augmenting Nennius's terse description of Arthur with details derived from folklore, saints' lives, topography, and doubtless his own imagination. The result is an Arthur who dominates Geoffrey's narrative, as well as much subsequent romance. While this composite Arthur is, in a sense, entirely Geoffrey's own, the king's place within the larger frame of the history is provided by Nennius. Other significant areas where Geoffrey relied heavily on Nennius include his accounts of the figures of Merlin (called Ambrosius in the *History of the Britons*) and the traitorous King Vortigern.

Geoffrey's borrowings from the Venerable Bede's *Ecclesiastical History* (*Historia ecclesiastica gentis Anglorum*) are far more limited, appearing almost entirely in the final two books of *The History*. In relating the history of the Celtic Britons, Geoffrey's project is, in a way, antithetical to that of Bede, who extols the virtues of the Christianized Anglo-Saxons; Geoffrey's British protagonists are Bede's heterodox antagonists. Moreover, as much as he draws upon Bede, Geoffrey is also committed to rewriting Bede's version of history, and he in fact extends the British tenure of the island some two hundred years in order to downplay the achievements of the Saxons and provide more space for the development of his own theme.[1]

In contrast, Geoffrey complements rather than competes with the polemic Gildas. Gildas' *Ruin of Britain* (*De Excidio Britanniae*) records in brief the history of the island during and after the Roman occupation, but his main objective is invective. As he upbraids the ancient Britons

---

[1]   Such is R. William Leckie's cogent argument in *The Passage of Dominion: Geoffrey of Monmouth and the Periodization of Insular History in the Twelfth Century* (Toronto: U of Toronto P, 1981).

for their arrogance and countless other sins, he depicts the invasions of Britain by the Scots, Picts, and Saxons as God's righteous vengeance upon an unrepentant people. Gildas also turns his attention to contemporary petty-kings, warning them that their sins might once again prove the undoing of their nation. Geoffrey draws on Gildas rather heavily in his account of the Roman withdrawal from Britain and for the names and details of King Arthur's sixth-century successors.[1] His most important borrowing from Gildas, however, lies in his adoption of Gildas' pessimistic view of British history. Like Gildas, Geoffrey narrates the ruin of the Britons (though, unlike Gildas, he sees little hope for their revival after the death of the last king, Cadwallader). The rhetoric of Gildas' moral condemnations thus infects Geoffrey's text at crucial moments. He quotes Gildas almost verbatim at points during the withdrawal of the Roman legions in Book Six or the reign of Malgo in Book Eleven, but a Gildas-like tone also informs many of the prophecies of Merlin as well. Generally speaking, the prophetic and Biblical tone of the Gildasian voice supplies Geoffrey the appropriate rhetoric with which to narrate the tragic downfall of the Britons, whose ruin, Geoffrey infers, is well-deserved.

Yet despite Geoffrey's substantial reliance upon these three historians, the vast majority of the material covered in *The History of the Kings of Britain* is attested in no surviving source. It is, of course, likely that Geoffrey simply conjured many episodes out of his own imagination, either to bridge gaps in the timeline of his narrative or to provide compelling anecdotes or descriptions. For example, many of the details of battles (which are numerous in *The History*) are not found in the chronicles of the day, and Geoffrey instead probably modeled them vaguely after the often gory descriptions of war in the French *chansons de geste*. Countless other episodes seem to draw loosely from Welsh folklore or documentary materials, but it is unlikely—if Geoffrey did draw upon any other Welsh or Anglo-Latin texts—that these texts are extant today. Nevertheless, we have enough knowledge of the Welsh accounts of the insular past that *were* in circulation in the twelfth century to confirm that Geoffrey draws fairly heavily, though randomly, upon similar materials.[2] Many of Geoffrey's characters are mentioned in the ample

---

[1] One should note, however, that Arthur is never mentioned by Gildas, a fact that most historians take as a sign of his non-existence.

[2] See Rachel Bromwich, ed., *Trioedd Ynys Prydein: The Triads of the Island of Britain,* 3rd ed. (Cardiff: U of Wales P, 2006); and Brynley Roberts, "Geoffrey of Monmouth and the Welsh Historical Tradition," *Nottingham Medieval Studies* 20 (1976): 29–40.

body of extant pre-twelfth-century Welsh literature, though they are often similar to Geoffrey's in name only. Several of the kings (Dunwallo Molmutius, Gorbonianus, Belinus, etc.) appear in the surviving Old Welsh princely genealogies and many of the other kings bear names that are at least patently Welsh (Guithelin, Eliud, Idwal, Peredur, etc.). The catalogue of King Locrinus's fifty children in Book Two is practically a handbook of contemporary Welsh names, as is the list of the nobility who attended Arthur's plenary court in Book Ten. The fragments of folklore contained in the Welsh triads, which were terse groupings of legendary material used as a mnemonic by bards, also suggest that Geoffrey may have been reworking native materials. For example, the triads allude briefly to a rich tradition of stories regarding the fateful Battle of Camlann, which Geoffrey describes at the beginning of Book Eleven. The triads attest it as one of "the three Futile Battles of the Isle of Britain," and as the scene of one of "the three Unfortunate Counsels of the Isle of Britain." Other triads mention heroic characters that were present at or survived the Battle of Camlann but are otherwise unknown. The triads thus reveal an entire network of native traditions about the insular past. In dealing with such legend and with local folklore, whether Welsh, Cornish, English or possibly even French, Geoffrey likely faced an embarrassment of riches. *The History of the Kings of Britain* is, in a way, as much a testament to the abundance of native tales about the insular past as it is a revision of them.

In the end, one can see that Geoffrey's relationship to his sources is omnivorous: he gleaned information rather indiscriminately from a variety of sources in order to provide the ancient Britons with the cohesive narrative history he felt they deserved. As his deep (if sometimes spotty) familiarity with the various Welsh traditions suggests, Geoffrey may have gathered a good deal of information for *The History* in the field. His upbringing makes it natural that he would be familiar with local folklore in the area around Monmouthshire, but he also seems to have known London well and shows a more than passing familiarity with Cornwall and southwest Wales, especially the areas around Tintagel and Caerleon.[1] In cases such as these, we can see one of Geoffrey's characteristic creative methods at work, for he seems to have invented stories and even kings to account for whatever information he encountered. The locale of Billingsgate mentioned in Book Three provides a typical example of this

---

[1]   See Tatlock 58–65; and Oliver Padel, "Geoffrey of Monmouth and Cornwall," *Cambridge Mediaeval Celtic Studies* 8 (1984): 1–27.

method in action. Knowing that a Billingsgate existed in twelfth-century London, for example, Geoffrey infers from the "Billings-" a fictional king named Belinus who must have built the gate, thankful in this particular instance that his reconstructed king's name also happens to correspond to Beli Mawr, a prominent figure in several of the early Welsh genealogical tracts. Having thus "invented" this king, he likewise reconstructs a plausible story for why the king built this particular gate—see Book Three of *The History* for the full story. Similarly, Geoffrey conveniently reveals a King Leir who founded Leicester, a King Coel who founded Colchester, a Queen Marcia who composed the so-called "Mercian" law code, and a Sabrina after whom the River Severn is named. Geoffrey may occasionally have even completely invented a particular episode. (I am personally suspicious of his account of King Bladud, who learns to fly, and of Merlin's transferral of Stonehenge from Ireland to Britain.) Again, although we can never know precisely to which traditions Geoffrey had access, it seems clear that he was dealing with a surplus of information and that he added, deleted, compressed, embellished, and rearranged as he deemed fit. Whatever Geoffrey's use of oral or written native traditions concerning the pre-Saxon past, scholars will continue to identify and interrogate the sources we do have—unless, that is, Geoffrey's alleged "certain very ancient book in the British tongue" ever turns up.

The History of the Kings of Britain

In attempting to enumerate the list of Geoffrey's source materials, one marvels not only at the range of Geoffrey's reading and the deftness of his skills as an editor and *compositeur*, but also at his stunning originality. As he weaves back and forth among his source materials—both oral and written—Geoffrey constructs a narrative with a grand vision in which the whole is far more than the mere sum of the parts. Indeed, more than just the haphazard accumulation of events that is real life or "real history," Geoffrey's *History* inheres as a series of interconnected thematic movements that narrate, in broad terms, the story of the rise and fall of the ancient Britons. The sequence of the history is steady and linear; Geoffrey rarely indulges in anecdote or digression. Yet the narrative movement is not monotonous, for it is punctuated periodically by colorful episodes or particularly weighty events. The British conquest of Rome in Book Three is one of these, as is the Roman occupation of Britain. Two figures, however, dominate the second half of Geoffrey's *History* in ways that dwarf all the other events and characters: the prophet/magician Merlin and the renowned King Arthur. Many, indeed, read Geoffrey of Monmouth solely for his account of these two, a practice that, while understandable, ignores the significance of these figures within the text as a whole. Only by comprehending the broader structures and themes of a narrative that relates events dating from the fall of Troy (c. 1200 B.C.E.) to 689 C.E. can one accurately assess the importance of any of the individual characters or events within it.

The first books of *The History* deal with the founding of Britain by a band of Trojan exiles under the leadership of Brutus and with the reigns of the earliest kings. Although Geoffrey adapts Brutus from Nennius, his account of the foundation of Britain contains thematic echoes from many classical sources, especially Virgil's *Aeneid* and Livy's *Ab Urbe Condita*. Whatever his influences, Geoffrey creates a myth of foundation for Britain, and he supplies his myth with all the requisite tropes: a man unjustly exiled, a period of wandering throughout the Mediterranean, and a divine prophecy—put into the mouth of the pagan goddess Diana—that finally leads, in true Biblical fashion, to the Promised Land of Britain. Of course, just as the Hebrews had to deal with the Caananites and other inhabitants of Palestine, so do the Trojans need to face the aboriginals, who here take the form of giants. Indeed, the climax of Book One can be said without much exaggeration to be the wrestling match between the robust Trojan Corineus and the leader of the giants, Gogmagog. Only after Corineus casts Gogmagog off a cliff and into the sea is the foundation of the realm complete, and only then is the island's name fittingly changed from Albion to Britain, after Brutus himself.

If the foundation of Britain is mythical, it is also violent, and it is precisely this tension between political stability and violence that characterizes much of the rest of the book. In fact, much of one's interpretation of *The History of the Kings of Britain* as a whole will rest upon whether one believes that Geoffrey is extolling the great works and deeds of the ancient Britons or denouncing their lamentable tendency toward internecine strife. The early books of *The History* give us plenty of founders and weighty deeds: Brutus's three sons establish Scotland, Wales, and Logres respectively; King Lud founds London; King Coel founds Colchester; King Leir founds Leicester; King Belinus founds Caerleon; King Dunwallo codifies the Molmutine Laws; and Queen Marcia creates the law code adopted centuries later by King Alfred. Good kings build cities, pave roads, and maintain the laws. Bad kings, on the other hand, quarrel with their vassals or their own kin. The story of Leir provides the most moving example of this, and its narration in Book

Two foreshadows later fraternal quarrels between Ferreux and Porrex, Belinus and Brennius, and others. It also adumbrates the events that lead to the ultimate downfall of Britain, especially the betrayal of Arthur by his kinsman Mordred. Despite the many ways in which Geoffrey repeatedly courts ambiguity elsewhere in the text, this much is clear: a kingdom that is united, as Britain was under Arthur or after the reconciliation of Belinus and his brother, is strong enough to conquer even Rome. A kingdom divided against itself, as Britain is in the wake of Caesar's invasion, will fall. The story of King Elidur in Book Three illustrates this point admirably: Elidur assumes the throne after the nobility deposed his tyrannical brother Archgallo. Coming across his now bereft brother in a forest five years later, Elidur takes Archgallo in out of brotherly devotion and contrives his return to the throne. Elidur's selfless dedication redeems Archgallo, who rules wisely to the end of his days. In this case, the integrity of the family underlies the integrity of the kingdom, a lesson of relevance to Geoffrey's own contentious day.

By far, most of *The History* is dedicated to the rulers of the island, some of whom are little more than names, though there are many compelling characters and episodes embedded throughout the text. But *The History* is also dedicated to narrating the transference of divinely-ordained power (*imperium*) from the Celtic Britons to their Germanic Anglo-Saxon successors.[1] Within the text, the usurper Vortigern provides the agency through which the passage of dominion commences; it is he who invites a band of Saxons led by Hengist and Horsa to serve as mercenaries in his own grab for power, though this hired army soon proves unmanageable, treacherous, and nearly impossible to extirpate. While providing the blow-by-blow account of which Saxon murders which king in true chronicle fashion, Geoffrey also furnishes his narrative with a more effective means of eliding this historical transition by introducing the figure of Merlin. Nearly as enigmatic as Geoffrey himself, the boy Merlin possesses magical powers and prophesises to Vortigern in a series of predictions that occupy almost all of Book Seven. This Merlin is based loosely on the figure of Ambrosius from Nennius, though Geoffrey changes the name in order to associate the character with an Old Welsh bard named Myrddin. This Myrddin putatively lived in the sixth century, but as time passed a number of prophetic poems in Welsh began to be attributed to him. The oldest of these that still survives, the *Armes Prydein*,

---

[1] For more on this aspect of *The History*, see Robert Hanning, *The Vision of History in Early Britain from Gildas to Geoffrey of Monmouth* (New York: Columbia UP, 1966).

dates from around 930 C.E., but the tradition was still alive in Geoffrey's own day. The Old Welsh Merlinic prophecies are explicitly political and their general message could not be clearer: they anticipated the day when the foreign Saxons would be uprooted from British soil and the island would revert to native Celtic rule.[1] While this must have seemed somewhat of a lost cause by Geoffrey's day, the prophecies of Merlin, perhaps because of their impressive rhetorical force, still evoked considerable interest in twelfth-century Norman audiences, who sought to legitimate their historical position as heirs to the dominion of Britain.

To most modern readers (and, frankly, to most medieval readers as well) *The Prophecies of Merlin,* a version of which Geoffrey had apparently written and circulated separately prior to the publication of *The History,* initially make little sense.[2] While it is currently unclear whether Geoffrey based the prophecies directly on a Latin or Welsh original, he certainly did little to ensure their proper interpretation. They are rife with animal imagery, astrological references, jeremiads, and opaque symbolism. If the host of medieval attempts to interpret the prophecies teaches us anything, it is that the prophecies themselves remained far from clear.[3] The first sequence of the prophecies, the so-called "Omen of the Dragons," proves the easiest to gloss: the Red Dragon (the Britons/Welsh) will rise from near-defeat to triumph over the White Dragon (the Saxons). This prediction, while simple enough, occupies only the first paragraph of the prophecies, which continue for another fifteen pages or so. One can discern (or trick oneself into thinking one discerns) references to events that will occur later in the text as well as historical events that seem to apply to Geoffrey's own day. The various medieval commentators agree almost universally, for example, that the Boar of Cornwall is King Arthur and that the Lion of Justice represents the Norman King Henry I. As one moves through the prophecies, however, even tentative interpretations such as these become more difficult, while the imagery takes a markedly

---

[1] One of the finest of these prophecies, *The Apple Trees,* is included in Appendix B. For an excellent overview of the Old Welsh prophecies, see A.O.H. Jarman, "The Merlin Legend and the Welsh Tradition of Prophecy," in *The Arthur of the Welsh,* ed. Rachel Bromwich et al. (Cardiff: U of Wales P, 1991), 117–45.

[2] Michael Curley, 48–74, has provided a clear and plausible explication of the prophecies, though we should be wary of taking even Curley's interpretation as representing Geoffrey's original meaning.

[3] I have argued elsewhere that they are deliberately obscurantist; see "Narrating the Matter of Britain: Geoffrey of Monmouth and the Norman Colonization of Wales," *The Chaucer Review* 35 (2000): 60–85. See also Julia Crick, "Geoffrey of Monmouth: Prophecy and History," *Journal of Medieval History* 18 (1992): 357–71.

apocalyptic turn. In the end, it is hard to know what to make of the prophecies at all.

We do know, however, that the initial circulation of *The Prophecies of Merlin* earned Geoffrey considerable repute and that many later readers of *The History* found Merlin's predictions in Book Seven a compelling read. They were even translated into Old Icelandic, and many spurious variants circulated in Middle English and other vernaculars for the remainder of the Middle Ages. Although the meaning of specific predictions will doubtless always elude us, it is easier to gauge their impact on *The History* as a whole. The prophecies, first and foremost, imply the idea that the future is, in some sense, pre-existent, and that its patterns are knowable by human beings. In regard to the history of Britain specifically, we can see that Geoffrey's placement of Merlin and his prophecies at a point very shortly after the advent of the Saxons provides a commentary on this historical transition. The sense of loss and anxiety engendered by the Germanic newcomers is balanced (or even elided) by the idea that history pre-exists and that it seems to fall into patterns. This is perhaps a meager consolation in the face of a pagan barbarian invasion, but the general obscurantism of the prophecies allows for any number of interpretations that might be more directly consoling or favorable to any particular reader. For example, a twelfth-century Welsh prince could read the prophecy "the island shall be called by the name of Brutus and its occupation by foreigners shall pass away" as a promise that the Normans, having vanquished their age-old enemies, the Saxons, would soon withdraw and leave the island under native control. A Norman bishop, on the other hand, might read the apocalyptic imagery at the end of the prophecies as a sign that the Normans would rule Britain until Judgement Day. In either case, the prophecies encourage the reader to take a larger interest in the teleology of events past and present. Finally, the prophecies promulgate the figure of Merlin as the authority on the interpretation of events and the meaning of history. Merlin's appeal perhaps led Geoffrey later in his life to compose his long hexameter poem *The Life of Merlin* (*Vita Merlini*).[1] This work, composed around 1150, presents further information about the prophet that Geoffrey likely gleaned from native Welsh sources. It describes Merlin's fall into a prophetic madness after a disastrous battle in which his lord is killed, as well as Merlin's subsequent sojourn in the wilderness. Most importantly, it presents several new prophecies—some

---

[1]   A new translation of Geoffrey's *Life of Merlin* appears in Appendix B of the present volume.

of them uttered by Merlin's sister Ganieda—that likewise engage readers and simultaneously defy easy interpretation. As with his initial appearance in *The History of the Kings of Britain*, Merlin thus again serves Geoffrey as a potent symbol for his own authority as a narrator of the past and, implicitly, as a shaper of future visions.[1]

Although the character Merlin perhaps most pointedly engages our understanding of Geoffrey as a historian and self-made authority, his King Arthur (whose life story takes up almost a fifth of the entire history) has proven to be of even greater interest to readers over the centuries. Arthur, like Merlin, acts as a bridge within the history between the advent of the Saxons and the downfall of the Britons. By focusing so closely on the figure of Arthur, Geoffrey revises Bede's simple account of the passage of dominion from morally reprobate Britons to Christianized Anglo-Saxons by positing one final and glorious reign of British greatness before the fall.

Geoffrey's Arthur is culled from a variety of sources, most obviously Nennius, but probably also from many oral Welsh folktales regarding this fabulous king and his entourage. Like the other admirable kings in *The History*, Arthur possesses "extraordinary prowess" (*probitas*)[2] as well as goodness (*bonitas*) and an unparalleled sense of generosity (*largitas*); also like previous strong kings, Arthur rebuilds cities and churches and confirms the validity of the laws. However, Geoffrey has done far more with the figure of Arthur than any of his predecessors, whether historians or oral storytellers: he situates his most exemplary of kings at a critical historical juncture, slowing down the pace of the narrative considerably to reflect the import of the events now unfolding. After a generation of Saxon occupation, it is King Arthur who vanquishes the foreigners and restores all of Britain to truly native rule. In part, Geoffrey was taking his cue from Nennius, who similarly sees Arthur as a vanquisher of Saxons. But where Nennius states that the defeated Saxons merely sent for reinforcements, Geoffrey makes Arthur's victories usher in an entirely new, albeit brief, era. After defeating the Saxons at Mount Badon, Arthur turns his attention to the perennially rebel-

---

[1] On Merlin as a figure for Geoffrey's authority, see Kimberly Bell, "Merlin as Historian in *Historia Regum Britanniae*," *Arthuriana* 10 (2000): 14–26.

[2] Geoffrey seems to reserve the Latin term *probitas* for a characteristic of the best of rulers. Difficult to translate, the semantic range of *probitas* spans from "probity" (its English descendant) to "prowess, courage," and "sense, wisdom" and even "temperance, moderation." I have translated *probitas* throughout in these various ways, according to the emphasis for which the text seemed to call at each given point.

lious Picts and Scots, subduing them easily before then conquering Ireland, Norway, Denmark, and Iceland. Expanding this nascent northern European empire, Arthur moves into France as well, defeating the Roman tribune Frollo in single combat. ·

The description of the plenary court at Caerleon that Arthur holds to celebrate these triumphs marks the pinnacle of the history of the ancient Britons as well as, in many ways, the climax of the book. First of all, it marks King Arthur as a figure of international repute, a British figure to rival the French Charlemagne or even Alexander the Great; as Geoffrey puts it, "There did not remain one prince of any merit on this side of Spain who did not attend this court when summoned. And this is no wonder, for Arthur's generosity was renowned all over the world, and this made all men love him" (175).The plenary court is also significant for the ways in which it both nods at previous traditions regarding Arthur while simultaneously inaugurating new ones. The long list of the nobles and knights in Arthur's service is a case in point, for it strongly resembles similar enumerations of Arthur's men in Welsh texts such as *Culhwch and Olwen*. At the same time, Geoffrey's presentation of an Arthur who presides over a band of worthy men anticipates the King Arthur of the French romances, which would be written down a generation or so after Geoffrey's. Indeed, many names that will be familiar to any student of Arthurian romance are present with Geoffrey's Arthur in Caerleon, including Gawain, Bedivere, Kay, Loth, and Urian.[1] The plenary court also appealed to the later romancers in its depiction of a court at play; at Arthur's court there are tournaments and jousting and other entertainments. Lastly, Geoffrey provides what is probably the first narrative record of "courtly love" in reference to the ladies of Arthur's court, who "would only grant their love to a man who had thrice proven his worth in battle. They were therefore made all the more chaste and the men all the more virtuous out of love for them" (176).

Geoffrey must have been aware of the rarity and fragility of moments of peace and political stability, for no sooner do the Britons attain the pinnacle of their cultural flowering at Arthur's plenary court, than that peace is threatened by angry demands from the Emperor of Rome. King Arthur's response is, one supposes, predictable: after one of his close advisors upbraids the court for its idleness, the king mobilizes his forces for war and the wheels of Geoffrey's history begin turning again in earnest.

[1]   Lancelot is absent and does not appear in any extant romances until Chrétien de Troyes's *Chevalier de la charrette* (c. 1180). Likewise, the Round Table only makes its first literary appearance in the *Roman de Brut*, Wace's Old French translation of *The History* (c. 1155).

Though Arthur is triumphant against the Romans, his victory is fruitless because of the same domestic unrest that, Geoffrey shows, has always plagued the Britons, this time in the form of the king's nephew Mordred, who has usurped the throne and committed adultery with Guinevere, the king's wife. The outcome of these events is well-known to audiences. Arthur defeats Mordred but is himself mortally wounded. Geoffrey curiously hedges his bets at this point, however. While in one sentence he states that the king is "mortally wounded," in the next he claims that Arthur is brought to the isle of Avalon to be healed. It would remain to later writers to interrogate the meaning of these lines. For his part, Geoffrey never mentions the idea that Arthur will return. Instead, he follows the downward trajectory of British history in the wake of Arthur's death. Indeed, as the narrative pace picks up again in the final book of *The History*, one is reminded that even King Arthur, in all his glory, is only a small part of a much larger story, the story of the rise—and inevitable fall—of the British people.

The ending of *The History of the Kings of Britain* forces one to make interpretive decisions, and it is precisely here that Geoffrey's characteristic ambiguity proves the most frustrating. Given the dismal end he provides for the Britons, one wonders whether he was ever on their side in the first place. The last British king, Cadwallader, fights an uphill battle in trying to wrest the island back from the Anglo-Saxons, who, having become Christians, are now far too difficult to villainize. The result of his efforts is a message from an angel of God, who tells him, in unequivocal terms: "God did not want the Britons to reign in Britain any longer, not before the day that Merlin had foretold to Arthur should arrive." Of course, *The History* contains no such prophecy; according to Geoffrey, Arthur and Merlin never even meet! It may not be too facetious to suggest that the Angel's condition amounts to saying "when hell freezes over." Geoffrey's brief account of the subsequent actions of the Britons certainly does not recommend them to any such privilege. In contrast to the Anglo-Saxons, who are now tilling the land and establishing churches and cities (as the exemplary British kings once did), the Britons themselves—in their "habitual barbarity"—retreat into the backwaters of the island and become the Welsh. As Geoffrey states in what are almost the last words of the entire book: "Having degenerated from the nobility they had enjoyed as Britons, the Welsh never again regained the kingship of the island. They instead persisted foolishly in their quarrels with the Saxons or among themselves and were hence constantly engaged in foreign wars and civil unrest" (217). The history of the ancient Britons and their kings dies not with a bang but a whimper, and supporters of the theory that Geoffrey of Monmouth held pro-Celtic sympathies, or even that he was a Welsh patriot, would do well to recall these final comments on the Britons. Despite Geoffrey's notorious ambiguity, and despite his apparent admiration for the ancient Britons—especially King Arthur—his *History of the Kings of Britain* would surely have found a warmer welcome among the Norman masters of Britain than among any of their conquered subjects, Saxon or Celt.

Truth and Reception

Although Geoffrey of Monmouth makes highly creative use of the sources available to him, fashioning a work with striking literary qualities, the historiographic impact of *The History of the Kings of Britain* cannot be underestimated, for the book essentially expands the narrated history of the isle of Britain by over a millennium. This achievement is even more remarkable when one considers the boldness of some of Geoffrey's inventions. Most audaciously, Geoffrey attributes to dark-age Britain an Arthurian empire that spanned much of western Europe (an empire entirely ignored by all previous historians). He also altered insular history to provide the ancient Britons with an additional two-hundred-year tenure, shifting the traditional date for the passage of dominion from the Britons to the Anglo-Saxons from 449 C.E. to 689 C.E.[1] Although a few of Geoffrey's near-contemporaries expressed some skepticism regarding the truth-status of *The History*, his account was accepted in the main, and his version of the insular past remained authoritative both in Britain and on the continent for the next several hundred years. Geoffrey's history proved the basis for almost all the English chroniclers from the thirteenth century on, and it was cited (and often mis-cited) to support dynastic claims and diocesan boundaries. It likewise supplies the basic understanding of the British past for medieval writers such as Geoffrey Chaucer, William Langland, the Gawain-poet, and even Sir Thomas Malory. Indeed, it was only after the Renaissance humanists applied the burden of proof to *The History of the Kings of Britain* that the book was generally deemed unreliable.

In light of the liberties that *The History* takes with established historical tradition and the bald inventiveness of some of its material, scholar Valerie Flint has suggested that *The History of the Kings of Britain* was

---

[1] Leckie 70–72.

composed as a deliberate parody of the new types of national histories being written by Geoffrey's contemporaries, men such as William of Malmesbury and Henry of Huntington.[1] On the one hand, it is true that Geoffrey references both of these writers in the conclusion to his work, defiantly declaring that his own history surpasses theirs in the antiquity of the material he is able to cover. It is also true that Geoffrey's *Historia* successfully achieves the same scope—and often the same feel— as the chronicles of his contemporaries. While the case can certainly be made that Geoffrey is therefore parodying medieval historiography *per se*, it seems more likely that he was instead writing history not as it could be reliably reconstructed from the documentary evidence (as William and Henry attempt to do) but history as he believes it should have been: vast in scope, high in drama, grand in vision—history, as we might put it today, as literature.

Although the distinction between fact and fiction in the Middle Ages could often be a blurry one, Geoffrey's work differs from the typical medieval chronicle in ways even a casual reader notices.[2] Most obviously, its range and pace are quite different. While William's *The Deeds of the Kings of the English* and Henry's *History of the English* both cover events from roughly the advent of the Saxons to the present (a period of approximately six hundred years), Geoffrey's *History of the Kings of Britain* traverses over double this period, beginning with the fall of Troy (c. 1200 B.C.E.) and continuing through to the seventh century of the Common Era: about 1900 years of history in all. Despite this scope, *The History* almost never feels rushed, and Geoffrey does an excellent job of maintaining a relatively constant pace throughout. Whereas William and Henry, as diligent historians, justly allow the sometimes plodding deeds of history to be their guides throughout, Geoffrey feels no such compunction; his coverage of material that was completely unknown to his contemporaries allowed him instead to pace the work as he saw fit.[3] The results may, in the end, be a matter of personal taste. A reader

---

[1] Valerie Flint, "The *Historia Regum Britanniae* of Geoffrey of Monmouth: Parody and Its Purpose. A Suggestion," *Speculum* 54 (1979): 447–68. In a similar vein, see Nancy Partner, *Serious Entertainments: The Writing of History in Twelfth-Century England* (Chicago: U of Chicago P, 1977).

[2] Monika Otter discusses twelfth-century fictionality and facticity in specific reference to Geoffrey of Monmouth in *Inventiones: Fiction and Referentiality in Twelfth-Century English Historical Writing* (Chapel Hill: U of North Carolina P, 1996).

[3] Unlike Geoffrey, I by no means intend to disparage William of Malmesbury, Henry of Huntington, or a score of other medieval chroniclers; their works are certainly compelling in ways that the more literary Geoffrey of Monmouth is not.

of William of Malmesbury can walk away from *The Deeds of the Kings of the English* having learned the detailed politics that led up to the Norman Conquest, for instance, and he may have gained from William a number of keen insights about the character and even physical appearance of William Rufus or Alfred the Great. Geoffrey's readers will be treated to far less verisimilitude. Geoffrey's style is less strictly mimetic: we never even learn what King Arthur looks like, and the motivations behind historical events bear far more resemblance to the impassioned desires of the characters in a *chanson de geste* or an epic like the *Aeneid* than to medieval *Realpolitik*. While William of Malmesbury and Henry of Huntington occasionally treat the reader to colorful anecdotes illustrating the manners and mores of the English court or recount dreams or omens portending some momentous event, Geoffrey gives us instead the story of the seduction of the wicked King Vortigern by a pagan princess as well as "actual" speech of King Arthur to his men before his battle against the Romans. It must have been easy for certain readers, such as the later historian William of Newburgh, to dismiss *The History* as romantic nonsense and Geoffrey as a prank. But time has proven the best judge. Today Geoffrey of Monmouth is far more widely read than his more reliable contemporaries.

By far, Geoffrey's most significant contribution to medieval ideas about the past lies in his account of King Arthur. Unlike his more sober predecessors, Geoffrey presents Arthur as a completely historical figure, as real as Alfred the Great or Julius Caesar. He even fixes Arthur's reign around a specific historical date (542 C.E.), a synchronization he rarely provides for his other kings. In contrast, the earliest British historians, Gildas and Bede, never even mention Arthur, let alone the celebrity of his court or the glory of his conquests. This historiographic absence has led modern historians to conclude, quite reasonably, that King Arthur never existed and that he is more an accretion of legend and half-truths that was propelled into "fact" by Geoffrey of Monmouth. Even the ninth-century *History of the Britons* describes Arthur only as a general (*dux bellorum*) and tells us little more than the names of his twelve battles against the Saxons. And while it is true that Arthur appears as a king in Welsh tales like *Culhwch and Olwen* from at least the tenth century, these Welsh traditions treat him as a fantastic hero whose verisimilitude would be unsatisfying by modern (and some medieval) standards. Only in *The Legend of St. Goeznovius*, a Latin saint's life of Breton origin dated tentatively at 1019 C.E. is Arthur mentioned (in passing) as someone whose existence is taken for granted (see Appendix C). One twentieth-century scholar, Geoffrey Ashe, posits that some legitimate Arthurian historical material underlies Geoffrey's "ancient book in the British tongue," identifying Arthur with a real fifth-century Romano-British general named Riothamus who waged a couple of successful campaigns in Gaul. However, Ashe's thesis, while tantalizing, is ultimately unprovable. What is certain is that Geoffrey of Monmouth—in defiance of earlier historians—debuts a King Arthur whose illustrious exploits have the veneer of being historically true. This "real" King Arthur flourished in the Middle Ages and persists in some circles into the present.

Much of the response to Arthur in particular and *The History of the Kings of Britain* in general was enthusiastic in Geoffrey's own century. In January 1139, the scholar Henry of Huntington famously marveled at the scope and breadth of *The History*. Within the first few years of its existence, copies of *The History* spread throughout Britain and France and perhaps beyond, and by 1155 there were already two translations into Old French verse: Geffrei Gaimar's *Estoire des Bretuns* (now lost) and Wace's famous *Roman de Brut*. The earliest English translation appeared around the turn of the thirteenth century in the form of Layamon's *Brut*. Wace's *Roman de Brut*, completed around 1155 and presented to King Henry II's court, proved the most influential of these translations. Audiences seemed particularly captivated by the figure of King Arthur, and, by the end of the twelfth century, the *matière de Bretagne*, the so-called Matter of Britain that was practically invented by Geoffrey of Monmouth, was the rage throughout much of Europe, from Italy to Iceland. Thus medieval writers such as Marie de France, Chrétien de Troyes, and Wolfram von Eschenbach owe at least an indirect debt to Geoffrey of Monmouth. While the more sedentary king of the Arthurian romances often bears only a passing resemblance to *The History*'s robust Arthur, we can still claim that Geoffrey of Monmouth inaugurated a genre that, to judge by recent films and the fantasy sections in bookstores everywhere, is still vibrant.

Not all of the reaction to Geoffrey of Monmouth was positive, however, as the writers represented in Appendix D of this volume demonstrate. Several years after *The History*'s publication in 1138, the Cornish scholar John of Cornwall published his own Latin version of the prophecies of Merlin, desiring perhaps to clarify and explain where Geoffrey had remained silent. Gerald of Wales, who lived a generation or so after Geoffrey, had a characteristically ambivalent attitude toward *The History of the Kings of Britain*. At one point in his *Journey Through Wales*, he insists that *The History* is nothing but falsehoods and fabrications. On the other hand, Gerald himself uses Geoffrey in passing as a historical source on several different occasions. He also evinced a particular interest in Geoffrey's *Prophecies of Merlin* and spent considerable time in search of other versions of the prophecies throughout Wales. Gerald's slightly later contemporary, the historian William of Newburgh, was less sanguine about Geoffrey of Monmouth's work. He considered it to be blatantly and probably deliberately untrue, and he especially condemned *The Prophecies of Merlin* as a piece of chicanery that carried no veridical force. William's comments were influential, and were quoted verbatim by the later scholars of the sixteenth and seventeenth centuries, men such as the humanist Polydore Vergil and the antiquarian William Camden. To these later writers, Geoffrey's *History* simply did not hold up to careful scrutiny. Most troublesome to them was the fact that the account of the British past that Geoffrey provides was, with the exception of details culled directly from authoritative sources such as Gildas and Bede, simply not verifiable, and it was not difficult to find contradictions between Geoffrey and other, more patently reliable historians. Nonetheless, at least one extremely influential English historian, Raphael Holinshed, mined Geoffrey for information in the compilation of his famous *Chronicles*. Had Holinshed followed the advice of his more sober contemporaries, we might now be deprived of such famous Shakespearean characters as Cymbeline, Cordelia, and Lear.

Since the Renaissance, and especially since the end of the Tudor dynasty, the claims to the throne of which rested in general terms on Geoffrey's account of British history, Geoffrey of Monmouth's status as a historian has suffered drastically. However, the value of *The History of the Kings of Britain* as "the food and drink of poets" (to use Geoffrey's own words) has been constant. Although John Milton famously abandoned his plan to write an English epic based on King Arthur (he wrote *Paradise Lost* instead), *The History*'s legend of Habren and the Severn River (Book Two) underlies his masque *Comus* (1634). When Alfred, Lord Tennyson, undertook his great Arthurian epic, *The Idylls of the King*, he relied not just on Malory's *Morte Darthur* but turned also to much of the antecedent material in the Galfridian tradition. Other nineteenth-century British writers such as Sir Walter Scott and Thomas Love Peacock were also familiar with Geoffrey's work, but the real resurgence of interest in *The History of the Kings of Britain* came in the twentieth century, hand-in-hand with the positivist pursuit of the origins of the Arthurian legends. While some scholars continue to mine *The History* for traces of facts regarding dark-age Britain, the use of

Geoffrey's book as a source for fiction writers desiring to explore the "historical" King Arthur is on the rise. Most notable of these is Rosemary Sutcliff, whose novel *Sword at Sunset* relies heavily on *The History* in its attempt to avoid the romantic post-Malory tradition and narrate a plausibly realistic Arthurian story. Other writers have followed in her wake, including Mary Stewart, Stephen Lawhead, and Bernard Cornwell. Finally, the modicum of interest in the "historical" King Arthur evinced in modern films such as *Excalibur* relies ultimately on Geoffrey's account of the period.

Despite its detractors over the centuries, Geoffrey of Monmouth's *History of the Kings of Britain* achieved enormous success both as fact and as fiction. Indeed, it is precisely its fusion (deliberate or not) of legend with truth, of invention with history, that supplies its perennial appeal: it offers readers a chronicle with an epic valence as well as a fictional narrative with all the trappings of historical verisimilitude. In this sense, the bearing away of King Arthur to be impossibly healed of a mortal wound in Avalon serves as the text's paradigmatic episode. It narrates the "historical fact" of the end of a glorious reign while simultaneously promising—albeit obliquely—a transcendence of the limits of history itself. Like Arthur, the ancient Britons and their deeds have the potential to live again in the minds of readers. Geoffrey of Monmouth's masterpiece thus ensures its own immortality by providing the kinds of truth that history too often fails to provide.

Geoffrey of Monmouth: A Brief Chronology

c. 1090–1105 Geoffrey is born in Monmouthshire, England.

1100 Henry I becomes King of England upon the death of his brother William II in a hunting accident.

1120 Prince William, son of Henry I and the only legitimate male heir to the throne of England, dies in a shipwreck on the English Channel.

1129 Geoffrey first appears in Oxford records, where he is probably a secular canon of the College of St. George.

1135 King Henry I dies. His nephew, Stephen of Blois, seizes the throne of England, displacing Matilda, Henry's daughter and legal heir.

c. 1135 *The Prophecies of Merlin* first published.

1136 The Welsh openly rebel against Norman rule. Morgan and Iorwerth ap Owein seize Norman castles at Caerleon and Usk. The Welsh make inroads against the Normans in south and central Wales as well.

c. 1138 *The History of the Kings of Britain* first published.

1139 The Anglo-Latin historian Henry of Huntington is impressed on finding *The History of the Kings of Britain* in the Norman abbey of Bec. Open civil war breaks out in England between the supporters of King Stephen and those of Matilda.

c. 1140-1150 An unknown (perhaps Welsh) redactor composes the Variant Version of Geoffrey's *History*.

1142 In an attempt to capture Matilda, King Stephen lays siege to Geoffrey's home city of Oxford.

c. 1145 Geffrei Gaimar bases his now lost Old French verse chronicle, *L'Estoire des Engleis*, on *The History of the Kings of Britain*.

c. 1150 Geoffrey composes his *Life of Merlin*.

1152 Geoffrey is appointed Bishop of St. Asaph's in North Wales, a position he never occupies.

1153 Geoffrey witnesses the Treaty of Westminster that ratifies the peace between Stephen and Matilda.

c. 1153 John of Cornwall publishes his *Prophecy of Merlin*, at least partially in response to Geoffrey's Merlinic prophecies.

1154   At Stephen's death, Henry Plantagenet, the son of Matilda, becomes King Henry II of England.

1155   Death of Geoffrey of Monmouth, according to a Welsh chronicle. Master Wace's Old French verse translation of *The History of the Kings of Britain* is completed.

A Note on the Text

The following translation is based on Bern Burgerbibliothek MS 568, a manuscript of Norman provenance from the late twelfth, or perhaps very early thirteenth century, now thought to represent the best single text of Geoffrey of Monmouth's *Historia regum Britannie*. The Latin text has been edited by Neil Wright (Cambridge: D.S. Brewer, 1984). I have also consulted Acton Griscom's edition of the Cambridge MS (London: Longmans, 1929), as & Green well as *The First Variant Version*, ed. Neil Wright (Cambridge: D.S. Brewer, 1988) and the printed Middle Welsh translation, *Brut Dingestow*, ed. Henry Lewis (Cardiff: U of Wales P, 1974). The present translation is the first to render the Bern MS in its entirety and thus the first to benefit from the monumental textual, archival, and bibliographical work done by Neil Wright and Julia Crick in the 1980s.

The issue of book divisions is one that has always vexed editors of Geoffrey of Monmouth. Throughout the present text I have retained in brackets the chapter numbers applied by Neil Wright to the Bern MS, hoping to facilitate reference to the Latin original and to allow readers to compare individual chapters to their corresponding passages in *The First Variant Version*, to which Wright has applied an identical numeration. However, a text of this length intended for general audiences as well as scholars can benefit from other sorts of division. For this task, previous editors have provided little guidance, and the manuscript tradition evinces no clear organization. The Bern MS has no book divisions at all, and the other earliest manuscripts, if they do possess book divisions, do not agree on whether *The History* should consist of four, nine, ten, eleven, or twelve books; a division into eleven books is the most prevalent (though by no means pervasive) practice in many of the most important early manuscripts.[1] However, we will, sadly, probably never know how Geoffrey originally intended his book to be divided, and all divisions by modern editors are thus at some level misleading. On the basis of several influential manuscripts, Acton Griscom in his 1929 edition of the Latin text partitioned Geoffrey's work into twelve books, while Lewis Thorpe in his 1966 translation breaks the narrative into

---

[1] Julia Crick summarizes the evidence for book-divisions in the early manuscripts in *The Historia Regum Britannie of Geoffrey of Monmouth IV: Dissemination and Reception in the Later Middle Ages* (Cambridge: D.S. Brewer, 1991), 152–53.

eight chapters, which he sees as corresponding to the text's major narrative movements. In the interest of at least maintaining a consistency with the ample body of literary scholarship of *The History* that has cited Griscom's edition, I have retained Griscom's twelve-book division.

While I aim at providing an accurate but readable text in this translation, I have especially tried to avoid the archaisms of previous translations yet still maintain some sense of the differences in verbal register within the text. The character of Merlin, for example, speaks in a markedly more formal register than the other characters, as does the narrator when reproducing letters or engaging in a Gildas-inspired invective. In order to make Geoffrey of Monmouth's long and heavily-subordinated Latin sentences more palatable to the modern reader, I have habitually split up longer sentences into shorter ones; in this I have followed the practice of the previous translator, Lewis Thorpe. I have done so not only for ease of comprehension, but also to avoid giving the impression that Geoffrey was a particularly ornate or imposing writer, the Henry James of the twelfth century. Geoffrey's Latin prose is, like Bede's, lucid and elegant, but it lacks the classical rhetorical luster of Gildas as well as the cold precision of a writer such as his contemporary Peter Abelard. Although Geoffrey himself professes to be writing in a "humble style," I can assure my readers that any lapses in eloquence in the translation that follows are entirely my own.

THE HISTORY OF
THE KINGS OF BRITAIN

DEDICATORY EPISTLE

[1] Tossing around a great many ideas, I set my mind on the history of the kings of Britain. But I noted in wonder how little I could discover on the subject beyond what Gildas and Bede wrote about in their splendid works.[1] And I could find nothing at all about the kings who lived here before the incarnation of Christ, not even about Arthur and the many others who succeeded him, though their deeds are worthy of everlasting fame and are joyfully recited out loud by the many people who know them by heart.

[2] While I was preoccupied by these matters, Walter the Archdeacon of Oxford, a man most expert in the art of oratory and in arcane histories, presented me with a certain very ancient book in the British language, which narrated in the most refined style an orderly and unbroken relation of the acts of all the kings, from Brutus the first king of the Britons to Cadwallader the son of Cadwallo. So I began at Walter's request to translate that book into Latin, content with my own lowly style and not seeking to gather gilded expressions from other writers' gardens. It would certainly annoy my readers if I attempted to render the original in flowery speech, since they would dwell more on unraveling my words than on understanding the history itself.[2]

[3] Therefore, Stephen, King of England, accept my little book and let it be set aright by your learning and probity so that it may no longer be considered the work of Geoffrey of Monmouth but instead the product of your own sagacity. Let it be published as the work of one whose uncle was the illustrious Henry, King of the English, of one accomplished in philosophy and the liberal arts, and of one whose innate prowess in war has put him in command of our armies. Britain now salutes you with such tender affection as if it had been blessed with a second Henry.[3]

---

[1] Gildas was the author of *The Ruin of Britain* (*De excidio Britanniae*), composed around 540. The great historical work of the Anglo-Saxon monk Bede (c. 673–731), *The History of the English Church and People* (*Historia Ecclesiastica Gentis Anglorum*), was the most well-known of Geoffrey's historical sources.

[2] Geoffrey perhaps alludes here to the highly decorous phraseology of Gildas, his historiographical predecessor.

[3] The Bern MS is the only extant manuscript to include this dedication to King Stephen, and the general scholarly consensus is that this dedication represents a displacement of Geoffrey's original dedication to Robert, the Earl of Gloucester (see below).

[4] You too, Earl Robert of Gloucester, who are the other pillar of our realm, should lend your effort to my task, so that this work will benefit marvelously from the guidance you both provide.[1] Because you too are sprung from that illustrious King Henry, Mother Philosophy has welcomed you to her bosom and has instructed you in the subtleties of her various arts. Moreover, in order to have you excel in military deeds amid our armies, she has brought you to the war-camps of kings, where, following in your father's footsteps, you have valiantly outdone all your comrades and have proven a terror to your enemies and a defender of your friends. Being such a loyal protector of your friends, welcome into your patronage your very own poet along with this book, which was written for your enjoyment. Only then, reposing under the shelter of such spreading boughs and far from the presence of the jealous and craven, shall I be able to play the reeds that truly belong to you, my muse, in perfect measure.

---

[1]   Robert of Gloucester (c. 1090–1147), the illegitimate son of King Henry I, was one of the most powerful magnates in England and a supporter of his half-sister Matilda's claim to the English throne. In most other manuscripts of *The History of the Kings of Britain*, Geoffrey makes the first dedication (made to King Stephen, above) to Robert of Gloucester, while reserving this second dedication to Waleran (1104–66), the Count of Meulun, another powerful baron.

BOOK ONE

[5] Britain is the best of isles, situated in the western ocean between France and Ireland.[1] Stretching eight hundred miles north to south and two hundred miles east to west, it supplies ceaseless abundance for every human necessity. It is rich in every type of metal and likewise has wide fields and hills, which are well-suited for widespread agriculture. The soil in its richness brings forth many types of crops, each in its proper season. The island also has forests filled with all types of wild beasts and pastures filled with domestic animals and with all colors of flowers that offer their nectar to the flying bees. It also possesses the greenest fields stretching pleasantly beneath lofty mountains, in which sparkling waters flow by in sweetly murmuring streams, promising sweet slumbers on their banks. Moreover, Britain is watered with lakes and rivers full of fish, and on its southern edge by a channel over which one can sail to France.

Three noble rivers—the Thames, the Severn, and the Humber—extend like three arms, bringing in the commerce of the sea from all countries. Twenty-eight cities once adorned the land. Some of these cities, their walls leveled, now lie in ruin; in others, still standing, there tower high the most beautiful steepled churches of the saints, in which groups of religious men and women give praise to God according to the Christian teaching. In latter days, five peoples have inhabited the island: the Normans, the Britons, the Saxons, the Picts, and the Scots. Of these, the Britons first settled the island from sea to sea, until divine vengeance, on account of their overweening pride, sent the Picts and Saxons to drive them out. The story of their origins and arrival now remains to be explained.

[6] After the Trojan War, Aeneas fled the fall of Troy with his son Ascanius and then sailed on to Italy. There he was most honorably received by King Latinus. Turnus, the King of the Rutuli, grew jealous and fought against him. They met together in combat, wherein Aeneas prevailed and slew Turnus, thus winning the kingdom of Italy, as well as the hand of Lavinia, King Latinus' daughter. After Aeneas had breathed his last, Ascanius took on the royal authority. He built Alba Longa on an island in the Tiber and had a son whose name was Silvius.

---

[1]   The description of Britain follows those of Gildas and Bede, often almost verbatim.

This son, indulging in secret pleasures, wed a certain granddaughter of Lavinia and fathered a child on her. When this was made known to Ascanius, he ordered his court wizards to ascertain the sex of the child. The wizards revealed, in no uncertain terms, that the girl would bear a son who would kill both his father and his mother, but that he would also wander in exile through many lands until he had finally achieved the highest honor. In this prophecy the wizards were not mistaken, for when the day of the child's birth arrived, the woman indeed bore a son and died in childbirth. The boy was taken by the midwife and named Brutus. When fifteen years had passed, this young man came upon his father while hunting and unintentionally killed him with an arrow: for it happened that, while his servants were leading a group of deer towards him, Brutus attempted to shoot at them, but his missile struck his father in the chest instead.[1]

[7] Brutus' relatives were horrified by the crime he had committed, and he was expelled from Italy. In exile, he traveled to Greece, where he discovered the descendants of Helenus, the son of Priam, who were still living in servitude among the Greeks under the authority of King Pandrasus. Pyrrhus, the son of Achilles, had captured Helenus and many others in the wake of Troy's destruction, carrying them off in chains. He had them kept in a state of slavery in order to avenge his father's death by Trojan hands.[2] Perceiving their distant kinship, Brutus lived for a time among these slaves. There Brutus began to grow so mighty in prowess and discernment that the kings and princes of that land loved him beyond all the other young men in the land.[3] Wise men considered him wise, and brave men held him to be brave. All the gold or silver or other riches he acquired in his various exploits he distributed among his soldiers.

When Brutus' fame began to be rumored throughout the entire land, the Trojans started to rally around him, begging him to be their leader and to liberate them from their Greek captors. They insisted that this would not be difficult to achieve, since they had by now multiplied

---

[1] Geoffrey's rendering of Brutus's youth elaborates greatly on Nennius's terse account (see Appendix A). Geoffrey's emphasis on the "hunting accident" would doubtless resonate with his contemporaries, since King William Rufus of England was also slain in a hunting accident in the New Forest in 1100.

[2] Achilles, according to Virgil's *Aeneid*, was slain by Paris, the son of the Trojan King Priam.

[3] I have rendered the Latin term *probitate* with the word "discernment" here. Throughout Geoffrey's text, *probitas* seems to signify all the general attributes of a good ruler: discernment, courage, wisdom, skill in battle, generosity, etc. Nearly every king of whom Geoffrey approves receives this descriptive term in one form or another.

so much that there were seven thousand of them, not even counting women and children. And there was now, what's more, a young Greek nobleman by the name of Assaracus who supported their cause. This Assaracus had been born of a Trojan mother and had the utmost confidence that the Trojans would be able to help him prevent being oppressed by the Greeks. His own brother, in fact, was opposed to him on account of three castles that their dying father had bestowed upon him. This brother was attempting to claim the castles on the grounds that Assaracus had been born of a slave-woman, while he himself was Greek on both his father's and mother's sides. He also asserted that the former king and many other Greeks had favored his claim. And so Brutus, realizing that both a multitude of men as well as Assaracus' three castles would be available to him, conceded to the Trojans' request.

[8] Assuming the leadership of the people, Brutus began to summon all the Trojans to him and fortified Assaracus' strongholds. Then he and Assaracus, with a great multitude of the men and women who flocked to him, took up their abode in the woodlands and hills. Brutus then sent letters to the Greek king containing these words: "Brutus, the leader of the remnant of Troy, sends his greetings unto Pandrasus, King of the Greeks. The people sprung from that illustrious Dardan stock, offended at being treated in your realm with less dignity than their lineage demands, will be withdrawing into the forests. That people would far prefer to live in freedom on a rustic diet of meat and herbs than to enjoy luxury under the yoke of your servitude. If this is offensive to the loftiness of your high office, do not hold it against them, for it is the desire of every slave to attain his freedom. Take, therefore, pity on them and grant them their former liberty. Allow them to dwell in that stretch of wilderness for which they forsook their servitude. Or, at the very least, give them your leave to depart for some other country."

[9] When this letter had been read aloud, Pandrasus was shocked that the people whom he had kept enslaved would have the gall to send him such a letter. He therefore consulted his advisors and began to assemble an army to hunt the Trojans down.

While Pandrasus was searching for them in the wastelands outside of Sparatinum, where they had said they would be, Brutus arrived with a force of three thousand men, catching Pandrasus off his guard. Brutus had in fact learned of the king's approach and had secured Sparatinum the previous night, so that he could launch an ambush while the Greeks were still unarmed and in disarray. Suddenly rushing out, the Trojans attacked most fiercely, pressing forward with great violence. The Greeks were dumbfounded and they fell back in every direction. In great haste they fled with their king across the River Akalon, which flowed nearby, though in doing so they risked being swept away by its currents. Brutus assailed them so relentlessly that some of them were drowned in the river and some of them met their doom on the shore. Running to and fro, the Greek host thus faced death on either side. When Antigonus, the brother of Pandrasus, learned of this situation, he was grieved beyond measure, so he called the scattered men together and led a swift charge at the raging Trojans. He deemed it better to go down in battle than to be sucked under by the murky waters. Ordering his soldiers into a tight formation, he bade them make a manly end and to cast their spears with all their might, even with their dying breaths. But this did little good. The Trojans were well-supplied with arms and men; the Greeks had nothing. For this reason the Trojans pushed on even more boldly and did not relent in their slaughter until almost all the Greeks were slain and they had captured Antigonus and one other soldier named Anacletus.

[10] Having secured this victory, Brutus then fortified Sparatinum with six hundred men and sent word to the woodlands, where the rest of the Trojan people were awaiting his instructions. Yet Pandrasus was most distressed at the routing of the Greeks and at the capture of his brother, and he managed to regroup his scattered forces that very night. By the time the sun had set the morning sky aglow, he returned and besieged the castle with a freshly organized army. He expected that Brutus would surrender to him before long and release his brother and the other prisoners. Assessing the castle's defenses, Pandrasus divided up his army and set them up in small brigades all around the fortress, commanding them to prevent anyone from leaving the castle. He also set separate groups to work diverting the flow of the river. And he ordered others to use battering rams and other engines of war to burst the castle walls at their seams. The Greeks carried out his orders with relish, putting all their effort into devising ways to press the siege more cruelly. At nightfall they selected the bravest men to guard their camps and tents against any sudden attacks from the enemy, so that those who had labored all day long could slumber in peace.

[11] The defenders meanwhile stood atop the walls, trying with all their might to repel the war engines of their enemies with devices of their own making. They shot out missiles and flaming sulphur in a concerted effort in order to defend themselves. When the enemy brought forth a protective shed and began to dig a tunnel under the castle walls, the defenders began to use Greek fire and boiling water to

force them to withdraw.[1] However, the besieged were finally worn down by a shortage of food and by their ceaseless efforts, and they sent a message to Brutus, entreating him to hasten to their aid. Indeed, they feared that they might have to abandon the castle because of their weakness. Brutus worried greatly about how he would break the siege, since he did not have enough soldiers to commit to a pitched battle. He therefore devised a cunning plan to approach the enemy by cover of night, mislead the sentries, and then kill the Greeks as they slept. Because this plan could not be carried out without some assistance from the Greek side, Brutus summoned Anacletus, Antigonus' comrade, and, drawing his sword, spoke to him thus: "A swift death will come for you and Antigonus both unless *you* agree to carry out my will faithfully. I intend to launch a surprise assault on the Greek camp this very night, but I fear that the night watchmen will discover my plan and repel me. It is therefore necessary that this line of defense be taken down first, and so I need you to deceive them so that my men may attack the others more effectively. You will perform this treacherous business: in the second hour of the night, go down to the siege-camp and distract them with whatever false words you can think of. Tell them that you have rescued Antigonus from my prisons and that you are keeping him in safety up in the underbrush. Pretend that he could flee no further because of the shackles about his feet. You will then lead them up into the woods as if to free him. There I will be armed and waiting to slay them."

[12] Anacletus, seeing the sword threatening his life as Brutus spoke, was thoroughly cowed and swore that he would execute this plan as long as Brutus granted Antigonus and himself a longer life. Anacletus pledged his loyalty, and the second hour of the night drew nigh. He arrived at the siege-camp as instructed. As he came at length into the vicinity of the camp, the sentries, who had been patrolling all the hidden pockets in that area, swarmed all about him. They asked him how he had made it there and whether he intended to betray the army. Feigning great joy, Anacletus answered them in these words: "By no means do I come as a traitor to my people. I have myself escaped imprisonment among the Trojans and come to you now to beg you to come to the aid of your Antigonus, whom I rescued from Brutus' custody. He is slowed down by the weight of the chains on his legs and lies concealed back among the fruit groves at the edge of the forest. He has ordered me to bring some men to free

---

[1] "Greek fire," also known in the Middle Ages as "liquid fire," was some kind of flammable chemical that had been in use by the Eastern Roman Empire as a secret weapon from as early as the seventh century. Its chemical composition is currently unknown.

him." They were unsure whether or not he was telling the truth until one of the guards recognized him, greeted him, and explained to the others that Anacletus was an ally. Now, wasting no more time, they summoned the other watchmen in the vicinity and went up to the wood where Antigonus was said to be hiding. Once they were all amid the fruit trees, Brutus sprang out with a band of armed men in sudden assault, attacking them most fearsomely. Brutus then proceeded on to the siege-camp, dividing his troops into three groups. He ordered them to attack only one part of the camp at a time and to do so quietly. They would thus avoid an all-out offense until he had come with his personal retinue to the king's pavilion and sounded his trumpet as a signal.

[13] Brutus gave each group its specific orders, and now, swiftly and silently, they made their way to the camp and took up their assigned positions, waiting for the signal. Brutus did not give it to them until he stood outside of Pandrasus' pavilion, which he desired to capture above all else. When they heard the trumpet signal, the men quietly drew their swords and entered the tents of the sleeping soldiers. They struck them over and over with deadly blows. They proceeded all through the camp in this way, granting no mercy. Some of the Greeks, awakened by the death-throes of their comrades, were like sheep suddenly surrounded by wolves and were astonished to see their slayers. The Greeks had no protection, since they had neither arms to seize nor the opportunity to flee. Completely unarmed, they rushed all around, wherever their terror impelled them. But more and more Trojans simply rushed in and cut them down. Some of the Greeks managed to escape half-alive, only to be dashed against the cliffs or the trees, thus spilling both their blood and their spirits. Others, protected only by a shield or some other covering, feared for their lives and rushed out in the dark night only to fall off of those same cliffs, breaking their arms and legs in the process. Those Greeks to whom neither of these dooms befell were drowned in the river, not knowing where else to flee. There were hardly any who escaped uninjured or without undergoing some misfortune. Moreover, when the besieged Trojans became aware of the arrival of their allies, they sallied forth and repaid twofold the slaughter they had been dealt.

[14] But when Brutus had reached the king's tent, as described earlier, he took care to bind the king and keep him safe, for he realized that Pandrasus would be more useful alive than dead. The soldiers who accompanied Brutus did not, however, cease their attack; they continued to slay everyone they found in their assigned areas. They passed the night in this manner and the light of dawn revealed the great ruin they

had inflicted. Brutus rejoiced that morning, and he allowed his men to reap the spoils of the massacre they had achieved, each according to his desire. He then entered the castle, leading the king with him, and waited for all the royal treasure to be distributed. Once everyone received their share, Brutus refortified the castle and ordered all the dead to be buried. Then, gathering together all of his men, he went back into the forest, blissful in his victory. Because such happiness filled their spirits, their renowned leader now summoned the more nobly-born of the Trojans to him and asked them what demands they should make of Pandrasus. For now that the king was in their power he would surely agree to whatever they asked if he were allowed to go free. But all the nobles desired different things. Some of them wanted to ask for a part of the kingdom to settle in. Others sought permission to leave Greece, along with the provisions to make such a journey. When they had stood a long while in disagreement, there arose one among them named Mempritius, who called for silence and addressed them thus: "Why do you waver, fathers, about these affairs that, I believe, are so vital to your well-being? There is only one thing to ask for if you wish your descendants to have everlasting peace: permission to leave. If you grant Pandrasus his life in exchange for a part of Greece to dwell in alongside the Danaans, never will you enjoy a lasting peace. The brothers and sons and grandsons of the men whom you have slain would be your neighbors and countrymen. They will always remember the murder of their kin and will hate you forever. They will seek out the flimsiest of pretenses upon which to avenge themselves on you. Nor do your meager people have sufficient force to resist an uprising against them. And if dissension should ever arise among you, then their numbers will increase daily, while yours decrease. I recommend, therefore, that you request that Pandrasus give his eldest daughter, whom they call Ignogen, as a gift to our leader, along with gold and silver and ships and grain and anything else that might speed you on our way. And if we can obtain these things, we should then seek out other countries with the king's leave."

[15] When Mempritius had finished saying these and similar things, the entire crowd agreed that Pandrasus should be brought among them and threatened with a most terrible death unless he granted their requests. He was led there without delay and placed in a seat higher than the others. Assessing the situation, Pandrasus replied in this way: "Since the unfriendly gods have placed me and my brother Antigonus into your hands, your demands must be met. Indeed, should you be denied, both of our lives are forfeit. Nothing do I hold more precious or more wonderful than life

itself, and it should come as no marvel that I desire to purchase it with material possessions. And so, though I am unwilling, I shall obey your commands. I will have to find solace in the fact that I am giving my daughter to a young man of such magnificence. His reputation is well known to us, as is the nobility that pulses through his veins, being a descendant of the line of Priam and Anchises. Who else could release the exiles of Troy from their servitude when so many of their own princes were in chains? Who else could lead them against the king of the Greeks or could with so few men bring battle against such a mighty force of armed soldiers and defeat their king? Since, therefore, such a youth possesses the prowess to defeat me, I will give him my daughter Ignogen. I will also give him gold, silver, ships, grain, and anything else you deem necessary for this journey. And if by chance you do decide to remain here among the Greeks, I will grant you a third of my kingdom to dwell in. If not, I will see to it that my promises are fulfilled; so that you may rest assured, I will remain among you as a hostage until all these things are carried out." Once this settlement was made, emissaries were sent through all the coastlands of Greece collecting ships. When all of these were gathered together, there were three hundred and twenty-four ships in total, and they were laden with all kinds of grain. Pandrasus' daughter was married to Brutus. Every man was given gold and silver according to his rank. The king was released from prison once all these things came to pass, and the Trojans departed from his lands upon the first favorable winds.

But Ignogen stood upon the ship's highest deck and fainted over and over again in Brutus' arms. Shedding many a tear, she bewailed having to abandon her home and family, and she did not look away as long as the Greek shores were still in sight. Brutus comforted her, coaxing her now with soft embraces, now with sweet kisses. He did not stop until her grief finally succumbed to slumber.

[16] And so it passed that they followed a kind wind for two days and one night, making for an island named Loegetia that had long ago been laid waste by pirates and now lay empty.[1] Brutus therefore sent three hundred armed men to see if anyone might yet be living there. Discovering no inhabitants, they hunted the many types of beasts that they found amid the woods and meadows. They eventually happened upon a deserted city in which there stood a temple dedicated to Diana. Within it there stood a statue of the goddess that would answer queries if anyone

---

[1] The resemblance between the name *Loegetia*, the first stop of the wandering Trojans, to the name *Loegria*, their final destination, is surely not accidental.

should ask. Burdened with the fruits of their hunt, the men headed back to the ships and told their compatriots about the lay of the land and about the city. They suggested that Brutus, as their leader, should go to temple, pour libations, and ask the goddess in what land they should make the seat of their house. Everyone agreed to this plan, and Brutus, accompanied by the augur Gero and twelve nobles, went up to the temple with everything necessary for a proper sacrifice. When they reached that place, they bound fillets about their brows and, before entering the temple, performed the ancient custom and built fires to the three gods: Jupiter, Mercury, and Diana. They then poured out one libation at a time. Standing before the altar of the goddess, Brutus himself in his right hand held aloft a vessel filled with wine mixed with the blood of a white stag. Turning to the silent statue of the goddess, he poured out the libation with these words:

Mighty goddess of the forest groves, O terror of the woodland boars,
You whose winding path leads you up to the loftiest heavens
And down to the deepest abodes of hell, reveal now an earthly matter
And declare in which lands you wish us to dwell.
Declare that constant seat from which we shall ever worship you,
Where, amid virgin choirs, I shall dedicate your temples.

Brutus pronounced these lines nine times, circled the altar four times, then poured out the wine which he held into the fire. Then he laid a deerskin out before the altar and laid down upon it. He soon attained a much-desired sleep. It was by then almost the third hour of the night, when the sweetest slumber comes to mortal men. He suddenly saw the goddess standing before him and she spoke to him in this way:

Brutus, beneath the setting sun, beyond the kingdoms of Gaul,
There is an island [encircled by the sea,
There is an island,] once inhabited by giants,[1]
But now it is deserted, ready to receive your people.
Seek it out: for it shall be your everlasting seat.   .
It shall be a second Troy unto your descendants.
There kings shall arise from your line, and unto them
Shall all the lands of the earth be subject.

Awakening from this vision, Brutus was unsure whether what he had

---

[1]   The bracketed words are absent in the Bern MS but present in other early mss.

seen had been a dream or whether it was indeed the voice of the living goddess foretelling what land he must seek.

Calling all of his comrades together, he explained to them exactly what had happened while he slept. [17] Greatly cheered, they suggested that they return to the ships, cast out to sea while the wind was still up, and, upon the swiftest of sails, seek out the land that the goddess had proclaimed. And so, hurrying back at once to their companions, they made for the high seas. They kept a straight course for thirty days and eventually came to Africa, but they did not know in which direction to set their prows from there. They arrived in due course at the Altars of the Philistines and the Sea of Salt, and they sailed between Russicada and the Mountains of Zaree. There they suffered great peril from a pirate attack, but the Trojans prevailed and acquired great wealth from the defeated pirates' plunder. Then, sailing past the mouth of the Malve, they came ashore in Mauretania. Constrained by their shortage of food and drink, the Trojans disembarked there in several groups and raided the land from end to end. Returning at last to their ships, they set sail for the Pillars of Hercules, where there appeared to them those sea-monsters known as the Sirens. Even though they allowed the Sirens a wide berth, the Trojan ships barely managed to escape.[1]

Somehow in their flight they made their way to the Tyrrhenian Sea. On the shores of that region, they discovered four generations of exiles from Troy, descendants of those who had fled with Antenor.[2] Their leader was Corineus, a man of unassuming demeanor but of most learned counsel and of great strength and courage. Whenever Corineus came upon a giant, he would throw it down at once, as if wrestling with a mere boy. Perceiving their ancient kinship, the Trojans quickly allied themselves with this Corineus and with the people whom he governed. It was from this leader that the name of Cornwall was later derived; Corineus indeed proved more helpful to Brutus than any other ally in a fight.

Then they came together to Aquitaine, where they dropped anchor in the mouth of the River Loire. They tarried there for seven days while exploring that realm. [18] In those days Goffar the Pict was king in the land of Aquitaine.[3] When news reached him that a foreign armada had

---

[1]   The Mediterranean wanderings of the Trojans allude directly to Virgil's *Aeneid*, in which Aeneas and his band of Trojan exiles are similarly seeking a new homeland.

[2]   Livy's *Early History of Rome* (*Ab Urbe Condita*), notes that Aeneas and Antenor were the two noble Trojans to escape the burning of the city; Livy's Antenor settles in the vicinity of Venice.

[3]   Geoffrey here associates the Picts (*Picti*) with the Poitevins (*Pictavienses*), the people of Poitou in France, on the basis of the similarity of their names in Latin.

landed on the borders of his realm, he sent messengers to find out whether they sought peace or war. The messengers therefore made their way toward the fleet, but they first came across Corineus, who was out hunting in the forest with a band of two hundred men. They asked him at once by whose leave he had slain beasts within the king's forest, for the law of old had been that no one should hunt there without the express permission of the king.[1] When Corineus answered that he required no one's permission to do anything, one of the messengers, by the name of Himbertus, stepped up and, drawing his bow, shot an arrow at him. Corineus, dodging the arrow, ran up to Himbertus and smashed his head in with his bow. The other messengers fled immediately, barely escaping Corineus' clutches and reporting the death of their comrade to Goffar as soon as they could. Grieved by these tidings, the leader of the Picts assembled a great host to avenge the death of his messenger.

Brutus, now forewarned of the approach of the Picts, fortified the ships and ordered the women and children to remain on board. He then marched out with a great force of hardy men to intercept the Pictish army. Meeting in battle, both sides inflicted grave damage on one another. After the better part of the day had been spent in such slaughter, Corineus was ashamed that the Aquitanians could resist so valiantly and that the Trojans could not secure a victory. Therefore, summoning all of his courage, he regrouped his men upon the right-hand side of the battlefield and, arraying his company in tight ranks, rushed down upon the enemy. Because the Trojan force was now pressing forward in such dense formations, Corineus did not cease to slaughter the enemy until he had penetrated straight to the heart of their army and set them all to flight. Brutus marveled, the Trojans marveled, and the enemy too marveled at the bravery and strength of Corineus. As he swung his axe among the fleeing troops, he taunted them fearlessly, crying, "Where are you going, you cowards? Where are you going, you lazy fools? Come back here! Come back and do battle with Corineus! Oh, for shame that so many thousands run away from me alone! Well, at least you can find comfort in the fact that the man you're running away from is the same man who single-handedly set all the giants of the Tyrrhenian Sea to flight, who sent them down to hell three and four at a time!"

Hearing these taunts, a consul named Suhard, who was leading three hundred men, turned face and attacked Corineus. Corineus warded off

---

[1] Medieval British audiences would doubtless detect an allusion here to the restrictive forest policies of the Norman kings.

the blow with his shield, and he did not neglect the battle-axe he was carrying. Raising his weapon, he struck Suhard upon the crest of his helmet with such force that the man was split in two from his head to his toes. In a sudden onslaught, he then turned his axe on the others, wreaking great havoc. He ran about here and there, never shying away from a blow nor flagging in his attack on the enemy. He cut the arm and hand right off one man, and severed the shoulders from another. Another man got his head cut off by a sweep of Corineus' axe, and another still lost his leg. All the Picts rushed at him, but he held them back single-handedly. When Brutus saw this, he was moved by a great affection for his comrade and hastened to help Corineus with a troop of soldiers. Then there arose a tremendous clamor between the two peoples. A torrent of blows fell, and on both sides there was grievous bloodshed. The Trojans quickly mastered the field and set King Goffar and the Picts to flight.

[19] Barely escaping from that battle alive, Goffar made his way throughout Gaul seeking assistance from his friends and relatives. In that time there were twelve kings in Gaul who governed the land in equal shares. These kings received Goffar warmly and agreed unanimously to help him repel this foreign people from the confines of Aquitaine.

Brutus, however, rejoiced in the victory. Distributing the spoils among all of his companions, he regrouped his troops, and led them through the countryside, seeking to pillage it and to fill his ships up with plunder. And so he put their cities to the torch and made off with all their treasures. He ravaged their husbandlands, inflicting great carnage on the farmers and the townsfolk alike, and hoping to destroy the wretched inhabitants down to the last man. When he had visited this slaughter throughout almost all of Aquitaine, he came upon that place which is now the city of Tours, which Brutus himself in fact later built there, as Homer attests. Since he had been seeking out possible locations for a refuge, he had laid out a camp in that place as a retreat, if need should arise. Indeed, he was concerned about the approach of Goffar and the other kings and princes of Gaul, who were leading a massive army to that very place, hoping to engage him in battle there. Setting up camp, Brutus awaited Goffar for two days, trusting in his own counsel and in the youthful audacity that still flourished within him.

[20] Goffar, who had learned of the location of the Trojans, did not cease his march by night or day until he could make out Brutus's encampment. Gazing down at the camp with a grim light in his eyes, Goffar smiled and said, "Alas! How sad this fate is! Baseborn exiles have pitched their tents in my kingdom. Arm yourselves, men, arm your-

selves and cast down their teeming battalions. We will capture these half-men in no time at all and sell them off them like so many sheep throughout our domains." Thereupon they all armed themselves and marched down in twelve columns to meet the enemy. Brutus was not at all dismayed at the enemy's advance. Instead, he exhibited wisdom in arranging what each company should do and how each might carry out its own offense and defense. As the battle began, the Trojans were at first successful, inflicting great carnage upon the enemy. At least two thousand Gauls fell, and the rest, terrified, began to turn to flee. However, Victory tends to favor those with greater numbers. Since the Gauls did outnumber the Trojans threefold, they managed to regroup after the initial assault, now pressing the attack on all sides and breaching the Trojan lines. Winning the field, they pinned the Trojans within their camp. They now believed the Trojans could never escape, and, being surrounded, either would submit their necks to chains of slavery or, weakened by hunger, would suffer a most painful death.

That evening, Corineus took counsel with Brutus. He wanted to leave the camp that very night by hidden ways and await the sunrise under the cover of a nearby wood. At daybreak, Brutus should engage the enemy, while Corineus himself would press the assault from the rear and inflict great slaughter. Brutus approved of this plan. And so Corineus, leading three thousand men, withdrew secretly and hid in the woods. As the next day dawned, Brutus organized his men into companies and, leaving their defenses, they came out into the open to fight. The Gauls hurried toward them in tight formation. Many thousands of men fell, for both sides inflicted grievous wounds and granted no quarter. There was there a certain Trojan named Turnus, Brutus' nephew, stronger and bolder than anyone except Corineus. [Armed only with his sword, he slew six hundred men, but he met an untimely death at the hands of the Gauls, who rushed headlong upon him.][1] It is from this Turnus that the aforementioned city of Tours derives its name, for he was buried there. While both armies were in the midst of bitter combat, Corineus suddenly emerged from the wood and attacked the Gauls from behind. The other Trojans then grew more daring and struggled all the more to press their assault. The Gauls were astonished at the great cry that Corineus' men made as they came up from behind and, believing that there were even more men now coming than were already there, they quickly abandoned

---

[1]   The bracketed sentence is absent from the Bern MS, though it is well-attested among other manuscripts. In this edition of *The History*, Neil Wright, lvi, suggests that it may have been suppressed by the Bern's Norman scribe.

the field. The Trojans hounded them in pursuit, and many a Gaul was slain in their retreat.

Although such a victory gave him the utmost joy, Brutus was still very worried, since the Trojans' numbers were decreasing daily, while the Gauls were steadily multiplying. He doubted whether he should wage war against them any longer and decided to return to the ships while the majority of his men were still unscathed. Indeed, with a recent victory in hand, he now thought it prudent to seek out the island that the goddess had spoken of. His men agreed. They returned to the fleet, filled their ships with all the riches they had acquired, and set sail without delay. Escorted by fair winds, they landed at Totnes, on the shores of their promised island.

[21] In those days, the island was named Albion, and was uninhabited except by a few giants.[1] It was a beautiful place, filled with forests and with rivers that teemed with fish. It inspired Brutus and his companions with a great desire to settle there. As they explored the various regions of the island, the Trojans discovered giants who had fled to caves in the mountains. With the approval of their leader, the Trojans then partitioned the land among themselves. They began to cultivate the fields and construct buildings, so that, after a short space of time, you would think that they had lived there forever. Then Brutus called the island Britain, after his own name, and he called his comrades Britons. In devising these names, he hoped to be remembered forever. Thus in later days, the language of the people, which was originally called Trojan or crooked Greek, was known as British.[2]

But Corineus called the portion of the realm that fell by lot to him Corinea after himself, and his people followed his example and called themselves the Corineans. When all the provinces of Britain were to be divided up, Corineus had been allowed to choose his portion before everyone else, and he preferred that region which is now called Cornwall, either from the fact that it is the horn of Britain or from corruption of the word Corinea.[3]

---

1   The name *Albion* is an ancient one, known to the Greeks and Romans. It is unclear, however, whether the indigenous peoples of Britain ever used the term at such an early date.

2   Geoffrey uses the word *Britannica* in describing the British language, a term that in twelfth-century Latin was regularly used to describe the Celtic languages of Wales, Brittany, and Cornwall alike. The term "crooked Greek" here derives from a Welsh folk etymology in which the name of the Welsh language, *Cymraeg* in Welsh, is derived from *cam groeg*, "crooked Greek."

3   Geoffrey's usual Latin term for Cornwall is *Cornubia*, and he usually refers to its inhabitants as *Cornubienses*, though here he employs the appellation *Corineienses* in order to emphasize the derivation of their name from Corineus. Historically, the name of the land

Corineus himself took great relish in fighting against the giants who seemed to thrive in his homeland more than in that of any of his comrades. There was among them a certain giant by the name of Gogmagog who stood some twelve cubits tall. This Gogmagog was so strong that he once uprooted an oak tree as if it were a hazel-shoot. One day, when Brutus was celebrating a feast at the place where the Trojans had first landed, Gogmagog came with twenty other giants and caused great slaughter among the Britons. The Britons managed to band together and defeat the invaders, killing all of them except for Gogmagog. Brutus insisted that he be kept alive, for he greatly desired to see a wrestling match between him and Corineus, who enjoyed fighting giants above all other sport. Corineus arrived most jubilantly. He rolled up his sleeves, threw aside his weapons and provoked the giant to wrestle. At first Corineus, then the giant, prevailed as they struggled together, locked in each other's embrace. The very air vibrated with the groaning of their mighty breaths. Eventually Gogmagog exerted all his strength on Corineus and broke three of his ribs, two on the right side, and one on the left. This infuriated Corineus: he put forth all of his own strength, slung the giant over his shoulders, and made as fast as he could under the weight to the edge of the sea. There, at the pinnacle of a great cliff, he shook himself out of the giant's grip, heaved up the deadly creature that he carried on his shoulders, and cast him into the sea. Gogmagog, falling against the sharp rocks below, was dashed into a thousand pieces. The tide was red with his blood. That place derived its name from the giant's fall and is still called Gogmagog's Leap up to the present day.

[22] After dividing up the realm, Brutus decided to build a city. To carry out this plan, he traveled all around the island looking for the perfect location. Coming eventually to the River Thames, he wandered its banks until he found a spot that was well suited to his purposes. He built a city there and called it *Troia Nova*, New Troy.[1] From this name it was called in latter days, through the corruption of tongues, *Trinovant*. But in years to come, Lud—the brother of that Cassibelaunus who fought against Julius Caesar—took control of the kingdom, and he surrounded that city with mighty walls and towers constructed with the most cunning artifice. He ordered the city to be called Kaer Lud after himself. There afterwards arose great strife between him and his

---

likely derives from the *Cornovii*, a Celtic British tribe mentioned by Roman authorities. The resemblance of the shape of the Cornish peninsula to a horn has led some to claim that the Celtic term *corn*, "horn" underlies the word.

[1]   This New Troy on the Thames is, of course, London.

other brother Nennius, who bore it ill that Lud should want to erase the name of Troy from their land. The historian Gildas describes the dispute between them at length; I shall therefore choose to pass over these matters, lest I spoil with my humbler diction that which such a great writer discusses so elegantly.[1]

After Brutus built this city, he dedicated it to the citizens as their birthright, and he gave them a law code with which they could maintain the peace. In those days, the High Priest Eli ruled in Judea, and the Ark of the Covenant was captured by the Philistines. In Troy, the sons of Hector reigned, having expelled the descendants of Antenor. Silvius Aeneas, the son of Aeneas, ruled in Italy. He was Brutus' uncle and the third king of the Latins.

---

[1] Gildas' account of the relations between Rome and Britain in his *Ruin of Britain* makes no mention of this fraternal strife.

BOOK TWO

[23] Brutus knew his wife Ignogen, and by her he fathered three illus-
trious sons, whose names were Locrinus, Kamber and Albanactus. In
the twenty-third year after his settling in Britain, they buried their father
in the city that he had founded. Then they divided the kingdom of
Britain among themselves and each brother ruled over his own terri-
tory. Locrinus, the eldest, possessed that part of the island that was later
called Logres after him. Kamber received the area that lies beyond the
Severn River and which is now called Wales, but which was called for
a long time Cambria after him, which is why the people of that land
who speak the British tongue still call themselves Cambrians.[1] And
Albanactus, the youngest, ruled over that land which is now called
Scotland in our tongue, but he named it Alban after himself.[2]

[24] With these matters settled, the three reigned in peace for a long
time until Humber, the king of the Huns, landed in Alban. He waged
war against Albanactus and slew him, forcing the people of that land to
flee to Logres. Upon hearing this news, Locrinus allied himself with his
brother Kamber. He gathered all the young warriors of the land and
went against the king of the Huns at the river that today is called the
Humber. Humber himself fled into the river and was drowned in its
currents, thus bestowing his name upon it. Having secured victory,
Locrinus distributed the booty among his allies, keeping nothing for
himself except for the silver and gold that he found in the Hunnish
ships. He also decided to keep for himself three girls of extraordinary
beauty, one of whom was the eldest daughter of the king of Germany.
Humber had carried her off along with the other two when he was
pillaging their homeland. The girl's name was Estrildis, and she was of
such great beauty that she could not easily be compared to any other

---

[1] In fact, the terms *Wallia* and *Cambria* were both common in twelfth-century Latin docu-
    ments. The twelfth-century Welsh did refer to themselves as *Cymry*, though they also
    employed the term *Britanyeit*, "Britons."
[2] Alba is a traditional term for Scotland in the various Celtic languages, and Geoffrey renders
    the word in Latin as *Albania*. To avoid association with the Eastern European nation of
    the same name, and to maintain Geoffrey's studied Celtic flavor, I translate *Albania* as *Alban*
    (the Welsh form of the word) throughout. I reserve the term *Scotland* for places where
    Geoffrey instead uses the Latin word *Scotia*.

woman.[1] The whiteness of her skin indeed surpassed that of ivory or the lily or the freshly fallen snow. Locrinus was completely smitten with love for her. He desired to lie in her bed and to unite with her in marriage.

When Corineus received word of this he was indignant beyond measure, for Locrinus had been betrothed to his daughter. So, with his double-bladed axe in his left hand, he went up to the king and addressed him in this way: "Is this how you repay me, Locrinus, for all the wounds I incurred battling against foreign peoples in your father's service? By jilting my daughter in favor of some barbarian concubine? You will not do this without retribution, not so long as there is still strength in my left arm here, which has snatched the joy of living out of many a giant all along the Tyrrhenian shores!" At this he shook his axe as if he were going to strike him, but their friends held him back. Calming Corineus down, they persuaded Locrinus to carry through with what he had promised. So Locrinus married the daughter of Corineus, a girl by the name of Gwendolen.[2]

The king, however, was still completely in love with Estrildis. He had an underground chamber devised for her beneath Trinovant, and had his most privy servants treat her with dignity. He could at least make love with her secretly there; out of fear of Corineus he did not dare flaunt her openly. So, as I just said, he concealed Estrildis in a cave, and he visited her there for seven whole years. No one shared in the secret except for his closest circle of friends. Whenever he wanted to go to her he would pretend that he was going to make a private sacrifice to his gods. He thus deceived everyone into believing something that was false. After a while, Estrildis became pregnant and bore him a daughter of marvelous beauty whom she named Habren. Gwendolen became pregnant as well, and she gave birth to a son to whom she gave the name of Maddan. He was sent to his grandfather Corineus to be reared.

[25] But time wore on, and after Corineus passed away, Locrinus abandoned Gwendolen completely and made Estrildis his queen. Gwendolen was offended beyond measure and went to Cornwall to muster all the youth of that realm in war against Locrinus. With the armies on either side thus deployed, they met in battle on the River Stour. There Locrinus

---

[1]   J.S.P. Tatlock in "The Origin of Geoffrey of Monmouth's Estrildis," argues convincingly that this episode derives from an account in William of Malmesbury's *Deeds of the Bishops of England* (*Gesta Pontificum Angliae*) of the similarly ill-fated Elfildis, the clandestine lover of an unnamed Norwegian king.

[2]   The name *Gwendolen* is unattested in medieval Britain outside of Geoffrey's text. It is perhaps invented on a misreading of the Welsh masculine name *Gwendoleu*.

was struck by an arrow and so forsook the joys of this life.[1] With Locrinus out of the way, Gwendolen, exhibiting her father's propensity for excess, seized control of the kingdom. She had Estrildis and her daughter Habren thrown into the river that is now called the Severn. Gwendolen then decreed that the river should be known by the name of the girl throughout all Britain. She decided to grant Habren this eternal honor since the girl was her husband's daughter. Thus it happens that even today that river is named Habren in the Welsh tongue and has been corrupted in the other language to Severn.[2]

Gwendolen reigned for fifteen years after the death of Locrinus, who himself had reigned for ten years. And when she saw that her son Maddan had reached adulthood, she handed the scepter over to him and was content to live out the remainder of her days in Cornwall. At that same time the prophet Samuel reigned in Judea, Aeneas Silvius was still living in Italy, and Homer was a famous orator and poet.

[26] Maddan was most distinguished and had two sons by his wife: Mempricius and Malin. He governed the kingdom with peace and wisdom for forty years. After his death, strife arose between the two brothers, since both of them wished to exert control over the entire island. Mempricius, seeking to accomplish his own purposes, arranged a meeting with Malin, purporting to make peace. However, roused by the flame of treachery, he killed his brother right in front of his very ambassadors. Then, seizing control of the entire island, he exercised such tyranny over the people that he had almost all the noblemen executed. He despised and feared even his own offspring, and, through force or treachery, he disposed of anyone at all who could succeed to his power. He even forsook his own wife, who had borne him the illustrious boy Ebraucus, and he gave himself over to the pleasures of sodomy, preferring unnatural delight to natural desire. But one day, in the twentieth year of his reign, while he was out hunting, he became separated from his companions in a little hollow. There he was surrounded by a ravenous band of wolves and most hideously devoured. In that same time Saul reigned in Judea and Eristenus in Sparta.

[27] At the death of Mempricius, his son Ebraucus, a man of great stature and marvelous strength, inherited the rule of Britain, and he held power for thirty-nine years. He was the first king since Brutus to lead

---

[1]   Harold, the last Anglo-Saxon king, met a identical fate at the Battle of Hastings in 1066.

[2]   *Hafren* is still the Welsh name for the Severn River, the traditional border between England and Wales. The term *Severn* derives from the Anglo-Saxon name *Sæfern,* in turn derived from the Late Britonnic form *Sabrina.*

a fleet over to Gaul. He brought war to the provinces of the Gauls, meting out slaughter to men and ceaseless oppression to the cities there. Thus enriched by an abundance of gold and silver, he returned home in triumph. Beside the River Humber he then built a city, which he named Kaer Ebrauc—that is, York—after himself.[1] At that time David reigned in Judea, and Silvius Latinus reigned in Italy, and Gad, Nathan, and Asaph prophesied in Israel.

The next thing Ebraucus did was to build the fortified city of Alclud near Mount Agned by the Scottish border; Alclud is now called the Castle of Maidens, and Mount Agned is called the Dolorous Mountain.[2] Ebraucus fathered twenty sons on his twenty wives, and thirty daughters as well, and he ruled the kingdom of Britain most capably for sixty years. These were the names of his sons: Brutus Greenshield, Margadud, Sisillius, Regin, Morvid, Bladud, Lagon, Bodloan, Kincar, Spaden, Gaul, Dardan, Eldad, Ivor, Cangu, Hector, Kerin, Rud, Assarac, and Buel. The names of his daughters were Gloigin, Ignogen, Oudas, Gwenllian, Guardid, Angharad, Guenlodoe, Tangustel, Gorgon, Medlan, Alethahel, Ourar, Mailure, Kambreda, Ragan, Gael, Ecub, Nest, Chein, Stadud, Gladys, Ebrein, Blangan, Aballac, Angaes, Galaes—she was the most beautiful of all the women who then lived in Britain or Gaul—Edra, Anor, and Stadiald.[3] Their father sent all these girls to Silvius Alba in Italy, who was the king there after Silvius Latinus. There they were offered in marriage to the more noble of the Trojans, whose beds were then being refused by the Latin and Sabine women. In the meantime, Ebraucus' sons, led by their brother Assarac, led a fleet into Germany. Enlisting the help of Silvius Alba, they seized that realm and subjugated its people.

[28] Brutus Greenshield remained in Britain with his father and, assuming governance of the kingdom after him, ruled for twelve years. He was succeeded by his son Leil, a lover of peace and justice. Leil, taking note of the prosperity of his kingdom, built a city in the northern part of Britain;

---

[1] The name Ebraucus recalls both *Eboracum*, the Latin name for the old Roman *castrum* which would become the city of York, as well as *Caer Efrawg*, the Welsh term for that same place.

[2] Geoffrey's Alclud corresponds to the present city of Dunbarton. Tatlock, *The Legendary History of Britain*, 15, notes that the inhabitants of Dunbarton were still called Welshmen into the twelfth century.

[3] Geoffrey likely derived these names from a Welsh genealogy. Several of them, like *Angharad, Gwenllian,* and *Nest*, were common names in twelfth-century Wales. As it stands, the list in the Bern MS is defective, enumerating only twenty-nine of Ebraucus' thirty daughters. The Cambridge MS, in agreement with the published Welsh *Bruts*, lists Egron as the thirtieth daughter. Geoffrey's Norman audiences would certainly have felt the "Welshness" of the names in this list.

it was called Kaer Leil after his own name.[1] At that time Solomon began to erect a Temple to the Lord in Jerusalem, and the Queen of Sheba came to consult his wisdom; and Silvius Epitus succeeded his father Silvius Alba in Italy. Leil lived on for twenty-five years after assuming the throne, but he ruled the kingdom rather feebly towards the end. As the king's health slowly debilitated, civil unrest arose in the realm.

[29] Leil's son Rud Hud Hudibras ruled after him for thirty-nine years. After he had led the people back from domestic strife to concord he built Kaer Keint, that is, Canterbury. He also built Kaer Guenit, which is Winchester, and the stronghold of Paladur, which is now called Shaftesbury.[2] That was the place where the Eagle spoke in those days, while the wall was being built. If I believed the Eagle's prophecies to be true I would not refuse to make mention of them as I have of other things.[3] In those days Capys son of Epitus reigned in Italy, and Aggeus, Amos, Ieu, Joel, and Azarias were prophesying.

[30] Bladud the son of Rud Hud Hudibras succeeded him and governed the kingdom for twenty years. He built the town of Kaer Badon, which is now known as Bath, and there he made hot baths ready for the use of men. He dedicated them to the goddess Minerva and placed inextinguishable fires in her temple, fires whose flames never failed, since when they began to die down they were turned about on stone spheres. In those days Elijah prayed that no rain would fall upon the earth and it did not rain for three years and six months.[4] This Bladud, however, was a most clever man and taught necromancy throughout the island of Britain. Not content with mere illusions, he had wings made for himself in an attempt to attain the zenith of the sky. But he fell to his death atop the Temple of Apollo in the city of Trinovant, consumed by vain error.

[31] With Bladud thus consigned to his doom, his son Leir was elevated to the kingship and ruled the land for sixty years. Leir built a city on the banks of the Soar which derives its name from him in the British tongue as Kaer Leir and in the Saxon tongue as Leicester. Denied

---

[1]   Carlisle is doubtless meant here.

[2]   The Bern MS names the first of these cities as *Kaer reint*. I have emended this, based on the reading of the Welsh *Bruts*, in order to preserve Geoffrey's sense of a comprehensible Celtic British analogue to the twelfth-century English name. The term Paladur also becomes more comprehensible in light of the Welsh *Bruts*, where Rud Hud Hudibras is known instead as Run Paladr Bras.

[3]   The prophecies of the Eagle of Shaftesbury seem to have had a vogue independent of Geoffrey. Geoffrey's attestation of their inaccuracy serves as an implicit authorization of his own prophecies of Merlin (see Book Seven).

[4]   Luke 4.25; 1 Kings 17.10–16.

any male offspring, he nonetheless had three daughters whose names were Goneril, Regan, and Cordelia.[1] Their father loved them all greatly, but he loved his youngest daughter, Cordelia, most of all. And so, when he began to grow old he thought about how to divide his kingdom among them and he sought to find such husbands as would share the rule of the land with them. In order to determine which of his three daughters was more worthy of the greater part of the kingdom, he went and asked them one by one who loved him the best. Posed this question by her father, Goneril the eldest daughter took the gods in heaven as witness that she bore for him a greater love than she bore for the soul that was in her own body. Her father then said to her, "Since in my old age you place me above all else, I shall marry you, my most beloved daughter, to whatever young man you should choose, and I shall give you a third of the kingdom of Britain." Then Regan, the second daughter, taking heed of her sister's example and hoping to insinuate her way into her father's good graces, answered him with many oaths, swearing that she could by no means express how much she loved him, except to say that she loved him above all other creatures. Thus gulled, her father granted her the same dignity as her sister and promised to find her a husband and give her another third of his kingdom.

But when Cordelia, the youngest daughter, perceived that her father was content with her sisters' flattery, she thought she would test him and decided to answer him quite differently. "Is there, my father," she asked, "a daughter anywhere who can presume to love her father more than is fitting? I do not think that there is any daughter who would dare to confess this, unless she is seeking to conceal the truth with empty words. Indeed, I have always loved you as my father and even now my feelings do not waver. And if you insist on wrenching any more out of me, remember the constancy of the love I have held for you and cease your questioning. You truly have as much of my love as you are worth: that's how much I love you." Then her father grew exceedingly angry and indignant about this answer that she had given from the bottom of her heart. He did not delay in expressing himself thus: "Because you hold your aged father in such contempt and do not deign to love me as your sisters do, I refuse to let you share any part of this realm with your sisters. Since you are my daughter, however, I am not saying that I wouldn't

---

[1]   Geoffrey's account of Leir and his three daughters is the earliest known version of the story that formed the basis of Shakespeare's *King Lear*. The story passed from Geoffrey into the writings of various medieval chroniclers, before finding its way into Holinshed's *Chronicles*, Shakespeare's primary source for the history of Britain.

marry you off to some foreigner if Fortune should permit it. But I assure you that I shall never seek to marry you with the same honor that I showed your sisters. Of course, while I had loved you until today more than your sisters, you have in fact loved me far less than they do."

Without delay, Leir followed the advice of his noble counsellors and married his two oldest daughters to the duke of Cornwall and the duke of Alban, along with half the island to rule between them as long as he lived. After his death, they would possess sovereignty over all of Britain.

Then it happened that Aganippus, the king of the Franks, having heard great tidings of Cordelia's beauty, sent messengers to the king asking for his daughter's hand in marriage.[1] Her father, steadfast in his anger, answered that he would give her to him freely, but without land or dowry, for he had already partitioned his kingdom, along with all his gold and silver, to his daughters Goneril and Regan. When this settlement was announced to Aganippus, he was even more greatly inflamed with love for the girl. He sent again to Leir, saying that he had gold and silver and lands enough, for he possessed a third of Gaul. So he obtained the girl in this way in order to produce heirs with her. When the agreement was reached, Cordelia was sent to Gaul and married off to Aganippus.

After a long space of time, old age began to wear Leir down, and the dukes to whom he had partitioned the kingdom and married his daughters rose up against him. They seized from him the kingdom and the sovereign power that he had hitherto wielded bravely and gloriously. They avoided an all-out civil war, however, because one of his sons-in-law, Maglaurus the duke of Alban, maintained Leir with one hundred forty knights so that the king would not appear dishonored. When two years had passed with Leir in residence there, his daughter Goneril became impatient with the great crowd of her father's retainers because they made trouble with her own servants, always insisting on more sumptuous rations. Her husband therefore decided that her father should be content with a retinue of thirty, and he dismissed the remainder.

Leir became so indignant at this treatment that he left Maglaurus and sought out Henwin, the duke of Cornwall, to whom he had married his second daughter, Regan. Although the duke welcomed him honorably, not a year had passed before there was again friction between the household and Leir's attendants. Regan became angry because of this and ordered her father to dismiss all of his men, except for five who

---

[1] Geoffrey's use of the term Franks rather than Gauls to refer to the inhabitants of France probably reflects less his awareness of the historical sequence of peoples in that land than his possible use of a different source for the Leir story.

should remain to serve him. Her father was then greatly anguished, and he went back to his first daughter to see if he could move her to pity and allow him to keep all of his retainers. But Goneril was not moved at all and rekindled her former hostility. She swore by the gods in heaven that he could not lodge with her unless he dismissed all his men and were content with a single retainer. She chided the old man, who now had nothing, for expecting to maintain such a following. Since she would in no way agree to anything he wanted, he yielded to her and dismissed the others and remained with one single servant.

But when Leir cast his memory back upon his former dignity, he began to detest the misery of his current state and thought about going to entreat his youngest daughter who lived across the ocean. He feared that she would not help him at all since he had married her off so ungraciously, yet he could tolerate his abjection no longer and set sail for Gaul. While crossing the sea, he noticed that he was accounted third among the princes there on the ship, and he lamented with crying and sobbing in these words: "O, you unbendable chain of Fate! you who keep to such an unswerving and narrow path! Why did you ever elevate me to an unstable happiness when it is a greater pain to revisit good times lost than to be oppressed by the sorrows to come? Indeed, the mere memory of that time when I was attended by a hundred thousand knights, when I was accustomed to cast down city walls and lay waste the lands of my enemies, grieves me more than the calamity of my present state. Fate has driven those who once lay beneath my feet to forsake me now in my weakness. O vengeful Fortune, will the day ever come when I will be able to repay those who have deserted me in my present state of poverty? O Cordelia, how true were those words you spoke when I asked what kind of love you bore me! You said 'I love you with as much of my love as you are worth.' While I was still able to give, I was worth much to them who were friends not to me but to my gifts. All the while they loved me but loved my riches more, for when the handouts went away so did they. But, dearest daughter, how will I dare to beg from you? Because of your words, I chose to marry you off more poorly than your sisters, who now, after receiving their inheritance, have reduced me to an exile and beggar."

Leir was saying these and similar things, and he came to Karitia where his daughter was dwelling.[1] Waiting outside the city, he sent a messenger ahead to announce how he had fallen upon such hard times.

---

[1] Karitia corresponds to no known city. Tatlock, *The Legendary History of Britain*, 93, notes that the Latin term *caritia* could mean "kindly cherishing." Thus Karitia provides a suitable locale for the reconciliation between Leir and Cordelia.

And since Leir had neither food nor clothing, the messenger begged her to grant mercy upon the king. When her father was presented in this way, Cordelia was moved to bitter tears and she inquired as to how many men he had with him. He sent answer that he had only the one man who waited outside with him. At this, Cordelia seized all the gold and silver at hand and gave it to the messenger, instructing him to bring her father to a nearby city. There the messenger should treat the king as if he were ill, and he should provide Leir with baths, food, and shelter. Cordelia also arranged that her father retain forty well-dressed and fully-armed knights and that, after a time, he should send for King Aganippus and his own daughter.

When the messenger returned to King Leir, he brought him to another city and hid him there, carrying out all the things that Cordelia had commanded. As soon as Leir was arrayed in kingly attire and had established his new household, he sent messages to Aganippus and Cordelia, explaining that he had been cast out of Britain by his own sons-in-law and that he was coming now to seek their aid in recovering his realm. And so Aganippus and Cordelia came to him with their counselors and retinue, and they treated him with great honor and restored him to the power and high dignity he had once commanded in his own kingdom. In the meantime, Aganippus sent messengers all throughout Gaul to muster every armed soldier for assistance in restoring the kingdom of Britain to his father-in-law. Once Aganippus had done this, Leir led Cordelia and the assembled host and fought against his sons-in-law and defeated them. Three years after he had regained all of his former power, he died. Aganippus, king of the Franks, had also died by then. So Leir's daughter Cordelia assumed the governance of the kingdom, and she buried her father in an underground chamber which she had had built beneath the River Soar downstream from Leicester. This crypt was built in honor of the two-faced god Janus. There, on the god's feast day, all the craftsmen of the city came to begin the first of the works that they would undertake for the entire year.

[32] After Cordelia had reigned tranquilly for fifteen years, the peace was broken by Margan and Cunedag, the sons of her two sisters who had been married to Maglaurus and Henwin. Both of these youths had upstanding reputations. Maglaurus had fathered the first of them, Margan, while Henwin had fathered Cunedag. Having succeeded after the deaths of their fathers to their respective duchies, these two grew outraged that Britain was now subject to a woman. Therefore, mustering their armies, they rebelled against the queen. They did not cease

their hostilities until, having laid many provinces to waste, they finally met the queen in battle. At the last they captured her and cast her in prison, where, because of her grief at having lost the kingdom, she killed herself.[1] Then the two men divided the island up between themselves: Margan received the part that extended from the River Humber towards Caithness, while Cunedag received the lands that stretched from the other side of the river towards the setting of the sun.

When two years had passed, certain men came to Margan who wished to see the realm in turmoil, and they insinuated to Margan that it was a crime and a disgrace that he, being the firstborn of the two cousins, did not rule the entire island. Aroused by this and a variety of other means, Margan led an army through Cunedag's provinces and began to set all his lands aflame. The peace now broken, Cunedag and his entire host met the onslaught with adequate force and set Margan to flight. Then he hounded Margan from province to province. Cunedag finally caught up with him in a village in Wales which, because of Margan's slaying there, the locals ever after called Margon.[2] Secure in this victory, Cunedag assumed the kingship over the entire island and ruled it in great glory for thirty-three years. At that same time Isaiah was making his prophecies and Rome was founded on the eleventh day of May by the twin brothers Romulus and Remus.

[33] After Cunedag died, he was succeeded by his son, Riwallo, a peaceable and most fortunate young man who governed the realm with great diligence. In his time it once rained blood for three days and men perished from an infestation of flies. After Riwallo, his son Gurgustius succeeded to the throne; after him Sisillius; after him Iago, the grandson of Gurgustius; then came Kimarcus, the son of Sisillius, and, after him, Gorboduc. To Gorboduc were born two sons, who were named Ferreux and Porrex. As their father grew old, dissension arose between the brothers over who would inherit the kingdom. And so Porrex, induced more powerfully by greed, laid his snares and planned to kill Ferreux. When Ferreux learned of this plot, he avoided his brother and sailed over to Gaul. Enlisting the aid of Suhard, King of the Franks, he came back and fought against his brother. However, Ferreux, along with

---

[1]   The rebellion of Margan and Cunedag against their legitimately-ruling aunt doubtless recalls the circumstances of Stephen's accession to the English throne in 1135; although Henry I's daughter Matilda had been legitimately designated as her father's heir, her cousin Stephen seized the throne shortly after the old king's death. Open war did not erupt until Matilda led an insurrection against Stephen in 1139.

[2]   There was a Cistercian abbey at Margam in Wales during Geoffrey's lifetime.

all the entire army he brought with him, was killed in battle. Then Judon, the mother of Ferreux and Porrex, learning the news of her son's death, was moved beyond measure in hatred against her other son, for she had loved Ferreux more than Porrex. She was enflamed with such wrath at her one son's death that she sought to avenge herself upon his brother. So, choosing a time when Porrex lay sleeping, she came upon him with her handmaidens and chopped him to pieces. From then on, civil strife afflicted the people and the kingdom itself fell under the control of five kings who waged constant war on each other.

[34] As time passed, great virtue arose in a certain young man named Dunwallo Molmutius.[1] He was the son of Cloten, the king of Cornwall, and he surpassed all the other kings of Britain in both beauty and valor. When he succeeded to the Cornish kingship after his father's death, Dunwallo rebelled against Pinner, the king of Logres, and slew him in battle. Then King Rudauc of Wales and King Stater of Alban, having solidified a mutual alliance, led their armies into Dunwallo's lands, despoiling both town and countryside. Dunwallo, however, came against them with thirty thousand men and pitched battle. After they had fought for many days with neither side claiming the victory, Dunwallo gathered the six hundred bravest youths he could find and ordered them to gird themselves with the weapons of their fallen enemies. Even Dunwallo himself cast off the arms he bore and clad himself like his men. He then led them into the midst of the enemy battalions, falling back as if they were the enemies' own men. When they finally reached that place where Rudauc and Stater were, Dunwallo gave the order to attack. The two kings perished in this onslaught, along with a great many of their men. Dunwallo Molmutius, fearing that he might be mistakenly killed by his own soldiers, returned with his companions and disarmed. Then, taking up again the arms that they had previously laid aside, he urged his allies to bear down upon the enemy, and he himself fought most fiercely. He swiftly gained the victory, forcing his enemies to scatter and flee. He then pushed on into the lands of the slain kings, overthrew their cities and towns, and made their people acknowledge his dominion.

When he had thus subdued the entire island, Dunwallo made for himself a crown of gold, and restored the kingdom to its former state.

---

[1] Certain early Welsh princely genealogies, such as those collected in Harleian MS 3859, mention a Dumngal Moilmut, the son of Garbaniaun. Later traditions, perhaps drawing tangentially on Geoffrey's account, identify this Dumngal Moilmut (or *Dyfnwal Moelmud*) as a pre-Roman king of Dumnonia in southwest Britain. The phrase "great virtue" here is the translation of the Latin term *probitas*.

It was Dunwallo Molmutius who instituted among the Britons those laws that are still known among the English as the Molmutine Laws. Dunwallo also made a decree, which the blessed Gildas recorded much later, that the cities and the temples of the gods should enjoy the special privilege that, should any fugitive or criminal flee to them, his enemies had to forgive his wrongdoings when he came out. Dunwallo declared that this law applied as well to the roads that led to these cities and temples, and he also ratified the farmers' ownership of ploughs. In his days, highwaymen ceased to draw their swords, the rapacity of robbers was quelled, and no one committed any violence against anyone else. At long last, some forty years after taking the crown, Dunwallo passed away. He was buried in the city of Trinovant outside the Temple of Concord, which he himself had erected as a surety of his own laws.

BOOK THREE

[35] Not long after King Dunwallo's death, his two sons, Belinus and Brennius, were plagued with the greatest strife, for both of them desired to inherit the realm and they quarrelled over which of them should should be honored with the crown.[1] However, after there had been many disputations between them, their mutual friends intervened and brought them to an agreement. These friends recommended that the brothers divide the kingdom between them. Since Trojan custom dictated that the eldest son receive the greater inheritance, Belinus should hold sovereignty over the entire island along with Logres, Wales, and Cornwall in particular. But since Brennius was the younger and should defer to his brother, he should receive Northumbria from the River Humber all the way to Caithness. They drew up a treaty with these provisions and for five years they ruled the land with peace and justice.

However, because strife is always seeking to insinuate itself into prosperity, certain flattering liars came one day to Brennius, saying "Has idle cowardice taken such a hold of you that you are submitting to Belinus? Do you not spring from the same father and mother? Were you not born with the same noble blood? Recall how skilled you are in making war, you who have so often repelled the incursions of Duke Cheulf of Moray, forcing him to flee from your realm. Break this treaty that is so unfair to you and take to wife the daughter of King Elsing of Norway so that you may receive his aid in restoring your lost dignity." After young Brennius' mind was corrupted with these and many similar thoughts, he gave in to these flatterers, went to Norway, and married the king's daughter just as they had advised.

[36] When this news finally reached Belinus, he was offended because Brennius had acted against him and had left the kingdom without leave. Belinus therefore attacked Northumbria, seizing the border cities and fortifying them with his own men. Learning of his brother's actions, Brennius in turn sailed back towards Britain leading a great force of

---

[1]   Belinus and Brennius, who are paired for the first time by Geoffrey, have antecedents in Welsh folk tradition and genealogies. Belinus perhaps corresponds to Beli Mawr, a shadowy figure in Welsh folklore, while Brennius corresponds to a certain Bran map Dumngal Moilmut in a genealogy recorded in Harleian MS 3859, as well as to a Welsh mythological figure, Bran son of Llyr, who appears in *The Mabinogion*.

Norsemen. As he was crossing the ocean with a favorable wind and thought himself safe from assault, he was intercepted by Guthlac, king of the Danes, who had been pursuing him. Guthlac had been madly in love with the girl whom Brennius had married; in his torment he had raised a fleet, gathered an army, and was now hunting down Brennius in the swiftest of ships. Attacking him at sea, Guthlac bore down upon the vessel in which the girl was being kept, grappled it with iron hooks, and towed it by force into the midst of his fleet. Then, as the two fleets began to clash together back and forth on the high seas, an adverse wind drew up a sudden storm, blowing all the ships off course. The fleets were thoroughly scattered and forced to land on sundry shores. The hostile king of Denmark was tossed about for five days by strong winds until he and the girl came ashore with trepidation in Northumbria, though he did not realize what unexpected fate awaited him there. When the locals recognized him, they seized them and led them to Belinus, who was in that region anticipating the landfall of his brother. Along with Guthlac's ship there also happened to be three other vessels that had been part of Brennius' fleet. When these men explained who they were to the king, Belinus rejoiced that this turn of events had transpired even while he was seeking to avenge himself on his brother.

[37] After several days, Brennius managed to rendezvous with his fleet, and he came ashore in Alban. There he was informed of the capture of his wife and men and of Belinus' occupation of the kingdom of Northumbria. So he sent messengers to his brother and demanded that his wife and lands be returned. He threatened to ravage the island from sea to sea and to slay his brother if the opportunity ever arose. When Belinus heard these threats, he refused the demands completely and, gathering all his soldiers, marched on Alban to make war. But Brennius, realizing he would be repelled trying to attack his brother in the north, intercepted Belinus in the forest of Calaterium and fought with him there.[1] The combat pressed on for much of the day, for there were very valorous men fighting at close quarters on both sides. There was great slaughter all about: weapons were wielded with great force and many fatal blows were struck. Just as fields of grain fall low beneath the mower's scythe, so did the men of both armies fall wounded. At long last, the Norsemen, their battalions torn to pieces, fled back to their ships and the Britons won the day. As the Norsemen fled, Belinus pursued them

---

[1]   Cf. The Prophecies of Merlin in Book Seven, prophecy (39). The forest of Calaterium has not been successfully indentified.

and meted slaughter without quarter upon them. Fifteen thousand died in battle that day, and less than a thousand of the survivors escaped without a wound. However, as fortune had it, Brennius himself managed to flee with a single ship and sought asylum on the shores of Gaul. The other men whom he had led into Britain went into hiding.

[38] After Belinus had secured this victory, he summoned all of his vassals to York, seeking to receive their counsel about what to do with the king of the Danes. Having been cast into prison, Guthlac declared that he would submit both himself and the Danish kingdom to Belinus. He also promised to pay a yearly tribute if only he and his beloved could be set free. He even agreed to send hostages in good faith of this treaty. The noblemen whom Belinus had summoned all agreed that Belinus should accept Guthlac's terms. Belinus therefore relented, and Guthlac and his lover were released and returned to Denmark.

[39] Since there was now no one in the kingdom of Britain to resist him, Belinus took control of the entire island from sea to sea. He confirmed all the laws that his father had instituted and he made arrangements for the abiding dispensation of justice throughout the kingdom. Most importantly, he ordered that the cities, as well as the great roads that led into them, should enjoy the same privileges that Dunwallo had granted them. Discord, however, arose over the issue of these roads, since there was no one who could now say what their precise confines were. Therefore, wishing to remove any ambiguity from his laws, Belinus brought together all the workmen of the entire island and ordered that a new road be made, paved with cement and stone, that would run the length of the island, from Cornwall's sea to the shores of Caithness, in a straight line through each of the cities. He also ordered that a second road be built across the breadth of the kingdom, from St. David's on the Irish Sea all the way to Southampton and passing through all the cities along the way. Two other roads he had constructed running diagonally through other cities.[1] Then Belinus hallowed these roads with great honor and privileges, decreeing that any violence committed upon them would be punished by the king's law. If anyone desires to know more about all the works accomplished by Dunwallo and Belinus, let him read the Molmutine Laws which the historian Gildas translated from British to Latin and that King Alfred later translated from Latin into English.[2]

---

[1] Geoffrey certainly has in mind the old network of Roman roads that once crisscrossed Britain and were still in place in the twelfth century.

[2] No such work by Gildas is now extant; claims that Alfred's laws derive from any source but the Mercian Law are unsubstantiated.

[40] While Belinus was reigning in peace and tranquillity, his brother Brennius, forced to bide his time on the Gallic shore, was wracked with anguish; he bore it ill that he was exiled from his homeland and had no hope of returning there in force to regain his former dignity. Not knowing what to do, he took a retinue of a mere twelve knights and sought out the various princes of Gaul. Although he explained his misfortunes to each of them in turn, he was unable to obtain any assistance from them. But he came last to Seginus, the duke of the Allobroges, who welcomed him with great honor. Brennius enjoyed this hospitality for a long while, and he grew so friendly with the duke that he was favored above all others in the court. In the affairs of both peace and war, Brennius demonstrated such great probity that Seginus grew to love him as a son. Brennius was, indeed, fair of face, tall and graceful of body, and most skilled in the hunting of bird and beast. Therefore, when he had become a close friend to the duke, it was arranged that Brennius should wed the duke's only daughter. If the couple should have no son, then Brennius would receive the kingdom of the Allobroges along with this daughter. If, however, a son should be born, Seginus pledged his aid in making that child the king of Britain. The girl was married to Brennius at once, the nobles of the land paid him their homage, and Brennius was given the throne of the kingdom.

Less than a whole year had passed when the duke's final day arrived and he departed from this life. Then Brennius, although he had already obtained the obedience of the vassals through friendship, opened the duke's treasury and treated them to lavish gifts that had been hoarded there since the days of their forefathers. And what's more—the thing that the Allobroges considered the best of all—he was most generous in giving out food and turned no one away from his door.

[41] Having obtained the favor of the Allobroges, Brennius now gave thought to how he could avenge himself on his brother. When he addressed this desire to his subjects, they all agreed to follow him into whatever kingdom he chose to lead them. Assembling a great army from his allies, he made a treaty with the Gauls to move unhindered through their provinces on his way to Britain. Passing through Gaul, he fitted a fleet on the shores of Normandy, set sail on the first favorable wind, and crossed over to Britain.

When his brother's landing was made known, Belinus gathered all the youth of his realm together and prepared to pitch battle against him. But suddenly, when the soldiers on both sides were just about to clash together, the mother of both Belinus and Brennius, who was still alive, rushed in between the two battalions. Her name was Conwenna and she hastened to look upon the son whom she had not seen in a very long time.[1] Making her way step by tremulous step to the place where Brennius was standing, she cast her arms about his neck and covered him with loving kisses. Then baring her breasts to him, she spoke to him amid her sobs: "Remember, my son, remember these breasts which gave you suck. Remember your mother's womb, where the Creator shaped you into human form; the womb from which with terrible pains I brought you into the world! Recalling the torments I suffered for you, hear my plea! Put aside your anger and seek pardon from your brother. You must hold nothing at all against him who has given you no insult. What makes you think that you have been wrongly ousted from your homeland? If you resolved to consider the chain of events more carefully, you would find nothing there to call unjust. Your brother's forcing you to leave did not cause something worse to befall you elsewhere. Instead, his action has made you abandon your former position for something much nobler indeed. Under your brother you possessed only part of a kingdom. But now that you've given that up, you have gained the kingdom of the Allobroges and are now your brother's equal. What has happened, after all, except that you have gone from ruling a petty kingdom to being a king of high position? Besides, don't forget that this bad blood arose on your part, not your brother's, and that it was *you* who hastened to rebel against *him* and that in this you enlisted the aid of the king of Norway."

Hearing these things that his mother uttered amid her tears, Brennius obeyed her most humbly and, taking off his helmet, went with her to his brother. When Belinus realized that Brennius was approaching him with the face of peace, he put aside all of his war gear and ran to kiss his brother. They made peace at once and their men disarmed and entered the city of Trinovant. Then, consulting about what they would now do, they decided to lead their united armies over to Gaul to bring all of those lands under their power.

[42] When a year had gone by, they crossed over to Gaul and began to ravage the countryside. The people there soon got word of this and so they gathered all the petty-kings of the Franks together to intercept the Britons and do battle with them. But Belinus and Brennius triumphed and the Franks retreated, their battalions wounded and broken. Although

---

[1]   The figure of Conwenna may have been inspired by the legendary Roman woman Veturia, the mother of the rebellious Coriolanus in Livy's *Ab Urbe Condita*, 2.40; like Conwenna, she appears on the battlefield at the eleventh hour in order to stem her son's violence against the state.

the Britons and Allobroges had secured this victory, they did not flag in their pursuit of the fleeing Gauls, but captured their kings and forced them to surrender. Within a year the Britons had overthrown all the fortified cities and had gained control over the entire kingdom.

[43] After they had finally compelled all the various provinces to surrender, they pushed on toward Rome with all their strength, laying waste the cities and towns all throughout Italy.[1] At that time there were two consuls in Rome, Gabius and Porsenna, to whom the governance of the land had been entrusted. When the consuls realized that there was no one who could withstand the onslaught of Belinus and Brennius, they obtained the Senate's permission to approach the brothers and ask for peace and friendship. The consuls offered Belinus and Brennius many gifts of gold and silver as well as a yearly tribute if they could continue to rule their own lands in peace. King Belinus and King Brennius thereupon granted the Romans a reprieve, taking hostages and leading their own forces into Germany.

As soon as the Britons and their allies began to attack Germany, the Romans regretted the pact they had made. They revoked the treaty with great boldness and sent military aid to the Germans. When Belinus and Brennius received word of this, they bore the news very gravely and took counsel together about how they might be able to fight both peoples at once. Indeed, the Italians were coming with such an enormous army that the Britons had cause for great consternation. They decided that Belinus would continue to wage the war against their enemies in Germany. Brennius meanwhile would lead his forces to punish Rome itself for breaking the treaty. Some of the Italian soldiers in Germany realized Brennius' strategy and deserted the Germans, hastening to intercept Brennius' march on Rome. Belinus, however, heard of their plan in turn and withdrew his own army from Germany. He forced his troops to march all through the night until he came upon a certain valley which he knew the enemy would be passing through. The Britons halted there and awaited the Romans' arrival. At sunrise on the very next day, the Romans in their journey south marched down through that place. When the Romans made out the glittering of spears in the valley before them, they were quite confused and immediately supposed that Brennius and the Gauls were approaching. As soon as Belinus caught sight of the Romans, the Britons fell upon them and

---

[1]   Geoffrey's account of the British invasion of Rome probably derives from Livy, 5.36–49, and he seems to identify his own Brennius with the Gallic chieftain Brennus, who led an army of Gauls against Rome and sacked the city in 386 BCE.

fought with them most bitterly. The Romans panicked, for they were defenseless and had not been arrayed for battle, and they quickly deserted the field. Belinus pursued them relentlessly, cutting them down without mercy until nightfall.

Secure in this victory, Belinus then sought out Brennius, who had already been besieging Rome for three days. Combining their armies, they assaulted the city from all sides and attempted to cast down the walls. And, to inflict even greater damage, they built gallows before the gates of the city and announced that they would hang the Roman hostages unless they surrendered. But they put aside all pity for their sons and grandsons and were determined to defend the city to the last. And so they began to destroy the Britons' siege-engines with similar devices of their own, and they began to drive the Britons away from the walls with missiles of various sorts. When Belinus and Brennius saw this, they seethed with rage and commanded twenty-four noble hostages to be hanged in the sight of their families. In retaliation, the Romans pushed their counter-attack even more fiercely, placing their hope in messages from the consuls Gabius and Porsenna, who were promising to arrive the following day with aid. The Romans therefore resolved to come out of the city and meet their enemies on field of battle. Just then, even as they were arranging their battalions more effectively, the consuls arrived ahead of schedule. They had reunited all of their scattered forces and were ready to fight. Closing their ranks, the Romans rushed down upon the Britons and Allobroges. When Belinus and Brennius perceived the great danger to their troops in this sudden onslaught, they at once began to urge their men to fall back into formation. Charging into the thick of battle, the two kings forced their enemies back. At long last, after thousands of men had fallen dead on either side, the brothers were granted the victory. Having slain Gabius and captured Porsenna, the Britons occupied the city and distributed the hidden treasures of the Romans among themselves.

[44] With this victory in hand, Brennius remained in Italy and ruled the people there with an unusual severity. Since the Roman histories already describe his other deeds and his eventual death, I have chosen not to treat these affairs here, lest I make this work too long or get myself off track by needlessly retelling what others have already discussed.[1] Belinus, in any case, returned to Britain and lived out the rest of his days

---

[1] Geoffrey's "Roman histories" included Livy's *Ab Urbe Condita*, and perhaps the *Historia Romana* of Landulphus Sagax.

in his homeland in great tranquility. He rebuilt all the walled cities that had collapsed and constructed many new works as well. Among other things, he established a city on the River Usk near the Severn Sea. It was in the archdiocese of Demetia and was for many years called Kaerusk, but its former name was displaced by the name Caerleon, the City of Legions, a name taken from the Roman legions who once used to winter there.[1] Belinus also constructed upon the banks of the Thames in Trinovant a new gate of great craftsmanship; this gate was named after him, and the people even in his day called it Billingsgate. Atop it he built a tower of remarkable height, and at its bottom he built a gate for ships to pass through. He renewed the laws of his father throughout the kingdom, devoting himself to the righteous dispensation of justice. In his days, moreover, the people enjoyed more riches than they ever had before or would ever have again in later days. At last, when the king's final day arrived and he was snatched from this life, his body was burned and his ashes were placed in a golden cask that was kept in the city of Trinovant in the same lofty tower that he had constructed.

[45] His son Gurguint Barbtruc succeeded him, a man both modest and wise. He loved peace and justice and ratified all of his father's acts. And when neighboring peoples rebelled against him, he likewise followed his father's example and brought dire war against his enemies, reducing them to servitude. Among other things, it happened that a certain king of the Danes who once paid tribute to his father, neglected to render Gurguint the same tribute, rejecting his former subjugation. Gurguint took this matter very seriously and led a fleet into Denmark. In a number of fierce battles, he attacked the people there and killed the king, renewing his sovereignty over that land.

[46] At that time, coming home after this victory through the Isles of Orkney, he discovered thirty ships full of men and women. When he inquired about the reason for their journey, their leader, a man by the name of Partholoim, approached.[2] Showing Gurguint great honor, he begged peace and pardon. He explained that he had been exiled from the lands where the Spaniards dwelt and that he was sailing through those seas in search of a place to dwell. He even asked the king

---

[1] Geoffrey seems to take pains here to identify the Latin *Urbs Legionum* with Caerleon-on-Usk rather than with the city of Chester, its traditional referent in earlier annals and chronicles.

[2] Certain Old Irish histories, such as those recorded in the *Lebor Gabála Erenn*, mention Partholim as the ancestor of one of the five successive migrations of peoples who populated Ireland. Later in the twelfth century, Gerald of Wales must have had access to similar accounts when composing his *History and Topography of Ireland*.

for a portion of Britain to settle in so that he no longer would have to wander on the hateful paths of the sea. A year and a half had passed since he had been exiled and had been sailing the ocean with his confederates. When Gurguint Barbtruc learned that they had come from Spain and were called Basques, and had heard their request, he sent them on to Ireland, which at that time lay empty of all inhabitants. Then they increased and multiplied and they continue to hold that island in the present day. Gurguint Barbtruc, for his part, lived out his days in peace and was buried in Caerleon, which, since his father's death, he had labored to improve with walls and edifices.

[47] After him Guithelin received the crown of the kingdom. He ruled benevolently and with restraint throughout all the days of his life. He had a noble wife by the name of Marcia who was learned in all the arts. Among the many brilliant things she devised in her great wisdom was the law code which the Britons called the Marcian Law. Alfred later translated this very law into the language of the Saxons and called it the Merchenlage.[1] And when Guithelin eventually died, the governance of the realm fell to the queen and to her son, whose name was Sisillius. Sisillius was then only seven years old and at this age could not be expected to rule the kingdom with any sense of judiciousness. So his mother, who was mighty in counsel and wisdom, took control of the entire island, and by the time she finally departed this life, Sisillius was ready to assume the crown of the kingdom. After him his son Kinarius obtained the kingdom. Kinarius' brother Danius succeeded him.

[48] At the death of King Danius, Morvidus was chosen king; he was Danius' son by the concubine Tangusteia. Morvidus would have been most famous for his great probity had he not also been given to excessive cruelty. When angered, Morvidus showed mercy to no one, preferring to kill a man if his weapons were near at hand. Yet Morvidus was also fair of face and most generous in the giving of gifts. Nor was there any man in the land with the strength to withstand him in combat. In his days it happened that a certain king of Moray attacked Northumbria with a great force and began to ravage the countryside. Morvidus, assembling all the young warriors that he could, rushed forth and met him in battle. Morvidus by himself was a greater force in battle than the most part of the army that he led forth. And after he obtained the victory, no

---

[1] The laws of the West Saxon King Alfred do acknowledge the influence of Mercian law, though they make no mention of Marcia; Geoffrey's account is probably apocryphal. See Tatlock, *The Legendary History of Britain*, 283.

living man escaped death at his hands. Morvidus commanded that the prisoners be brought before him one by one, and he entertained his cruelty by slaying each one personally. When fatigue finally forced him to pause, he ordered the men who were left to have their hearts torn out and their carcasses burned. While he committed these and other atrocities, a misfortune struck him that put an end to his evil. There emerged out of the Irish Sea a creature of unheard-of ferocity that was continually devouring the people who lived near the shore. When word of this reached Morvidus' ears, he approached the beast and fought with it. But when in vain he had spent all of his spears on the creature, the monster rushed at the king, opened its gaping jaws, and gobbled him up as if he were a mere school of fish.

[49] Morvidus fathered five sons, the eldest of whom, Gorbonianus, inherited the throne of the kingdom. There was no one in his day who was more just or a greater lover of the law than he. Nor was there anyone who ruled the common people with a greater sense of duty and compassion. It was ever his custom to pay due honor to the gods and to dispense justice to all the people. He rebuilt temples in all the cities throughout the kingdom of Britain and constructed many new ones as well. Throughout all the days of his life the island enjoyed a greater abundance of riches than all the neighboring countries. He encouraged the common folk to till the earth, and he protected them from the abuses of their lords. He even enriched young warriors with silver and gold so that they would have no need to attack anyone else. After these and many other deeds that revealed his inborn goodness, he paid his debt to nature and departed from this life. He was buried in the city of Trinovant.

[50] After Gorbonianus, his brother Arthgallo was invested with the royal diadem. In all of his actions he proved himself quite the opposite of his brother. He strove constantly to depose members of the nobility, setting up ignoble men in their places. He managed to accumulate vast hoards of treasure by stealing the wealth from others. The chief men of the kingdom finally refused to tolerate this any longer, and they rebelled and overthrew Arthgallo. They then set up his brother Elidur on the throne of the realm. This Elidur in later days would later be called "the Faithful" because of the great mercy he showed to his brother. For after he had ruled the kingdom for five years, he was out hunting in the Forest of Calaterium when he came upon his dispossessed brother. Arthgallo had been wandering through the neighboring kingdom looking for aid in regaining his former dignity. But he found no help. And when he was no longer able to bear his poverty any longer, he

came back to Britain, his retinue a mere ten knights. He had been seeking out those whom he had once called friends when Elidur happened upon him quite unexpectedly. On seeing Arthgallo, Elidur rushed over and took his brother in his arms, showering him with countless kisses. After he had bewailed Arthgallo's wretched state for a while, he led his brother into the city of Alclud and concealed him in his bedchamber. Then Elidur pretended to lie ill there, and he sent his messengers all throughout the realm, beckoning the nobles to come and visit him. And when they had all arrived in the city where he lay, he ordered them to come into his bedchamber one by one, taking care not to make any noise. He claimed that the voices of so many people crowding in would exacerbate his suffering. Each nobleman accepted this request and they entered the chamber one after another. But Elidur had ordered his servants to decapitate the men one by one unless they would swear anew their allegiance to Arthgallo. This he did, one by one, to all of them, and so by manipulating their fear he made peace between Arthgallo and all the nobility. After the oaths had been sworn, Elidur then led Arthgallo to York, and there he removed the royal crown from his own head and set it upon his brother's. And so it was that Elidur earned the name of the Faithful, since he kept faith with his brother. Arthgallo reigned for ten years, and he never again lapsed into his former evil. Reversing his previous policies, he deposed the ignoble and promoted the magnanimous. He allowed everyone to possess his own goods freely, and he assured that appropriate justice was always done. Eventually, he fell into a coma and died. He was buried in the city of Kaer Leir.

[51] Elidur was then made king once more and restored to his former dignity. However, although Elidur followed his eldest brother Gorbonianus in all his good works, his two youngest brothers, Ingenius and Peredur, went about assembling an army to topple him. Victorious, they seized Elidur, locked him in a tower in the city of Trinovant, and placed guards all about him. They then divided the kingdom in two. The lands lying west of the River Humber fell by lot to Ingenius. Peredur received the other portion, as well as all of Alban. After seven years, Ingenius died and the entire kingdom passed to Peredur. Having gained control in this way, Peredur set about governing the realm with peace and moderation. He hoped in this way to surpass his older brothers, though no one ever mentioned Elidur. However, since no man may evade death forever, death caught up with Peredur and snatched his life away. Elidur was then released from prison and set on the throne of the

kingdom for a third time. And after he had lived out all of his days in goodness and justice, he at last forsook this life. He stood as an example of loyalty for all his successors.

[52] After Elidur had died, the son of Gorbonianus took the crown of the kingdom, and he set about imitating his uncle's good sense and wisdom.[1] Casting off all vestiges of tyranny, he treated all the people with justice and mercy, and he never strayed from the path of righteousness. After him reigned Margan, the son of Arthgallo. He too was illuminated by his family tradition, and he governed the Britons most peacefully. His brother Enniaunus succeeded him. Enniaunus was so different from Margan in the way he ruled the people that he was deposed from the royal seat during the sixth year of his reign. For Enniaunus far preferred tyranny to justice, and it was this that caused his removal from the throne. His cousin Idwal, the son of Ingenius, took his place. Keeping the downfall of Enniaunus ever in his mind, Idwal cherished justice and righteousness. Rhun, the son of Peredur, succeeded him. After him came Geraint the son of Elidur. After him came Kadell his son. After Kadell came Coel, after Coel came Porrex, and after Porrex came Cherin. To Cherin were born three sons— Fulgenius, Edadus, and Andragius. They all reigned in succession after him. Then Urianus the son of Andragius took the throne, then Eliud, then Cledauc, then Cloten, then Gurguint, then Merianus, then Bledud, then Cap, then Oenus, then Sisillius, then Bledgabred. Bledgabred was the greatest singer of ancient days, and he surpassed all others in every mode and musical instrument to such an extent that he was called the God of Minstrels. After him reigned his brother Arthmail. After Arthmail came Eldol. Redion succeeded him, then Redech, Samuil, Penissel, Pir, and Capoir. Capoir was succeeded by his son Cligueillius, a man who was both moderate and wise in all of his deeds. He upheld justice as highest thing for all of his people.

[53] After Cligueillius, his son Heli inherited the kingdom and ruled for forty years. Heli had three sons: Lud, Cassibelaunus, and Nennius. Lud, the eldest, received the kingship after his father. He was a renowned founder of cities, and he renovated the walls of the city of Trinovant and erected countless towers going all around atop them. He also ordered that even the common folk build such houses and buildings that the city of Trinovant would have the fairest edifices in all the

---

[1]   This king remains unnamed in all of the manuscripts I have examined, as well as in all the published Welsh translations.

far lands of the kingdom. Lud was a warlike man and he gave lavish feasts. And although he possessed a great many cities, he loved Trinovant most of all, spending the better part of his reign there. Thus Trinovant came to be called Kaerlud after him, and, in later times, it was known through the corruption of tongues as Kaerlundein. As even more time passed and men's speech changed even further, it was called Lundene, and afterwards Londres by the foreign invaders who conquered the land.[1] When Lud died, his body was preserved in this city next to the gate that is now named after him: Portlud in the British tongue and Ludesgata in the Saxon.

Lud had two sons, Androgeus and Tenvantius. Since they could not rule after them because of their young age, Lud's brother Cassibelaunus was promoted to the kingship. Shortly after he received the crown, his reputation for generosity and righteousness began to increase so much that his fame was rumored throughout many distant lands. And so it happened that he retained the kingship for his own and did not cede it to his nephews. However, moved by his deep sense of loyalty, Cassibelaunus did not want the two youths to be deprived of their inheritance, and so he granted the greater part of the realm to them. He invested Androgeus with the city of Trinovant and the duchy of Kent and gave Tenvantius the duchy of Cornwall. But Cassibelaunus himself remained High King of the entire island and held sway over these two princes.

---

[1]   Some of the Welsh *Bruts*, translations of Geoffrey's *History*, insert the Welsh story known as *Cyfranc Lludd a Llefelys* (*The Tale of Lludd and Llefelys*) at this point in the narrative.

BOOK FOUR

[54] Amid all these events, it happened, as one reads in the Roman histories, that Julius Caesar came to the coastlands where the Ruteni lived, having subjugated all of Gaul.[1] Gazing out across the ocean, he espied the isle of Britain, and he asked those who were standing near him what country it was and what people dwelt there. When they told him the name of that realm and its people, Caesar declared, "By Hercules! We Romans and these Britons are sprung from the same root, for we both came out of Troy. After the destruction of Troy, Aeneas was our first father; and their Brutus descends from Silvius the son of Ascanius the son of Aeneas. However, unless I am mistaken, they are certainly degenerates compared to us. Nor do I think they can know much about military affairs, since they live across the ocean at the edge of the earth. It should be easy to force them to pay us tribute and to render eternal homage to the power of Rome. We must first inform them that, though they have been hitherto out of touch with the Roman people, they must nevertheless pay taxes since all other peoples pay a tribute to the Senate. If they refuse, we may have to offend the ancient nobility of our common ancestor Priam by spilling the blood of these our remote kinsmen."

Caesar sent this message off to King Cassibelaunus, who became enraged and sent him back a letter that said: [55] "Cassibelaunus, King of the Britons, greets Gaius Julius Caesar. I marvel, Caesar, at the rapacity of the Roman people and at their enormous thirst for gold and silver. Although we dwell beyond the perils of the great ocean at the very ends of the earth, the Roman people cannot suffer us to exist without needing to acquire our property, which we have until now possessed in peace. Nor will this alone suffice unless we also cast aside our freedom for subjugation and submit ourselves to eternal servitude. You have sought to offend yourself, Caesar, since the blood of common nobility flows from Aeneas through the veins of Britons and Romans alike. Our shared lineage should make us the firmest of friends. Friendship, then, not servitude, should you be asking of us, for we

---

[1] Despite Geoffrey's claims to be consulting the Roman histories for his information on Caesar's invasion of Britain, his account here is based largely on Bede, I.2–3, and on Nennius' *History of the Britons*, though Geoffrey has fleshed out both of these terser narratives considerably.

would rather extend our friendship than take on the yoke of servitude. Indeed, we are now so used to our freedom that we no longer know how to be servile. If the gods themselves attempted to take our freedom from us, we would still strive with all our might to resist them and to retain our liberty. Do give up your plans, Caesar, for if you try to conquer the island of Britain, as you have threatened, you will have to contend with us for our land and liberty alike!"

[56] Reading this letter, Gaius Julius Caesar prepared a fleet and waited for just the right winds so that he could carry out the threats he had made in his letter to Cassibelaunus. Choosing an opportune moment, he raised his sails and landed his army in the estuary of the River Thames. As the rafts were in the process of bringing the Roman army ashore, Cassibelaunus was ready, hastening to meet him with all of his forces. Once there, Cassibelaunus entered the fortress of Dorobellum and took counsel with the nobles of the kingdom how they could defend themselves against this enemy for any length of time.[1] His two nephews were there, Androgeus, duke of Trinovant, and Tenvantius, duke of Cornwall; he also had three subject kings with him: Cridous of Alban, Gueitheit of Venedotia and Britahel of Demetia. Since these led many others with them who were ready for combat, they advised the king to attack Caesar's forces at once and attempt to expel him from the island before he was able to capture any cities or strongholds. They believed that if Caesar were able to establish a foothold in Britain, it would be all the more difficult to oust him in the future, since he would discover where they and their allies were. Everyone agreed to this plan, and they made for the shore where Julius Caesar had set up his camp and defenses.

The two sides formed their lines of battle, and then the Britons began to assail their enemies, returning spear-thrust for spear-thrust and sword-blow for sword-blow. Wounded in the clash, the soldiers began to run about to and fro, spilling their entrails. The blood and gore of the dying men soaked the very ground, just as when the south wind forces the ebbing tide back onto the shore. As the armies were thus engaged, it happened that Nennius joined forces with Androgeus' men from Kent and Trinovant, right by the place where the Emperor's bodyguard stood. As the Britons advanced, the Imperial guard was slowly forced to give ground to the Britons, who pushed forward with their powerful assault. Then, although the fighting was redoubled, fortune granted Nennius hand-to-hand combat with Julius Caesar himself. Rushing towards him,

---

[1] Dorobellum may perhaps correspond to Dover.

Nennius rejoiced beyond measure to be able to deal this man even a single blow. When Caesar noticed the oncoming attack, he held up his shield and parried the blow, and then he struck Nennius's helmet with his naked sword with as much force as he could muster. Then, raising his sword, he tried to follow up his first strike by dealing a lethal wound. Nennius, infuriated, blocked the blow with his shield. Caesar's blade, bouncing off Nennius's helmet, lodged itself in his shield with such great force that he could not draw it out when the battle began to sweep the two of them apart. Having obtained Caesar's sword in this way, Nennius cast aside the sword he was carrying and, pulling Caesar's out of his shield, rushed back into the fray. Everyone whom Nennius struck with the sword either got his head chopped off or else was so wounded as Nennius passed that he had no hope of ever recovering. The Roman tribune Labenus, rushing furiously at Nennius, was slain in this way. Thus, as the better part of the day passed, God granted the field to the Britons, who kept advancing in tight formation and dealt mighty blows to the enemy. Caesar withdrew all the wounded Romans back to the camp and onto the ships. He spent all that night regrouping his men. They boarded the ships and Caesar was glad to have the sea so close at hand. And since his men dissuaded him from pushing the fight further, he heeded their advice and returned to Gaul.

[57] Cassibelaunus rejoiced, thanking God for this great victory. Then he gathered his men together and bestowed great gifts upon those who most deserved them. At the same time, he was grieved by the fact that his brother Nennius was lethally wounded and lay dying. Julius Caesar had struck Nennius in the fight described above and had dealt him an incurable wound. He gave up this life fifteen days after the battle and is buried next to the north gate of the city of Trinovant. At his funeral they placed the sword that he had won in his battle with Caesar in the tomb with him. The name of that sword was Golden Death, since no one who was struck by it could survive.

[58] Turning his back on Britain, Julius Caesar returned to the shores of Gaul to find that the Gauls had grown unruly and now sought to overthrow his dominion, for they deemed that he was now so weakened that they need no longer fear him. The rumor everywhere was now one and the same: that the sea was now thick with the ships of Cassibelaunus in pursuit of Caesar. The boldest Gauls even planned how they would expel Caesar from their lands altogether. Julius Caesar understood clearly that it would be unwise to fight a war on two fronts against such belligerent foes. Instead, he approached some of the more noble Gauls and bought

peace from them, one at a time, with treasure from his coffers. He also promised freedom for the masses, as well as the return of their seized property and the manumission of those whom he had enslaved. At one time, aflame with leonine ferocity, Caesar had taken everything away from the Gauls; now, in a voice as humble as a meek little lamb's, he was happy to give them back as much as he could. He continued in such a spirit of kindness until he had pacified all the Gauls and restored his tottering power. And he brooded on nothing in the following days except on his own narrow escape and the victory of the Britons.

[59] After two years had passed, Caesar prepared to traverse the ocean once again and avenge himself on Cassibelaunus. When Cassibelaunus heard of Caesar's approach, he fortified all the cities, rebuilt the crumbling walls, and set up armed soldiers at all the gates. He also set up thick rows of stakes made of lead and human thigh bones just below the water line in the bed of the River Thames. Caesar would have to traverse this river on his way to the city of Trinovant, and his ships would be dashed to pieces against these stakes. Cassibelaunus also mustered all of the island's young men and built a barracks near the shore where they would await the enemies' arrival.

[60] As soon all of his own preparations were in place, Julius Caesar set off across the sea again with a countless host of soldiers, in great hopes of inflicting terrible violence upon the people who had previously repelled him. He would, without a doubt, have been able to achieve this if his fleet had been able to land intact. However, as the ships approached Trinovant up the Thames, disaster struck as they reached the stakes that the Britons had set up there. The soldiers drowned by the thousands as the river filled up their tattered vessels.[1] When Caesar realized this situation, he turned his sails with the utmost haste and made for land. The few men who had managed to escape this peril clambered onto the shore with him. Cassibelaunus awaited them on the shore, rejoicing in the sinking of the ships, though dismayed that so many Romans had escaped. Then, giving the signal to his men, he commenced the assault against the Romans. But the Romans who had avoided being drowned in the river and had now made it to shore, repelled the attack of the Britons valiantly. Although courage was their only defense, they still put up a good fight. In the end, however, they suffered far more than their enemies. Having already faced a great ordeal in the river, there were far fewer Romans

---

[1]   In Bede's account in his *Ecclesiastical History*, 1.2, the Romans perceive the British trap and avoid it.

now left, and the Britons, gaining new troops by the hour, soon outnumbered them by three to one. The Britons thus attained victory because of the weakness of their foes.

Seeing that defeat was imminent, Caesar fled with a few men back to the ships and made it to the protection of the sea without a fight. Great winds blew up at once, and Caesar raised his sails and headed for the shores of the Moriani. Then he established a base in a tower there known as Odnea, which he had constructed during his previous invasion of Britain. He was concerned about the faith and instability of the Gauls, lest they attack him again just as they had done when they rose up against him the last time he needed refuge from the Britons.

[61] Cassibelaunus thus obtained a second triumph against the Romans, and he rejoiced greatly. He declared an edict that all the noblemen of Britain should come to Trinovant with their wives to pay the solemn debts they all owed to the gods of their land for the victory they had won over a such a commander as Caesar. And when they had all assembled, they killed many cattle and made other types of sacrifices as well. They offered up a total of forty thousand cows and one hundred thousand sheep and so many different types of birds that it is impossible to enumerate them all. In the meantime, they also rounded up three hundred thousand wild beasts of various kinds. As soon as they had made these sacrifices to the gods, they celebrated a great feast with the remainders of the animals, as was their custom after a sacrifice. For the remainder of that night and the next day, the Britons competed in various games together.

During these festivities, it happened that two youths, one the nephew of the king and the other the nephew of Duke Androgeus, were tied in a wrestling-match and they began to argue about who had won. The name of the king's nephew was Hirelglas, and the other's name was Cuelinus. As their argument escalated, Cuelinus snatched up the sword of the king's nephew and cut off his head. The court was most dismayed at this slaying, and the news soon reached Cassibelaunus. Persuaded by the intervention of his friends, Cassibelaunus ordered Androgeus to bring Cuelinus into his presence at the court. Once there, Cuelinus should submit to whatever sentence the court declared, lest Hirelglas remain unavenged if he had been unjustly slain. But Androgeus doubted the king's intent; he told the king that he would hold his own court and that it should determine what punishment one of his own men should receive. If Cassibelaunus insisted on prosecuting Cuelinus, he would have to do it in Trinovant, according to the ancient custom. Cassibelaunus, then, unable to obtain the satisfaction of his desire, threatened Androgeus, declaring that he would put Androgeus' lands to fire and the sword if his request were not granted. Indignant, Androgeus withdrew the offer he had made. Cassibelaunus, growing furious in turn, wasted no time in ravaging Androgeus' lands. Androgeus sent word daily through friends and relatives, begging the king to temper his wrath. But since nothing was able to mitigate the king's fury, he began to deliberate over how he could best withstand Cassibelaunus. Therefore, having no other hope, he decided to seek aid from Caesar, sending letters to him that expressed the following:

"Duke Androgeus of Trinovant, who once wished death upon Gaius Julius Caesar, now wishes him good health. I do regret having participated in the battles that you fought against my king. If I had not been present at those engagements, you surely would have defeated Cassibelaunus. Indeed, he grew so haughty after repelling you that he has invaded my lands to rid himself of me, through whom he had gained his triumph. Should not these outrages be repaid? I enriched him, yet he is now trying to disinherit me. I restored him to his kingdom twice, and now he wants to rid himself of me. I did all of these things for him by fighting against you. With the gods as my witness, I swear that I did not deserve his wrath unless, I suppose, that I did not hand over my nephew, whom he wanted to condemn to an unjust death. Allow me to explain the cause of this quarrel for your consideration. It happened that, in our triumph, we were giving our most solemn thanks to the gods of our land. While we were making the ritual sacrifices, our young men were competing in various athletic games. During one of these games, our two nephews were wrestling together, following the example of the other young men. When my nephew had won the match, the other was filled with an unjust anger and went to strike him. But, avoiding the blow, my nephew seized the fist that held the other's sword and sought to take it from him. In the meanwhile, it happened that the nephew of the king stumbled upon the blade and met his untimely end. When this entire affair was made known to the king, he commanded me to hand over my boy to him so that he could be punished for the slaying. When I refused this command, he came with a great army and laid my lands waste. I am therefore imploring you for your assistance. If you restore my lands to me, you shall be the master of Britain. Do not doubt me in this matter: I have no thought for treachery. Mortal men, after all, are governed by such chance conditions: great friendships may arise after great enmity, and those who once fled may yet return in triumph."

[62] Pondering this letter, Julius Caesar took counsel with his companions. They advised him not to accept this duke's invitation to come to Britain unless Caesar were given hostages to assure his safe arrival. Androgeus at once sent him his son Sceva and thirty young nobles of his personal acquaintance. Caesar felt assured by these hostages. He regrouped his army, set sail as soon as possible, and landed in Richborough.

In the meantime, Cassibelaunus had laid siege to the city of Trinovant and was pillaging the outlying villages. But when he received the news that Julius Caesar had returned, he abandoned the siege and hurried to intercept the emperor. As he was entering a valley near Canterbury, he spied the Roman army setting up its tents and defenses there. Androgeus had led them to that very place in order to make a secret attack upon the city. As soon as the Romans became aware of the approach of the Britons, they armed themselves quickly and got into their battle formations. For their part, the Britons also readied their arms and fell into their ranks. However, Androgeus took five thousand armed men and hid in a nearby wood, so that he could rush to Caesar's aid by ambushing Cassibelaunus and his men with a surprise attack. When the two armies began to skirmish, they did not shirk from casting deadly missiles and dealing lethal blows. The troops rushed together and much blood was spilled. On both sides, the wounded fell like the leaves of a tree in autumn. As the armies were clashing together, Androgeus burst out of the woods and attacked Cassibelaunus's vanguard, upon which the entire outcome of the battle depended. Before long, the vanguard could no longer hold its ground, for it had already been decimated by the Romans and now faced an attack from its own fellow-Britons. When the vanguard troops had been scattered in this way, Cassibelaunus turned in flight and abandoned the field.

Nearby there was a hill whose top was covered by a dense thicket of hazel trees. Cassibelaunus fled there with his men after he had been defeated on the lower ground. Reaching the summit, he defended himself valiantly and inflicted great slaughter on any of the enemy who followed him up there. Indeed, the Romans and the men of Androgeus attempted to pursue him, cutting down his men as they fled. These enemies made many charges up that hill, but they could not manage to reach the top. The Britons made such a defense with the rocks of the mountain and the steepness of the slope that they were able to inflict considerable harm on their foes as they tried to advance up the hill. As night began to settle, Caesar finally laid siege to the entire hill, cutting off all escape. Indeed, Caesar hoped to defeat the king with hunger since he could not do so with arms. O, how remarkable the Britons were in those days, for they had twice set to flight that man whom the entire world feared! Though the entire world could not resist him, the Britons did so now, even in desperate measures: they were ready to die for their homeland and their freedom. Thus did Lucan sing their praises when he wrote of Caesar that

He fled from the Britons whom he had come to conquer.[1]

As the second day passed, Cassibelaunus feared that he would succumb to his hunger and be captured by Caesar, since there was now nothing left to eat. Therefore he sent word to Androgeus, asking him to make peace with Caesar lest the honor of his native people be sullied by the captivity of its king. He also pointed out that Androgeus should not want to kill him, even if he had caused Androgeus some distress. When the messengers announced this, Androgeus declared: "We should not cherish a king who is meek as a lamb in war and fierce as a lion in peace. O gods of heaven and earth, now my lord implores me whom he once commanded! Does he wish to make peace and do homage to Caesar, who once begged mercy of him? He surely must have feared that I, who helped repel that commander from his kingdom, would be able to bring him back. I should not have been treated so unjustly, for I had the power to transfer my loyalties from one to the other. He is indeed a fool who insults and dishonors the very men with whose aid he triumphs. No leader is truly victorious except through them who shed their blood fighting for him. Nonetheless, I will make peace if I can, since the insult and injury he gave me is now sufficiently vindicated in his begging me for mercy."

[63] After these things, Androgeus hastened to Julius Caesar and, embracing his knees, spoke to him in this manner: "You have avenged yourself enough on Cassibelaunus; now have mercy on him. What more is there for him to do now but surrender and pay homage to the majesty of Rome?" When Caesar did not reply, Androgeus spoke again: "I promised you only one thing, Caesar: that once Cassibelaunus was defeated I would labor to subdue Britain for you. And behold, Cassibelaunus is defeated and Britain subdued through my assistance. What more do I owe you? The Creator of all things does not want my liege lord to beg for mercy or be carried off in chains, now that he atones for the insult

---

[1] Lucan, *Pharsalia*, II, 572. One wonders how much Geoffrey appreciated Lucan's scurrilous irony.

he gave me. It is no light matter to kill Cassibelaunus while I yet live, for I would not hesitate to lend him my aid, unless you would yield to my counsel." Held back, then, by his fear of Androgeus, Julius Caesar made peace with Cassibelaunus, who agreed to pay a yearly tribute. The tribute that he pledged was three thousand pounds of silver. Then Julius Caesar and Cassibelaunus became friends and exchanged gifts. Caesar spent that winter in Britain, then crossed the Channel and returned to Gaul the next spring. Not long afterward, Caesar organized an army of men of all different races and he rushed back to Rome to oppose Pompey. And when seven years had passed, Cassibelaunus died and was buried in York.

[64] He was succeeded by Tenvantius, the brother of Androgeus; for Androgeus himself had gone off to Rome with Caesar. Invested with the royal crown, Tenvantius ruled the kingdom most diligently. He was a warlike man and one who insisted on the full measure of justice. His son Cymbeline was elevated to the royal throne after him.[1] This Cymbeline was a mighty soldier whom Augustus Caesar had reared and decorated. He enjoyed such a great friendship with the Romans that, although he could have withheld payment of the annual tribute, he paid it willingly. In those days was born our Lord Jesus Christ, whose precious blood redeemed mankind, which had been in the thralldom of demons.

[65] When Cymbeline had governed Britain for ten years, he fathered two sons, the elder of whom was named Guiderius and the younger Arviragus. After the days of Cymbeline's life were spent, Guiderius held the governance of the realm. When he denied the tribute that Britain owed to the Romans, Claudius, who had been elevated to the Emperorship, arrived unexpectedly. There came with him an officer of his legion by the name of Lelius Hamo, who advised Claudius on how to wage all of his battles. As soon as they landed near Portchester, Hamo had that city's gates blocked with a wall, thereby preventing the townsfolk from leaving, for he desired that, forced by hunger, they would surrender to him or else die most cruelly.

[66] Learning of the arrival of Claudius Caesar, Guiderius assembled the entire soldiery of the kingdom and marched out to meet the Roman army. Joining battle, Guiderius attacked most fiercely, doing more damage with his own sword than the better part of his army combined. Claudius made for his ships at once and the Romans were quickly dispersed. But

---

[1]   Geoffrey's account of King Cymbeline is, via Holinshed's *Chronicles*, the ultimate source for William Shakespeare's *Cymbeline*. The name itself derives from the Welsh *Cynfelyn* (Britt. *Cunobelinos*), a figure mentioned in some of the early genealogies.

then, the cunning Hamo, casting aside his raiment, took up British arms and began to fight against his own men. He urged the Britons to follow him, promising them a swift victory. Indeed, he spoke their language and knew their customs, for he had been raised among British hostages in Rome. And so he moved very gradually closer to the king and, once he reached him, he fearlessly cut his throat. Falling back among the charging lines of his enemies, he returned to his own people with this nefarious victory in hand. But Arviragus, seeing Guiderius slain, quickly dropped his own arms and took up the arms of his brother the king. He raced here and there among the Britons, pretending he was Guiderius and encouraging them to remain steadfast. Not knowing of the death of their king, the Britons heeded his words and stood their ground, fighting and inflicting great slaughter.

At last the Romans were split into two groups, and began deserting the field most shamefully. Claudius sought the safety of the ships with one half of the army, while Hamo fled to the woods since there was no way for him to get to the ships. Arviragus, thinking that the Emperor was escaping with Hamo, hastened in pursuit. Following him from one place to another, Arviragus did not relent until he caught up with him near the shore that is now called Hampton after Hamo himself. There was, moreover, a harbor in that place, most suitable for merchant ships to moor in. Hamo attempted to enter the harbor, but Arviragus defeated him and slew him at once. From that day on, the harbor has been called Southampton.

[67] In the meantime, Claudius had regrouped his soldiers and was attacking the city mentioned above, which was then called Kaer Peris but is now called Portchester. Without delay, he ripped down its walls and subjugated its people. He then pursued Arviragus, who had taken refuge in Winchester. Claudius then laid the city under siege and sought to destroy it by means of various siege-engines. Arviragus, realizing he was trapped, ordered his men into battalions and, throwing open the city gates, went out to meet Claudius on the battlefield. But although the Britons were attacking, Claudius sent messengers to Arviragus, proposing a truce. Indeed, Claudius was fearful of the daring of the king and of the strength of the Britons: he preferred to quell the Britons with sense and wisdom rather than by engaging in a battle whose outcome seemed uncertain. Claudius therefore proposed a treaty to Arviragus, promising to give him his daughter if the Britons would simply acknowledge the suzerainty of Rome. While the hostilities were suspended, the nobility of Britain persuaded Arviragus to accept Claudius' offer. They claimed that it would not be ignoble to submit to

the Romans, since the entire world was under their sway. Mollified by these words and many similar arguments, Arviragus yielded to his counselors and made his formal submission to Claudius Caesar.

[68] Claudius sent to Rome for his daughter at once, and, with the help of Arviragus, he brought the Orkneys and all the other outlying isles under his power. When the winter had passed, the legates returned from Rome with the girl and delivered her to her father. The girl's name was Genvissa, and she was of such great beauty that everyone gazed upon her in admiration. Moreover, once their marriage had been legally consummated, she inspired the king with such ardent love that he preferred her company above all other things.[1] Because Arviragus desired that the place where they were married should always be remembered, he suggested to Claudius that they build a new city there, which would keep ever fresh the memory of his wedding day. Claudius agreed, and he built a city that was named Kaer Glou after him. Gloucester it is called in the present day, and it is located on the borders of Wales and England, on the banks of the River Severn.[2] Some people claim that the city takes its name from Duke Gloio, whom Claudius sired there and to whom Arviragus later entrusted the overlordship of Wales. After this city had been built and the island had been pacified, Claudius returned to Rome and ceded the governance of the insular provinces to Arviragus. Around that same time, Peter the Apostle founded the church at Antioch. After that he came to Rome and held the bishopric there, sending Mark the Evangelist to Egypt to preach the Gospel which he had written.

[69] Once Claudius had departed, Arviragus began to display his great judgment and wisdom, rebuilding the cities and towns. He governed the people of the realm with such a respect for the law that he was feared by kings and peoples far and wide. He then grew so haughty that he scoffed at the power of Rome and refused to pay the annual tribute to the Senate any longer, preferring it for himself. When Claudius got word of this, he sent Vespasian to pacify Arviragus and restore his submission to Rome. Just as Vespasian began to land at Richborough, Arviragus was there to meet him and prevented him from entering the harbor. He had led such a great host of armed men there that the Romans were terrified and did not dare to come ashore

---

[1]   Geoffrey's depiction of Arviragus as a lover may perhaps underlie the character of Arveragus in Geoffrey Chaucer's *The Franklin's Tale*.

[2]   The Latin name of Gloucester, *Claudiocestria*, explicitly suggests this connection with the Emperor Claudius.

for fear of being attacked. So Vespasian withdrew from the harbor, turned sail, and headed for Totnes. Making landfall, he marched on to lay siege to Kaer Penhuelgoit, which is also called Exeter. When he had besieged Exeter for seven days, Arviragus arrived with his army and they met in battle. Both sides were cut to pieces that day, yet neither achieved victory. On the following morning, Queen Genvissa negotiated a truce between the two leaders, and they sent their troops over to invade Ireland together.

When the winter had passed, Vespasian returned to Rome and Arviragus remained in Britain. Feeling old age set in, Arviragus grew to respect the Roman senate and governed his realm in peace and tranquility. He confirmed the traditional laws and even established some new ones, all the while bestowing gifts upon the deserving. His fame spread throughout all of Europe, and the Romans loved him and feared that his word was worth more in Rome than that of any other king. This is why Juvenal in his book mentions that a certain blind man, talking with Nero about a turbot that had been caught, told the Emperor that

Either you will capture a particular king or Arviragus
Will fall headlong from the British chariot-pole.[1]

No one was fiercer in war than Arviragus, nor more gentle in times of peace. No one was merrier than he, or more generous in the giving of gifts. And when the days of his life had drawn to a close, he was entombed in Gloucester in the same temple that he had dedicated in honor of Claudius.

[70] Arviragus was succeeded by his son Marius, a man of great sense and wisdom. During his reign, a certain king of the Picts named Sodric came down with a great fleet out of Scythia and landed in the northern part of Britain in what is now called Alban, and he began to lay that region waste.[2] Gathering his folk together, Marius sought Sodric out, slew him in battle, and won the day. He then erected a stone as a sign of his victory in that region, which was afterward named Wistmaria after him.[3] On the stone was engraved a memorial to this battle, which can still be read in the present day. Although Sodric was slain, Marius nonetheless allowed the conquered people who had come with him to

---

[1] Juvenal I. iv. 126–127. A turbot is a type of salt-water fish similar to the halibut.
[2] On many medieval maps, Scythia appears far closer to Britain than it actually was. It was usually located just east or southeast of Scandinavia.
[3] Presumably Westmoreland.

settle in that region of Alban which is now called Caithness. It was deserted in those days, long devoid of any inhabitants. Since that folk did not have any wives, they asked to wed the daughters and other female relations of the Britons. But the Britons disdained marrying off their daughters to such a people. Thus refused, the Picts sailed over to Ireland and married the women of that land, and through their offspring their numbers were greatly increased. But I shall stop here, since I did not intend to relate the history of the Picts or of the Scots, who trace their descent from this union between the Picts and the Irish.

After Marius had brought the entire island to peace, he nurtured such an admiration for the Roman people that he always paid the tribute that they required from him. Spurred on by his father's example of peace and justice, Marius cultivated the laws and all other honest pursuits throughout his kingdom. [71] When the days of his life had drawn to an end, his son Coilus obtained the governance of the realm. Since he had been raised in Rome since his early childhood, he was well-versed in Roman customs and maintained a great friendship with that people. He too always paid the tribute, not wanting to cause any trouble. Indeed, he realized that the entire world was subject to Rome and that their power exceeded that of any other city or nation. He therefore paid the tribute they demanded so that he could retain the peaceful possession of his lands. Of all the British kings, no one displayed a greater respect for the noblemen of the realm, since he either left them peacefully to their own devices or lavished them with gifts.

[72] One son was born to Coilus, by the name of Lucius. When, at the death of his father, he was invested with the royal crown, he imitated all of his father's good deeds so that everyone considered him to be a second Coilus. And, in hopes that his ending would surpass his beginning, Lucius sent letters to Pope Eleutherius asking that he might receive the Christian faith from him.[1] Indeed, the miracles that Christ's servants were performing throughout all the nations soothed his mind. Thus, breathless in his love of the true faith, his pious request was granted. Acknowledging Lucius' devotion, the Holy Pontiff sent him two great teachers of the religion, Fagan and Duvianus. These men, preaching the incarnate word of God, cleansed him with holy baptism and converted him to Christ. Soon after that, all the people of the land were rushing to follow the example of their king, and they were

---

[1] Eleutherius was Pope from c. 174–89. Bede, 1.4, mentions an exchange of letters between this Pope and a British king named Lucius.

cleansed by the same baptism and restored to the Kingdom of Heaven. When these two blessed teachers had delivered almost the entire island from paganism, they rededicated the temples, which had been founded to honor many gods, to the One God and his saints, and they filled them with various religious orders. At that time in Britain there were twenty-eight pagan *flamens* and three *archflamens*, who had power over the judges of morals and the temple officials.[1] At the Pope's command, these men as well were snatched from idolatry. Where there had been *flamens* there were now bishops, and where there had been *archflamens* there were now archbishops. Moreover, the seats of the three *archflamens* had been in the three noblest cities: London, York, and the City of Legions, whose ancient walls and buildings testify that it was situated in Glamorgan on the River Usk.[2] Once these three were cleansed of superstition, they took control of the twenty-eight bishoprics. The parishes were redistributed. Deira and Alban were apportioned to the archbishopric of York, since the great River Humber separated them from Logres. Logres and Cornwall were assigned to the archdiocese of London. The Severn separates these last two provinces from Cambria, or Wales, which belonged to the archdiocese of Caerleon.[3]

After all these deeds had been performed, the two legates returned to Rome and requested that the most Holy Pope ratify everything they had done. Once they received this confirmation, they returned to Britain with many other companions. Through their teaching, the Britons were speedily converted to faith in Christ. Their names and deeds can be found in the book that Gildas wrote concerning the victory of Aurelius Ambrosius.[4] Since he treated these matters so lucidly, there is no need to repeat them here in my own inferior style.

---

[1] Geoffrey seems to imagine the pagan Britons worshipping something similar to the Roman pantheon, and he describes the British priesthood using the Latin names of particular Roman religious offices.

[2] Geoffrey again takes pains to identify the City of Legions (*Urbs Legionum*) with Caerleon-on-Usk rather than with Chester, as other authorities had done.

[3] Caerleon-on-Usk was not an archbishopric see in the twelfth century, and the entirety of Wales was under the jurisdiction of the Archbishop of Canterbury. Later medieval attempts to establish Caerleon as an archdiocese used Geoffrey's text as an authority on the matter.

[4] If Gildas wrote such a book, it is no longer extant.

BOOK FIVE

[73] In the meantime, when that glorious King Lucius saw the cultivation of the True Faith within his realm, he was filled with great joy and consigned all the lands and possessions which had previously belonged to the pagan temples to pass into the hands of the churches of the faithful, who put them to much better use. And since he desired to extend the highest honor possible to these churches, he added to their holdings even greater lands and buildings and bestowed every type of legal privilege upon them. After all these deeds, he finally gave up the ghost in the city of Gloucester. He was buried with great honor in the archdiocesan church in the 156th year after the Incarnation of Our Lord. Lucius left no offspring to succeed him; hence great dissension arose among the Britons after his death, and the power of Rome was weakened.

[74] When word of these events came to Rome, the Senate dispatched Senator Severus and two legions to restore Roman sovereignty in Britain.[1] As soon as he landed, Severus made war with the Britons, subjugating many of them. Moreover, he strove to plague those Britons whom he had failed to subdue with such dire oppression that they were forced to flee through Deira and up into Alban. But a certain nobleman named Sulgenius resisted Severus with all his might, and he frequently harassed both the Romans and his own countrymen. Sulgenius led as many men of the island as he could find to assist him, and thus he achieved many a victory. Because his incursions were growing ever greater, the Roman commander ordered a wall to be built between Deira and Alban in order to prevent any attacks from penetrating further south. With this command issued, they made the wall stretch from sea to sea so that they would be able to hold back the enemies' progress for a long while. But Sulgenius, realizing that he could no longer resist Severus, sailed over to Scythia to seek out the aid of the Picts in regaining his honor. Enlisting every young man that he could in that land, Sulgenius returned to Britain with an enormous fleet and laid siege to York. When news of this spread throughout the various folk of Britain, a great part of the people deserted Severus and joined up with Sulgenius. This turn of events did not divert Severus from his plans. Instead, he gathered together all the Romans and

---

[1] Bede, I.4, is Geoffrey's primary source for Severus' activities in Britain.

all the Britons who were still loyal. Then he headed for the siege and fought with Sulgenius. However, as the battle grew more ferocious, Severus and many of his men were killed, though Sulgenius too was lethally wounded along with many of his own men. Severus was then laid to rest in York, a city which his legions had occupied.

[75] Severus left two sons, Bassianus and Geta. Geta's mother was of Roman blood, but the mother of Bassianus was a Briton. At the death of their father, the Romans elevated Geta to the kingship, favoring him because he was Roman on both sides. The Britons scoffed at this and chose Bassianus as their king, because of his kinship with them on his mother's side. On this account, strife arose between the brothers; Geta was killed, and Bassianus gained the kingdom.

In that time there was in Britain a young man by the name of Carausius who was sprung from a lowly bloodline.[1] Having demonstrated his great prowess in many battles, he traveled to Rome and sought leave from the Senate to protect Britain from the attacks of barbarians with a fleet of ships.[2] If his request were granted, he promised them that he would perform such deeds that the Roman state would be strengthened more than if he had given them the entire kingdom of Britain. Since the Senate was enticed by his promises, he obtained what he had asked for and returned to Britain with sealed charters. As soon as he had assembled the fleet, he gathered together a mighty force consisting of many young men of the land, and he went to sea, sailing all the shores of the kingdom and causing great unrest among all the people. Meanwhile, landing on some of the outlying islands, he set about plundering the fields, sacking the cities and towns, and carrying off all the islanders' possessions. Because of this activity, many men who coveted the possessions of others began to flock to him, so that, after a short while, Carausius commanded an army that no neighboring prince would be able to withstand. He therefore grew swollen with pride. He told the Britons that they should make him their king and that, by killing and exterminating the Romans, he would liberate the entire island from alien peoples. After he had achieved this, he at once made war with Bassianus and, slaying him, took up the governance of the realm. Bassianus was, in fact, betrayed by the very Picts whom Sulgenius, his own mother's brother, had led into Britain. For, although the Picts owed Bassianus their allegiance, they were corrupted by promises and bribes from Carausius, and in the final battle they abandoned

---

[1]   As with Severus, Bede (I.5) provides the source for Geoffrey's description of Carausius.

[2]   Despite his humble origins, Carausius displays the kingly virtue of *probitas*, translated here as "great prowess."

Bassianus' side and began to attack their comrades. The rest of Bassianus' men were dumbfounded because they did not know friend from foe. Their army fell apart and Carausius won the field. Once he had gained this victory, he granted the Picts a dwelling-place in Alban where they mixed with the British and remained throughout the subsequent ages.

[76] When word of Carausius' insurrection was made known in Rome, the Senate sent Allectus with three legions to kill the tyrant and restore Roman power in Britain. As soon as he landed, he pitched battle against Carausius, slew him, and seized the throne of the kingdom.[1] He then inflicted great slaughter upon those Britons who had abandoned the Roman state and supported Carausius. The Britons took this ill and set up Asclepiodotus, the duke of Cornwall, as their king. United in a common cause, they pursued Allectus and provoked him to battle. Allectus was then in London celebrating a feast to the gods of the land, but when he learned of the approach of Asclepiodotus, he interrupted his sacrifices and went out against him with all his strength, offering him a most bitter fight. Asclepiodotus won the day, scattering the Roman forces and setting them to flight. Many thousands fell as Asclepiodotus pursued them, and he killed Allectus personally.

As soon as Asclepiodotus had secured this victory, Luvius Gallus, one of Allectus' lieutenants, gathered all the remaining Romans into the city. They barred the gates and built towers and other fortifications; Gallus thought that by staving off Asclepiodotus in this way he would be able to avoid an almost certain death. However, when Asclepiodotus realized what Gallus was doing, he at once laid siege to London and sent word to all the lords of Britain that he had slain Allectus and thousands of his men and that he was now besieging Gallus and the remaining Romans in London. He entreated them most humbly to hasten to his aid. It would be an easy thing, he said, to extirpate the Roman people from Britain if they attacked with their combined strength. In response to his request came men from Demetia and Venedotia, from Deira and Alban, and from many other tribes of the Britons. And when they all had assembled before him, the duke ordered innumerable war-machines to be made to cast down the walls of the city. Every man obeyed him immediately and they attacked the city most fiercely. As soon as the walls fell, they entered the city and began to slaughter the Romans. But when the Romans saw that they were being slain without quarter, they persuaded Gallus to surren-

---

[1] Bede's version of the story has Allectus, there one of Carausius' associates, betray him rather than defeat him in battle.

der and begged Asclepiodotus for pardon so that they could escape with their lives. Indeed, almost all of them had already been slain except for one legion that had held out to the last. Gallus finally assented, and he surrendered himself and his men to Asclepiodotus, who was prepared to grant them mercy. However, an organized contingent of men from Venedotia intervened and, in a single day, decapitated all of the Romans near a stream that ran by the city, which in later days was named Nantgall in the British tongue after their leader, or Galabroc in Saxon.[1]

[77] With this victory in hand, Asclepiodotus took the crown of the kingdom and placed it upon his own head with the consent of the people. For the next ten years he ruled the land with peace and appropriate justice, protecting the people from the rapacity of bandits and the blades of thieves. In his days there occurred the persecutions ordered by the Emperor Diocletian, which almost completely wiped out the Christian faith that had been safe and flourishing in Britain since the time of King Lucius. Maximianus Herculius, one of the emperor's generals, had arrived in Britain. He had all the churches toppled, and all the sacred Scriptures that could be found were handed over to him and burnt in the middle of the city squares. Furthermore, all the elected priests were executed, along with the faithful souls who were their wards, so that they must most certainly have hastened to the joyous kingdom of Heaven in great throngs, taking their long-awaited seats. Yet in that time of persecution, God indeed increased His mercy toward us, for, as a freely-given gift, He lit the brightest lamps of holy martyrdom so that the British people would repent and not be lost in the heavy darkness of black night. The tombs of these martyrs and the places of their deaths would even now inspire the great ardor of godly love in those who looked upon them, if only they had not been lost to their countrymen by the grievous neglect of barbarous peoples. Among the martyrs of either sex who stood in the army of Christ and suffered death courageously were Albanus of Verolamium, and Julius and Aaron of Caerleon. This Albanus, aglow with the grace of God's love, concealed in his own house his confessor Amphibalus, saving him from persecution and arrest; finally, exchanging clothes with Amphibalus, Albanus offerred himself up to be condemned to death, thus imitating Christ who gave up His life for His flock.[2] The other two, Julius and Aaron, were most violently torn from

---

[1] Tatlock, 75, identifies *Nantgall* with a small river named *Nant y Gall*, a tributary of the River Monnow not far from Geoffrey's home city of Monmouth.

[2] Geoffrey's description of Albanus' life and martyrdom differs markedly from Bede's, and he seems to have been drawing on an independent life of the saint.

limb to limb before the gates of Jerusalem, and their martyred souls flew swiftly up to Heaven in triumph.

[78] In the meantime, Coel, the duke of Kaercolum (that is, Colchester), rose in rebellion against King Asclepiodotus. Meeting him in battle, Coel slew the king and took the crown of the kingdom for himself.[1] When this was made known to the Senate, they rejoiced on account of the death of that king who had been such trouble to the power of Rome. Reflecting on the damage they had incurred from the loss of their domains, they dispatched Senator Constantius, a wise and brave man who had subdued all of Spain for them and who had striven for the improvement of the Roman state above all else. When Coel, king of the Britons heard the news of his coming, he shirked from doing battle with this man, whose reputation held that not even a king could withstand him. Therefore, as soon as Constantius came ashore on the island, Coel sent messengers to him, suing for peace and promising submission; in return for continuing to rule the kingdom of Britain, he would not have to pay anything in respect of Rome except for the traditional tribute. When this had been announced, Constantius agreed to these terms and took hostages, and they confirmed the peace. But after a month had passed, Coel succumbed to a grave illness and was snatched away by death within eight days. At his passing, Constantius assumed the crown of the realm and married Coel's daughter, whose name was Helen. Her beauty exceeded that of all the damsels of the land, nor was there another woman more skilled at playing musical instruments or more learned in the liberal arts. Her father had no other heir to whom he could pass the throne of the kingdom; he had therefore taken great care to instruct her in the ruling of the realm so that she could run things more easily after his death.

So Constantius took Helen in marriage, and he fathered a son on her named Constantine. After eleven years had passed, Constantius died at York, granting the kingdom to his son. Constantine ascended to the throne of the realm, and, within a few years, began to develop great prudence, to display a leonine prowess, and to uphold justice among the people. He diminished the rapacity of thieves, trampled the savagery of tyrants, and strove to restore peace everywhere.

[79] In that time, there was a certain dictator in Rome by the name of Maxentius, who attempted to disinherit the nobility and the noblest citizens, plaguing the Roman state with the worst sort of tyranny.

---

[1]   This legendary King Coel, the father of Helen, is likely the source for the old nursery rhyme "Old King Cole." Geoffrey's account, sadly, makes no mention of the fiddlers three.

Oppressed by his cruelty, many of the Romans who were exiled fled to Constantine in Britain, and there they were welcomed most honorably. When a great number had thus flocked to him, they incited in him a hatred for that dictator, and they would quite often say things to him like "Why do you tolerate our misfortune and exile, Constantine? Why do you delay in restoring us to our native lands? You are the only man of our race who can oust Maxentius and give us back what we have lost. For what other prince could be compared with the king of Britain either in the power of his robust warriors or in his abundance of silver and gold? We implore you: restore to us our possessions and our wives and our families by bringing your army to Rome with us." Upon hearing many such pleas, Constantine grew incensed; he went to Rome and subjugated the city for them, thus obtaining sovereignty over the entire world.[1] Helen's three uncles,—Ioelinus, Trahern, and Marius—accompanied him, and he installed them as senators.

[80] In the meantime, Octavius, duke of the Gewissei, rose in rebellion against the proconsuls in whose keeping the rule of the island had been entrusted because of their status as Romans.[2] He killed them and usurped the throne. When this was reported to Constantine, he sent Helen's uncle Trahern with three legions to restore the island to Roman rule. As soon as Trahern had come ashore near the city known in the British language as Kaer Peris, he attacked that city and captured it within the first two days. When news of this victory spread among the British tribes, Octavius mustered every man who could bear arms and intercepted Trahern not far from Winchester upon a plain that in the British tongue is called Maisurian. He defeated Trahern in battle there. Trahern then withdrew his tattered forces and led them back onto the ships. They sailed off to Alban, where he was able to ravage the land unimpeded.

When this was made known to King Octavius, he regrouped his men and went off in pursuit. He fought against Trahern in that province which was called Westmoreland, but he fled the field without victory. Trahern, on the other hand, as soon as he realized that Octavius was fleeing, pursued him in turn, and he did not relent until he had wrested from him not only all the cities of Britain, but the crown of the kingdom as well. Grieving for the loss of his realm, Octavius sailed off to Norway and

---

[1] Geoffrey intends this Constantine to correspond to the Roman Emperor Constantine the Great, who hailed from Britain and whose mother was also named Helen.

[2] Octavius is derived from Welsh traditions about Eudaf Hen (*Eudaf=Octavius*), a character who figures prominently in the Welsh genealogies as a famous king and ancestor of several of the later Welsh princely dynasties.

sought aid from King Guthbert there. For the time being, Octavius had left his men with the order to spare no effort in attempting to assassinate Trahern. The head man of one particular town, who loved Octavius more than any other, did not hesitate to carry out these wishes. For one day, while Trahern was riding out of London, this man lay in ambush with a hundred soldiers in a certain wooded glen that Trahern would have to pass through. He made a surprise attack as Trahern passed by, slaying him and his bodyguards. When this was made known to Octavius, he returned to Britain, scattered the Roman forces, and regained the royal throne. Within a short time he had displayed such prowess and had gained such an abundance of silver and gold that he feared no man. He ruled the kingdom of Britain quite happily until the days of Gratianus and Valentinian.

[81] Later on, weakened by old age, Octavius desired to set his affairs in order for his people. He asked his counselors which of his offspring they wished to make king after his death. He had only a single daughter and lacked a male heir to whom he could commit the rule of the kingdom. There were some among his counselors who urged him to give his daughter—along with the kingdom—to some Roman nobleman so that it could flourish in a more secure peace. Others advised him to appoint his nephew, Conan Meriadoc, to the throne of the realm, and to wed his daughter with a dowry of gold and silver to the prince of some other land. While these plans were being debated, Caradoc, the duke of Cornwall, came forth and recommended that they call in a certain Senator Maximianus and that they give him both the girl and the kingdom, and thus they would enjoy an abiding peace.[1] This Maximianus was, moreover, a Briton, since Constantine's uncle Ioelinus, whom I had mentioned earlier, was his father. He was also a Roman by birth on account of his mother and thus sprung from royal blood on both sides of his family. For that reason, such a marriage promised a lasting peace, for Caradoc knew that Maximianus, both because he was of the line of the emperors and because he had blood-ties among the Britons, would uphold the laws in Britain.

When the duke of Cornwall had given this counsel, the king's nephew Conan grew furious. He argued most strenuously that he

---

[1] Geoffrey's Maximianus corresponds to Maxen, a figure in Welsh legend and, like Octavius (Eudaf Hen), the ancestor of a number of later Welsh dynasties. In the Welsh *Dream of Maxen* (*Breudwyt Maxen Wledic*), the Roman emperor Maxen Wledig has a vivid dream in which he crosses the sea to Britain, where he beholds the most beautiful woman in the world. Upon his awakening, his advisors recommend that he seek out Britain, which he does, obtaining the hand of Elen, Eudaf Hen's daughter.

should rule the kingdom, setting the entire court astir in the process. But Caradoc refused to back down from his position, and he sent his son Mauricius to Rome to explain the situation to Maximianus. This Mauricius was of fine build and possessed great sense and bravery; he was accustomed to settling any criticism of his judgments by challenging his opponent to single combat.[1] When he came into the presence of Maximianus, he was received as is proper and granted a place of honor among Maximianus' companions.

There was at that time great unrest between Maximianus and the two emperors, Gratianus and his brother Valentinian, since Maximianus had been expelled from the third portion of the empire that he had desired. Therefore, when Mauricius saw that Maximianus was so mistreated by these emperors, he spoke these words to him: "How is it that you fear Gratianus, Maximianus, when it is clear to you how you would be able to snatch the empire from him? Come to the isle of Britain with me, and you will receive the diadem of the kingdom. King Octavius is worn down by old age and sloth, and he desires nothing else but to find a man to whom he can give his daughter and his kingdom. For he has no male heir, and he sought advice from his counselors about upon whom he should bestow his daughter and kingdom. He favors the opinion of these men and has decided to grant both the girl and the realm to you. They have sent me to you to apprise you of this situation. If you come with me now and embark on this enterprise from the beginning, you will be able to return to Rome with an abundance of gold and silver from Britain and a host of the experienced warriors who dwell there. You will be able to expel the emperors and subjugate Rome. Your kinsman Constantine did this very thing, as have many other of our kings who have ascended to the emperorship."

[82] Persuaded by his words, Maximianus headed for Britain, subduing the cities of the Franks along the way and seizing from them much silver and gold. Soldiers everywhere flocked to his banner. From there he crossed the sea and arrived at Southampton upon an auspicious wind. When his arrival was made known, King Octavius grew very frightened, believing in his senility that a hostile force had come. He therefore summoned his nephew Conan and ordered him to gather every armed soldier in the island and intercept the enemy. So Conan assembled all the youth of the realm and came to Southampton where Maximianus had

---

[1]   Mauricius' propensity for dueling would have seemed admirable, rather than pugnacious, to Geoffrey's audiences.

pitched his tents. When Maximianus caught sight of the approach of such a great host, he was deeply worried and did not know what to do. His own army had far fewer men, and he feared both the number of the approaching force as well as their boldness, for there seemed no hope for peace with them. He summoned the elder men of his company, as well as Mauricius, and began to ask them what should be done in this situation. Mauricius responded: "We must not do battle with so great a host, for we have not come here to subjugate Britain in war. We must ask for peace and gain leave to camp here until the king's will can be ascertained. Let us say that we have been sent from the emperors to deliver a message to Octavius, and thus we will mollify these people with clever words."

When they had all agreed on this course of action, Maximianus took twelve snowy-haired and wise retainers with him, and they approached Conan, holding out olive branches in their right hands. When the Britons espied these men of venerable age carrying the olive branch as a sign of peace, they stood forth to honor them and made way for them to approach the king more easily. As soon as they were in the presence of Conan Meriadoc, they greeted him in the name of the emperors and the Roman Senate and declared that Maximianus had been sent to King Octavius bearing messages from Gratianus and Valentinian. To these words, Conan replied, "Why do you then come with such a great host? This is not the customary method of ambassadors. You seem more like a conquering army that has come to do us harm." Mauricius answered, "It does not befit so worthy a man to come here without the proper escort, especially one who is deemed hateful by many kings due to the power of Rome and the deeds of his ancestors. Indeed, if he had made the journey here with a meager force, he might have been slain by the enemies of the Roman state. In peace he comes and peace it is that he seeks; this must be judged by his behavior alone. From the moment that we landed, we hold that we have done harm to no man at all. We have paid all of our debts like men of peace, purchasing all our supplies and taking nothing by force." While Conan hesitated, unsure whether to commit to war or peace, Duke Caradoc of Cornwall and several other nobles approached him and dissuaded him from doing battle after hearing such a petition. Although Conan would have preferred to fight, he put aside his arms, granted them peace, escorted Maximianus to the king in London, and explained the entire affair to him.

[83] Then Duke Caradoc of Cornwall, accompanied by his son Mauricius, ordered all of the bystanders to step aside, and he addressed the king in these words: "Behold, through God's will the thing that we

who have been true and kept our faith with you in loving obedience have long desired has now come to pass. You had commanded your men to give their counsel about what should be done with your daughter and your kingdom, once your great old age prevents you from governing your people any longer. Some of these leaders recommended that the crown be given to your nephew Conan and that your daughter be married honorably in some foreign country. Swayed by their own fear, these men would have brought ruin upon their fellow citizens if a prince of some other nation had come to rule over us. The other counselors agreed that, after your death, the kingdom should pass to your daughter and to some other nobleman who speaks our language. A majority of us thought it well to send for one of the kinsmen of the emperors to whom both the girl and the crown should be given. They promised that a stable and abiding peace would be established with the Roman power to back it up. Now behold: God had deemed you worthy enough to send this young man to you, who is Roman by birth but also descends from the royal line of the Britons. It is my counsel that you should not hesitate to marry your daughter to this man. If you were to deny him, what law in the kingdom of Britain could you bring against him? He is truly of the blood of Constantine and is the nephew of our king Coel whose daughter Helen, we must admit, should possess the kingdom by the strict law of inheritance."[1]

When Caradoc had explained these matters, Octavius acquiesced, followed the general consensus, and bestowed both his daughter and the kingdom of Britain upon Maximianus. Seeing these things, Conan Meriadoc grew angrier than can be thought possible. He withdrew to Alban, where he had the opportunity to assemble an army to harass Maximianus. With a great band of confederates, he approached the Humber and began to ravage the lands on both sides of the river. When this was made known to Maximianus, he gathered a force together and hastened to intercept him. He met Conan in battle and returned victorious. However, Conan's forces were not so reduced that he could not regroup and threaten the lands with destruction once more. Maximianus therefore returned and they fought many battles: in some he triumphed and in others he suffered defeat. After they had done a great deal of damage to one another, Maximianus and Conan, at the urging of their friends, finally made peace.

---

[1] Caradoc's advocacy of inheritance through the female line suggests Geoffrey's sympathy with the cause of the Empress Matilda, the only legitimate heir of King Henry I, in her bid for the English crown against the claims of her cousin Stephen, Henry's nephew.

[84] After fifteen years had passed, Maximianus grew haughty on account of the endless measure of gold and silver that flowed to his coffers daily, and he fitted a fleet and assembled every armed soldier in Britain. Crossing the Channel, he came at first to the kingdom of Armorica, which is now called Brittany, and he began to make war with the Frankish people who dwelt there. Then the Franks, led by Duke Imbalt, came to meet him, and they pitched a battle against him, but the greater part of their host abandoned the field, considering themselves in great danger. After he had inflicted considerable harm upon the Franks, Maximianus rejoiced, for he knew that the country would now be easy to subdue because of the ruin of these men. He summoned Conan to him from among the battalions and, with a faint smile upon his lips, said: "Look! Now that we have subjugated one of the petty kingdoms of Gaul, we can hope to conquer others. Let us hasten to capture cities and towns before news of our threat spreads to the far parts of Gaul and stirs all the peoples to take up arms against us. If we are able to keep a hold on this kingdom, I do not doubt that we can bring all of Gaul into our power. Do not be ashamed that you ceded the island of Britain to me, even though you had your hopes set on possessing it, for now I shall restore to you in this land whatever you may have lost. I will make you the king of this realm and it will be a second Britain, and we shall expel the natives and fill it up with our own people. It is indeed a land of fertile fields and fish-thronged rivers, of the most beautiful forest groves and the loveliest mountain glades; there is, in my judgment, no finer land anywhere."[1] At these words, Conan bowed his head and gave thanks, promising that he would hold the land faithfully as long as he lived.[2]

[85] After that, Maximianus assembled his troops and they made for Rennes and captured it on the very same day. The citizens of Rennes, having heard of the ferocity of the Britons and of the fall of their countrymen, fled the city in great haste, leaving behind their women and children. Following their example, the others did the same in their cities and

---

[1] Maximianus' description of Brittany echoes the description of Britain in Book I. It should be noted that either Maximianus, or more likely Geoffrey himself, lets his rhetoric get away from him here, for there are no significant mountains in Brittany.

[2] Welsh traditions associate the hero Conan (Welsh *Cynan*) with Brittany from at least the tenth century on, where Conan figures as a Breton messiah in various Welsh prophecies. Cynan also appears as the founder of Brittany in the later *Dream of Maxen (Breudwyt Maxen Wledic)*. No text earlier than Geoffrey attests the sobriquet *Meriadoc* being appended to this hero's name.

towns so that they lay completely open to the Britons. In whatever city they occupied, the Britons slew all the males, sparing only the women. Afterwards, when they had destroyed almost all the native inhabitants of that land, they built cities and castles for the soldiers of Britain, situated on various high points throughout the region. Once word of the viciousness of Maximianus was spread throughout the provinces of the Gauls, the dukes and princes were struck with such an excessive fear of him that they had no other hope but to pray. And they therefore fled from all the countryside, heading for the cities and castles and any other place that could offer them safe refuge. Taking heed of their fear, Maximianus continued with an even greater boldness, and he hastened to increase the size of his army with profuse bribes. Moreover, he allied himself with men who were eager to seize the property of others, and he did not hesitate to secure their loyalty with silver and gold and other gifts.

[86] Maximianus had finally gathered up such a great host of men that he believed he would be able to subjugate all of Gaul. However, he put aside his warlike spirit for a time until the realm he had already captured was secure and he was able to repopulate it with Britons. And so he made an edict that one hundred thousand common men from the island of Britain should be mustered and report to him. Furthermore, he demanded thirty thousand soldiers as protection for those who were to remain in Armorica. Once he had done these things, he distributed these men all throughout the lands of the realm of Armorica, thus creating a second Britain. This he gave to Conan Meriadoc. Then, with the rest of his men, he marched further into Gaul, subjugating it, and Germany as well, after achieving victory in a series of fierce battles. Setting up the throne of his empire at Trèves, he then unleashed his wrath upon the two emperors, Gratianus and Valentinian, killing the former and driving the latter from Rome.

[87] In the meantime, the Gauls and Aquitanians began to attack Conan and the Armorican Britons, plaguing them with frequent raids. Conan withstood their assaults, and returned slaughter with slaughter, defending his new homeland valiantly. When he had finally achieved victory, he desired to give his men wives so that heirs could be born to possess the land of Armorica forever. In order not to intermingle with the women of Gaul, he decided that women should instead come from the island of Britain to marry his own men. He sent his messengers to King Dionotus of Cornwall, who had succeeded his brother Caradoc in that realm, and he charged Dionotus with arranging this matter. This Dionotus was noble and powerful, and Maximianus had entrusted the

governance of the island to him while he himself was engaged in the deeds of conquest mentioned above.[1] Dionotus, what's more, had a daughter of exceeding beauty whom Conan cherished above all else.

[88] Upon receiving Conan's messenger, Dionotus was eager to obey orders, and so he selected the daughters of noblemen from throughout the various provinces of Britain, to the number of eleven thousand, to which he added forty thousand women of lesser birth.[2] He commanded them all to gather together in the city of London. Then he had ships sent from various ports in order to convey these brides-to-be across the Channel. Although these marriages abroad might have been pleasing to many of the women in that company, it displeased many of the others, for they bore an ardent love for their families and native country. There were also some women who did not even heed the summons, preferring a life of chastity over marriage; they were prepared to forego their lives among the people rather than obtain riches in this world. Indeed, the various wishes of all these women could have been granted, if only they had been able to do what they so desired. Instead, when the fleet was made ready, the women embarked and set off down the Thames and out to sea. After the ships had turned their sails toward Armorica, ill winds began to blow and, within a short space of time, the entire fleet was scattered. The ships were thus placed in peril of the open sea and were for the most part sunk.[3] Those few ships that escaped this peril were cast away upon various islands, and the women were either slain or were sold into slavery by the barbarous inhabitants. In fact, the women had happened upon the nefarious army of Wanius and Melga, who, under order from the Emperor Gratianus, were harassing Germany and all the northern shores with great carnage. This Wanius was the King of the Huns, and Melga the King of the Picts. Gratianus had retained these men and had sent them to Germany to harass the supporters of Maximianus. Prowling the seas, they came across some of the maidens who had come ashore in those parts. When they espied the great beauty of these girls,

---

1   This Dionotus corresponds to the *Dunawt*, a king of Cornwall or Dumnonia according to early Welsh triads and genealogies.

2   Tatlock, 237, notes that the following legend is based loosely on that of St. Ursula: Ursula, the daughter of a British king named Deonotus, is betrothed to a continental pagan prince and departs from Britain accompanied by 11,000 virgins; after a series of adventures, she is martyred by Huns at Cologne.

3   The sinking of the ships carrying the virgins across to Armorica would have resonated with Geoffrey's aristocratic audiences because of the notorious shipwreck of the White Ship in 1120, which had been conveying many noble youths and maidens, including King Henry I's only legitimate son, across the Channel.

they desired to have their wanton way with them. But because the girls refused them, the Ambrones attacked them, slaying most of them in no time at all. Then Wanius and Melga, the wicked leaders of these Picts and Huns, who were supporters of Gratianus and Valentinian, discovered that the island of Britain was emptied of all of its armed men. They made their way there in all haste, and, allying themselves with the men of the neighboring islands, landed in Alban. Arraying their host, they invaded the British kingdom, which now lacked any ruler or protector. They completely slaughtered the peasantry. As was mentioned above, Maximianus had taken away all the young warriors who could be found; only unarmed and infirm farmers remained behind. When Wanius and Melga attacked, these husbandmen were unable to put up any resistance, and so the invaders inflicted great carnage upon the cities and farmlands as if they had been so many sheepfolds.

When this disaster was reported to Maximianus, he dispatched a certain freedman, whose name also happened to be Gratianus, with two legions to render assistance in Britain. When this force arrived on the island, they fought a battle with their enemies and, dealing them a most bitter slaughter, forced them to flee to Ireland. In the meantime, Maximianus was slain in Rome by friends of the Emperor Gratianus, and the Britons in his entourage were either slain or scattered. Those who did manage to escape came back to their comrades in Armorica, which was now called Second Britain.

BOOK SIX

[89] When Gratianus the freedman learned of the death of Maximianus, he seized the crown of the realm and declared himself king. From that moment on, he oppressed the people with such great tyranny that the common folk organized themselves and attacked and killed him.[1] As word of this event reached other countries, the abovementioned enemies, Wanius and Melga, returned from Ireland. Leading an army of Scots, Norsemen, and Danes, they ravaged the kingdom with fire and sword from sea to sea. Because of this terrible infestation and oppression, messengers were sent to Rome with letters, tearfully imploring the Romans to lend military aid so that they could avenge themselves; they also vowed their own eternal subjection to Rome, if only their enemies could be held at bay. In response, a legion that had not been involved with the recent ills in Britain was dispatched at once. It was shipped across the ocean to Britain and engaged the enemy in hand-to-hand combat. Overthrowing that great host, they drove the rest of the foreigners out of the land and thus delivered the oppressed people of Britain from destruction. The Romans then advised the Britons to construct a wall between Alban and Deira stretching from coast to coast. Though requiring a multitude of workers, such a wall would protect them from their enemies and would instill fear in any invaders, thus providing a defense for the Britons. Indeed, Alban in those days was completely overrun with barbarians, and any enemy force that landed there could always find a warm welcome. Therefore, drawing upon both private and public support, the local inhabitants pressed on in their labor and erected the wall.

[90] The Romans then announced that they would by no means be troubled any longer with such costly expeditions and that it was beneath them to waste their military forces on land and sea dealing with unruly pirates. Instead, they said, the Britons should get into the habit of relying upon their own forces; they should act like men and defend their own lands, riches, women, children, and, above all, their freedom and way of life. Having issued this warning, they summoned all the men of the island who could bear arms back to London, for they themselves were preparing to return to Rome.

---

[1] Geoffrey's description of Gratianus is based on a similarly terse account in Bede, I.11.

When all the men were assembled, word was sent to Guithelin, the bishop of London, who addressed the Britons with these words: "Because of the command of the princes gathered around me, I feel obliged to address you. But I feel more like weeping than giving you some fancy speech; for I bewail the weakness and lack of guidance that has beset us since Maximianus bereaved this realm of all its armed forces and young men. You, a people unskilled in the waging of war, are all that is left, you whose real business lies in the tilling of fields or the trading of wares. When invaders came from foreign lands, you went running like sheep without a shepherd, abandoning your folds until the power of the Romans restored your possessions. Will your hope always lie in outside protection? Will you not equip your own hands with shields and swords and spears against thieves who would by no means be stronger than you if you would only shake off your own sloth and sluggishness? The Romans have grown weary of running constantly about and taking the trouble to fight our enemies for us. They would rather forego whatever tribute they used to collect than continue to waste their efforts defending us by land and by sea. So now what? If you had only been a humble folk back when you were at the height of your former military power, do you think that all mankind would have fled from you? Can real men not be born of humble stock? Can a soldier not be born into a farmer's family, or a farmer from a military family? A soldier can indeed come from a shopkeeper's family and a shopkeeper from a soldier's. Since it is not unusual, then, that a man of one type can come from a different type of stock, I do not believe that you people can forget how to be real men. Since you are men, act like men! Call upon Christ to grant you the courage to defend your own homes!" When he had finished speaking, the people broke out in such a clamor that you might say that their courage was restored in that very moment.

[91] After this, the Romans gave the timid Britons some good advice and left plans for the construction of defenses. They recommended that the Britons build a series of watchtowers at fixed intervals all along the southern coast of the ocean, for that is where the Britons kept their merchant fleet and therefore where they should most fear a barbarian attack. But it is easier to make a kite hunt like a sparrow-hawk than to instruct a farmer in the art of war. He who tries to explain complex matters to such a person might as well toss a pearl among swine. For as soon as the Romans bade their farewell, never to return, their old enemies emerged once again from the ships in which they had fled to Ireland. They brought with them hideous hosts of Scots and Picts and Norsemen

and Danes and many others, and they captured all of Alban down to the Wall. Now that they had learned about the withdrawal of the Romans and their intention never to return, they were far more confident and threatened to ravage the entire island. The farm-folk defended the walls against them, but they were useless in battle, unable even to flee because of their faint-heartedness, and a poor defense they made perched up in their look-out posts all day and all night. All the while, the enemy continued to shoot the wretched Britons with barbed missiles, which flung them from the walls and dashed them to the ground. This untimely death was actually a blessing, for with such an end they avoided the awful torments that their brethren and loved ones would soon suffer. O how God punishes past evils! Alas, that Maximianus in his folly took away so many strong warriors! If they had been there when such a disaster hit, there would have been no enemy host that could not have been repelled. What was now clear about the Roman occupation is that they had been able to protect far-off lands with their military might and that they had ruled Britain peacefully. This is what happens when the defense of a kingdom falls upon its common-folk. What more can I say? Once their cities and the High Wall were abandoned, all the usual exiles swiftly followed, as did desperate dispersions, and persecution by the enemy, and the cruelest slaughter. The miserable Britons were plucked off by their foes like sheep by a wolf.

And so once again, the miserable remnant sent letters to Agitius, a powerful man among the Romans, imploring him thus: "O Agitius, thrice consul, hear the groans of the Britons!" And after saying a few more words, they added: "The sea drives us toward the barbarians and the barbarians drive us into the sea. Two different modes of death await us: we will either be drowned or get our throats slashed."[1] But, not receiving any aid from the Romans, the messengers returned home sadly to relate the sorry news to their countrymen.

[92] Taking counsel together, the Britons decided that Guithelin, the Archbishop of London, should go to Brittany, which was then called Armorica or Letavia, to seek help from their fellow Britons there. At that time, Aldroenus was king of Brittany, the fourth since that Conan to whom Maximianus had granted that land, as has been related above. Seeing a man of such high reverence as Guithelin approaching, Aldroenus welcomed him with great ceremony and asked the reason for his visit.

---

[1] The letter of Agitius is taken almost verbatim from Gildas' *The Ruin of Britain*. See Appendix A.

Guithelin answered: "It is clear enough that pity can move you and your noble retainers to tears over what we, your fellow Britons, have suffered since Maximianus despoiled our island of all its soldiers and ordered them to inhabit the land which you rule. May you yet rule over it in peace for many long years. However, all the peoples who dwell near our island have risen up against us, the destitute remainder of your own British people. They have completely emptied our island realm of its store of riches. The British folk now have no food at all except what they can catch by hunting. There is no one who can stop them since no one remains among us who is skilled in the arts of war. You see, the Romans grew weary of defending us and went home, depriving us of all support. We are now bereft of all other hope, and we come to beg for your mercy. We beg you to take command and defend from barbarian invasion the kingdom that rightfully belongs to you. Who else but you whom we implore should wear the crown of Constantine and Maximianus, the crown your own grandfathers and great-grandfathers wore? Prepare your fleet and come: I place the kingdom of Britain in your hands."

To these words Aldroenus responded: "There was once a time when I would not have refused the isle of Britain if it had been offered to me. Truly, I do not deem any country more prosperous than Britain when it enjoyed peace and tranquillity. But now that misfortune has overtaken the land, it becomes less appealing to me and completely loathsome to my vassals. Above all, the evil power of the Romans has harmed Britain, so much so that no king can now maintain his power there unless he abrogates his freedom and accepts servitude to Rome. Who, then, would not prefer to reign quietly but freely over another land rather than possess the riches of Britain under the yoke of servitude? The kingdom that is now under my power is one I hold honorably, paying no homage to anyone higher than myself. I cherish it above all other lands, for I govern it in liberty. However, since my grandfathers and great-grandfathers did indeed once hold sway over the island of Britain, I will send with you my brother Constantine and two thousand soldiers so that, by God's mercy, he may liberate the country from the barbarian upstarts and attain the crown of the kingdom for himself.[1] In fact, this very brother of mine, whose name I have already mentioned, is most skilled in the affairs of war and in many other matters. I do not hesitate to

---

[1]   Geoffrey derived the character of Constantine from Bede, I.11, though in this case he has altered his source significantly. Bede's Constantine is "a common trooper of no merit" who moves from being a tyrant over Britain to the Roman Emperorship, where he is soon executed.

commit him to you, along with the abovementioned number of troops, if you are pleased to receive him. I can dispatch no more troops than that because the unruliness of the Gauls poses a constant threat."

As soon as he finished speaking, the archbishop thanked him, and, summoning Constantine, smiled and said: "Christ triumphs, Christ is king, Christ reigns! Behold the king of desolate Britain, with the help of Christ! Behold our defense! Behold our hope and joy!" What more can I say? While the fleet was made ready, soldiers were mustered from the various parts of Brittany and handed over to Guithelin. [93] When everything was in order, they crossed the sea and landed in the port of Totnes. They at once mustered together the remaining youth of the island and, meeting their enemies in battle, were led to victory by the merits of that blessed man. Then the Britons, who had been scattered all about, began to flock together. Convening at Silchester, they made Constantine their king and placed the crown of the realm upon his head. They also gave him a wife from a noble family, whom Guithelin had personally raised. And when he knew her, she produced three sons whose names were Constans, Aurelius Ambrosius, and Uther Pendragon. The eldest, Constans, was dedicated to the Church of Amphybalus in Winchester and took monastic orders there.[1] The other two, Aurelius and Uther Pendragon, were committed to Guithelin for their fostering. But later, after ten years had passed, a Pict in Constantine's service sought to have a private conversation with the king. Once the king was separated from all his other companions in a thicket of trees, the Pict stabbed him to death.

[94] Upon the death of Constantine, there was unrest among the nobility over who was to be elevated to the throne. Some of them proclaimed Aurelius Ambrosius, some proclaimed Uther Pendragon, while others still supported various other relatives. While they were arguing for one over the other claimant, Vortigern, the leader of the Gewissei and a man who exerted every effort to obtain the throne for himself, came forth.[2] He went to the monk Constans and spoke to him

---

[1]   As with Constantine, Geoffrey derives Constans from Bede, I.11, but elaborates greatly on Bede's brief description. Bede describes Constans merely as "a monk whom Constantine had created Caesar" and who was assassinated by a rival, presumably in Rome.

[2]   Vortigern, a figure known under the name of *Gwrtheyrn* in the Welsh genealogies as one of the ancestors of the Welsh rulers of Powys, is the first figure in *The History of the Kings of Britain* to have been mentioned extensively in other historical sources, appearing in Bede and Nennius, as well as in the work of Geoffrey's contemporaries William of Malmesbury and Henry of Huntington.

in these words: "Your father has died and your brothers cannot take the throne because of their young age. I can see no one else of your blood-line whom the people can take as their king. If you heed my advice and increase my power and possessions, I can instill in the people the desire to elevate you to the throne and, since your religious affiliation precludes such an office, to get you out of your monastic orders."

When Constans heard this plan, he was filled with great joy and prom-ised on oath to give Vortigern whatever he wanted. Vortigern then took Constans and led him to London, endowing him with the royal regalia and making him king, though this was hardly done with the people's approval. By that point in time Archbishop Guithelin had died, and there was no one else who would dare anoint Constans, since he had forsaken his monastic vows. Nonetheless, Vortigern, acting as the archbishop himself, placed the crown upon Constans' head with his own hands.

[95] Thus elevated to the throne, Constans committed the overseeing of all justice in the kingdom to Vortigern, and he gave himself over to Vortigern's counsel so completely that he found he could do nothing without his permission. It was, in fact, Constans' own weakness of char-acter that caused this state of affairs, as well as the fact that he had learned nothing in his cloister about how to run a kingdom. Assessing the situa-tion, Vortigern began to plot how he himself could be made king, for that is what he desired above all else. He was only waiting for the perfect moment in which his desire could most easily be achieved. For now all the realm was essentially under Vortigern's control, and Constans himself could only be called the shadow of a king. Indeed, Constans seemed to lack both stringency and a sense of justice, and was feared neither by neighboring peoples nor by his own folk. Furthermore, his two young brothers, Uther Pendragon and Aurelius Ambrosius, still lay in their cradles and were unable to be elevated to the kingship. One more misfor-tune had occurred as well: all the elderly statesmen of the realm had died off and now Vortigern seemed to be the only person who was experi-enced and wise in counsel. Almost all the other noblemen were either adolescents or young boys and, since their fathers and grandfathers had all perished in the wars of recent years, they held their ancestral lands practically by chance. Recognizing the opportunities in this state of affairs, Vortigern gave thought to how he could carefully and cleverly depose the monk Constans and set himself up in his place. However, he decided to postpone his plan until he had gained the allegiance and friendship of other countries. And so he began to place funds from the king's treasury into his own keeping, using the money to fortify certain

cities, claiming that there was a rumor that some of the neighboring peoples were planning an attack. After he had achieved this, he placed his personal friends in all those cities, men who would keep their allegiance to him. Next, setting his treacherous plans in motion, he went to Constans and told him that he needed more men in order to repel foreign invaders more effectively. Constans said: "Have I not entrusted the entire running of the kingdom to you? Do whatever you want, as long as you keep your faith with me." Vortigern answered: "I am told that the Picts are planning to bring Norsemen and Danes to inflict heavy losses upon us. For that reason, let me recommend what I think is the most prudent course of action: retain some Picts here in your court to serve as mediators between you and their compatriots. If it is indeed true that the Picts wish to make war, these mediators will explain to you the plans and wiles of their countrymen and you will thus be able to resist them more effectively."

Alas, for the treacherousness of a false friend! Vortigern did not advise this course of action so that good things would befall Constans but instead because he knew that the Picts were a volatile people and open to committing any kind of crime. If they were inebriated or moved to anger, they could be easily used against the king and would kill him without hesitation. If this should happen, Vortigern would be able to set himself up as king, as he had long desired. Sending messengers into Alban, Vortigern invited one hundred Picts and placed them in the king's household. Vortigern himself welcomed them more than anyone else, and he gave them many gifts. He more than sated their desire for food and drink, so that they began to consider him their king. During their meals, they would sing out of affection for him: "Vortigern is worthy of power and worthy of the scepter of Britain; Constans, on the other hand, is not worthy." Hearing these words, Vortigern tried to tame them more and more, so that they would continue to prefer him. When he had completely gained their love, he got them drunk. He pretended that he wished to leave Britain in order to rule over a greater territory elsewhere. He also claimed that the trifling possessions he currently held were not enough to support even fifty soldiers. Then, feigning sadness, he left them and retired to his chambers, leaving them alone to drink in the hall. Seeing him in such a state, the Picts were saddened beyond belief, thinking that what he said was true. Murmuring among themselves, they said: "Why should we suffer this monk to live? Why don't we kill him so that Vortigern can have the throne of the kingdom? Who would succeed that monk anyway? Vortigern is worthy of power and honor, and especially worthy too of our honor, since he has not ceased to enrich us."

[96] With these words, the Picts burst suddenly into the king's bedchamber and killed him. Then they carried Constans' head to Vortigern. When Vortigern saw it, he began weeping as if he were truly grieved, even though he had never been happier in his life. What's more, he summoned together all the people of London (for that is where he happened to be) and urged them to hold the Picts responsible for this crime and to have their heads cut off for the wickedness they had perpetrated. However, there were some who believed that this treachery had been hatched by Vortigern, and that the Picts would have done nothing at all without his consent. There were even some who would not hesitate to convict Vortigern himself of such a crime. With the outcome of affairs in such doubt, the custodians of the king's brothers Aurelius Ambrosius and Uther Pendragon fled with their charges to Brittany, fearing that Vortigern would put the boys to death. King Budicius welcomed them and raised them with the honor that they merited.

[97] Now that Vortigern now saw no rival in the kingdom, he placed the royal crown upon his own head, declaring his authority over all the other nobles. When his treachery was made known, the peoples of the neighboring islands, whom the Picts had invited into Alban, rose up against him. The Picts were angry indeed that their compatriots had been executed on account of the death of Constans, and now they sought vengeance. Because of this, Vortigern worried every day about his army sustaining heavy losses in a battle against the Picts. He was also concerned about Aurelius Ambrosius and his brother Uther Pendragon, who, as was related above, had fled to Brittany because of him. Every day, moreover, rumors filled his ears that these two were now grown up and that they were building a fleet and preparing their return to their rightful kingdom.

[98] In the meantime, three *ceolas*, which we call longships, came ashore in Kent.[1] They were filled with armed men under the leadership of the two brothers Horsa and Hengist. At that moment, Vortigern happened to be in Durobernia, which is now called Canterbury, for habit often led him to visit that city. When messengers came to him announcing that an unknown people of mighty stature had landed in longships, he granted them safe transit and ordered them to be brought before him. As soon as they arrived in his presence, his eyes fell upon the two brothers, for they stood out among the rest on account of their noble bearing. After he had looked long and hard upon the rest of them, he asked what country they were from and why they had come

---

[1] Geoffrey borrows the Anglo-Saxon term *ceolas* from Nennius.

into his kingdom. Hengist began to answer for them, for he was older and wiser than the rest: "Most noble king of foreign peoples, the land of Saxony reared us, which is one of the regions of Germany. The cause of our coming is to offer our service to you or to some other foreign prince. Indeed, we have been exiled from our homeland for no other reason except that the custom of that land demands such an action. For the custom of our homeland is that, whenever there is a surplus population of men, the princes of the entire realm gather together, bringing the youth of the realm with them. They then cast lots to decide who among the stronger and more experienced of us must seek his fortune in another country. In this way our country is relieved of its excess population. Our land has just recently become overpopulated again, and so our leaders have cast lots and chosen the band of young men whom you see before you, and they ordered us to honor that custom passed down from ancient times. We two brothers are the leaders of these men, for we are born of a noble house: I am Hengist and this is Horsa.[1] Obeying our hallowed ancient traditions, we have sailed the sea and, by the will of Mercury, we have come upon your kingdom."

At the mention of Mercury, King Vortigern raised an eyebrow and inquired about their religion. Hengist replied: "We worship the gods of our country, including Saturn, Jove, and all the others who govern this world. But the greatest god of all is Mercury, whom we call Woden in our tongue.[2] To him our forefathers dedicated the fourth day of the week, which we even today know by the name of *Wodnesdei*. After him we venerate the most powerful of the goddesses. [Her name is Frea and to her we have dedicated the sixth day of the week,] which we call *Fridei* in honor of her."[3] Hearing this, Vortigern said: "Your belief—or, rather, unbelief—grieves me terribly. But I do rejoice in your arrival, for either God or some other power has sent you to me in the hour of my need. My enemies are pressing upon me from all sides, and, if you would care to share the labor of my battles, I will treat you honorably here in my kingdom and will give you gifts and land." The barbarians agreed to these terms, a treaty was drawn up, and they took up residence in Vortigern's court.

---

[1] Geoffrey borrows the figures of Hengist and Horsa from Bede (1.16), though he expands upon their characters considerably. Hengist and Horsa also appear in Nennius' *History of the Britons* (see Appendix A).

[2] Since at least as early as Tacitus' *Germania* (first century C.E.), it had been customary to equate the Germanic gods with those of the Roman pantheon.

[3] The bracketed passage is absent from the Bern MS.

The Picts soon after sent out a great force from Alban and began to ravage the northern regions of the island. When this news was related to Vortigern, he mustered his troops and crossed the Humber to engage them. They met in close, hand-to-hand combat; back and forth, the Britons and their enemies fought most bitterly. But the Britons themselves did not need to fight much, for the Saxons who had accompanied them fought so valiantly that they speedily repulsed the Picts, who had hitherto been so used to winning.

[99] Securing this victory through the aid of the Saxons, Vortigern distributed generous gifts among his Saxon allies, and he granted their leader Hengist broad tracts of land in Lindsey where he could maintain his men. Then Hengist, who was a wise and clever man, recognizing the friendship that the king was offering him, addressed Vortigern in these words: "Lord, your enemies are everywhere burning with hatred for you and for your subjects who love you. Everyone is threatened, and now you are told that Aurelius Ambrosius will be leading a force of men from Brittany to oust you and set himself up as king. By your leave, allow us to send word to our homeland and invite soldiers from there, so that our numbers will be able to support you in a fight. There is one more request I would beg to ask you in your clemency, if I did not fear it would be refused." To this, Vortigern answered: "Go ahead and send word to your allies in Germany and invite whom you will. Now tell me what else you desire and you will not be denied." Hengist bowed his head and thanked the king. Then he said: "You have invested me with great lands and estates, but not, however, with the honor that befits a leader of noble blood. Perhaps along with these other things I should also be given cities and castles so that I will be respected by the other peers of your realm. The title of Earl or Prince should be granted to me, seeing as I spring from a people that has both of these ranks." Vortigern answered: "I am forbidden to give you a gift of this sort, for you and your men are both foreign-born and pagans. And I do not yet understand your customs and character well enough to consider you the equal of my people. Even if I considered you to be true citizens, I could never treat you as such because of the disapproval of the British nobility." "Then at least," Hengist said, "grant to me, your servant, as much land as can be encircled by a single thong on which I can build a fortress and where, if the need arises, I can find safe refuge. I am loyal to you, and I have been and will continue to be loyal to you. What I now desire to do, I shall likewise do in complete loyalty to you."

The king was moved by these words to acquiesce to this request. Hengist sent messengers into Germany to invite more warriors from that land to come quickly and lend their aid. As soon as the messengers had departed, Hengist took the hide of a bull and made it into a single leather thong. Then, in a rocky place which he had chosen with much thought, he walked around with this thong and began to build a castle within this measured-out space. Once built, it took its name from the thong with which it had been surveyed. For it was later called Kaer Carrei in the British tongue, Thanchester in the Saxon tongue, and Castrum Corrigiae in Latin.[1]

[100] In the meantime, the Saxon messengers had returned from their mission, bringing eighteen ships full of the choicest soldiers. They also brought with them Hengist's daughter Renwein, whose beauty was second to none. After their arrival, Hengist invited King Vortigern to his house to inspect the new fortress and fresh soldiers. Coming there in secret, the king praised how quickly the castle had been erected, and he retained the soldiers who had been invited. Once the royal feast had been served, the girl Renwein came out of her chamber carrying a goblet of wine. Approaching the king, she curtsied and said: "*Lauerd king, Waesseil!*" When Vortigern saw the girl's face, he marveled greatly at her beauty and grew inflamed with desire for her. Then he asked his interpreter what the girl had said and how he should answer. The interpreter explained: "She called you 'lord king' and honored you with a word of greeting. You should answer '*Drincheil.*'" The king said "*Drincheil,*" and commanded the girl to drink. He then took the goblet from her hand, kissed her, and drank. From that day until the present time it has been the custom of the table in Britain that whoever drinks should say "*Waesseil*" to his fellow. And whoever receives the drink next should say "*Drincheil.*"

Vortigern got rather drunk because of the different types of drinks he had imbibed. At that point Satan entered his heart, and he fell in love with the girl and asked her father for her hand. I say that Satan entered his heart because, though he was a Christian, he desired to sleep with a pagan woman. Hengist, who was no fool, had taken note of the king's mood. He consulted with his brother Horsa and with the other elders who were there over how they should respond to the king's request. They were all of one mind that the girl should be given to the king and that they should be given the province of Kent as a bride-price. She was thus given to the king at once and Hengist was invested with Kent,

---

despite the fact that Earl Gorangon currently held those lands.[1] The king wed the pagan girl that very night, for he found her pleasing beyond measure. Because of this, he earned the immediate enmity of both his vassals and his sons, for Vortigern had already sired three sons whose names were Vortimer, Katigern, and Paschent.

In that time, Saint Germanus, the Bishop of Auxerre, and Lupus, Bishop of Troyes, came to preach the word of God to the Britons, for their Christian faith had been corrupted both by the pagans and by the heretic Pelagius, whose words had poisoned them for many days. By the preaching of these two blessed men, the true faith was restored among the Britons. Germanus and Lupus manifested the faith almost daily through many miracles. Through these two men God revealed many miracles, as Gildas has recorded so eloquently in his treatise.[2]

[101] Once the girl had been wed to the king, as mentioned above, Hengist said to him: "I am now your father and should act as a counselor to you. Do not scorn my advice, for you conquered all your enemies by the strength of my people. Let us now invite my son Octa and his younger brother Ebissa: they are seasoned warriors indeed. Give them lands in the northern reaches of Britain by the Wall between Deira and Alban. They will hold back any attack from the barbarians so that you yourself may have peace south of the Humber." Vortigern agreed, and he had Hengist's sons invited, along with anyone they knew who could help them. Messengers were dispatched, and Octa, Ebissa, and Cerdic soon arrived with three hundred ships full of armed men.[3] Vortigern gave them a warm welcome, lavishing many gifts upon them. He was, in fact, able to defeat all of his enemies through their assistance, and he emerged the victor in every battle.

Hengist, meanwhile, was inviting even more ships—a few at a time—and the strength of his forces increased daily. The Britons were alarmed when they perceived his audacity, and they asked the king to expel the Saxons from his kingdom. Pagans, they argued, should not have commerce with the Christians nor should they be allowed to settle in a Christian realm, for the Christian Law forbade it. Most of all, such

---

[1] Bede documents the fact that Kent was the initial area of Anglo-Saxon settlement in Britain.

[2] These saints do not appear in Gildas' *The Ruin of Britain*, nor in the work of Nennius, who was routinely confused with Gildas in the Middle Ages. Bede, however, does give an account of Germanus and Lupus and their struggle against the Pelagian heresy in 429 C.E.

[3] Hengist had not mentioned his third son, Cerdic, in his previous request. The Anglo-Saxon kings of Wessex, incidentally, claimed descent from this Cerdic.

a great multitude of pagans had now come that the Britons were terrified of them. No one could tell any longer who was a pagan and who was a Christian, since the pagans were mingling with their daughters and other kinswomen. Protesting all these things, they tried to persuade the king not to retain these Saxons, lest the British people be overcome by some kind of treason. But Vortigern gave little heed to their entreaties, for he loved the Saxons above all others on account of his wife. When the Britons realized this, they deserted him at once and, in their anger, promoted his son Vortimer to the kingship. Vortimer agreed to address their concerns, and he began to expel the barbarians, attacking them and fighting fiercely against them. He fought four great battles against them and was victorious at every turn. The first battle occured at the River Derwend, and the second at the ford at Eppingford, where Horsa fought against Katigern, Vortigern's other son, and they slew each other in the fray. The third battle took place on the shore of the sea, where the pagan ships fled in a most unmanly fashion, taking refuge on the Isle of Thanet. Vortimer besieged them there and persistently engaged them in naval warfare. When the Saxons could no longer withstand the British assault, they sent King Vortigern, who had been with them through the entire campaign, to entreat his son Vortimer to allow them to retreat to Germany unscathed. While Vortigern and Vortimer were meeting, the Saxons set to sea and returned to Germany for a time, leaving their women and children behind.[1]

[102] Achieving these victories, Vortimer ordered the possessions that had been confiscated from the Britons to be restored. He loved and honored the people, and, at the request of Saint Germanus, he rebuilt the churches. But the Devil, who had entered the heart of his step-mother Renwein, was jealous of Vortimer's goodness and incited her to murder him. Putting forth all of her skills in the dark arts, Renwein gave Vortimer poison to drink, by means of one of his servants whom she had corrupted through countless bribes. As soon as that famous warrior drank the poison, he was seized with great sickness, so that he no longer had any hope of living. He commanded all of his soldiers to come to him at once and, announcing his imminent demise, he distributed his gold and silver and the other treasures of his ancestors among them. They all wept and lamented, but Vortimer consoled them, explaining that he was only embarking on the way of all flesh. He

---

[1]   Geoffrey omits information about Vortimer's fourth battle against the Saxons. The list is derived from Nennius.

exhorted all the brave and warlike young men who had accompanied him in all his campaigns to fight for their homeland and to protect it constantly from alien incursion. Then a bold plan occurred to him. He commanded a monument of brass to be built at the port where the Saxons were accustomed to land. After his mortal body had perished, he would be buried atop that monument so that, spying his grave, the barbarians would turn their sails back to Germany. He declared that no Saxons would dare to come any closer once they had caught a glimpse of his grave. Oh, the great courage of this man, who chose to terrorize even while dead those in whom he had inspired such fear while still alive! However, once Vortimer had died, the Britons acted otherwise and buried his body in the city of Trinovant.[1]

[103] After Vortimer's death, Vortigern was restored to the throne. At his wife's bidding, he sent messengers to Hengist in Germany, inviting him to come back to Britain. However, he requested that he come back quietly and with only a few men, fearing that, should Hengist return in full force, the hatred between the Britons and barbarians would be renewed. Hengist, on the other hand, had already heard about the death of Vortimer. Acting on his own, he gathered together a naval force of three hundred thousand armed men and returned to Britain. When the approach of such a great host was made known to Vortigern and the vassals of the realm, they were greatly angered. Taking counsel, they decided to fight Hengist and repel the Saxons from the coasts. But as soon as Hengist got word of this plan from messages sent by his daughter, he immediately gave thought to how he could best act against it. Considering many different types of plans, Hengist finally decided to betray the Britons under the guise of making peace. He sent his messengers to the king and ordered them to announce that he had not led such a great host of men with him to make settlements or to attack them. He had only brought them, he said, because they believed Vortimer was still alive. He had wanted to fight against Vortimer if Vortimer had continued to oppose him. But now, since that man was now dead, Hengist

---

[1] The proposed deposition of Vortimer's body in a brass monument has an analogue in the burial of Bran's head in the Second Branch of the *Mabinogion, Branwen verch Lyr.* "And from that moment on, they could find no rest except in carrying the head toward London. However long they were on the road, the came at last to London, and they buried Bran's head in the White Mount. And their burying it was one of the Three Fortunate Concealments, and its eventual finding proved one of the Three Unfortunate Disclosures; for no oppression could come to this island from across the sea so long as that head remained buried."

would place himself and all his men under Vortigern's command. Vortigern could choose how many to keep in his kingdom; Hengist would lead the rest back to Germany without delay. If this plan seemed acceptable to Vortigern, then Hengist asked the king to name a time and place in which they could meet and arrange these matters according to the king's will. When matters were announced to the king, he was most pleased, since he did not wish to have Hengist depart.

Vortigern then declared that the Britons and the Saxons would meet at Mount Ambrius on the first day of May, which was rapidly approaching, so that all these matters could be settled. [104] Both sides agreed. Then Hengist, hatching his next plan, ordered each of his men to carry his customary long knife at his side and await Hengist's word. When the Britons became engrossed in the discussion at hand, Hengist would give them this signal: "*Nemet oure saxas!*"[1] Each man would then stand by a Briton, boldly draw his knife and quickly cut his victim's throat.

The appointed day soon arrived. Britons and Saxons alike gathered in the aforementioned place and began to discuss peace. When Hengist saw the perfect moment for his plan, he cried out, "*Nime oure saxas!*" And then he himself seized Vortigern and held him by his robe. Hearing the signal, the Saxons drew their knives at once and attacked whatever leader was standing next to them. The Britons were expecting nothing of this sort. The Saxons cut the throats of about four hundred and sixty barons and earls; the blessed Eldad later gave their bodies a Christian burial in a place not far from Kaer Caraduc, which is now called Salisbury, in the cemetery beside the abbey of Ambrius, who had founded it there long ago. In any case, the Britons had all come unarmed, for they had only expected to be talking peace. For this reason, the foreigners were able to slaughter them all the more easily.

[105] However, the pagans did not achieve this treachery completely unscathed; many of them were killed even as they tried to assassinate their victims, for the Britons began to pick up rocks and sticks off the ground, striking the traitors with them in self-defense. The earl of Gloucester, whose name was Eldol, was also there.[2] Beholding the treachery, he seized a wooden stake, which he had come across by

---

[1]   *Nime oure saxas*: a Latin rendering of the Anglo-Saxon *Nimeth eowre seaxas*, "Take out your blades!" Nennius provides a less plausible version of the signal, "*Nimader sexa!*" This short, one-edged sword (A-S *seax*), Geoffrey suggests, was the eponymous weapon of the Saxons.

[2]   Geoffrey's special focus on the feats of Eldol, the earl of Gloucester, reflects his patronage by Robert, the twelfth-century earl of Gloucester. The character is unattested in all of *The History*'s known sources.

chance, and began to defend himself with it. If anyone approached him, he struck him so hard that his limbs would break and he would be dispatched straight to Hell. Eldol smashed heads and arms and shoulders and legs, inspiring the Saxons with great terror. Before he left that spot, he had slain seventy men with that stake. However, since he could not hold back the entirety of the Saxon force, he finally withdrew and retreated to his city.

Though many fell on both sides that day, the Saxons still had the victory. For the Britons had come unarmed, not expecting any treachery, and hence they were powerless to resist. Once they had perpetrated their wickedness, the Saxons wanted to slay Vortigern as well. Instead, they tied him up and threatened him with death, demanding his cities and fortresses in exchange for his life. Vortigern agreed to whatever they asked so that he would be allowed to escape alive. When he had sworn oaths, they released him from his chains. They arrived first at London, capturing the city. Then they seized York, Lincoln and Winchester, ravaging the lands all around. They fell upon the native Britons everywhere like wolves upon sheep whom the shepherd has deserted.

When Vortigern beheld all of this devastation, he retreated into Wales, not knowing how to stop this wicked people. [106] Summoning all his court magicians, he asked their advice and ordered them to tell him what to do. They declared that he should build the strongest tower he could to be his defense, since he had forfeited all his other strongholds. He considered various locations that might be suitable for such a fortress, and he came at last to Mount Eryri, where he gathered masons from all over the land and commanded them to build a tower.[1] Coming together, the stoneworkers began to lay the foundations. However, whatever work they accomplished on a given day sank into the earth by the next, in such a way that they did not know where their work had disappeared to. When this was announced to the king, he consulted his magicians again to explain the reason behind it. They told him that he must find a youth without a father and that he should kill him so that the boy's blood could be mixed in with the cornerstones of the tower's foundations. Doing this, they assured him, would stabilize the foundations. Messengers were sent throughout the land at once in search of such a person. At long last, when they came to the city that was called Carmarthen, they saw some children playing before the city gates and went to watch their game. Weary from their journey, they sat down in a circle, hoping yet to discover what they

---

[1]   Eryri is the Welsh name for Mount Snowdon in North Wales.

were looking for. After much of the day had passed, an argument broke out between two of the children, whose names were Merlin and Dinabutius.[1] In the midst of their argument, Dinabutius suddenly said to Merlin: "Why do you even bother fighting with me, you fool? We two will never be of the same rank. I am sprung from a line of kings on both sides of my family. It is not even known who you are, since you have no father." At these words, the messengers raised their heads, and, gazing attentively at Merlin, asked all the bystanders who the boy was. The messengers were told that no one knew who the boy's father was. His mother, however, had been the daughter of the king of Demetia and she now dwelt in that same city, among the holy sisters of the Church of Saint Peter.

[107] The messengers went at once to the prefect of the town and ordered him in the king's name to have Merlin and his mother sent to the king. When the prefect realized the reason behind their errand, he sent Merlin and his mother to Vortigern so that the king could do with them as he pleased. And when they had been led into the king's presence, Vortigern welcomed the woman gladly, for he knew that she was of noble blood. Then he began to ask her about the boy's father. She responded: "By my living soul, my lord king, and by your living soul too, I knew no man who could have conceived this child in me. But I can tell you that once, when I was among my sisters in the cloister, a man in the likeness of a beautiful youth appeared to me. He would often take me within his arms and kiss me. After he had tarried with me for a while, he would disappear completely, and I would be able to find no trace of him. And many times he would talk with me while I sat alone, though he would not become visible. When he visited me in this way, he would often take the shape of a man and have intercourse with me. And he left me pregnant. Know in your great wisdom, my lord, that I have known no other man but the one who fathered this boy."

Marvelling greatly, the king ordered his sage Maugantius to be summoned so that he could decide if what the woman had said could have really happened. Maugantius was brought forth, and, on Vortigern's

---

[1] The figure of Merlin, one of Geoffrey's most compelling, is a composite of at least two semi-historical figures. The first is the sixth-century Welsh bard Myrddin, the Latinized version of whose name would be *Merdinus* or *Merlinus*. To this bard were attributed (probably incorrectly) a number of political prophecies, some of which are appended to this volume. The second source for Geoffrey's Merlin is the enigmatic figure of Ambrosius from Nennius's *History of the Britons*. For a full discussion, see A.O.H. Jarman, "The Merlin Legend and the Welsh Tradition of Prophecy," in *The Arthur of the Welsh*, ed. Rachel Bromwich et al. (Cardiff: U of Wales P, 1991): 117–40.

command, he explained to all who were listening: "I have discovered in the writings of our philosophers, and in many histories as well, that many men are sired in this manner. For, as Apuleius asserts in his *De deo Socratis*, many spirits that we call *incubi* dwell between the Earth and the Moon.[1] They take somewhat after human beings and somewhat after angels. They can assume human form when they so desire and have intercourse with human women. Perhaps one of these spirits appeared to this woman and begat this boy on her." [108] And when Merlin heard all this, he approached the king and asked, "Why have my mother and I been led into your presence?"Vortigern answered: "My wizards have advised me that I need a man without a father whose blood I may sprinkle on my edifice so that it will stand firm." Then Merlin replied: "Tell your magicians to come with me and I will demonstrate that they are lying."

Still in amazement at these words, the king summoned his magicians and had them sit by Merlin. Merlin said to them: "You do not know what is interfering with the foundation of the tower which these men have begun, yet you have recommended that my blood be mixed with the mortar, hoping in that way to stabilize the building. But tell me now what lies underneath that foundation. For the thing that lies beneath it is what prevents it from standing." The magicians were most afraid, and remained silent. Merlin, who was also known as Ambrosius, continued: "My lord king, call your workers and tell them to dig down into the earth and you will find a underground pool. That is what is preventing the tower from standing." When this had been done, a pool was indeed discovered underground, which had been making the ground unstable. Merlin Ambrosius turned once again to the magicians and said: "Flatterers and liars! Tell me what lies at the bottom of this pool." They did not utter a word, and remained completely silent. "Have the pool drained," Merlin said, "and at the bottom you will find two hollow stones and within the stones two sleeping dragons." The king believed his words since he had been right about the pool, and he commanded it to be drained. He marveled surpassingly at Merlin. Everyone else who was there also marveled at his great knowledge, and they believed that some sort of supernatural spirit was with him.

---

[1]   Lucius Apuleius (c. 123–70 C.E.) was a Roman writer and philosopher, best known for his novel *The Golden Ass* (*Metamorphoses*). He had a reputation, even in his own time, as an authority on magic and the occult. Geoffrey is likely referring to the following passage in Apuleius' *De Deo Socratis*, VI: "[There are] ... certain semi-divine spirits situated in the realm of the air between the Ether on high and the Earth below.... The Greeks call them *daemons*, and they are the messengers and interpreters of our prayers and wishes to the gods."

BOOK SEVEN

[109] I had not yet reached this point in my history when my associates, hearing Merlin discussed everywhere, urged me to publish his *Prophecies*; I was particularly inspired by Alexander, the bishop of Lincoln, a man of the highest piety and wisdom.[1] There was no one among either the clergy or the populace at large who was attended by more noblemen, for his holiness and good-natured generosity attracted them to his service. Because I desired to satisfy that man, I translated the prophecies and sent them to him with this letter: [110] "O Alexander, Bishop of Lincoln, the regard which I hold for your nobility compels me to translate the prophecies of Merlin from British into Latin before continuing the history of the deeds of the British kings which I have already begun. I had originally intended to complete that work before then applying myself to this shorter one, lest my judgment start to flag from working on both at the same time. However, since I am reassured by the subtle discretion of your wisdom, I have pressed the rustic reed to my lips and, with pastoral melodies, I now interpret this language which is unknown to you.[2] Yet I remain completely awed that you have deigned to commit this task to my humble pen, when the staff of your power commands so many men who are more learned and worthy than I, men who would caress your Minerva-like sense with their more refined music. And yet, passing over all the wise men of Britain, I am not ashamed to confess that it is you alone, above all others, who should pick up the merry harp and sing along with me, should your high office not beckon you to other duties. Therefore, since it pleases you that Geoffrey of Monmouth should pipe out these predictions, do not forget to favor his music and, should any of it sound uneven or dissonant, please do not spare the rod in correcting its rhythm."

---

[1]   Alexander, the Anglo-Norman bishop of Lincoln from 1123 to his death in 1147 or 1148, was a known patron of letters and presided over one of the most splendid Episcopal courts in Britain.

[2]   No single source has been found, either in Latin or "the British tongue," from which Geoffrey's version of Merlin's prophecies derives. There had been a thriving tradition of political prophecy attributed to the bard Myrddin in Welsh, and perhaps in Cornish as well, and several of Geoffrey's prophecies are echoed in some of the extant Welsh texts. One of these Welsh prophecies of Merlin, *The Apple Trees* (*Yr Afallennau*) is included in Appendix B this volume, as is Geoffrey's later revisiting of the genre of prophecy in his *Life of Merlin*.

★ ★ ★

[111] While Vortigern, the king of the Britons, sat there by the side of the now-emptied pool, two dragons emerged from it, one white and the other red. Whenever one approached the other they fought bitterly, spewing out flames at one another. At first the white dragon seemed to prevail, and the red dragon fled back to the depths of the pool. But when it felt itself wounded, it made a sudden charge at the white dragon and forced it back.[1] While they were fighting in this way, the king ordered Merlin Ambrosius to explain what this battle between the dragons portended. Merlin at once burst into tears, and, summoning the spirit of prophecy to him, he spoke:

(1) [112] "Woe to the Red Dragon, for its death hastens! The White Dragon, which refers to the Saxons whom you have invited here, will occupy its caves. The Red Dragon stands for the people of Britain who shall be oppressed by the White Dragon. The mountains will be made level with the valleys, and the rivers of the valleys will flow with blood. True worship will be destroyed, and the churches will lie open to ruin.

(2) But the oppressed shall prevail and resist the viciousness of the foreigners. Indeed, the Boar of Cornwall will be swift to offer his aid and he will trample their hills beneath his feet. The isles of the Ocean itself will submit to his power and he will possess the forests of Gaul. The House of Romulus will tremble at his ferocity, and his end will be cloaked in uncertainty. He will be celebrated by the voice of the people and his deeds will be food for poets.[2]

(3) Six of his line shall hold the scepter after him but after them the German Worm will arise. The Sea-Wolf that was nourished amid the groves of Africa will subdue it. Religion will be destroyed once again, and there will be a redistribution of arch-bishopric sees. The dignity of London will adorn Canterbury and the seventh bishop of York will tarry in the kingdom of

---

[1]   The omen of the two dragons is first attested in Nennius' *History of the Britons* (see Appendix A). Medieval commentators agree that the Red Dragon represents the Britons and the White Dragon the Saxons. The Red Dragon still appears on the flag of Wales today.

[2]   Merlin later identifies the Boar of Cornwall as King Arthur, who will be born in Cornwall at Tintagel Castle (Book Eight). The prophecy describes his maritime and continental conquests, as well as his attempted conquest of Rome.

Armorica. Menevia will be endowed with the metropolitan pall of the City of Legions, and the preacher from Ireland will be silent on account of a child still growing in the womb. The skies will rain blood and a grave famine will afflict mortal men.

(4) The Red Dragon shall bemoan the passing of these events, but it will wax strong with great travail. Misfortune will then befall the White Dragon, and its mansions and gardens will be destroyed. Seven kings will perish and one of them will be made a saint. The wombs of mothers will dry up and children will be born dead. A monster will serve as a surety unto men that the natives will be restored. The man who accomplishes these things will erect a bronze statue of a man, and for many years it will protect the gate of London upon its bronze horse.[1]

(5) After that, the Red Dragon shall revert to its old ways, and shall strive to inflict violence upon itself. But the vengeance of the Thunderer will prevail, since every field will betray those who plow it. A plague will afflict the people and it will empty out all the lands. The survivors will desert their native soil to cultivate foreign fields. A blessed king will ready his ship and will be counted among the twelve in the Heavenly Hall. The desolation of the kingdom will be grievous indeed and the threshing-houses will be overgrown with fruit-laden forests.

(6) The White Dragon shall rise again and invite the daughter of Germany. Our gardens will be filled once more with the seed of foreigners and the Red Dragon will languish at the far end of the pool.

(7) Then the German Worm shall be crowned and the bronze prince will be buried deep. A time limit is set for the Worm that it cannot escape: [113] it will remain for one hundred and fifty years of unrest and oppression, and then will rule for three hundred more.

(8) Then the North Wind shall blow against him and snatch away the flowers that the West Wind had quickened. The temples will be adorned with gold, and swords will not lose their sharpness. The German Dragon will scarcely reach its cave before vengeance for its crimes overtakes it.

(9) The Worm shall thrive only a little longer until the decimation

---

[1] The prophecy of the bronze horseman, one of the clearer of the prophecies, seems to refer to King Cadwallo. See Book Eleven, paragraph 201.

of Neustria harms it.[1] A people clad in iron tunics will arrive in a ship, and they will wreak vengeance upon the Worm for its crimes. This people will restore the lovely mansions of the natives and will mete out ruin to the foreigners. The seed of the White Dragon will be completely uprooted from our gardens, and the remainder of its race will be decimated. They will bear the yoke of perpetual servitude and will wound their mother with mattocks and plows.

(10) Two dragons shall succeed to the throne. One of them will choke to death on the sting of envy, and the other will return under the shadow of a name.

(11) The Lion of Justice shall then succeed, and the towers of Gaul and the dragons of the islands shall tremble at his roar.[2] In his days, gold will be twisted from the lily and myrtle, and silver will flow from the hooves of cattle. Men with attractively groomed hair will dress in new styles of woolen garments, and their outer dress will reflect their inner state. The feet of barking dogs will be cut off. The wild beasts will enjoy peace, but humankind will mourn its dire straits. The rapacity of goats will diminish, and the teeth of wolves will grow dull.

(12) The Lion's Cubs shall be transformed into fish and his Eagle will make a nest upon Mount Aravius.[3] Venedotia will be red with its mother's blood and the house of Corineus will slay six brothers. The island will spill tears in the night because everyone will be provoked to all sorts of deeds.

(13) [114] The latter-born shall try to fly far aloft, but the favor given to new men shall be greater still. Piety will not approve of him who has inherited goods from the impious until he adopts his father's style of dress. He who is girded with the teeth of the boar will ascend higher than the mountain peaks and the shadow of the helmeted man.

(14) Alban shall grow haughty and, summoning its allies, will not hesitate to spill blood. In its maw will be found a bridle fashioned in

---

[1] Neustria was an older name for Normandy. The Worm's decimation at the hands of Neustria suggests the Norman Conquest of England in 1066.

[2] Most twelfth-century commentators on Merlin's prophecies agreed in identifying the Lion of Justice as King Henry I.

[3] The transformation of the Lion's cubs into fish may signify the drowning of Henry I's only legitimate son in the sinking of the White Ship in 1120. This, according to Rupert Taylor, 13, is the latest datable event mentioned in *The Prophecies of Merlin*.

the Bay of Armorica. The Eagle of the Broken Covenant will cover it with gold and will rejoice in her third nesting.

(15) The Lion's Cubs shall be watchful and shall hunt in the woods beyond the walls of the cities. They will inflict great slaughter upon whoever stands in their way, and they will cut out the tongues of bulls. The necks of the lions will then be burdened with chains and they will restore the times of their grandfather.

(16) After that, from the first to the fourth, from the fourth to the third, from the third to the second shall the thumb be rolled in oil.

(17) The Sixth King shall undermine the walls of Ireland and shall transform the forests into open plains. He will reduce sundry provinces into one and will be crowned with the head of the lion. His beginning will succumb to his fickle disposition, but his ending will soar to the heavens. He will restore the traditional seats of the blessed throughout the land, and he will place priests back in their proper places. He will endow two cities with the metropolitan pall, and he will give virginal gifts to the virgins. The favor of the Thunderer will be granted to him, and he will be reckoned among the blessed.

(18) [115] A piercing light shall issue from him that shall portend the ruin of his own people. Because of this light, Neustria will both lose the island and be deprived of its former dignity.[1]

(19) Then the native citizens shall return to the island; for the downfall of the foreigners shall commence. The white-haired old man upon the snow-white horse will divert the flow of the River Periron, and he will measure out a mill with his white staff.[2]

(20) Cadwallader shall summon Conan and invoke an alliance with Alban.[3] Then there will be a great slaughter of the foreign-born, and the rivers will flow with blood. Then the hills of Armorica will crumble, and he will be crowned with the diadem of Brutus. Wales will be filled with joy and the oaks of Cornwall

---

[1] Instead of "light" here, many of the other manuscripts read "lynx" (the Latin words *lux* and *linx* could be easily confused). *Lux*, "light," however, seems to make more sense of the accompanying adjective *penetrans*.

[2] The River Periron, a tributary of the Severn, lies in Gwent not far from the city of Monmouth. The tenth-century Welsh Merlinic prophecy *Armes Prydein* features the mouth of the River Peryddon as the site of a confrontation between the Welsh and the steward of the English king.

[3] Cadwallader and Conan appear as prophesied saviors of the Britons as early as the tenth-century *Armes Prydein*.

will flourish. The island will be called by the name of Brutus and its occupation by foreigners will pass away.

(21) From Conan shall arise a warlike Boar who will test the sharpness of his teeth amid the forests of Gaul. He will cut down even the mighty oaks and offer protection to the lesser ones. The Arabs and the Africans will fear him, for the force of his onslaught will extend even to distant Spain.

(22) A goat of the camp of Venus shall succeed him, and he will have horns and a silvery beard that will puff down from his nostrils like a cloud overshadowing the entire surface of the island.

(23) There shall be peace in his time, and the crops will multiply in the fruitful soil. Women will turn continually into serpents and all of their concourse will be filled with pride. The camps of Venus will be renewed and the darts of Cupid will not cease to wound. The source of the River Amnis will turn to blood and two kings will fight a duel on account of the Lioness of Stafford. All the land will grow decadent and mankind will fornicate ceaselessly.

(24) Three hundred years it will take for these things to pass until the kings buried in London are exhumed.

(25) Famine and plague will come again; the people will mourn the desolation of the cities.

(26) A Boar of Commerce shall then arrive who will recall the scattered flocks to their former pasture. His bosom will be their food, and his tongue will satisfy the thirsty. From his mouth there will issue rivers that will water men's parched gullets.

(27) And atop the Tower of London there shall spring a tree that will shade all the surface of the island with the spreading of its leaves, though it will only have three branches. The North Wind will be an enemy to it and it will break off the third branch with its treacherous blowing.

(28) The two remaining branches shall take the place of the one that was blown away until one begins to strangle the other with the density of its leaves. Then the one branch will take the place of both the other two and will provide a home for foreign birds. Then the native birds will deem that tree hostile, for they will lose the freedom of flight out of their fear of the tree's shade.

(29) Then the Ass of Wickedness shall come to power, acting swiftly against the shapers of gold but slowly against the viciousness of wolves.

(30) [116] In those days, the oaks shall burn in the forests and acorns grow upon the boughs of the lindens. The Severn Sea will flow through seven mouths, and the River Usk overflow for seven months. Its fish will die from the heat and serpents will be born from them. The hot springs of Bath will freeze and their normally healthy waters will breed death. London will bemoan the slaughter of twenty thousand, and the Thames will be changed to blood. The hooded monks will be eager to marry and their cries will resound in the Alps.

(31) Three fountains shall burst forth in the city of Winchester whose streams will divide the island into three parts. He who drinks from the first stream will live long and will not be burdened with any disabling weakness. He who drinks from the second will die of an insatiable hunger, and paleness and terror will be evident on his face. He who drinks from the third will suffer a sudden death, but his body will never rest in a tomb. Whoever would avoid such a hideous end will attempt to cover the spring up with various types of coverings. But any kind of weight placed upon it will take the form of some other substance. If the dirt is heaped upon it, the dirt will turn to stones; stones would turn into liquid; wood into ashes; ashes into water.

(32) At this time, a Maiden shall be sent out of a city in Canute's Forest to heal with her leechcraft. Employing all of her craft, she will dry up all of these noxious fountains with a mere breath.

(33) After that, when she has refreshed herself with a wholesome draught, she shall bear the forest of Celidon in her right hand and the ramparted walls of London in her left. And as she proceeds, her every step will burn with brimstone and fume with a double flame. That smoke will arouse the Ruteni, and it will provide food for those who dwell under the sea. She will shed tears of mercy, and she will fill the island with her terrible cry.

(34) A stag with ten tines shall slay the Maiden; four of its tines will be crowned with gold. The other six will turn into the horns of oxen, and they will disturb the three isles of Britain with a horrible uproar.

(35) The Forest of Dean shall be aroused and shall burst forth in a human voice, crying: "Come, Wales, and bring Cornwall with you, and say to Winchester: 'The Earth will swallow you up. Transfer the bishop's seat to where the ships dock, and let the

limbs follow the head. The day is hastening in which the people must perish for their wicked crimes. The whiteness of wool has harmed you, as have the many colors in which it is dyed. Woe to this wicked race, for the great city will fall because of it.'''

(36) Ships shall rejoice because of this increase, and one will be made from two. Laden with apples, the Hedgehog will rebuild the city, and birds from many different forests will fly toward the fragrance of the apples. He will also build a great palace there and will fortify it with six hundred towers.

(37) London shall be envious of this city and build up its own walls threefold. The River Thames will surround it on every side, and the rumor of this event will pass beyond the Alps. The Hedgehog will hide his apples within it and will devise many underground passages.

(38) In that time the stones shall speak, and the sea over which one sails to Gaul shall be narrowed to a short space. A man will be able to hear another man on the other side, and the island's firm land will be made broader. Things hidden beneath the sea will be revealed, and Gaul will tremble in fear.

(39) After these things have passed, a Heron shall emerge from the Forest of Calaterium and fly around the island for two years.[1] Crying at night, she will summon the birds, and every type of fowl will ally itself with her. They will rush down upon the fields of mortal men and devour all types of grain.

(40) Famine shall afflict the people, and a grave plague shall follow the famine. And when these disasters have ceased, an odious bird will come to the Vale of Galabes and will raise it up, making it a lofty mountain.[2] Upon its summit the Heron will plant an oak and will nest in its branches.

(41) Three eggs shall be laid in that nest, and from these eggs a Fox, a Wolf, and a Bear will hatch. The Fox will devour its mother and will wear the head of an Ass. In this monstrous guise he will frighten his brothers and send them fleeing into Normandy.

(42) But in Normandy the brothers shall arouse the tusky Boar and, returning by ship, they will meet the Fox in battle. During this battle, the Fox will play dead, moving the Boar to pity. He will

---

[1] The Forest of Calaterium is the site of one of the campaigns in the fraternal strife between Belinus and Brennius in Book Two.

[2] Merlin is said to frequent the Springs of Galabes in Book Eight.

then approach the Fox's corpse and, standing over it, will breathe upon the Fox's eyes and face. But, not forgetting her former cunning, the Fox will bite off his left foot and rip it from his body. Jumping upon him, she will also tear off his right ear and his tail and will then go hide herself in the mountain caves.

(43) Thus deluded, the Boar shall demand that the Wolf and the Bear repay him for his missing limbs. These two brothers will seek to satisfy the Boar, and they will promise him the two of the Fox's feet, as well as both of her ears and her tail. They will combine these into a pig's hide to make him whole again. The Boar will agree to this and await the fulfillment of their promises.

(44) In the meantime, the Fox shall come down out of the mountains and transform herself into a Wolf. And she will come to the Boar as if to parley and, using all her craft, will gobble him up. Then she will transform herself into a Boar and, pretending to be without limbs, will lie in wait for the two brothers. But after they come, she will slay them with her teeth at once, and she will be crowned with the head of the Lion.

(45) In those days a Serpent shall be born who will threaten men with death. The length of its body will surround London, and it will devour all the passersby.

(46) The Mountain Ox shall assume the head of the Wolf and shall whiten his teeth in the smithy of the Severn. He will ally himself with the flocks of the Scots and Welsh, and together they will dry up the Thames.

(47) The Ass shall summon the long-bearded Goat and shall take on his appearance. The Mountain Ox will grow angry over this and will call the Wolf to his side and transfix him with his horn. Having unleashed this viciousness, he will gobble up their flesh and bones, but he himself will be buried atop Mount Urianus.

(48) The embers of the pyre shall be transformed into swans that will swim on dry land as if it were a river. They will devour fish when among the fish, and they will glut themselves on men while among men. But when old age catches up with them, they will become sea-lords and will engage in piracy. They will sink ships and gather no small store of silver.

(49) The Thames shall then flow once again and, mustering all of its currents together, it will exceed the confines of its riverbed. It will flood the nearby cities and overturn any hills that stand in its path.

(50) It shall wend itself with cunning to the source of the Galabes,

which is filled with wickedness.[1] From it there will arise a great sedition that will provoke the Venedotians to war. The oaks of the forests will gather together and will fight against the axes of the Gewissei. The Crow will soar with the Kite, and it will devour the bodies of the slain.

(51) An Owl shall nest atop the walls of Gloucester, and an Ass will spring from its nest. The Serpent of Malvern will build him up and will encourage him in various types of treason. Assuming the crown, he will ascend on high and will frighten the people of the land with his horrific bleating.

(52) In his days the Mountains of Pacau shall totter, and the lands will be stripped of their forests. Indeed, a fire-breathing Worm will come who will set the trees ablaze with the exhalation of its breath.

(53) From the Worm shall spring seven Lions who will be disfigured with the heads of goats. They will corrupt the women-folk with the stench from their nostrils, and they will make their own wives into common whores. A father will not know his own son because of these wanton and bestial habits.

(54) Then there shall arise the Giant of Wickedness, who will terrify everyone with the keenness of his eyesight. The Dragon of Worcester will rise against him and try to slay him. In this fight the Dragon will be vanquished and will be enslaved by the evil of his conqueror. The Giant will climb upon the Dragon and, casting aside his robes, will sit upon him naked. The Dragon will carry him up and, with his tail up, will strike the Giant in his nakedness. Then, regaining his strength, the Giant will pierce the Dragon's innards with his sword. Tangled up in his own tail, the Dragon will die from its own poison.

(55) The Boar of Totnes shall succeed him, oppressing the people with dire tyranny. Gloucester will send out a Lion who will continually molest him in various types of warfare. He will trample the Boar under his feet and will terrify him with his gaping maw.

(56) After a time this Lion shall come into conflict with the entire kingdom and will climb upon the backs of the nobles. A Bull

---

[1] I have emended the Bern MS's *fortes Galahes* (the strong men of the Galahes) to *fontes Galabes* (the source of the Galabes), a phrase that not only makes more sense here but that also occurs elsewhere in the text (Book Eight). The Bern scribe likely misread the *n* of *fontes* for an *r*, a common and understandable slip, as is the confusion of the *b* of *Galabes* with an *h*.

will then enter the fray and will strike the Lion with his right foot. He will pursue the Lion through all the taverns in the kingdom, but the Bull will break his horns on the walls of Exeter.

(57) The Fox of Caerdubal shall avenge the Lion and shall devour the Bull with its teeth.

(58) The Serpent of Lincoln will coil itself around the Fox, making his presence known to the many dragons by his horrible hissing. Then the dragons will fight and will tear one another to shreds. The one with wings will oppress the one without wings and will rend the other's cheeks with its poisonous claws. Still more dragons will come to the battle, and the one will slay the other.

(59) The fifth one shall succeed the slain; he will destroy the rest with various schemes. He will climb atop the back of the third and chop the head from the body with his sword. Casting off his robes, he will mount the next one and will grasp its tail with both his right and left hands. Naked will he vanquish him, since he could accomplish nothing when robed. Thus mounted, he will torment the others and scatter them all throughout the realm.

(60) The Roaring Lion shall overcome and he will be feared because of his dreadful ferocity. Thrice five portions will he reduce into one and he alone will govern the people.

(61) A snowy-colored Giant shall shine forth; from his seed will spring a white people.

(62) Pleasure will weaken the princes and, thus subdued, they will turn into beasts. From among them will arise a Lion who is glutted on human flesh. The Reaper will assist the Lion at this harvest; but when the Reaper becomes confused, the Lion will overpower him.

(63) The Charioteer of York shall pacify them and, overthrowing his master, he will climb upon the chariot he drives. With drawn sword, he will threaten the east and the tracks that his wheels make will fill up with blood. Then he will become a fish of the sea and will couple with the Serpent, allured by her hissing.

(64) From this union there shall be born three thundering Bulls who, having eaten down their pastures, will be transformed into trees. The First Bull will carry in a scourge made of vipers and he will turn his back upon the Second Bull. The Second Bull will seize the whip, but it will be snatched away by the Third Bull. They will avoid each other's faces until they cast away the poisoned goblet.

(65) A Husbandman from Alban shall succeed them, though a serpent will be hanging down his back. He will have time to till the soil so that the fields of his homeland turn white. The serpent will strive to spread its poison so that the grasses and crops never grow back. The population will decrease because of a deadly calamity, and the city walls will stand empty.

(66) Gloucester shall be offered as a remedy and shall promote the Foster-Daughter of the Scourger. She will carry the Scales of Healing, and within a short space of time the island will be restored.

(67) After that, two shall follow the scepter, and the Horned Dragon will wait upon them both. The first will arrive clad in iron and riding a winged serpent. He will sit naked upon its back and grasp its tail with his right hand. The very seas will grow tempestuous at the rumor of his approach, and they will inspire the second with fear.

(68) The second shall then ally himself with the Lion, but strife will arise between them and they will quarrel. They will wound each other, but the ferocity of the beast will prevail.

(69) A single man shall stand forth with a harp and drum, and he shall pacify the Lion's ferocity. The peoples of the realm will make peace and they will persuade the Lion to come to the Scales. Once there, he will be diligent in balancing the weights, but he will extend his palms to Alban. The Northerners will mourn and they will unbolt the temple gates.

(70) A Wolf bearing the banner shall lead the armies, and he will encircle Cornwall with his tail. A knight in a chariot will resist him, transforming that people into a Boar. The Boar will then ravage many lands, but he will hide his head in the depths of the Severn.

(71) A man shall embrace the Lion in wine, and a golden lightning will blind the onlookers. Silver will glitter as it goes round and it will vex the wine presses. [117] Consuming the wine that is given to them, mortal men will become drunk and, forsaking Heaven, they will fix their gazes upon the earth.

(72) Then the stars shall turn their faces from them and stray from their fixed paths. Because of the stars' wrath, the crops will all wither and dew will not alight upon the ground. Roots and branches will change places and the novelty of this affair will be a great wonder.

(73) The light of the Sun shall fade in the amber of Mercury. Stilbon of Arcadia will change his shield, the helm of Mars will summon Venus.[1] The helm of Mars will cast a shadow, Mercury's wrath will make it surpass its fixed bounds. Iron Orion will bare his sword, watery Phoebus will harass the clouds. Jupiter will abandon his true course and Venus will leave her ordained track behind. The star Saturn will set balefully and will slay men with his curved sickle. The twelve houses of the Zodiac will lament the waywardness of their guests. The Twins will forget their customary embraces and they will summon the Water-Bearer to the fountains. Libra's weights will hang crookedly until the Ram supports them with his curved horn. The Virgin will climb upon the Archer's back, forsaking her maidenly flowers. The Scorpion's tail will engender lightning and the Crab will contend with the sun. The chariot of the Moon will set the Zodiac all awhirl, and the Pleiades will burst out weeping. No one will then perform his duty, but the closed gate at the piers will conceal Ariadne.

(74) In a stroke, the seas shall rise up, and the dust of the ancients shall be revived. The Winds shall contend with dire blowings, and their clamor shall resound among the stars.

---

[1] The use of the obscure term Stilbon for the planet Mercury suggests Geoffrey's considerable familiarity with the jargon of medieval astrology.

BOOK EIGHT

[118] When Merlin had finished revealing his prophecies concerning these and many other things, the bystanders marveled at the ambiguity of his words. Vortigern was even more astonished than the others, and he praised the youth's discernment and predictions, for in those days there was no one who would dare to speak such words in front of a king. Desiring to hear about the end of his life, Vortigern pressed Merlin to tell him what he knew. Merlin replied: "Flee from the fires of the sons of Constantine, if you are able. At this very moment they are preparing their fleet, at this moment they are casting off from the shores of Armorica, at this very moment *they spread their sails across the waves.*[1] They will come to the isle of Britain, they will attack the Saxon people, they will subjugate that wicked race. But first they will burn you alive within a tower. In your wickedness you betrayed their father and invited the Saxons to this island. You invited them as allies, but now they prevail and demand your service in turn. Two deaths lie in wait for you, and it is unclear how you will be able to avoid either of them. On the one hand, the Saxons are laying your kingdom waste and threatening your life. On the other hand, the two brothers, Aurelius and Uther, are coming and will attempt to avenge their father's death. Try to flee them if you can; they will come ashore at Totnes tomorrow. The faces of the Saxons will run red with blood, Hengist will be killed, and Aurelius Ambrosius will take the crown. He will restore peace to the land and rebuild the churches, but he himself will succumb to poison. His brother Uther Pendragon will succeed him, but his days will also be cut short by poison.[2] Your offspring will be behind this treachery, but the Boar of Cornwall will devour them."

[119] As the next day dawned, Aurelius Ambrosius came ashore.[3]

---

[1] The original Latin here is in the last half of a hexameter, which suggests that Geoffrey may have been working with some kind of Latin verse source, now lost.

[2] Like many of Geoffrey's other characters, the figure of Uther Pendragon is absent in previous histories but well-attested in early Welsh triads and other poetry, where he is occasionally linked to Arthur. In no source clearly predating Geoffrey, however, is Uther described as a king of Britain. See Rachel Bromwich, *Trioedd Ynys Prydein: The Triads of the Island of Britain* (Cardiff: U of Wales P, 2006), 512–15.

[3] Geoffrey's source for the campaigns and reign of Aurelius Ambrosius draws ultimately from the figure of Ambrosius Aurelianus from Gildas' *The Ruin of Britain*. Gildas makes a brief mention of this victorious fifth-century general as a descendant of the old Roman elite and a worthy role model for what Gildas saw as his own decadent times.

As the news of his arrival spread, the Britons, who had been scattered all about after the recent devastations, rallied together. Bolstered by the fellowship of their countrymen, the Britons regained their usual high spirits. The clergy were then summoned. They anointed Aurelius as their king, and the people paid homage to him according to their ancient customs. The Britons were at that point quite eager to attack the Saxons, but the king dissuaded them, for he desired to root out Vortigern first of all. Indeed, Aurelius grieved so much at the treachery done to his father that he would do nothing at all before avenging himself on Vortigern.[1] Carrying out this plan, he led his army into Wales and came to the castle of Genoreu. This castle lay in the land of Erging on the River Wye atop a great hill called Cloartius.[2] As Aurelius Ambrosius made the final approach, recalling the betrayal of his father and brother, he turned to Eldol, the duke of Gloucester, and said: "Now let's see, my noble duke, whether any cities or castle walls will be able to protect Vortigern, for I myself shall plunge the point of my sword into his innards. He deserves death. Nor, I suppose, can you be unaware of how he has earned this fate. O, that most wicked of all men! He is worthy of unspeakable torture! First he betrayed my father Constantine who had rescued him—and this entire land—from the invasion of the Picts. Then he betrayed my brother Constans, whom he had made king. After that, when he had attained the throne for himself through his stratagems, he brought pagans into the land to mingle with the natives and to root out all those who were loyal to me. But now, through the grace of God, he has unwittingly fallen into the trap that he had laid for his allies. And when the Saxons learned of his wickedness, they drove him out of the kingdom; that, at least, is the one thing for which we can thank the Saxons. In my opinion, what is most deplorable is that this wicked people whom that wicked man invited here has destroyed the noble cities, laid waste the fertile fields, destroyed the holy churches, and rooted out almost all the Christian faith from sea to sea. But now, my countrymen, let us act bravely and

---

[1]   The text incorrectly suggests that Aurelius Ambrosius holds Vortigern responsible for his father Constantine's death. Though Vortigern had machinated the murder of Aurelius' brother Constans, it was in fact an unnamed Pict who slew Constantine. Vortigern does not even appear in *The History of the Kings of Britain* until the paragraph after Constantine is killed. Geoffrey has either conflated two separate traditions concerning Constantine's death or has simply confused his story, though not without dramatic effect.

[2]   Tatlock, 72, speculates that Geoffrey understood these locations to be in the vicinity of Monmouth, while Lewis Thorpe places them in the region of Snowdon in North Wales. The Welsh *Brut Dingestow* gives the castle's name as *Goronwy* and the hill's as *Clorach*.

avenge ourselves first upon the man who brought all these deeds to pass. Only after defeating Vortigern should we turn our forces against the other enemies who threaten us, and we shall liberate our land from their clutches!" Without delay, the Britons brought forth various types of siege-engines and attempted to demolish the castle walls. At last, when the other siege tactics had failed, they made use of fire. When the fire finally blazed up, it did not cease until it had consumed the entire tower and Vortigern along with it.

[120] When these events were related to Hengist and the Saxons, they grew most anxious, for they feared the prowess of Aurelius Ambrosius. Indeed, that man possessed such strength and valor that, when he had lived in Gaul, there was no man who dared to meet him in a fight. If anyone did try to ride against him, Ambrosius would either unhorse his opponent or run him through with his spear. Moreover, he was also generous in dealing out gifts, diligent in his devotion to God, and modest in all endeavors; he shunned falsehood above all else. He was a mighty warrior on foot, even mightier on horseback, and a brilliant military commander. So great were his deeds while he abode in Brittany that his fame had already spread on the swiftest of wings throughout the entire island. The Saxons were terrified of him and retreated across the Humber River. There in the North they fortified the cities and castles, for that region had always provided a refuge for them. Its vicinity to Scotland also afforded them protection, since the Scots were in the habit of inflicting damage of all kinds upon the Britons. Scotland was indeed a dreadful place in which to dwell; having been deserted by the Britons, it now offered a safe harbor for all kinds of foreigners.[1] Because of its geographical position, it lay open to the Picts, the Scots, the Danes, the Norse, and others who had landed there in order to ravage the entire island.

The Saxons therefore fled towards Scotland, secure in their relationship with that land so that, if the need arose, they could retreat there as if to their own castle. When Aurelius Ambrosius learned of their retreat, he was encouraged by the hope of victory. He quickly mustered the Britons to reinforce his army and set out towards the North. However, as he was passing throughout the countryside, he was grieved to see that the land had been deserted and, above all, that the churches had all been destroyed. He vowed to restore them if he emerged triumphant.

---

[1] Geoffrey uses the standard Latin name *Scotia*, rather than his usual archaicized *Albania* to refer to Scotland here; hence, I have translated it as *Scotland* rather than the usual *Alban*.

[121] But Hengist learned of his approach. Selecting his very best men, he went about encouraging them one by one, urging them all to defend themselves valiantly and not to shirk from battle with Ambrosius. He also told them that Ambrosius had only taken a few men with him from Brittany and that their total numbers did not exceed ten thousand. Hengist indeed saw the insular Britons as worthless, since he had defeated them so many times in battle. He consequently promised his men victory and safety because of their greater numbers. There were gathered there two hundred thousand armed men. And when Hengist had encouraged them all in this manner, he went to intercept Aurelius Ambrosius at the field called Maubet, which Aurelius Ambrosius was about to pass through.[1] For Hengist desired to ambush the Britons when they were least expecting an attack. But Aurelius Ambrosius was not deceived. For that reason, he did not hesitate to pass through the field, but pushed on all the more swiftly. As soon as he sighted the enemy, he arrayed his troops for battle. He commanded three thousand of the Armorican cavalry to stand their ground, while the rest of the Armoricans assembled with the Britons in a wedge-formation. He assigned the men of Demetia to positions on the hills and the men of Venedotia to occupy what woods were there. The reason for this was that, if the Saxons should try to flee, his men could cut off their escape.

[122] In the meantime, Eldol, duke of Gloucester, approached the king and said: "This day alone would suffice for all the days of my life if God would allow me to meet Hengist in battle. For certainly one of the two of us will fall when we lock swords together. I recall that day when we had met as if to make peace. Although Hengist was arranging a treaty, he betrayed everyone who was there, killing them all with knives except for me, who alone had discovered a wooden pole and escaped. Four hundred and eighty barons and earls perished that day, having come unarmed. Amid that disaster God granted to me that pole with which I made my escape." Such were Eldol's words. Aurelius urged his troops to place all of their trust in the Son of God, and then to attack the enemy bravely and to fight unswervingly for their homeland.

[123] Hengist began to deploy his warriors against the Britons, assigning them positions and giving them specific orders for the battle. He then circulated among his men so as to inspire them all with the same lust for battle. At last, when the men on both sides were in their battle forma-

---

1   The Cambridge MS names this place as *Maisbeli*. Neither the Bern's *Maubet* nor *Maisbeli* have been successfully identified as real places.

tions, their front lines began to clash together, sword to sword, inflicting great carnage. Britons and Saxons soon lay dying upon the field. Aurelius urged on his Christian troops, while Hengist threatened his pagans. And all the while as the armies fought together, Eldol kept seeking out an opportunity to fight with Hengist. But it never came. For as Hengist saw his men falling dead and the Britons prevailing through the will of God, he made haste to flee and took refuge in the castle of Kaer Conan, which is now called Cununoeburg.[1] Aurelius followed him there, imposing death or servitude upon whomever he found along the way. When Hengist realized that Aurelius was pursuing him, he was reluctant to enter the castle itself. Instead, he positioned his folk for battle again. He well knew that the castle defenses would not be able to resist Aurelius for long, and that his only real defense consisted of the sword and spear. When Aurelius finally came up the road, he arrayed his men as well, and the two sides met in a most bitter battle. The Saxons defended themselves as if with one mind, but they were mortally wounded in turn. Blood was spilled on both sides, and the groans of the dying urged the living to greater wrath. In the end, the Saxons would have won the day if the Armorican cavalry had not arrived. For Aurelius had made use of these horsemen, just as he had done in the first battle. As the cavalry rushed in, the Saxons withdrew and were so scattered that they were unable to reform their lines.[2] Then the Britons pushed forward all the more fiercely, attacking their enemies relentlessly. Aurelius never ceased calling out orders to his men, nor did he cease wounding those Saxons who approached him or pursuing those who fled from him. In this way he proved a great benefit to his soldiers.

Eldol too ran to and fro, meting grievous wounds upon his foes. In whatever he did, he yearned constantly to meet Hengist face-to-face in battle. [124] As various battalions pressed this way and that in the course of the fight, Eldol and Hengist finally came together by chance and at once began to trade sword blows. O how these men were mighty in battle above all others! As they dealt stroke after stroke to each other,

---

[1]   Tatlock, 26, convincingly equates Cununoeburg with the town of Conisborough in the West Riding of Yorkshire, where an impressive twelfth-century Norman castle still stands. Later tradition identified this castle as the site of Hengist's grave; Sir Walter Scott popularized this Conisborough for later audiences in his historical novel *Ivanhoe* (1820).

[2]   The tactical advantage of the Armorican cavalry over the Saxon infantry—a detail unique to Geoffrey—resembles the superiority of William the Conqueror's mounted knights over the English foot-soldiers at the momentous Battle of Hastings in 1066. It is perhaps with a sense of poetic justice that Geoffrey shows the Saxon ancestors of the English suffering a similar defeat several centuries earlier.

sparks flew up from their blades like thunder and lightning. For a long while it was unclear which of the two possessed the greater strength: first Eldol would press forward and Hengist would fall back, then Eldol would lose ground while Hengist prevailed. As they fought in this way, Gorlois, the duke of Cornwall, rushed forward with the battalion he commanded. When Eldol saw him, he grew more assured of himself. He seized Hengist by the noseguard of his helmet and, exerting all his strength, dragged him back behind the British lines. With the greatest joy, Eldol then cried aloud: "God has granted my wish! Press on, soldiers, press on! Destroy the Ambrones! Victory is now within your grasp! With Hengist defeated, you have won!" And so the Britons persisted in cutting down the pagans, rushing in more and more fiercely, attacking even more intensely as the Saxons retreated. They did not cease fighting in this manner until they had won the field. The pagans all fled, every man for himself. Some escaped to various cities, others headed for the forested highlands. Others still fled in ships across the sea. Hengist's son Octa retreated with a great force to York, which his kinsman Eosa had fortified with countless armed soldiers.

[125] In triumph, Aurelius Ambrosius captured the city of Kaer Conan, which I have discussed above, and he rested there for three days. During this time he ordered the dead to be buried, the wounded to be healed, the weary to rest, and everyone to take what leisure they could. Then he summoned the leaders of the army together to decide what to do with Hengist. Eldol's brother Eldad, the bishop of Gloucester, was present there, and he was a man of the utmost wisdom and piety.[1] When he beheld Hengist standing there before the king, he ordered the others to be silent and spoke these words: "Even if you all had agreed to set this man free, I myself would cut him to pieces. In this I take my example from the prophet Samuel. When he had Agag, the king of Amalek, within his power, he cut him to pieces, saying: 'Just as you have bereft mothers of their children, so shall I make your mother childless above all other women.'[2] That is how you should treat this man, who is truly a second Agag." At that, Eldol took up his sword, led Hengist outside the city walls and chopped off his head, sending Hengist's spirit to Hades. But Aurelius Ambrosius, who was moderate

---

[1]   There was no bishop of Gloucester until the sixteenth century. Geoffrey's creation of this
       office probably reflects the patronage he received from Earl Robert of Gloucester.
[2]   See 1 Samuel 15.33: "And Samuel said, 'As your sword has made women childless, so shall
       your mother be childless among women.' And Samuel hewed Agag in pieces before the
       LORD in Gilgal."

in all matters, ordered Hengist to be buried and for a mound to be raised over his body according to the custom of the pagans.[1]

[126] Aurelius Ambrosius then led his army to York in order to root out Octa, Hengist's son. Although he held the city, Octa doubted that he would be able to defend it against so great a host. Therefore, after consulting his advisors, he came out of the city, accompanied by a retinue of his noblest men. He carried a great chain in his hand and had sprinkled his head with dust. He presented himself to the king with these words: "My gods have been vanquished, and I admit that your God reigns above all, for he has compelled so many noble men to come to you in this manner. Accept us as captives, then, along with this chain, and, if you choose not to show mercy, have us bound and we will submit willingly to whatever punishment you deem fit." Aurelius was moved to pity at this, and he convened his council to decide what to do with them. While they were debating their various options, Bishop Eldad stood up and pronounced these words: "The Gibeonites came of their own free will to beg mercy of the Israelites and their request was granted.[2] Shall we Christian men be worse than the Jews and deny them mercy? Mercy they seek, and mercy they shall find. The isle of Britain is wide and is uninhabited in many regions. If nothing else, let us at least take these men as allies and allow them to inhabit some of these empty lands. In this way they will serve us forever." The king agreed with Eldad's proposal, and he granted the Saxons mercy. Seeing Octa's example, Eosa and the others who had fled also received amnesty. The king gave them the land bordering on Scotland and accepted them as allies.

[127] Having thus subdued their enemies, the barons and princes of the realm assembled at York; the king ordered them to restore the churches that the Saxons had destroyed. Aurelius himself began to rebuild the metropolitan see at York as well as the other bishoprics in the land. After fifteen days of dispatching artisans on various assignments, he came to the city of London, which had not been spared from the assaults of the enemy. Bemoaning the fall of that city, Aurelius summoned its scattered citizens and undertook its restoration. At the same time he also

---

[1] Geoffrey brings to bear some knowledge of the authentic pre-Christian Saxon tradition of raising a burial mound over a fallen leader. The burials at Sutton Hoo represent perhaps the most stunning examples of this practice.

[2] See Joshua 9.3–15. The Gibeonites, hearing of the might of the Israelites, make a deceptive peace with the Israelites, a peace confirmed under oath. Although the Gibeonites' deception is eventually revealed, the Israelites honor their oath and allow the Gibeonites to live among them, albeit as a servant class. Bishop Eldad's citation of this story may therefore reveal an abiding distrust of the Saxons.

began to set his realm in order, reviving the neglected laws and restoring men to their ancestral possessions. Those lands that were left with no heirs because of the recent upheavals he distributed among his own men. His entire mind was set upon the restoration of the kingdom, the reestablishment of the churches and the dispensation of justice.

Departing from London, Aurelius Ambrosius traveled to Winchester in order to rebuild that city as he had the others. And when he had done what he had to for the restoration of that town, he took the advice of Bishop Eldad and visited Kaer Radoc, which is now called Salisbury, where there lay buried the nobles and princes whom the war-mongering Hengist had slain.[1] An abbey of three hundred monks stood there atop Mount Ambrius; Ambrius was the name of the man who had once founded that house, as the stories tell. As Aurelius looked upon the place where the dead lay buried, he was moved to great pity and burst out in tears. For a long time he considered many different ideas about how to memorialize this site, for he felt that some kind of monument should grace the soil that covered so many noblemen who had died for their homeland.

[128] Aurelius Ambrosius therefore summoned master carpenters and masons from across the kingdom, ordering them to exert all their skills in the building of a structure that could stand forever as a memorial to so many men. But when these craftsmen foundered in their efforts and admitted defeat, Tremorinus, the bishop of Caerleon, approached the king and said: "If anyone could accomplish this task, it is Merlin, Vortigern's soothsayer. Indeed, I do not think there is anyone else in your realm who has greater insight into the affairs of the future or greater skill in the contrivance of cunning devices. Command him to come and exert his great craft in building the monument you desire." And after Aurelius had inquired much about this Merlin, he sent messengers throughout the various parts of the land who were to find that man and convey him to Salisbury. Traveling far and wide, they eventually found him in the country of the Gewissei near the spring of Galabes, which he liked to frequent. Explaining what they wanted, they led him to the king. The king gave Merlin a glad welcome and asked him to tell the future, desiring greatly to hear of wondrous things. Merlin replied: "Such hidden matters must not be revealed unless the greatest need demands it. For if I were to declare such things for amusement or vanity, the spirit which instructs me would fall silent and

---

[1]   Salisbury is equated in Book Six with Kaer Caradoc, of which Kaer Radoc is a corrupted form.

would remain silent when I most required it." Later, when Merlin had likewise refused everyone else there, the king did not wish to bother him any longer with future affairs but instead to speak about the construction of the memorial. Merlin said to him: "If you wish to honor the grave of these men with something that will last forever, send for the Ring of Giants which is in now atop Mount Killaraus in Ireland. This Ring consists of a formation of stones that no man in this age could erect unless he employed great skill and ingenuity. The stones are enormous, and there is no one with strength enough to move them. If they can be placed in a circle here, in the exact formation which they currently hold, they will stand for all eternity."[1]

[129] At Merlin's words, Aurelius burst out laughing, asking how it could come to pass that such great stones could get to his kingdom from so far away. Did not Britain itself, he wondered, possess stones that would accomplish his purpose just as well? To these questions, Merlin answered: "Laugh not in vain, O king, for it is not in vain that I tell you these things. These stones are magical and possess certain healing powers. The giants brought them long ago from the confines of Africa and set them up in Ireland when they settled that country. They set the Ring up thus in order to be healed of their sicknesses by bathing amid the stones, for they would wash the stones and then bathe in the water that spilled from them; they were thus cured of their illness. They would even mix herbs in and heal their wounds in that way. There is not a stone among them which does not have some kind of medicinal power." When the Britons heard Merlin's words, they agreed to send for the stones and to attack the people of Ireland if they tried to withhold them. At last they chose Uther Pendragon, the brother of the king, along with fifteen thousand armed soldiers to carry out this business. Merlin was also chosen so that they could be guided by his wisdom and advice. When the ships were ready, they set sail, and, with prosperous winds, made for Ireland.

[130] At that time there ruled over Ireland Gillomanius, a young man of great prowess. When he heard that the Britons had landed in Ireland, he gathered a great army together and set out to meet them. Discovering the reason for their coming, he laughed and said to his companions: "I do not wonder that a barbarous race like the Saxons was able to over-

---

[1]   The Ring of Giants that Merlin advises setting up near Salisbury is to be identified as Stonehenge, though Geoffrey's account of the megaliths' construction is untrue. Not only did Stonehenge stand on Salisbury Plain far earlier than it does in Geoffrey's history (modern archeologists date its construction as early as 2800 B.C.E.), but the stones themselves were quarried not in Ireland but in the Preseli Mountains in Wales.

run the island of Britain, given how stupid and doltish these Britons are. Has anyone ever heard of such foolishness? And how could the rocks of Ireland be so much better than those of Britain that they would attack our kingdom for them? Arm yourselves, men, and defend your land, for they shall not remove a single one of the stones of the Ring while there is still life in me."

When Uther saw the Irish preparing for battle, he quickly arranged his own troops in battle formation. The Britons soon won the field and the Irish were cut and killed and Gillomanius was put to flight. Having achieved this victory, the Britons went up Mount Killaraus and gazed at the ring of stones in gladness and wonder. As they all stood there, Merlin came among them and said: "Use all of your strength, men, and you will soon discover that it is not by sinew but by knowledge that these stones shall be moved." They then agreed to give in to Merlin's counsel and, through the use of many clever devices, they attempted to dismantle the Ring. Some of the men set up ropes and cords, and ladders in order to accomplish their goal; but none of these things was able to budge the stones at all. Seeing all of their efforts fall flat, Merlin laughed and then rearranged all of their devices. When he had arranged everything carefully, the stones were removed more easily than can be believed. Merlin then had the stones carried away and loaded onto the ships. Uther's fleet returned in joy to Britain, carried on favorable winds. They came ashore and brought the stones to the graves of the men. When Aurelius was informed of their arrival, he sent messengers throughout Britain to summon the clergy and the common folk. As they gathered together, they went up to the tombs upon Mount Ambrius with great joy and reverence. At Aurelius' bidding there also came priests and abbots, together with the king's subjects of every rank. Once everyone was assembled on the appointed day, Aurelius set the royal crown upon his own head. Then, in kingly fashion, he celebrated the Feast of Pentecost, and took his leisure for the next three days. During this time, he distributed among his personal retinue any lands that were currently lordless in order to repay his men for their service. There were also two metropolitan sees lying vacant at York and Caerleon. Heeding the advice of the common people, he installed Samson, a man renowned for his piety, at York; for Caerleon he selected Dubricius, whom divine Providence had already chosen for promotion there. After deciding these matters and a great many others, he requested that Merlin place the standing stones that he had brought from Ireland around the graves. Merlin carried out the king's desire, and the stones were set up in a circle around the graves exactly as they had been arranged on Mount Killaraus in Ireland. Merlin thus proved that his craft was indeed better than mere strength.

[131] At that time Vortigern's son Pascent, who had fled to Germany, began stirring up enmity against Aurelius Ambrosius among his men, desiring to avenge his father. He promised his soldiers an endless supply of gold and silver if they would help him subdue Britain. When he had corrupted all the young men of Germany with his promises, he fitted a great fleet and landed in the northern parts of the island and laid those regions waste. Aurelius Ambrosius soon learned of this and summoned up an army to meet them, soon provoking that barbarous host to a pitched battle. They came out to meet him, and engaged the folk of that country in combat. However, with the grace of God, the Germans were defeated and forced to flee.

[132] Routed in this manner, Pascent did not dare to return to Germany, but set sail instead to Gillomanius in Ireland, and he was welcomed there. After he had explained his misfortunes to Gillomanius, the Irish king was moved to pity and agreed to assist him in his conquest, for he himself still remembered the affront dealt to him by Uther Pendragon, Aurelius' brother, when he had demanded the Giants' Ring. Making a pact between them, Pascent and Gillomanius fitted their ships, embarked on their journey, and soon came ashore at the city of Menevia. When news of their arrival spread, Uther Pendragon gathered a contingent of armed soldiers and rushed into Wales to fight them, for his brother Aurelius lay stricken with an illness in Winchester and so could not go himself. When Pascent and Gillomanius and the Saxons learned of this, they rejoiced greatly, believing that Aurelius' weakness would make the kingdom all the easier to conquer. While speculation of this sort spread among the people, a man by the name of Eapa approached Pascent and said: "How would you reward the man who kills Aurelius Ambrosius for you?" Pascent replied: "If I knew of anyone brave enough to accomplish such a deed, I would give him a thousand pounds of silver along with my everlasting friendship. And if Fate allows me to wear the crown of this realm, I would make that man a centurion and confirm him by oath." To these words, Eapa answered: "I have learned the British tongue and the customs of that people, and I also know something about medicine. If you will fulfill the promises you just made, I will pretend that I am a Christian and a Briton, and I will go to the king disguised as a doctor, and I will give him a potion that I will have concocted, and it will kill him. In order to come to him more quickly, I will pretend to

be a most pious monk, one most learned in scholarly matters." When Eapa proposed this course of action, Pascent drew up a pact with him and confirmed by oath what he had already promised.

And so Eapa shaved off his beard and assumed a monk's tonsure and habit. Then, carrying cases with various medicines, he made his way toward Winchester. At last entering the city, he was greeted by the king's retainers and found favor among them. They desired few things more than a physician. Thus welcomed, Eapa was led into the presence of the king and offered to restore the king's health if he imbibed his potions. At once he ordered the potion to be made, and he mixed poison into it and gave it to the king. As soon as Aurelius had taken the potion and swallowed it, that wicked Ambrone advised the king to climb in bed under his blankets and go to sleep in order that hateful potion might be more effective. The king deemed that traitor's advice reasonable, so he went right to sleep, hoping to regain his health. Death, which spares no man, soon followed, creeping with the poison throughout all the king's pores and veins as he slept. In the meantime, that traitor had slipped away among the courtiers and was nowhere to be found.

[133] While these events were occurring in Winchester, a star of great size and brightness appeared, shining forth in a single beam. At the end of the beam was a globe of fire shaped like a dragon, and from the dragon's mouth two more beams were emanating. The length of one of the beams could be seen stretching out beyond the shores of Gaul; the other stretched toward the Irish Sea in seven smaller beams. This star appeared three times, inspiring fear and wonder in all who beheld it. Even the king's brother Uther, who was engaging the enemy force in Wales at the time, was struck with considerable trepidation, and he sought out wise men to explain what the star portended. He especially desired that Merlin be summoned, for Merlin had come with the army in order that their war strategies could benefit from his counsel. When Merlin stood before him, Uther ordered him to explain the meaning of the star. Merlin began weeping, but then, summoning forth his spirit, exclaimed: "Woe for the irreversible damage! Woe for the orphaned folk of Britain! Woe for the passing of our most noble king! That renowned king of Britain, Aurelius Ambrosius, has died; we shall all perish with him unless God lends us His aid. Hasten now, Uther, our most noble leader! Do not shirk from the fight against your enemies now. The victory will be in your hands and you will be the king of all Britain. Indeed, this star signifies you, as does the fiery dragon beneath the star. That beam which is stretched out toward the shores of Gaul

indicates your future son, a most powerful man, whose might shall hold sway over all the lands he will protect. The other ray signifies a daughter, whose sons and grandsons will later rule the kingdom of Britain."[1]

[134] Then Uther, though he doubted whether Merlin really spoke the truth, advanced on the enemy host in hopes of capturing it. And he came into the vicinity of Menevia, where he intended to rest for half a day. When Uther's presence there was reported to Gillomanius, Pascent, and the Saxons who were there, they left the city to fight with him. As soon as the two hosts spied each other, they both drew up their battle-lines and fell upon each other in close combat. Clashing in that way, soldiers of both sides were slain left and right, as would be usual in such a battle. Uther finally prevailed and seized the victory, but only after most of the day had passed and he had slain both Pascent and Gillomanius. The barbarians fell back to their ships as quickly as they could, but the Britons cut them down as they fled. With Christ's favor, a complete victory was granted to Uther, who then made his way as speedily as he could to Winchester, for messengers had arrived announcing that the king had indeed died and that he had just been buried near the abbey of Ambrius within the Ring of Giants which, in life, he had had erected. Hearing of the king's death, the bishops and abbots and all the other clergy of that region had gathered in the city of Winchester and had overseen his funeral rites, as befitted such a king. Because Aurelius had once commanded that he be buried in the cemetery that he himself had established, they carried him there and buried him with royal pomp.

[135] And so Uther, the brother of Aurelius, in the presence of both the clergy and the common folk, took the crown of the island and was elevated to the kingship. Remembering Merlin's explanation of the star, Uther ordered two dragons to be fashioned from gold in the likeness of the dragon that he had seen in the beam of the star. These were made with wondrous skill. He presented one to the parishioners of the cathedral church of Winchester; the other one he carried with him into battle. And it was from that time on that he was called Uther Pendragon, by which in the British tongue we mean "head of the dragon."[2] Uther received this title on account of the fact that Merlin had foreseen his kingship in the dragon.

---

[1] Merlin's prophecy refers to the continental conquests of Uther's future son, King Arthur, and to the reigns of Arthur's successors.

[2] Geoffrey's translation of *Pendragon* is strictly inaccurate. A better rendering, suggested by Bromwich, *Trioedd*, 513, would be "chief of the dragons" (the Welsh term *dragon* had also been a poetic synonym for "leader, chieftain" since at least the tenth century).

[136] Meanwhile, Octa, the son of Hengist, along with Eosa his kinsman, broke the treaty they had made with Aurelius Ambrosius. They strove at every turn to foment unrest and to overrun King Uther's lands. First they aligned themselves with those Saxons whom Pascent had brought with him, and then they dispatched messengers to enlist more Saxons from Germany. Assembling an enormous host, they invaded the northern regions of Britain. They took no respite from their pillaging until they had destroyed all the cities and highlands from Alban down to Yorkshire. At last, just when Octa had begun to lay siege to the city of York itself, Uther Pendragon arrived on the scene with all the military might in his realm, forcing Octa to battle. The Saxons made a brave defense, suffering the onslaught of the Britons until they were able to drive their enemies back. Obtaining this victory, the Saxons pursued the Britons as long as daylight allowed, driving them to take refuge upon Mount Damen. That hill was indeed a difficult ascent: on the top there was a hazel grove, and halfway up there were jagged rocks that provided perfect dens for wild animals. The Britons set up camp there and took shelter all night amid the hazels and the rocks.

But when the Bear began to revolve around the Pole, Uther summoned counts and princes together in order to figure out how to break the enemies' lines. They all came at once into the presence of the king, and he commanded them to give their counsel. They asked Gorlois, the duke of Cornwall, to proffer his advice first. He was a man wise in counsel and mature in years. "We have no time now," he said, "for long speeches or vain words while the night still lingers. We must now use all our strength and valor if we desire to enjoy our life or freedom any longer. That enormous pagan horde is spoiling for a fight, but we are far, far fewer. If we place any hope in lasting the night, I do not deem it useful to try to fight with them. Come then, while the shadows of night are still with us, let us rush down in thick ranks and make a surprise attack on their camp. Although these Saxons seem not to waver, they certainly won't be expecting us to come down upon them in that way. If we attack together, exerting all of our boldness, we will certainly achieve the victory." His words pleased the king and everyone else, and they yielded to his counsel. Arranging themselves in dense formation and taking up their arms, they made their way toward the enemy camp and rushed down upon them, attacking in unison. But as the Britons had drawn closer, the enemies' sentries had spotted them and began to blow their horns to alert their sleeping comrades. The Saxons were thrown into complete confusion. Some of them tried to arm themselves hastily, while others were seized with fear and ran in whatever direction impulse took them. But the Britons, pushing slowly forward in tight formation, finally arrived at the Saxon camp. Once they had found a way into the camp, they drew their swords and rushed in among the enemy. The Saxons, taken unawares, did not offer much resistance. The Britons, on the other hand, gained boldness because of their surprise attack. Then they made an even more determined advance in order to cut the enemy down. They slew the pagans by the thousand. When they had at last captured Octa and Eosa, the rest of the Saxons were completely routed.

[137] After this victory, Uther headed for the city of Alclud, restoring order in that region and renewing peace everywhere. He even made a tour of the territories of the Scots, and he delivered that unruly people from their barbarity. Indeed, he enforced the laws in those lands far more than any of his predecessors had done. The Scots were fearful during Uther's reign, and those who tried to rise up against him received no mercy. After pacifying the northern parts of the realm, Uther went to London and ordered Octa and Eosa to be kept in prison.

As Easter approached, Uther summoned all the nobility of the realm to London so that he could receive the crown and celebrate the holy day with honor. All the nobility gathered just before the feast day, arriving from all the various cities of the kingdom. The king celebrated the feast itself with great solemnity as he had planned, and then made merry with his vassals. All the guests enjoyed themselves, for Uther had welcomed them gladly. The noblemen had even brought their wives and daughters to that joyous feast. Among the nobles present there was Gorlois, the duke of Cornwall, with his wife Igerna, whose beauty surpassed that of all the other women of Britain.[1] When the king beheld her there among the other women, he was suddenly consumed with such love that he forgot all else and could think of nothing but her. Igerna alone it was to whom Uther continually directed the serving trays, Igerna alone it was to whom he sent his personal attendants with goblets of wine. He smiled at her many times, and engaged her in pleasant conversation. When her husband noticed this, he became quite angry and left the court without permission. No one there could persuade Gorlois to stay, for he feared losing the one thing that he loved above all else. Uther grew furious and ordered Gorlois to return to the

---

[1]   Readers familiar with Malory's *Morte Darthur* will recognize Igerna as Igraine, King Arthur's mother. A Welsh version of this figure, *Eigr*, appears in a number of genealogies and triads, which may possibly have influenced Geoffrey. *Eigr* appears in the verse of the later medieval Welsh poets, the *cywyddwyr*, as an appellation for any beautiful woman.

court so that Uther could render judgment for the insult he had suffered. But Gorlois continued to flee, and this infuriated Uther even more. He swore that he would ravage all of Gorlois' lands unless the duke gave him immediate satisfaction. While this feud was still hot between them, Uther wasted no time in assembling a great army, and he made for Cornwall, setting flame to every city and town along the way. Gorlois, however, did not dare to engage Uther in battle, since his own army was far smaller; instead, he decided to fortify his castles until help could arrive from Ireland. Because he was more concerned about his wife's safety than his own, he placed her in the castle of Tintagel by the sea, for it was his best-protected stronghold. He, on the other hand, took refuge in the castle of Dimilioc so that, if any misfortune occurred, they would not both be in danger.[1]

When this was announced to the king, he came to the castle where Gorlois was and laid siege to it, barring every exit. Uther still remembered his love for Igerna, and so, after a week had passed, he summoned his old comrade-at-arms, Ulfin of Rhyddcaradoc, and told him what he was feeling in these words: "I burn with love for Igerna, and I hold myself in bodily peril unless I can have her. Advise me as to how I can quench my desire, or else I shall perish from this torment within." Ulfin answered: "What advice can anyone give you? There is no way to get to where Igerna is kept in the castle of Tintagel. That fortress is surrounded by the sea on three sides, and there is no means of access other than a narrow causeway. It only takes three armed knights to defend that approach, even if you brought the entire kingdom of Britain against them. If only the prophet Merlin would set his mind to this problem. Only then do I think you will be able to achieve your desire."

The hopeful king then summoned Merlin to him; for even Merlin had come along with Uther's army. Merlin soon stood before the king, who commanded him to offer his advice as to how he could sate his desire for Igerna. When Merlin perceived the torment that the king suffered for his great love of that woman, he said: "For your wish to be fulfilled, it will be necessary to employ new arts that are unheard of in this day and age. By means of certain concoctions of mine, I will be able to give you the appearance of Gorlois, so that you will look exactly like him to all eyes. If

---

[1]   Geoffrey's geography of the northern coast of Cornwall is reasonably accurate and would seem to rely upon personal knowledge; it is quite possible that Geoffrey himself had visited the region. See Oliver Padel's discussion in "Geoffrey of Monmouth and Cornwall," *Cambridge Mediaeval Celtic Studies* 8 (1984): 1–27. Both Tintagel Castle and Dimilioc Castle existed in Geoffrey's day.

you follow my instructions, I shall make you look just like him, and I shall make Ulfin look like Jordan of Tintagel, Gorlois' servant. I too shall assume a different guise and come with the two of you. In this way, you will be able to gain safe access to Igerna in her castle."

The king agreed to this plan, and followed all of Merlin's instructions diligently. After handing over command of the siege to his officers, he submitted himself to Merlin's craft and was transformed in appearance to look just like Gorlois. Ulfin was changed into Jordan, and Merlin himself took on the form of Britahel so that no one would be able to perceive who they really were. They then took the road up toward Tintagel and reached the castle at dusk. Once the warden there was notified that the duke had arrived, the castle gates were opened and the three men were allowed to pass inside. Who would have thought anything but that Gorlois himself had come home? The king spent the entire night with Igerna, making love with her and thus sating his desire. Indeed, even Igerna herself was taken in by the false shape that the king had assumed. He deceived her with many lying words that he had taken great care in devising. He also told her that he had come secretly from his besieged stronghold at Dimilioc just to check up on his beloved wife and his castle. She, of course, believed everything that Uther told her. That very night they conceived Arthur, that renowned man who in later days won great repute for his extraordinary prowess.

[138] In the meantime, when it was noticed that the king was not present at the siege of Dimilioc, the army, acting without permission, attempted to raze the walls and thereby provoke the besieged duke to battle. Acting just as rashly, Gorlois issued forth with his troops, thinking that he would be able to fight off so many armed men with his meager force. Gorlois, however, was among the first to be killed in the course of the skirmish, and his soldiers were scattered. Castle Dimilioc was then captured, though the treasure there was divided most unevenly, for everyone just snatched up whatever spoils he could according to his own strength or good fortune. Only after these outrageous acts of violence had settled down did messengers come to Igerna to inform her of the death of the duke and the outcome of the siege. But when they beheld the king, who sat next to Igerna still wearing the duke's form, they turned red and marveled greatly that the man whom they had left for dead could have gotten to Tintagel safe and sound. They knew nothing of the concoctions that Merlin had prepared. The king smiled at these rumors and embraced the duchess, saying: "I am of course not slain, but am still living, as you can plainly see. But I do regret the destruction of my castle and the slaughter

of so many of my men. We must be wary that the king does not come here and capture us in this castle. I will go now to meet with him and will make my peace with him so that nothing worse happens to us." He then left the castle and came to his own camp and, shedding the form of Gorlois, he turned back into Uther Pendragon. When he learned of all that had occurred, he did indeed bemoan the death of Gorlois, but he also rejoiced that Igerna was now freed from the bond of marriage. Returning to Tintagel, he captured the castle and took Igerna to him, thus achieving his desire. From that day on, Uther and Igerna lived together as equals bound by mutual affection, and they had a son and a daughter. The son's name was Arthur and the daughter's was Anna.

[139] As the days and years passed, the king was seized by an illness and lay in pain for many days. In the meantime, the wardens of the above-mentioned prison where Octa and Eosa were being held fled in their boredom to Germany, taking their prisoners with them and terrorizing the land. Rumors, in fact, were spreading that the Saxons were now stirring up Germany and were preparing a great fleet that would return to ravage the island. That is exactly what happened: they came back with an enormous fleet and countless warriors. Landing in Alban, they set both cities and townsfolk to the flame. Then, in order to protect the land from its enemies, the army of Britain was placed under the command of Loth of Lothian. He was the lord of Leis and a most experienced soldier, wise and mature. In token of his prowess, the king had given Loth his daughter Anna in marriage, and he entrusted the kingdom to Loth in his illness. But whenever Loth led his men against the enemy, his forces were repeatedly driven back, so that he had to take refuge within the cities. At other times, Loth was able to rout and scatter the Saxon forces, forcing them to flee into the wilderness or back to their ships. The outcome of the battles between them was always in doubt so that no one ever knew which side would gain the victory. Pride, moreover, afflicted the Britons, for they scoffed at obeying Loth's orders. They weakened themselves by doing this, and they were therefore unable to triumph once and for all over their wicked enemies.

[140] When it was made known to the king that the Saxons had ravaged almost the entire island, he grew so angry that even illness could not restrain him, and he summoned all his vassals in order to upbraid them for their arrogance and weakness. When they all were assembled before him, he censured them with scornful words and swore that he would now lead them against the enemy himself. He ordered that a litter be made to carry him, since his illness prevented him from moving in any

other way. He also demanded that all his men be ready to engage the enemy whenever the opportunity presented itself. The litter was prepared at once, the men prepared themselves for war, and the day for action arose.

[141] Placing the king in his litter, they hastened to Verulamium, where the Saxons were terrorizing all the folk. When Octa and Eosa learned that the Britons were approaching and that the king was lain out in a bier, they scorned to do battle with him since he had to be carried to the battlefield. They declared that he was already half-dead and that it would not befit men of their caliber to fight with someone in his condition. Then they withdrew into the city, leaving the gates wide open to show that they were not concerned with him. When this was reported to Uther, he commanded his men to besiege the city at once and to make an attack on the walls. The Britons made their siege-preparations and commenced an assault on the city walls. They made a great slaughter of the Saxons there and would have breached the very walls if their enemies had not resisted to the last. They managed to repel the Britons, who had been scaling the walls with various types of ropes and nets. Then night fell as they were still battling it out, forcing both sides to cease fighting. While many welcomed this respite, many others were still of a mind to destroy their foes.

The Saxons by now had realized how much their own insolence had harmed them and had almost led to a British victory. They therefore decided to make a sortie at dawn and challenge the Britons to an open battle. And that is what they did. As Helios[1] ushered the day in, the Saxons marched out of the city in battle-formation in order to carry out their plans. When the Britons realized what was happening, they organized their own soldiers and, intercepting the Saxons, began their attack. The Saxons held their ground, the Britons pressed forward, and both sides inflicted great slaughter on one another. After much of the day had passed, the king of the Britons won the field. Octa and Eosa were both slain and the rest of the Saxons fled. King Uther was so elated that, although he had been unable to get up by himself, he now sat up effortlessly in his litter as if he had suddenly regained his former health. Laughing, he cried out with a glad voice: "Those Ambrones called me a half-dead king just because illness has laid me out in this bier. And so I was. But I far prefer to be half-dead and victorious than to go into the next life healthy but defeated! It is always better to die with honor than to live on in shame!"

---

[1] *Helios* was a learned and poetic term for the sun, derived from the name of the Greek sun-god.

[142] Although defeated, as I have just related, the Saxons did not desist from their wickedness, but they withdrew into the northern regions of Britain and molested the people there ceaselessly. King Uther wished to pursue them as he had planned, but the nobles dissuaded him because a more serious illness had set in since the last victory. This made the Saxons grow even bolder, and they tried to conquer the land by any means conceivable; they even began to conspire about how they could kill the king through treachery. After other attempts to assassinate him had failed, they decided to murder him with poison. And this is exactly what they did: while the king was still lying at Verulamium, they sent out spies disguised as beggars to ascertain the state of things at the royal court. While they were learning about everything there, they discovered one particularly useful fact that they could exploit for their wicked plans: there was a fountain of the purest water near the king's hall from which the king preferred to drink, since he detested all other liquids because of his sickness. Those wicked men approached that fountain and sprinkled poison throughout the waters there so that it was all corrupted. When the king then drank from it, he succumbed to a swift death. One hundred other men also perished before this treachery was discovered. The Britons then covered over that spring with a mound of dirt. When the death of the king was made known, the bishops and clergy arrived, and they carried his body to the monastery of Ambrius. Uther was buried with royal pomp next to Aurelius Ambrosius within the Ring of Giants.

BOOK NINE

[143] After the death of Uther Pendragon, the leaders of all the various provinces of Britain gathered together in the city of Silchester. They urged Dubricius, the archbishop of Caerleon to consecrate Uther's son Arthur as the next king.[1] Indeed, necessity dictated this action, since the Saxons had heard of Uther's death and were now summoning more of their countrymen out of Germany under the leadership of Colgrim, and they hoped to exterminate the Britons. The Saxons had in fact already subdued all the lands that lay from the River Humber to where Caithness meets the sea.

Dubricius, greatly concerned about the calamity about to befall the land, summoned all the other bishops and invested Arthur with the crown of the kingdom. Although Arthur was only fifteen years old at the time, he was a youth of outstanding virtue and largesse. His innate goodness made him exhibit such grace that he was beloved by almost all the people. On being invested with the royal insignia, Arthur upheld the ancient custom and dispensed gifts to one and all. Such a great number of soldiers flocked to him that he began to run out of gifts to give them. Yet for a man in whom great generosity dwells in the company of great courage, such empty-handedness can last only for a time, and habitual poverty cannot afflict him. Thus Arthur, who indeed possessed both great courage and generosity, was determined to attack the Saxons so that he could distribute their riches among his men. Justice spurred him on as well, since by right of inheritance he ought to have had control over the entire island.

Gathering together all the young soldiers, he marched to York. When Colgrim got wind of his arrival, he mustered all the Saxons, Scots and Picts, and led them in a great host to intercept Arthur at the River Douglas. In the clash of battle that day both sides stood in great peril of their lives. The victory, however, belonged to Arthur. Colgrim fled the field and took refuge in the city of York, where he was besieged.

---

[1] Geoffrey's account of King Arthur is the first known attempt, aside from the brief cata-
logue of Arthur's battles in Nennius, to treat Arthur as an historical figure and to describe
the king's entire career from birth to death. Falling in line with certain Welsh traditions,
such as that recorded in *Culhwch and Olwen*, Geoffrey is the first historian to describe
Arthur as a king rather than as a victorious general.

Hearing of his brother's plight, Baldulf came up with six thousand men to break the siege and liberate Colgrim. While Colgrim had been engaging Arthur's men, Baldulf had been waiting for the arrival of Duke Cheldric by sea, who was coming from Germany to lend his aid. When his forces had come within ten miles of the city, Baldulf decided to continue to march by night and thus make a surprise attack upon Arthur's army. Learning of this plan, Arthur ordered Cador, the duke of Cornwall, to take six hundred knights and three thousand infantrymen and intercept Baldulf that very night. They seized the road by which Baldulf's men would pass and ambushed them. Killing many of the Saxons and wounding many others, Cador's men forced them to retreat.

Baldulf was greatly perturbed, for there was now no way he could come to his brother's aid, and he thought about how he might be able to send some message to him. Together, he reckoned, the two of them would be able to devise a safe means of escape, but he first had to speak with his brother face-to-face. Seeing no other alternative, Baldulf shaved his head and beard, took up a harp, and disguised himself as a minstrel.[1] He then wandered about the enemy camp, picking out little ditties on his harp as if he were a real musician. And when no one suspected him, he came slowly up to the city walls, still in disguise. When the Saxons within the city realized who he was, they hoisted him up over the walls with a rope and conveyed him to his brother. When Colgrim beheld him, he greeted him with kisses and embraces as if Baldulf had risen from the dead. They then tried to devise plans for escaping the city, but began to give up all hope.

At that point, messengers from Germany arrived, declaring that six hundred ships laden with strong soldiers had just landed in Alban under the command of Cheldric. When Arthur's counselors heard this news, they advised the king to abandon the siege because, if they were attacked by so great a host, the outcome of the battle would be uncertain at best. [144] Arthur heeded his privy council and withdrew to the city of London. There he summoned all the clergy and sought advice from all the primates within his jurisdiction on how he could most safely and effectively wage war against the pagans. They all agreed that messengers should be sent to King Hoel in Armorica notifying him of the disaster about to befall Britain. This Hoel was in fact the son of

---

[1]   Geoffrey perhaps bases this episode on a story that William of Malmesbury recounts in his *The Deeds of the Kings of the English* in which King Alfred disguises himself as a minstrel to spy on the Danes. See Tatlock, 283.

Arthur's sister by Budicius, the king of the Armorican Britons.[1] When Hoel heard of the calamities besetting his uncle, he ordered his fleet to be made ready. Then he gathered fifteen thousand armed soldiers and, setting sail on the first favorable wind, he landed in Southampton. Arthur welcomed him with due honor and they embraced one another many times.

[145] A few days later, they set out for the city of Kaer Luidcoit, which, as I had mentioned earlier, the heathen Saxons had besieged. This city is situated in the province of Lindsey atop a hill between two rivers, and it is also called Lincoln.[2] When the Britons arrived there with all their host, they pitched a battle with the Saxons, inflicting great slaughter upon them. Six thousand Saxons died that day: some of them drowned in the river, while many others were shot to death by arrows. Many of the rest, who were completely dumbfounded, abandoned the siege and took flight. Arthur pursued them all the way to the Forest of Celidon.[3] They regrouped themselves there and attempted to make a stand against the king. In that battle they inflicted great slaughter upon the Britons, defending themselves most valiantly. They were even able to avoid the Britons' arrows by taking cover in the trees. When Arthur realized this, he commanded that all the trees in that part of the forest be cut down; once felled, they would surround the area where the Saxons were and cut off all escape. Arthur was hoping that the Saxons would be trapped there for such a long time that they would die of hunger. To that end, he ordered his soldiers to surround the forest, and he waited there for three days. The Saxons, who required something to eat lest they starve to death, finally asked for a truce; in return for safe passage, they would leave behind all their silver and gold and go back to Germany with empty ships. They even promised to send Arthur tribute from Germany and to leave behind hostages. Consulting his

---

1 The name Hoel was in fact the name of several historical kings of Brittany. In terms of Hoel's relationship to Arthur, Geoffrey names only one sibling of Arthur's: his sister Anna, who later married Loth of Lothian. If we wish to endow Geoffrey with chronological or genealogical consistency, then Anna's age here would prohibit her being the mother of the adult Hoel. The wife of Budicius could possibly be an otherwise unmentioned half-sister, perhaps the child of Igerna and Gorlois of Cornwall. Sir Thomas Malory, writing in the fifteenth century but encapsulating a host of earlier Arthurian traditions, recognizes three such half-sisters: Morgause, Elaine, and Morgan le Fay.

2 Geoffrey has misidentified this city: Kaer Luidcoit was the Welsh name for Lichfield.

3 Celidon Forest (*Coed Celyddon*) figures rather prominently in certain Welsh traditions, being associated in particular with the bard Myrddin. See Geoffrey's further exploration of such material in his *Life of Merlin*, translated in Appendix B.

advisors, Arthur agreed to their request. He accepted their treasures and hostages as a surety and allowed them to depart empty-handed.

[146] However, as these Saxons were sailing home across the sea, they grew ashamed at the pact they had made, and so they turned their sails back toward Britain and landed in Totnes. Coming ashore, they ravaged all the land as far as the River Severn, dealing deadly wounds to all the country folk. From there, they made their way toward the region of Badon and laid siege to the city of Bath there. When this turn of events was announced to the king, he marveled at their great treachery, and he ordered that a speedy punishment be dealt to the hostages, who were summarily hanged. Postponing the campaign that he had just commenced against the Scots and Picts, he hastened away to break the siege of Bath. Arthur was, however, greatly worried, for in going to Bath he had to leave behind his nephew Hoel, who was very ill, in the city of Alclud. When at last his army reached the province of Somerset and drew near to the siege, Arthur said, "Because these nefarious, heathen Saxons have scoffed at their pledge to me, I shall place my trust in my God and shall endeavor to avenge the blood of my countrymen this day. Take up your arms, men! Take up your arms and valiantly attack these traitors! With God on our side, we shall certainly defeat them."

[147] After the king uttered these words, the holy Dubricius, archbishop of Caerleon, went up to the top of a hill and cried aloud: "O you men who are most distinguished in your Christian faith, may the love of your homeland and of your countrymen who have been slain by the pagans ever be a reproach to you unless you persevere in defending them. Fight for your homeland, even unto death, for such a death would itself be a victory and a balm for your souls. Whoever suffers death for his countrymen offers himself as a living sacrifice before God and does not hesitate to imitate Christ, who deemed it worthy to give up His own life for His brethren. Should any of you die in battle, let your death serve as a penance and absolution for all of your sins: in this way you will not hesitate to suffer death."

Roused by his blessing, these good men all hastened to arm themselves and to carry out their orders. Arthur too donned armor as befitted a king, along with a golden helmet with the carved likeness of a dragon upon the crest. And on his shoulders he bore the shield Pridwen, which had the image of the blessed Mary, mother of God, painted upon it, keeping him always mindful of her.[1] He also bore Caliburn, the great-

---

[1]   In the Welsh *The Spoils of Annwn* (ninth to twelfth century) and *Culhwch and Olwen* (eleventh century), *Prydwen* appears as King Arthur's marvelous ship.

est of swords, which had been made in the isle of Avalon, while in his right hand he carried the spear that was known as Ron:[1]

This spear was long and broad and keen in warfare.[2]

After arranging his troops in battle formation, Arthur fiercely attacked the Saxons, who were arranged in their usual formations. The Saxons fended off the Britons bravely all that day, while the Britons kept up their offensive. At long last, the sun began to set and all the Saxons occupied a single hill, where they intended to pitch their camp for the night.[3] Confident in their great numbers, they believed that the hill itself would provide sufficient protection. However, at the first light of day, Arthur and his men pushed upward to the summit, although many of them fell in the attempt, for the Saxons, rushing down from the hilltop, were able to inflict wounds upon them quite easily, since they could run down much faster than the others could scramble up. Once the Britons had with great effort reached the summit, they were immediately able to gain the upper hand. The Saxons turned to face them and exerted all their might in trying to fight them off. After much of the day had passed in this way, Arthur grew furious that the Saxons were still doing so well and that he had not yet won the field. And so, in the name of the blessed Mary, he drew the sword Caliburn and rushed in among the dense battle-lines of the enemy. Whomever he struck while calling out the name of the Lord fell with a single blow. He did not waver in his assault until 470 men had perished on Caliburn's blade. Seeing their commander in the midst of the enemy lines, the rest of the Britons followed suit, dealing out great slaughter left and right. Colgrim fell there, as did his brother Baldulf and many thousands more. Cheldric, on the other hand, perceiving the great peril to his men, turned and fled.

[148] Having achieved this victory, the king ordered Cador, the duke

---

[1]   Arthur's sword Caliburn, later known as Excalibur, appears as *Caledfwlch* ("hard-breach") in *Culhwch and Olwen* as well as in several of the Welsh triads. Arthur's spear Ron also has a parallel with the spear *Rhongomyniad* in *Culhwch and Olwen*.

[2]   In the Bern MS, this line is distinct from the main text and forms a hexameter line.

[3]   The assault of this hill outside Bath is doubtless Geoffrey's fleshing out of the Battle of Mount Badon, which appears in Nennius as Arthur's decisive victory against the Saxons. (In Nennius' version Arthur slays 960 men rather than Geoffrey's mere 470!) The *Annales Cambriae* also mention the battle under the year 516: "The Battle of Badon, in which Arthur bore the cross of our Lord Jesus Christ upon his shoulders for three days, and the Britons were victorious." Gildas records the battle as well, but ascribes it to the campaigns of Aurelius Ambrosianus.

of Cornwall, to pursue the Saxons while he himself made for Alban, for it had been announced to him that the Scots and Picts were besieging Hoel in the fortress of Alclud, where, as I mentioned earlier, he was lying ill. On this account the king hurried to his aid, lest the barbarians take the castle.

In the meantime, the duke of Cornwall, leading ten thousand men, decided not to pursue the retreating Saxons. His men instead speedily captured the Saxon ships in order to prevent their enemies' escape. As soon as they did this, they loaded the ships with all their best soldiers, who would repel the pagans if they tried to flee that way. Only then, following Arthur's commands, did Cador hasten off in pursuit of the enemy, mercilessly cutting down whomever he overtook. The Saxons, who had until recently burned with a lion-like ferocity, now fled timidly away. They made for the mountains, and there they took refuge in caves in order to give themselves a respite. Finally, when they could find no lasting protection anywhere else, they gathered their bedraggled forces together on the island of Thanet. But the duke of Cornwall pursued them even there, meting out ceaseless slaughter. He did not rest until Cheldric himself was slain and the rest were forced to surrender and give hostages.

[149] After he had secured this peace from the Saxons, Cador headed for Alclud, which Arthur had just liberated from a barbarian siege. He then led his army into Moray, where the Scots and Picts were now themselves besieged. They had been defeated in the third battle that they had fought against Arthur and his nephew and had now taken refuge in this area. They had come to Loch Lomond and occupied all the islands in the lake, thinking they had found a safe haven. This lake contains forty islands, and it takes in the water from sixty rivers, though only one river flows out of it down to the sea. Among the islands there are also sixty great rocks where one can find just as many eagles' nests.[1] Every year the eagles used to gather together there and, in a single lofty voice, foretell all the prodigious events that would happen in the kingdom.

It was among these islands that the Picts had taken refuge from their enemies, and now they took comfort in the natural protection of the lake. This strategy, however, did them little good, for Arthur had fitted

---

[1] Geoffrey's description of Loch Lomond derives directly from *The Wonders of Britain* (*Mirabilia Brittaniae*), a catalogue compiled in Gwent in the eighth century, transcribed by pseudo-Nennius, and appended to his *History of the Britons*: "The first wonder is Loch Lumonoy. In it there are sixty islands where men dwell, and around the islands are sixty rocks, and upon each rock there is an eagle's nest, and sixty rivers flow into the Loch, though only one flows out to the sea, and that is the River Lemn."

a fleet and now sailed around the rivers. He besieged them there for fifteen days and forced them to such hunger that they died by the thousands. While Arthur bore down upon them in this way, Gillamorius, the King of Ireland, arrived on the scene with a great host of barbarians, hoping to bring aid to the besieged Scots and Picts. Arthur raised the siege and turned his forces against the Irishmen, whom he cut down mercilessly and forced to go back home. Once he had defeated the Irish, Arthur was free to harry the Picts and Scots once again, which he did with an indescribable ferocity. However, just as he had made the decision to leave none of them alive, all the bishops and clergy of that wretched land approached the king barefoot, carrying all their saints' relics and other holy artifacts, hoping to obtain the king's mercy on their people. As soon as they were in the king's presence, they fell down on bended knees and implored him to have pity on their remorseful countrymen: they had already suffered enough, and there was no need to destroy the rest one by one. The bishops also asked that Arthur allow the besieged to have some little plot of land as their own, seeing that they would be bearing the yoke of servitude anyway. After they had pleaded with the king in this way, pity finally moved him to tears. He agreed to the request of those holy men and granted a general amnesty.

[150] While these matters were being settled, Hoel began to survey the terrain around the lake, marveling that there were so many rivers and rocks and eyries there. As he stood there in contemplation, Arthur came up to him and said that there was a pool in the district that was even more wondrous. It was twenty feet wide and just about as long, and five feet deep. No one knew whether it had been shaped into a square by nature or by the craft of men. It nourished four different kinds of fish in its four corners, and the fish from one corner never mingled with the fish from the others.[1] Down in Wales there was yet another pool that stood near the River Severn and which the locals called Linliguuam because, whenever the tide filled it up, it swallowed all the waters up like a whirlpool. Even though it took in all this water, it never overflowed, and its banks were never flooded. And whenever the tide went out, the

---

[1]   As with the description of Loch Lomond, Geoffrey also draws the description of this lake from *The Wonders of Britain*: "There is a spring by the name of *Ffynnawn Gwrheli*. No stream flows into it, nor does any leave it. When men go fishing in this spring, they catch a certain type of fish in the eastern part, a different type in the south, another type in the west, and a different type still in the north. A different kind of fish is thus caught from each different side.... the spring is knee-deep, twenty feet long and twenty feet wide, with banks on all four sides."

pool belched forth all of these waters like a mountain, and only then did the banks get wet. Whenever the people of all that region would turn their faces towards that pool, their clothing would get splashed by the waves and they were scarcely able to avoid being swallowed up into the pool; however, if they turned their backs to the pool, the rushing of the waters was not to be feared, even if one was standing right at the edge.[1]

[151] Having pardoned the Scots, the king headed for York to celebrate the feast of Christmas, which was drawing near. As he entered the city, he was grieved that all the holy churches had been abandoned, for Archbishop Samson had been driven out, as had all the other men of faith there, and the half-burnt churches no longer celebrated their services to God. The fury of the pagans had indeed prevailed there. Arthur therefore gathered the clergy and the people together and appointed his chaplain Piramus as the new archbishop. Arthur then rebuilt all the churches that had been destroyed and established communities of religious men and women there. He also restored titles and property to all those who had been driven out by the Saxon occupation.

[152] With him there were three brothers of royal blood: Loth, Urian, and Anguselus.[2] They had been eminent men before the coming of the Saxons and had had the governance of those regions. Desiring to honor the decrees of his own father, Arthur gave Anguselus royal power over the Scots, and he gave Urian the scepter of Moray. Back in the days of Aurelius Ambrosius, Loth had married the king's sister Anna, by whom he fathered Gawain and Mordred. Arthur now granted him the earldom of Lothian and the other neighboring lands that had once belonged to him. Finally, having restored the entire kingdom to its former state of pristine dignity, Arthur married a woman by the name of Guinevere, who sprang from a noble Roman family.[3] She had been brought up in the household of Duke Cador and surpassed all the other women of the island in beauty.

[153] The next summer, Arthur prepared a fleet and sailed over to Ireland, which he greatly desired to subdue. As he came ashore, King Gillamorius came against him with an enormous host, ready to do

---

[1]   This pool also derives from *The Wonders of Britain*.

[2]   The origins of the figures of Loth and Anguselus seems obscure, but Urian derives from the sixth-century Brittonic hero Urien Rheged. The poet Taliesin was connected to Urien's court and several of his poems in praise of Urien survive. See *The Poems of Taliesin*, ed. Ifor Williams, trans. J.E. Caerwyn Williams (Dublin: Dublin Institute for Advanced Studies, 1987).

[3]   This is the earliest extant mention of Guinevere in a Latin text. Geoffrey draws her name, at least, from Welsh traditions concerning Arthur's wife *Gwenhwyfar* (literally "White Phantom").

battle. No sooner did the fighting begin than the Irish, who were unarmed and not dressed for battle, began to get miserably slaughtered, and they fled into hiding. Gillamorius was at once captured and forced to surrender. The remaining Irish princes, who were abashed at what had happened to their king, surrendered in turn. Having thus conquered all of Ireland, Arthur then led his fleet to Iceland and subdued that unruly people. After that, the rumor spread among all the isles that no land could resist King Arthur, and so King Doldavius of Gotland and King Gunuasius of Orkney approached him of their own free will to offer tribute and pay homage. As the winter months passed, he returned to Britain and, settling all his realm into a state of abiding peace, he dwelt there for twelve years.

[154] King Arthur then invited all the bravest men from the far-flung reaches of his domains to join his household. In this way, he was able to cultivate such refinement in his court that people far and wide sought to emulate it. Every young nobleman was tempted to hang himself unless he could dress or bear arms like the knights of King Arthur's court. The fame of Arthur's great generosity and prowess then spread to the furthest ends of the earth, and great fear beset the kings across the sea that Arthur would invade them and seize the lands under their rule. Spurred on by these concerns, they refortified their cities and towers and built castles in strategic locations so that, in the event that Arthur attacked them, they would have a safe refuge. When Arthur learned of these things, he rejoiced at being universally feared, and he desired to submit all Europe to his rule. So he prepared a fleet and sailed first to Norway, hoping to bestow its crown upon his brother-in-law Loth. Loth was, in fact, the nephew of Sichelm, the king of the Norwegians, and should have inherited the throne when Sichelm died. But the Norwegians refused to accept him as their king, setting up a certain Riculf in his place. They believed they could fight off Arthur from within their fortified cities. At that time, Loth's son Gawain was only twelve years old and had been placed in the service of Pope Sulpicius, from whom he received his arms. When Arthur landed on the shores of Norway, as I had begun to say, King Riculf came out to meet him with all the people of his land, and they did battle. After much blood had been shed on either side, the Britons finally prevailed. Making one final advance, they were able to kill Riculf and many of his men. Once they had achieved this victory, they put the Norwegian cities to the flame and scattered the inhabitants with great ferocity until they had subdued not only all of Norway, but Denmark as well, to Arthur's rule.

[155] Once those lands were pacified and Loth had been established as king, Arthur sailed over to Gaul and, organizing his armies, began to ravage that land. Gaul was still in those days a province of Rome, and the tribune Frollo ruled there under the authority of the Emperor Leo.[1] When Frollo learned of Arthur's arrival, he mustered all the armies under his power and met Arthur in battle. But he hardly stood a chance, for Arthur led with him young men from all the islands that he had subjugated. What is more, it was said that Arthur had such a great army that it was nearly impossible to defeat it. It was even rumored that Arthur had won the allegiance of the greater part of the Gaulish legions through his enormous generosity. Frollo, when he realized that he was getting the worst of the battle, fled the field with a handful of his men and took refuge in Paris. There he regrouped his scattered men and fortified the city. He now wanted to do battle with Arthur again. But while his army was trying to enlist the help of his neighbors, Arthur arrived unexpectedly and laid siege to the city.

After the siege had lasted a month, Frollo worried that his people would die of hunger, and so he challenged Arthur to single combat. Whoever won would obtain the kingdom of the other. Frollo was a man of extraordinary stature and courage and strength, and, in proposing this fight, he was completely convinced that he would win. When the challenge was announced to Arthur, the king was extremely pleased and sent back messages to say that he was ready to meet Frollo on the appointed day. Making a truce, they met together on an island that lay just outside the city walls, so that the people could witness the outcome. Both men were fittingly armed, and both sat upon horses of wondrous speed. It was not at all clear which of the two would prevail. Taking their positions opposite each other, and raising their lances, they suddenly spurred their horses and clashed together with mighty blows. Arthur aimed his lance carefully and pierced Frollo in the chest. Frollo's own spear missed, and he was thrown to the ground with great force. With his sword now drawn, Arthur was rushing forward to attack his opponent again when Frollo suddenly leapt to his feet, brandished his lance and struck Arthur's horse with a lethal wound in the chest, causing the king to fall.

When the Britons saw their king lying on the ground, they feared that he was dead and could hardly hold back from breaking the truce

---

[1] There were two Leos who were successive rulers of the Eastern Roman Empire who ruled from 457–74. The second Leo only reigned for a single year, 474. The tribune Frollo is unattested elsewhere.

and rushing headlong upon the Gauls. However, just as all concern for the peace treaty was fading from their minds, Arthur got up slowly. He drew his sword and then rushed to attack Frollo. Coming together, they exchanged blows in close combat, each attempting to kill the other. At last, Frollo saw an opportunity and struck Arthur upon his forehead, thinking to deal him a mortal wound unless his helmet should deflect the blow. When Arthur, who was now bleeding profusely, saw the blood on his armor and sword, he was inspired with an even greater fury, and, lifting Caliburn, he struck Frollo with all his might so that he pierced all the way through the helmet. Frollo's head was cleaved in two. Frollo fell to the ground from this wound, beating the dirt with his heels, and his spirit was borne away with the breeze.

When Frollo's death was made known to the Gauls, the people in the city ran to open the gates, and they handed the city over to Arthur. Having achieved this victory, Arthur divided his army in two, placing half of it under Hoel and giving him orders to go subdue Guitard, the duke of Poitou. Arthur, commanding the rest of the army, would occupy himself with subjugating the provinces of Gaul that were still hostile to him. As soon as Hoel reached Aquitaine, he began to attack the cities of that land and finally forced Guitard, who was wearied by so many battles, to surrender. Hoel then set Gascony to the fire and sword, scattering its people and subjugating its princes. After nine years of conquest had passed, Arthur had finally made all of Gaul submit to his power, and he returned to Paris and held court there. He summoned all the clergy and common folk and confirmed his rule as peaceful and legal. At that time he gave Bedivere, his cup-bearer, the honor of Neustria, which is now called Normandy, and he gave his seneschal Kay the province of Anjou.[1] He granted many other provinces to the other noble men in his service. At long last, having pacified all the cities and peoples of Gaul, he returned to Britain at the first approach of spring.

[156] When the solemn feast of Pentecost began to draw near, Arthur, rejoicing in his triumph, decided to hold court and place the crown of the kingdom of Britain upon his head. He summoned all the kings and dukes who were subject to him to this feast so that he could celebrate it all the more honorably and renew the pacts with his vassals all the more effectively. Informing his household of his plans, he took their advice to

---

[1] Bedivere and Kay appear in early Welsh traditions as Arthur's closest companions, Bedwyr and Kei. For an example, see Appendix C2.

hold the court in Caerleon.[1] This city was located in Glamorganshire on the river Usk, at a lovely site not far from where the Severn empties into the sea. It had a great abundance of riches, above all that of the other cities, and thus was an excellent place to hold a high feast. On one side of the city, moreover, the noble Usk flowed in such a way that the kings and princes who were coming from across the sea would be able to get there by ship. On the other side, which was surrounded by fields and royal forests, the buildings were so impressive that the golden gables of their roofs seemed to rival Rome. There were also two great churches there. One had been erected in honor of the martyr Julius, and it was adorned with a choir of the most beautiful virgins who had dedicated themselves to God. The other church had been founded in the name of Aaron, the blessed companion of Julius. It was served by a house of canons and was the site of the third metropolitan see of Britain. It also had a school with two hundred philosophers who were most learned in astronomy and other arts. They diligently observed the motion of the stars, and, employing reasonable arguments, they would explain to King Arthur the omens of things to come. Caerleon, then, which was endowed with so many fine things, was made ready for the great feast.

And so messengers were sent to invite the vassals from the various realms. Both those from Gaul as well as those from the neighboring islands had to come to the court. And so there arrived Anguselus, the king of Alban, which is now called Scotland; and Urian, the king of Moray; Cadvan, the king of Venedotia, which is now called North Wales; Eddelin, the king of Demetia, which is now called South Wales; and King Cador of Cornwall. The three archbishops of the metropolitan sees of London, York, and Caerleon also came, and Dubricius was the archbishop of Caerleon. He was the foremost prelate in Britain, and he held the apostolic see with such piety that he was able to relieve the pain of the suffering through his very words. The earls of the noble cities also attended: Morvid, the earl of Gloucester; Mauron of Worcester; Anarawd of Salisbury; Arthgal of Kaer Gweir, which is now called Warwick; Jugin of Leicester; Cursalem of Chester; Kinmarc of Durham; Galluc of Winchester; Urbgennius of Bath; Jonathal of Dorchester; and Boso of Rydychen, that is, Oxford. In addition to these earls came other noble

---

[1]   Geoffrey's detailed description of the city of Caerleon probably reflects his intimate knowledge of the areas along the Welsh border. His association of King Arthur with Caerleon continues into the later romance traditions; Arthur's more famous court at Camelot does not appear until the romance *Lancelot, or, The Knight of the Cart* (*Le chevalier de la charrette*), written by Chrétien de Troyes in the later twelfth century.

heroes: Donaut map Papo; Cheneus map Coil; Pederur map Peredur; Gruffudd map Nogoid; Regin map Clawd; Eddelein map Cledauc; Kingar map Bangan; Kinmarc; Gorbonian Map Sgoit; Clofaut; Rhun map Neton; Kinbelin map Trunat; Cathleus map Cadell; Kinlith map Nethon; and many others whom it would take too long to enumerate here.[1] From the outlying islands came Gillamorius, the king of Ireland; Malvasius, the king of Iceland; Doldavius, the king of Gotland; Gunuasius, the king of the Orkneys; King Loth of Norway; and King Aschill of Denmark. From other distant lands across the sea came Holdwin, the duke of the Ruteni; Leodegarius, the count of Boulogne; Bedivere the Cup-Bearer, the duke of Normandy; Borrellus of Cenomannia; Kay the Seneschal, the duke of Anjou; and Guitard of Poitou; along with the twelve peers of the Gauls, who were led by Gerin of Chartres.[2] Duke Hoel of the Armorican Britons was also there with his vassals. They all came with such a train of equipment and mules and horses that it is well-nigh impossible to describe. There did not remain one prince of any merit on this side of Spain who did not attend this court when summoned. And this is no wonder, for Arthur's generosity was renowned all over the world, and this made all men love him.

[157] Once everyone had gathered together in the city in order to celebrate the solemn feast, the archbishops arrived at the palace to bestow the royal crown. Since Dubricius was the prelate of the diocese where the court was being held, he made ready to celebrate the high mass. The king, as soon as he was robed, was led with great ceremony to the church of the metropolitan see. On both his right and left he was escorted by an archbishop. Ahead of him marched the four kings of Alban, Cornwall, Demetia, and Venedotia. It was their duty to walk before him carrying golden swords. A great company of clerics also preceded him, chanting in wondrous harmony. From the opposite direction, the archdeacons and priests escorted the queen in all her regalia to the church of the devoted virgins. The four queens of the abovementioned kings came with her, carrying mourning-doves, as was the custom. All the other women who were there marched in her train

---

[1] All the "noble heroes" mentioned here have distinctively Welsh names, especially those with the Welsh patronymic *map* ("son of"). This list of Arthur's men resembles—in style, though not in content—the vast catalogs of Arthur's heroes in Welsh texts like *Culhwch and Olwen* or *The Dream of Rhonabwy*.

[2] The reference to "the twelve peers of the Gauls" alludes to the renowned Twelve Peers of France, who were Charlemagne's vassals and companions in the French Charlemagne cycles of *chansons de geste*. Geoffrey's inclusion of them here implicitly places Arthur above even Charlemagne.

with great delight. As the procession drew to a halt, there was such beautiful music and singing coming from both churches that the knights who were there did not know which church they should attend first. They crowded together first towards one, then toward the other; if the entire day had passed in this kind of celebration they would not have grown bored.

After the holy mass was celebrated in both churches, the king and queen put aside their crowns and adopted less formal garments. The king then retired to his hall to feast with the men, while the queen withdrew to hers with the women, for they still maintained the Trojan custom of celebrating feast days separately, the men with the men and the women with the women. Once they were all seated according to their proper rank, Kay the Seneschal, clothed all in ermine, brought in the food, accompanied by one thousand young nobles who were also clad in ermine. On the other side of the king's hall, Bedivere the Cup-Bearer, followed by another thousand young men all clad in miniver, distributed the drinks in different chalices of various styles and shapes. In the queen's hall, countless attendants in different types of fine clothing performed their duties, each having his own particular task. If I were to describe every detail of this feasting, I would draw my history out far too long.

Britain had at that point attained such a state of dignity that it surpassed all other kingdoms in its courtliness, in the extravagance of its fineries, and in the polished manners of its citizens. Every individual knight of fame and virtue in the kingdom bore a livery and arms of a unique color. The women of those days had a similar style of dress. And those ladies would only grant their love to a man who had thrice proven his worth in battle. They were therefore made all the more chaste and the men all the more virtuous out of love for them.

Finishing their meals, the men went down to the fields outside the city, organizing themselves into groups for the playing of various games. The knights quickly matched off for competitions on horseback and arranged a mock battle. The ladies looked on from atop the city walls: the games inspired them with the maddening flames of love. Some of the other men whiled away their time at archery, others with spear-throwing; some cast heavy rocks and stones, while others still played at dice and a host of other amusements. What's more, they had put aside all ill-will toward one another. Whoever achieved victory in a contest received the most generous gifts from Arthur himself. Three whole days passed by in this way. On the morning of the fourth day, Arthur summoned everyone to him who had performed service in whatever office that he held. Each man was granted possession of cities and castles, bishoprics and archbishoprics, and many other high honors.

Then the blessed Dubricius, desiring to live out his last days as a hermit, gave up the archbishopric see. In his place the king's uncle David was consecrated, whose life was an example of every type of goodness to those whom he had instructed.[1] Teilo, a famous priest from Llandaf was also appointed then in place of the holy Samson as Archbishop of Dol. He had been approved by King Hoel of the Armorican Britons on account of his exemplary life and morals. Maugan was appointed to the bishopric of Silchester, and Duiian to the bishopric of Winchester. Eledem, furthermore, was endowed with pastoral authority over Alclud.

[158] While King Arthur was busy arranging these ecclesiastical appointments, twelve very aged men with stern faces marched solemnly into the court, bearing olive branches in their right hands to indicate that they were messengers. Saluting the king, they delivered a letter from Lucius Hiberius, which read:[2] "Lucius, the protector of the Roman Republic, wishes upon Arthur, the king of Britain, exactly what he deserves. I am shocked at how impudently you have behaved in the course of your tyranny. Shocked, I repeat, shocked and appalled when I think about the offenses you have committed against Rome. And I am quite angered that you have abandoned your senses so much as not to realize this, or to comprehend that by your illegal actions you have offended the Senate, to whom, as you well know, the entire world owes allegiance. You have even presumed to defy our commands and hold back Britain's tribute, which Julius Caesar and other noble Romans have received for ages now. You have also snatched up Gaul and the territory of the Allobroges, and the islands of the Ocean, whose kings rendered my ancestors tribute when Roman power held sway in those lands. Since the Senate demands justice for the countless offenses you have committed, I command you to come to Rome by the middle of next August. There you will pay homage to your overlords, accepting whatever punishment their judgment deems fit. If you fail to come, I shall personally come to your lands and attempt to win back by the sword what you in your folly have stolen from Rome."

After these words had been read aloud in the presence of King Arthur and his nobles, they retired to an enormous tower near the

---

[1]   St. David, the patron saint of Wales, died in 589. A twelfth-century *vita* of St. David attributes a royal lineage to him, so the connection to King Arthur is not completely incredible.

[2]   The Roman general Lucius Hiberius is unattested in earlier sources.

palace gates in order to figure out how to answer such tidings. But as they began to go up the stairs, Duke Cador of Cornwall, who was in high spirits, addressed the following speech to the king, laughing as he spoke: "Until this moment, I had feared that the leisure of abiding peace would make the Britons idle cowards and that their martial prowess, which is so highly esteemed by other peoples, would be entirely neglected. Indeed, whenever the practice of arms is put aside and replaced by dice or the courting of women or by other pastimes, it is not surprising that virtue, honor, courage, and fame should be polluted by idleness. Almost five years have passed since we abandoned military training for these other pleasures. God, I believe, has inspired this aggression on the part of the Romans so that sloth does not weaken us and that we may restore our prowess to its former level."

[159] As Cador made this speech and continued saying similar things, the nobles all took their seats. Once they were gathered together, Arthur spoke to them with these words: "Comrades in prosperity and adversity," he began, "I have always valued your probity in matters of counsel and warfare. Summon up all your expertise and reveal to me what in your wisdom you think should be done about the Romans' demands. As the saying goes, whatever wisdom commends is more easily endured when the need for action arises. We will be able to withstand an attack from Lucius more effectively if we put our heads together and plan how we might best weaken him. I, for one, do not think we need fear his attack very much, since he demands this tribute from Britain on such a flimsy pretense. He claims that it should be given to him because it had been paid to Julius Caesar and his successors, who came here in armed force because of our forefathers' disputes, and who had once subdued our fickle and quarrelling homeland to their power with force and violence. Since they had obtained the tribute in this manner, they took it unjustly indeed. Nothing that is acquired by force or violence can be justly possessed by anyone. So Lucius now treats us with unreasonable threats, contriving a pretext whereby he can legally make us his tributaries. Since he presumes to make these unjust demands upon us, let us use a similar tact and demand tribute from Rome. Let the side that is stronger carry off whatever it wishes! For if Lucius declares that tribute must again be rendered to him merely because Julius Caesar and the other Roman kings once subjugated Britain, then I believe that the Romans should pay tribute to us, since my ancestors captured Rome in ancient times. The most noble Belinus, with the aid of his brother Brennius, the duke of the Allobroges, captured Rome and hanged

twenty noble Romans in the middle of the Forum. He held the city for many years. And let us not forget Constantine, the son of Helen, or Maximianus, both my near kinsmen: they were both kings of Britain who also ascended to the throne of the Roman Empire. Don't you all think, then, that we should demand tribute from the Romans? Lastly, we owe no tribute for Gaul or the islands of the Ocean, since they did not bother to defend those lands when we took them under our power."

[160] When Arthur had finished his speech, he commanded Hoel, the king of the Armorican Britons, to respond first. Hoel answered in these words: "If each and every one of us thought these matters through and spent time tossing them over in his mind, I do not think he would find any better plan than that which you, in your great cleverness and wisdom, now recommend. Lead us forward, then, since your speech (which was bedecked with a truly Ciceronian eloquence) has led us thus far.[1] We should always honor a man of such steadfast goodwill, of so keen a mind, and of such advantageous counsel as yourself. If you will lead us to Rome for such a cause, I have no doubt that we will triumph, so long as we preserve our liberty, so long as we act justly against our enemies who sought to make such unjust demands on us. Indeed, whoever attempts to take from another that which is not his shall lose what he seeks to gain. Since the Romans desire to take our possessions from us, we should, without a doubt, take from them what is theirs if we have the opportunity to meet them in battle. Yes, all the Britons long for this war! The Sibylline Prophecies[2] bear true witness that a third man shall be born in Britain who shall obtain the Roman Empire. This prophecy has already borne fruit, for it is clear that the first two to achieve the emperorship were, as you said, Belinus and Constantine. Now we have the third in you, to whom such a height of honor is promised. Hasten, then, to take what God Himself does not hesitate to offer you. Hasten to conquer what He wishes to be conquered. Hasten to exalt all of us, who, because you exalt us, will not hesitate to suffer wounds or give up our lives. In order that you may achieve these things, I commit ten thousand armed warriors to your command."

[161] When Hoel had finished speaking, King Anguselus of Alban began to explain how he felt about these matters: "As soon as I realized

---

1   Marcus Tullius Cicero (106–43 B.C.E.) was a famous Roman Statesman and orator.

2   The Sibylline or, more properly, pseudo-Sibylline prophecies were a loose collection of the purported vaticinations of the classical sibyls, compiled by early Christian writers between the second and sixth centuries C.E. They circulated in various forms throughout the Middle Ages, and it is quite possible that Geoffrey may have read one or more of them.

that my lord meant what he said, my spirit was filled with more joy than I can now express. All the campaigns we have fought against so many different kings all come down to nothing if the Romans and Germans remain unscathed, if we do not, like men, avenge ourselves for the slaughter they once visited upon our homeland. But now that we have the opportunity to fight with them, I rejoice indeed! I long for the day when we meet them in battle. I thirst for their blood as I would thirst for a fountain if I had been forbidden to drink for three days. O, let the light shine upon me, the light that will be the sweet wounds that I will either receive or mete out when we exchange blows in battle! Even death will be sweet when I endure it to avenge our fathers, to protect our liberty, and to exalt our king. Let us attack these half-men! Let us persist in this war until they are defeated and we can take all their lands in a joyous victory. I shall increase our army by two thousand armed knights, along with infantrymen to accompany them."

[162] After all the others said what needed to be said, one by one they pledged to Arthur whatever military service they owed him to the effect that, in addition to the men that the Duke of Armorica had promised, sixty thousand armed soldiers were rallied from the island of Britain alone. But since the kings from the other islands were not in the habit of maintaining military forces, they each pledged as many foot-soldiers as they owed, so that from the six islands—that is, Ireland, Iceland, Gotland, the Orkneys, Norway, and Denmark—one hundred twenty thousand men were counted. From the duchies of Gaul (the Ruteni, the Portivenses, the Angevins, the Poitevins) eighty thousand men were promised. And from the twelve counties of Gaul under the leadership of Gerin of Chartres, there were twelve hundred more. All in all, the force consisted of 183,200 men, plus the foot-soldiers, whose numbers were too difficult to tally.[1]

King Arthur accepted the pledges of his vassals, who were ready and able to render him service, and he ordered them to return at once to their homelands to muster the troops they had promised. Then they were to hasten to meet him by the beginning of August at the port of Barfleur. From there they would head toward the borders of the land of the Allobroges in order to meet the Romans. He then sent word back to the Roman Senate through their own messengers that he would never pay them tribute, nor was he coming to Rome to submit

---

[1] Geoffrey's arithmetic here defies final analysis, and Thorpe's suggestion that there has been some kind of scribal numerical error seems a reasonable one.

to their legal judgment. Instead, he claimed, he was coming to collect from them the very tribute they had hoped in all their legal wisdom to extract from him. The messengers went forth, as did all the kings and vassals, who did not fail to carry out Arthur's commands.

BOOK TEN

[163] When Lucius Hiberius heard the tone of King Arthur's letter of reply, he carried out the will of the Roman Senate and ordered the kings of the East to prepare their armies to come and subjugate Britain. There arrived at once Epistrophus, the king of the Greeks; Mustenar, the king of the Africans; Ali Fatima, the king of Spain; Hirtacius, the king of the Parthians; King Bolcus of the Medes; King Sertorius of Libya; King Pandrasus of Egypt; King Misipsa of Babylon; King Politetes of Bithynia; Duke Teucer of Phrygia; Evander of Syria; Echion of Boeotia; and Hyppolitus of Crete, along with all the lords and vassals subject to them. From the senatorial order arrived Lucius Catellus, Marius Lepidus, Gaius Metellus Cocta, Quintus Milvius Catulus, and Quintus Carutius. All in all, their numbers totaled 400,160. [164] Making all the necessary arrangements, they set out on the road to Britain at the beginning of August.

When Arthur heard of the Romans' advance, he yielded Britain to the custodianship of his nephew Mordred and Queen Guinevere.[1] Then he made his way with the army to Southampton, where he set out across the sea amid stormy winds. Around midnight that same evening, while the king's ship sailed amid the innumerable ships of his fleet as they plowed the waves with good winds and high spirits, a portentous dream befell the king. Sound asleep, Arthur dreamt that he saw a bear flying through the air, whose growling made all the coastlands tremble. Then he saw a terrible dragon flying towards him from out of the west, and the light from the dragon's eyes lit up all the land. As these two creatures came together, they engaged in a furious battle. But the dragon attacked the bear many times with his flaming breath, and the bear finally fell to the earth, burnt to a crisp. This awakened the king, and he immediately related his dream to those who were standing about. Interpreting the dream, they said that the dragon symbolized him, while the bear must represent some giant that he would fight with; the fight between the

---

[1] Mordred is mentioned in the *Annales Cambriae* as falling, along with Arthur, at the Battle of Camlann in 537. There, as elsewhere in the Welsh genealogies and triads, his name appears as *Medrawt*. The form *Mordred* is distinctly Cornish, which may indicate Geoffrey's familiarity with Cornish sources or local folklore. See Oliver Padel, "Geoffrey of Monmouth and Cornwall."

dragon and the bear portended the battle that would occur between them, and the dragon's victory, they claimed, indicated Arthur's victory. Arthur, on the other hand, believed that the vision referred to the imminent war between himself and the Roman emperor. As the night wore on and the red dawn approached, they landed in Barfleur. They pitched their tents at once and awaited the arrival of the kings of the islands and of the leaders of the provinces of Gaul.

[165] In the meantime, news came to King Arthur that a certain giant of marvelous size had come up from Spain and had kidnapped Helen, the niece of Duke Hoel of Brittany, fleeing with her to the top of that hill that is now called Mont-St.-Michel.[1] The knights of the region had gone in pursuit, but to no avail. Whether they attacked him by sea or by land, the giant would either sink their ships with heavy rocks or would finish them off with other sundry weapons. Indeed, he had even captured many of them and eaten them while still half-alive. So on the following night, two hours past midnight, King Arthur woke up Kay his seneschal and Bedivere his cup-bearer and secretly left the camp, stealing his way up toward the mountain.[2] For King Arthur possessed such strength and courage that he scoffed at bringing the entire army against such monsters. He wanted to impress his men by vanquishing the creature himself.

As they approached the mountain, they perceived a fire burning atop it and another fire on a hill nearby. So the king ordered Bedivere the Cup-Bearer to sail over to the mountain; there was no other way across since the hill rose up out of the sea. While he was attempting to climb up, Bedivere heard a woman's screams issuing from above him. At first he was struck with horror, fearing that the monster was drawing near. But his courage soon returned, and he drew his sword. When he reached the summit, at first he saw nothing at all except for the fire that he had sighted earlier. But then he noticed a recently dug grave and beside it an old woman who was moaning and bewailing. When she saw him, however, she ceased her lament at once and spoke to him thus:

---

[1] Mont-St.-Michel, which lies off the coast of France between Normandy and Brittany, was the site of an impressive abbey and town. Geoffrey's account reveals knowledge of the local topography, for Mont-St.-Michel is to this day surrounded by water when the tide is high. The story of the giant who plagued the area perhaps reflects Geoffrey's knowledge of local folklore, though no extant story antedates this one.

[2] Arthur's choice of Kay and Bedivere is consistent with the fact that these two (*Cei* and *Bedwyr*) appear as the most prominent of Arthur's companions in early Welsh poetry and in *Culhwch and Olwen*.

"O unlucky man! What ill fortune has led you to this place? Oh, you will suffer a death of the most unspeakable agonies! I do pity you, for this very night that most detestable monster will devour the flower of your youth! For soon that most wicked and nameless giant will be here. He carried the two of us up to this mountain—Duke Hoel's niece, whom I have just buried here, and myself her nurse—and without delay he will mete you out some unspeakable death."

"Alas!" she continued, "How terrible was my dear girl's fate! When this wicked creature gathered her into his embrace, such fear seized her tender breast that it ended her life, which should have seen many more years. However, since in unclean union he failed to lay with her—she who was my kindred spirit, my life, all my sweetness and light—he raped me instead. He did this, I confess, with great force and violence, in spite of God and my old age. Flee, my dear! Flee before he returns to have his way with me again. When he sees you he will tear you up most hideously."

Bedivere was moved as much as is humanly possible. He calmed the woman with kind words and promised to hurry back with help. So he hastened back to Arthur and told him everything that had happened, whereupon Arthur, groaning over the girl's fate, announced that he would attack the giant by himself and would call for them to assist him only if necessary. They then made their way to the higher hill and, entrusting their horses to their squires, began to climb up. Arthur led the ascent.

There by his fire was that inhuman creature, his mouth stained with the gore of half-eaten pigs. Some of them he had gobbled up, while others he had roasting on spits over the fire. The giant was caught off guard by the approach of the men and made immediately for his cudgel, which was itself so heavy that two young men could scarcely lift it off the ground. The king then unsheathed his sword, drew his shield up before him, and made a rush for the giant before he could get hold of the cudgel. But the giant noticed the king's hostile intention. He seized the club and struck the king against his shield with such force that the sound of the blow reverberated across the waters and caused the king himself to go deaf. The king now burned with a bitter anger. He lifted up his sword and dealt the giant such a blow that, though not lethal, made the blood gush all over his face and eyes, blinding him. The giant had, however, fended off the main force of the blow with his club and so avoided a mortal wound to his forehead. Unable to see because of the bleeding and now even angrier than before, the giant rose up and, just as a cornered boar will turn on the hunter, threw himself at the king's sword. He grabbed the king by his middle and forced him to kneel on the ground. Recovering his strength, the king quickly wriggled out of his grasp and began swiftly lashing out with his sword, now here, now there, not ceasing until he had dealt a mortal blow by driving his sword into the giant's head at that point where the brain is protected by the skull. The evil creature screamed and finally fell with the greatest tumult, like an oak uprooted by blasts of great winds.

The king then laughed in relief. Bedivere came up and cut off the giant's head and gave it to one of the squires to carry back down to the camp for everyone to behold. The king then said that he had never encountered anyone of such strength since he slew the giant Retho atop Mount Aravius.[1] This Retho had summoned Arthur to fight in single combat and had been collecting the beards of kings with which to make a fur coat. He had sent a message to Arthur that requested that the king rip his own beard out and send the ripped-out beard up to him. He promised that, since Arthur was eminent above all other kings, he would find Arthur's beard a place of honor among the other beards. If Arthur refused, he would challenge the king to combat: whichever of the two proved stronger would receive the loser's coat and beard. Arthur won the day soon after the contest began, and so he received the other's beard and coat. Since that day, Arthur maintained, he had met no one stronger than Retho.

Having secured this victory as noted above, they returned to their tents with the giant's head just before daybreak. The men all crowded around to see it, giving great praise to him who had freed the land from such a gluttonous monster. But Hoel, mourning over the death of his niece, ordered a church to be built upon the grave of that girl who now lay upon the hilltop. The church took its name from the girl's burial site, and is still called Helen's Tomb in the present day.

[166] Once all the forces that Arthur was waiting for had mustered together at Barfleur, he advanced on Autun, where he thought the Roman commander might be. As he came to the River Aube, however, it was announced to him that Lucius had made camp very close to their current position and was now advancing with such a great army that, it was reported, no one would be able to withstand it. Arthur did not waver, nor did he wish to deviate from his initial plans. However, he did set up a garrison on the banks of the river from which he could safely maneuver his men and where, if the need arose, they might take refuge.

---

[1]   The giant Retho appears in Welsh traditions as Rhita Mawr.

He also sent two of his vassals, Boso of Oxford and Gerin of Chartres, along with his nephew Gawain, as an embassy to Lucius Hiberius to explain that he should withdraw at once to the borders of Gaul or else Arthur would come to do battle to determine who had the more just claim to Gaul. The youth of Arthur's court, rejoicing greatly, began to urge Gawain to create some type of pretext for fighting with the Romans while he was visiting the emperor's camp.[1]

The delegation made its way to Lucius and ordered him to withdraw from Gaul or else meet them in battle the next day. While Lucius was in the process of replying that he would by no means withdraw but had instead come to rule that country, his nephew Gaius Quintillianus interrupted, and started saying that the Britons were far better-equipped with bragging and threats than they were with courage or skill in battle. Gawain was incensed at these words; he drew his sword, attacked Gaius, and cut off his head. The delegation then took to its horses and fled. The Romans pursued them with foot-soldiers and a cavalry force, sparing no effort in trying to avenge themselves on these fleeing messengers. But just as one of the Romans was starting to gain on them, Gerin of Chartres suddenly turned his horse and cast his spear at him, piercing right through the man's armor and body and pinning him to the ground. When Boso of Oxford saw the great feat that Gerin had performed, he turned his horse as well and threw his spear at the first Roman to approach. It pierced him through the throat and made him fall off his horse, lethally wounded. Then Marcellus Mutius, who was hoping to avenge Gaius Quintillianus, tried to attack Gawain from behind and was just beginning to lay his hands on him. But Gawain spun around and struck him with his sword right through the helm, cleaving his head all the way down to his chest. He told Mutius that, when he saw Quintillianus in Hell, he should tell him that this was why

---

[1]   The focus on Gawain partially reflects Welsh traditions like those found in *Culhwch and Olwen*, where the hero *Gwalchmei* (literally "Hawk of the Field") also appears as Arthur's nephew. Geoffrey was probably more directly familiar with the following account in William of Malmesbury's *The Deeds of the Kings of the English*, III: "At that time, in the province of Wales which is called Rhos, the tomb of Walwen [Gawain], who was not Arthur's degenerate nephew by his sister, was discovered. He ruled over that part of Britain which even now is called Walweitha. He was a warrior who was most renowned for his great valor, but he was slain by the brother and nephew of Hengist ... but only after inflicting great damage upon them in compensation for his exile; in this he can share in the praise given to his uncle, for they both staved off the downfall of their homeland for many years.... Walwen's tomb, which was fourteen feet long, was discovered upon the shore of the sea during the reign of King William. For this reason, some claim that he was wounded by his enemies and then shipwrecked; but others say that he was slain by his fellow-citizens at a

the Britons' boasting was not idle. Gawain then regrouped with his companions and urged them each to turn and attack their pursuers in this way. They agreed, and each of them threw down one Roman. But the rest of the Romans, who had up until this point been bent only on pursuit, now answered their blows with swords and lances. Yet they still could not catch them or cast them down. They chased them at long last into the vicinity of a certain forest, from which around six thousand Britons emerged. They had been watching the delegation's escape and had lain hidden in this wood in order to lend their aid. The Britons set spurs to their horses and the air was suddenly filled with their war-cries. Readying their shields for the attack, they rushed upon the Romans, immediately setting them to flight. The Britons followed them, unhorsing some of the Romans with their spears, while others they either captured or killed.

When this turn of events was reported to Senator Petreius, he hastened to the aid of his comrades with a force of ten thousand men. He forced the Britons to retreat back into the woods from which they had first issued, but not without a great loss to his own forces. Even as they fled, the Britons would turn amid the forest paths and inflict great damage upon their pursuers. As they fell back in this way, Hider, the son of Nuc, hurried to their aid with five thousand soldiers.[1] The Britons were there-fore able to hold their position, and they turned once more to valiantly oppose those whom they had been fleeing, striving to inflict heavy blows upon their enemies. The Romans also made their stand, now overthrow-ing the Britons, now being overthrown in turn. But the Britons, who burned with such a keen desire for war, did not care whether they stood or fell in battle. The Romans, on the other hand, acted more cautiously. Petreius Cocta, behaving as a good leader should, instructed his men expertly in when to advance and when to withdraw, and the Romans were thus able to inflict great harm on the Britons. When Boso realized this, he gathered around him the men he knew to be the boldest and spoke to them in this way: "Since Arthur does not know that we are engaged in this battle, we must take care, now that we have committed ourselves, lest the battle goes against us. For if we are defeated here, we will not only incur a great damage to our forces, but we will also make the king deplore us. Gather your courage together and follow me against the Roman lines so that, if Fortune favors us, we may kill or capture this Petreius."

---

[1]   The British champion Hider son of Nuc corresponds to the figure of Edern son of Nudd or Yder son of Nut of the Welsh and French Arthurian romances.

Then the Britons spurred on their horses and assaulted the enemy lines at the exact place where Petreius stood ordering his troops. Boso rushed up to him and grabbed him by the neck, just as he had planned, and the two of them fell to the ground. The Romans hurried over to extricate their leader from enemy clutches. The Britons rushed in to help Boso at the same time. There was great slaughter between them, and a great din, and great contention as the Romans tried to free their leader and the Britons tried to retain him. Each side inflicted wounds and was wounded in turn, overcame and was overcome. It seemed that anyone who had a spear or shield or bow might prevail in that fray. But then the Britons regrouped into a solid line and, fending off the onslaught of the Romans, carried Petreius back behind the strength of their own lines. Then they turned around once more and attacked those troops whose commander they had just kidnapped. The Romans were now greatly weakened and were just about ready to turn and run. Pressing their advantage, the Britons now attacked from behind as well. They threw down those whom they attacked and plundered those whom they had cast down before passing on in pursuit of the rest. They also took many prisoners, whom they hoped to present to the king.

At last, after they had put themselves in enough danger, they withdrew from the field with their spoils and captives to their stronghold by the river. There, rejoicing greatly in their victory, they explained what they had accomplished and presented Petreius Cocta and the other prisoners to King Arthur. Arthur congratulated them, and he promised to grant them further lands and titles since they had acted with such prowess even without him. Since the king desired to place the captives in prison, he summoned some men to escort them to Paris the next day, where they would remain in the custody of the city jailers for the time being. He also ordered Duke Cador and Bedivere the Cup-Bearer, as well as the two counts Borellus and Richerius, to accompany the convoy to Paris so that it need not fear any Roman ambushes.

[167] The Romans, however, got wind of these arrangements for the prisoners and, at the emperor's command, selected fifteen thousand of their men who would set out on the road that night, attack the convoy, and attempt to liberate the captives. Two senators, Vulteius Catellus and Quintus Carutius, were placed in command, along with King Evander of Syria and King Sertorius of Libya. That night they took control of the road as ordered and concealed themselves in a position by which they thought the Britons would pass. The next morning, the Britons did in fact come up the road with their captives, and even as they drew near they did not realize what

kind of trap the Romans had laid for them. Just as they began to pass by, the Romans suddenly jumped out unexpectedly and began to harass and attack them. But although the Britons were at first taken by surprise and scattered, they soon began to regroup and hold their ground valiantly. Some of them remained to guard the captives, while the rest arranged themselves in battle-formation and attacked their enemies. The guard that was established to watch the prisoners was under the command of Richerius and Bedivere. Duke Cador of Cornwall and Borellus took command of the rest. The Romans, on the other hand, all rushed upon them without any clear plan, and they did not bother arranging their men in battle-lines. They assailed the Britons with all their might while the Britons were still struggling to get into formation and defend themselves.

Because of their great tactical weakness at this point, the Britons might well have lost the captives they were guarding, had not Fortune hastened to their aid. Guitard, the duke of the Poitevins, realizing the trap his comrades had walked into, suddenly appeared on the scene with three thousand knights. With their assistance, the Britons were able to turn the tide of battle and repay the bloodshed to their shameless assailants. However, they had still lost many of their men during the first stage of the battle. They lost Borellus, that famous count of the Cenomanni, who was pierced through the throat with a spear as he fought against King Evander of Syria, and he bled to death. They also lost four other noble vassals: Hyrelglas of Periron, Mauricius of Kaer Dorcanen,[1] Aliduc of Tintagel, and Er the son of Hider. There were no bolder men than they. Unwavering in their courage, they did not despair of the fight, and they exerted every effort in guarding the captives and overthrowing their foes.

In the end, the Romans were unable to best the Britons in battle, and they swiftly abandoned the field and headed back to their encampment. The Britons pursued them and continued to harass them with great slaughter and to capture a great many of them. They did not cease until they had slain Vulteius Catellus and King Evander of Syria and had completely scattered the rest. Secure in their victory, they sent the prisoners they had been escorting up to Paris, and they led the new prisoners before the king. This victory encouraged the king with the hope of ultimate triumph in the war, since so few Britons had utterly routed so mighty a force of their enemies.

[168] These defeats sat ill with Lucius Hiberius, and he was sorely vexed in his mind. Completely undecided, he did not know whether

---

[1]   Probably Dorchester.

he should stay and engage Arthur in battle or whether he should go into Autun and wait for reinforcements from Emperor Leo. Giving in to his fears, he led his troops toward that city, stopping that night in Langres along the way. When Arthur learned of this, he desired to take the road ahead of Lucius. So that same night, he entered a lowland by the name of Saussy, which Lucius would have to pass through on the left of the city. In the process of arranging his soldiers into battle-groups, Arthur ordered a single legion, under the command of Earl Morvid, to remain behind so that, if necessary, he would have someplace to retreat to in order to regroup his men and bring the battle back to the enemy. He divided the rest of his soldiers into seven battalions, placing five thousand five hundred and fifty-five well-armed men in each. One section of each battalion consisted of foot-soldiers, while the rest was made up of mounted knights. Their orders were to let the infantry advance while the cavalry attempted to break the enemy lines by coming in from the sides. The entire infantry was, moreover, arranged into a square with a right and left wing, the standard British tactic. The wings were under the command of King Anguselus of Alban and Duke Cador of Cornwall, one on the right and one on the left. The rest of the army was led by the renowned earls Gerin of Chartres and Boso of Rydychen, which is called Oxford in the Saxon tongue; the third battalion was led by King Aschill of the Danes and King Loth of Norway; the fourth battalion by Hoel, leader of the Armoricans, and the king's nephew Gawain. Behind these battalions there were four others, the first led by Kay the Seneschal and Bedivere the Cup-Bearer; the second by Duke Holdwin of the Ruteni and Duke Guitard of the Poitevins; the third by Jugin of Leicester, Jonathal of Dorchester, and Cursalem of Chester; the fourth by Urbgennius of Bath. After arranging the army in this way, Arthur himself took command of a legion, stationed it in a certain place, and raised his personal banner of the gold dragon there: if any of his men were wounded or fatigued in the battle, they could, if necessary, take refuge among Arthur's legion as if in a fortified camp. In the legion that Arthur personally led, there were six thousand six hundred and sixty-six men.

[169] Once he had organized all his troops in this way, King Arthur addressed them with these words: "O my friends, you who have made Britain the sovereign over thirteen different realms, I celebrate your prowess, which, I believe, never fails but grows greater and greater each day. Even though you have spent the last five years enjoying the pleasures of peace rather than honing your martial skills, you have nevertheless not

degenerated at all from your innate strength. No, you have kept that strength up and have even set the Romans to flight! In their pride, the Romans desired to deprive us of our liberty. They sought to overwhelm us in battle with their greater numbers, but they could not prevail against your power, and now they slink within that city there. Soon they will issue forth and enter this valley on their way to Autun, and you will be able to set upon them completely unexpectedly and slaughter them like beasts. You will indeed witness the cowardice of Oriental peoples as you subjugate them and make them pay tribute to your homeland. Do they know how you waged war against the Danes and the Norse and the leaders of the Gauls, all of whom you brought under my power, liberating them from their shameful overlords? We who have triumphed in these greater wars will surely triumph today in this lesser battle, as long as we set our minds on crushing these half-men. Think of the rewards that each of you will merit if, like loyal soldiers, you follow my commands and carry out your orders! Once this field-army is defeated, we will push on to Rome and capture and occupy that city. There you will receive gold, silver, palaces, towers, castles, cities, and all the other spoils of war." As soon as he finished saying these things, they all assented in a single great cry, and they were now more predisposed to dying in battle than to fleeing the field with their lives.

[170] But Lucius Hiberius, who had detected the ambush that they had laid for him, did not flee, though he wished to, but instead summoned his courage and decided to lead his men into the valley. But first he gathered his commanders together and spoke to them with these words: "Venerable fathers, whose power holds sway over both East and West, call to mind your forefathers who did not flinch from spilling their own blood when enemies threatened the Republic, but who have instead left you a heritage of goodness and courage and skill in war, and who have fought as if God had declared that they would not die in battle. Thus they triumphed often and evaded death, for there was no other death that could overtake them other than what the Providence of God decreed. The Republic grew stronger, as did the prowess of the Roman people. Straightforwardness and honor and magnanimity all became a matter of course to them, and, as these qualities flourished, the dominion over all the earth fell to them and to their descendants. Wishing to inspire these same values in you, I urge you now to recall the virtue of your forefathers. Keeping this in mind, you should push on through the valley in which they have trapped you and wrest from them what is yours. Do not think that I had retreated into that city because I feared facing them in battle. No, I expected that they would

foolishly attempt to engage us, but that we would be able to turn on them unexpectedly and inflict great slaughter upon them as they fled pell-mell. Now, however, since they have not done what we thought they would, we must alter our tactics. Let us seek them out and boldly attack them. Or else, if they should make the first move, let us hold our lines steadfastly and withstand their initial assault, for after that we shall surely triumph. Experience in many battles shows that he who can prevail in the first assault most often wins victory in battle."

As Lucius finished making this speech, all his men agreed with his plan. Raising their hands, they swore oaths and then hurried to their weapons. Girded for battle, they left Langres and came into the valley where Arthur was ready with his troops. Then they arranged themselves into twelve wedge-shaped battalions of infantry, all of which themselves formed the entire force into a wedge shape, in the Roman fashion. Each battalion contained six thousand six hundred and sixty-six men. Each battalion was given its own commander, along with the orders to attack and to hold steady when under attack. The first battalion was under the command of Lucius Catellus and Ali Fatima, the king of Spain; the second was commanded by Hirtacius, the king of the Parthians, and by Senator Marius Lepidus; the third by Boccus, king of the Medes, and Senator Gaius Metellus; the fourth by Sertorius, king of Libya, and Senator Quintus Milvius. These four battalions were assigned to be the vanguard of the Roman forces. There were four more battalions behind them: the first was under the command of Xerxes, king of the Ituri; the second under Pandrasus, the king of Egypt; the third under Duke Politetes of Bithynia; the fourth under Duke Teucer of Phrygia. Behind these there were four more battalions serving as a rearguard: the first of these was placed under the command of Senator Quintus Carutius; the second under Lelius Hostilius; the third under Sulpicius Subbuculus; the fourth under Mauritius Silvanus. Lucius Hiberius himself moved all throughout the army, inspiring the troops and giving orders. Among them he brought their standard, the golden eagle, and he ordered it to be planted firmly in the midst of them, and warned them that, whatever befell, they should strive to bring it back if it was lost.

[171] At long last the Britons and the Romans stood opposite each other, each side brandishing its spears. At the sound of the battle-trumpets, the battalion under the command of the King of Spain and Lucius Catellus rushed rushed forward and boldly attacked the British soldiers under the King of Scotland and the Duke of Cornwall. But no matter how fiercely the Romans attacked, they could not scatter the Britons.

Then the regiment led by Gerin and Boso fell upon the attackers and, while the other band was defending itself, it came down with a sudden onrush of horses and cut right through the Roman lines, so that the battalion under the King of the Parthians now had to face the men under Aschill, king of the Danes. These two armies clashed together, each penetrating the other's lines and bringing on a great fight. The slaughter between them was wretched indeed. Amid the great din of battle, men were thrown headlong to the ground, and the earth was soaked with the life-blood of men from both sides.

The Britons suffered the greatest damage at first, since Bedivere the Cup-Bearer was slain and Kay the Seneschal was mortally wounded. When Bedivere had come up against Boccus, the King of the Medes, he was pierced by a spear and fell dead among the enemy troops. Then Kay the Seneschal, attempting to avenge him, was surrounded by a company of Medes and received a lethal wound. However, like the good soldier he was, Kay still would have led his division all the way back through the enemy lines, slaying and scattering the Medes along the way, if he had not come up against the King of Libya's battalion, whose sudden onslaught scattered all of his troops. However, he still managed to make his way with a few men back to the standard of the Gold Dragon, bearing Bedivere's body. How great were the laments of the Neustrians when they saw the body of their lord Bedivere so badly wounded! And how great were the cries of the Angevins when they understood that Kay, their count, had taken so many wounds! But there was no time for mourning, for the bloody battle raging all around them allowed them no opportunity to lament because they had to defend themselves.

[172] Then Bedivere's nephew Hirelglas, grieving beyond measure at his uncle's death, gathered three hundred of his men to him and, like a boar amid a pack of hounds, led a mounted charge straight into the enemy lines. He headed for where he had seen the banner of the king of the Medes, giving little thought to how he would be able to avenge his uncle. When he reached the banner, he slew the king there and carried him away. Then, laying him aside Bedivere's corpse, he tore the king's body to pieces. After that, he gave a great cry and urged his comrades to attack their enemies and to harry them constantly, for a new courage now blazed within them, while the spirits of their foes began to waver. In hand to hand combat, the Britons were arrayed more wisely than the Romans, and they were thus often able to inflict more dire harm. Spurred on by Hirelglas's encouragement, the Britons attacked the enemy all about, and both sides experienced great slaughter.

Among the countless warriors who fell on the Roman side were King Ali Fatima of Spain and Misipsa of Babylon, as well as the senators Quintus Milvius and Marius Lepidus. On the Briton side fell Holdwin, Duke of the Ruteni, and Leodegar of Boulogne, as well as the three earls Cursalem of Cicester, Gualac of Salisbury and Urbgennius of Bath. [173] Eventually, the companies that they led were weakened beyond measure and had to retreat until they came to the battalion led by Hoel of the Armorican Britons and Gawain. These two men suddenly burned like a flame and led a charge against the enemy. Regrouping the soldiers who were retreating, they forced those Romans who had just a moment ago been in pursuit to turn and flee. Catching up with the retreating Romans, they cast them down and slew them and did not cease massacring them until they came up against the emperor's personal battalion. The emperor, seeing the great peril of his comrades, lent his aid immediately. The Britons were greatly weakened in this battle. Cinmaroc, the Count of Tréguier, fell there, along with two thousand of his men. Three famous noblemen also fell— Richomarcus and Bloccovius and Iagwivius of Bodloan. If these three men had been princes of their own realms, future ages would have sung their fame on account of their prowess. While Hoel and Gawain made their charge, no enemy whom they attacked could escape, but had his life snatched away by either sword or spear. But when their company had come into the midst of Lucius' men, they were completely surrounded by the Romans and they fell in battle just as their comrades had. Hoel and Gawain, however, were the greatest of all the knights of old, and when they beheld the slaughter of their companions they fought on all the more fiercely. Pushing ahead now on one side, now on the other, they harried Lucius' personal bodyguard. Gawain, always aflame with a vigorous courage, sought to do battle with Lucius man to man. As this bold knight advanced, he would throw down and slay his enemies. Shining no less brightly, Hoel pressed the attack on the other side, urging on his companions and wounding the enemy. He received their blows most valiantly in turn, never shirking. He attacked and was attacked. It was not easy to say which of the two—Hoel or Gawain—was the mightier knight.

As Gawain cut his way through Lucius' bodyguard, as was mentioned before, he finally reached his goal and rushed upon the commander himself, forcing him to single combat. But Lucius was still in the prime of his youth. He possessed great courage and strength and skill in battle; he desired nothing more than to test his prowess against such a knight. When he withstood Gawain's initial assault, he was joyous and exultant, for he had heard of Gawain's fame. The battle between the two lasted a long time. They showered each other with mighty blows and warded off the blows with their shields, all the while struggling to kill each other. While they were fighting bitterly in this way, the Romans began to make a comeback, and they rushed upon the Armorican Britons and came to their commander's aid, forcing Gawain and Hoel and their men back until they suddenly found themselves back among Arthur's battalion.

[174] When King Arthur himself heard that his men were suffering such slaughter when only moments before they had been on the offensive, he drew Caliburn, the best sword in the world, and addressed his soldiers in a lofty voice, saying: "What are you doing, men? Are you going to let these mere women get away unscathed? Let not one of them escape alive! Remember your own right hands, which have, in so many battles, subdued thirty kingdoms to my dominion. Remember your ancestors, too, whom the Romans, when they were stronger, made pay tribute. Remember as well your freedom, which these half-men hope to take away from you. Let not one of them escape with his life, not one of them! What will you do?" Crying out these and many other things, he rode out toward the enemy, cast them down, and slew them. If anyone tried to stand in Arthur's way, he killed either a horse or a man with every single stroke. They began to flee from him like beasts from a fierce lion whose hunger has spurred him to devour whatever he comes across. Their armor did little to protect them from Caliburn, which, wielded in the right hand of such a mighty king, forced them all to pour their souls out along with their blood. Two kings, Sertorius of Libya and Politetes of Bithynia, had the misfortune of getting in Arthur's way. He cut off their heads and sent their souls to Hell.

When they beheld their king fighting in this way, the Britons regained their courage and rushed out against the Romans, advancing in tight formation. While the British infantry harried the Romans from one side, the cavalry strove to throw them down and break their lines from the other direction. The Romans held out bitterly. At the command of the illustrious king Lucius, they did their best to return the blows they received from the Britons. Both sides fought as vigorously as if the battle had only just begun. On the one side, Arthur continued striking down his foes and urging his fellow-Britons to persevere. On the other side, Lucius Hiberius kept the Romans in line and continued to perform many daring deeds. He never took a respite from the battle, but rode about through all his battle-lines, slaying any enemy he came upon with his sword and lance. Terrible carnage befell both sides as both Britons and Romans sought to prevail over their foes.

[175] Many thousands of Romans fell that day. Lucius, the commanding officer, was finally attacked in the midst of all his troops and slain, pierced through by someone's spear. Though the Britons pushed on to victory, it was only attained through great toil.

The Romans were scattered, and their forces were broken up. Some out of fear took refuge in the forest groves and hidden byways; others fled to the cities and fortresses and other strongholds. The Britons exerted every effort in hunting them out, meting out death and slaughter. They also captured and plundered those whom they could, since many of the Romans unmanfully surrendered themselves just so they might be able to live a little longer. Divine providence governed the day, for the Romans in ancient times had attacked the forefathers of the Britons with unheard-of violence; but now the Britons defended their freedom, which the Romans desired to take away, and they denied the tribute that was so unjustly demanded of them.

[176] Having achieved this victory, Arthur commanded the bodies of his own chief vassals to be separated from the enemy corpses. Once this was done, he had their bodies prepared for burial as if they were kings, and then had each carried to the abbey of his native territory and honorably interred. Bedivere the Cup-Bearer, however, was carried off by the Neustrians with great lamentation to the city of Bayeux, which his great-grandfather, Bedivere I, had founded. There he was laid to an honorable rest in a cemetery in the southern part of the city near the walls. Kay, on the other hand, who was grievously wounded, was brought to Chinon, a fortress that he himself had built. He succumbed to his wounds shortly thereafter, and was buried, as befit the leader of the Angevins, at an anchorage in the forest, not far from his castle. Holdwin, the duke of the Ruteni, was borne to Flanders and laid to rest in his city of Thérouanne. Other earls and vassals, on Arthur's orders, were brought to nearby abbeys. Taking pity on his enemies, Arthur ordered their bodies to be buried in their native soil as well, and he had the body of Lucius conveyed to the Roman Senate, telling them to expect no other tribute from Britain.

King Arthur wintered in those parts and spent his time subduing the cities of the Allobroges. As summer approached, he desired to head for Rome. However, just as he was about to cross the mountains, news reached Arthur that his nephew Mordred, in whose keeping he had left the governance of Britain, had proven himself to be a tyrant and a traitor. Mordred had seized the throne of Britain and now took his wicked pleasure with Guinevere, who had broken her marriage vows.

BOOK ELEVEN

[177] My noble Earl, Geoffrey of Monmouth does not fall silent here. Instead, drawing on the abovementioned source in the British tongue as well as on the assistance of Walter of Oxford, a man most expert in historical matters, I will now in my humble style briefly relate the battles that this famous king fought with his nephew upon returning to Britain after his great victory.

When the news of the wicked deed reached King Arthur's ears, he immediately postponed the campaign that he had hoped to wage against Leo, emperor of the Romans. Placing Hoel, the duke of the Armorican Britons, in charge of the armies in Gaul in order to pacify those regions, Arthur returned to Britain accompanied by only the insular kings and their forces. Meanwhile, that most wicked traitor Mordred had sent the Saxon Chelric into Germany in order to muster whatever allies he could and to bring them back as swiftly as possible to Britain. He even promised to give Chelric that part of the island that lay north of the Humber up to the borders of Scotland, as well as all the domains in Kent that Hengist and Horsa had once held under King Vortigern. Chelric, fulfilling his side of the bargain, brought eight hundred ships filled with armed pagan men, who obeyed that traitor as if he were the real king. Mordred had also made alliances with the Scots, Picts, and Irish, all of whom had long nurtured a hatred for his uncle. All counted, Mordred's troops numbered around eighty thousand and were composed of pagan and Christian alike.

Placing his trust in the enormous army he had amassed, Mordred marched out to meet Arthur as he attempted to land in Richborough. The two forces met in battle, and Mordred's troops inflicted great slaughter on the others, who were still in the process of disembarking. King Anguselus of Alban, the king's nephew Gawain, and countless others fell on the field of battle that day. Anguselus was succeeded in Alban by Ywain, the son of his brother Urian.[1] This Ywain later distinguished himself through many valiant deeds during the wars that followed. At last, through great effort, Arthur's forces managed to come

---

[1] Owein ap Urien is a historical, sixth-century Welsh hero. The figure of Ywain would later appear prominently in the cycle of Arthurian romances, beginning with *Yvain* by Chrétien de Troyes (c. 1175).

ashore, returning the terrible onslaught that they had suffered and setting Mordred's army to flight. Being used to constant warfare, they had arranged their forces partly on foot and partly on horseback: whenever the infantry needed to attack or retreat, the cavalry would charge at an angle, thus attempting to break the enemy lines and force them to withdraw. The traitor Mordred regrouped his troops and entered Winchester the next night. When this was reported to Queen Guinevere, she gave up hope and fled from York to Caerleon, where she joined the nuns at the Church of St. Julius the Martyr and was determined to live chastely.

[178] Arthur was now kindled with an even greater wrath, having lost so many hundreds of his men. Three days later, after having given his fallen warriors a decent burial, he approached Winchester and besieged the wretched traitor who had taken refuge there. But Mordred did not wish to abandon all of his plans yet, and so, exhorting his men in various ways, he issued out of the city with his troops in formation and pitched a battle against his uncle. As the fighting began, great slaughter befell both sides. But Mordred's men got the worst of it, and he was forced to abandon the field. Caring little for the burial of his dead, Mordred at once took to flight by boat, making his way towards Cornwall.[1] Arthur, on the other hand, was greatly concerned that so many of the enemy had escaped. He pursued them with great haste into Cornwall and awaited their arrival at the River Camlann.[2] Mordred, since he was a bold man and ever swift to attack in battle, quickly arranged his troops. He hoped either to be victorious or to perish in the attempt, not desiring to flee any longer. Sixty thousand armed soldiers still remained of his allies, and he placed them in six battle-groups, assigning 6,666 to each group. Then he formed one last group from the remainder. He assigned commanders to all of the divisions, and took personal command of the last division. With the troops now arranged, Mordred encouraged them, promising them the possessions of their enemies if they were able to emerge triumphant from this battle.

---

[1]   Geoffrey's geography is a bit murky here. Winchester is neither on the sea nor on a major waterway. Moreover, the traditional sites for the subsequent Battle of Camlann place that battlefield on the northern side of Cornwall, surely out of Mordred's direct escape route.

[2]   Camlann was, according to long-standing Welsh traditions, the site of Arthur's last battle; the *Annales Cambriae* states that it occurred in the year 537 and that both Arthur and Mordred fell there. Geoffrey seems to be the first to identify the spot with the River Camel in Cornwall. Certain Welsh traditions pre-dating Geoffrey attribute the cause of the battle to a dispute between Gwenhwyfar (Guinevere) and an otherwise unknown woman named Gwenhwyfach.

Arthur was also arranging his troops on the other side of the field. He divided them into nine companies of infantrymen, each of which was arranged in a square, with a left wing and a right wing. Then, appointing commanders to each division, he urged them all to destroy the thieves and traitors who had been brought to their land by his treacherous nephew and who still hoped to take away all of their possessions. He told them that many of these barbarians from various kingdoms were unwarlike by nature and completely ignorant of the arts of war. It would be nothing at all, he said, for worthy men as expert in war as themselves to emerge victorious if they rushed bravely onto the field and fought valiantly.

Both Arthur and Mordred exhorted their own troops in this way. Then, in a sudden onslaught, the two armies advanced upon the field and strove to inflict one another with many dire blows. Great carnage was suffered on both sides, countless groans issued from the dying men. Indeed, the clashing of these warriors is almost too grievous and laborious to describe. Men all around inflicted wounds and were wounded in turn, killed and were killed.

After they had passed much of the day in this way, Arthur rushed in with a battalion of 6,666 men against the company where he knew Mordred to be. Clearing the way with their swords, they penetrated Mordred's bodyguard and inflicted the most fearsome slaughter. The traitor finally fell there, and many thousands with him. However, the rest of the enemy force did not flee the field because of Mordred's death, but instead gathered together from all around the battlefield and made a last stand with all the boldness they could muster. They fought most bitterly, for almost all the commanders from both sides were there with their men. On Mordred's side there fell that day the Saxon leaders Chelric, Elafius, Egbrict, and Bruniggus; the Irish leaders Gillapatric, Gillabor, Gillafer, and Gillarum; as well as all the Scottish and Pictish leaders along with everyone they commanded. On Arthur's side, there fell King Olberic of Norway, King Aschill of Denmark, Cador Limenic, and Cassibelaunus, along with many soldiers of both British and foreign origin whom he had brought with him. However, even the illustrious King Arthur was mortally wounded. He was carried away to be healed of his wounds on the isle of Avalon, and he gave the crown of Britain to his kinsman Constantine, son of Duke Cador of Cornwall, in the year of our Lord 542.[1] May his soul rest in peace.

---

[1]   The mystery surrounding Arthur's end is notorious. In Book Seven, Merlin had prophesied that the end of the Boar of Cornwall would be shrouded in doubt. An early Welsh

[179] Upon Constantine's coronation, the Saxons, led by the two sons of Mordred, revolted, but they could not prevail against the king. After many battles, one of them fled to London, while the other went to Winchester, and they seized control of these two cities. At that time, the holy Daniel, the bishop of Bangor and a most reverend priest, died and the bishop of Gloucester was appointed to the archdiocese of London.[1] David, the archbishop of Caerleon, also died at this time at his abbey in the city of Menevia. He had cherished this abbey above all others because the Blessed Patrick, who had prophesied David's own birth, had founded it. While he was abiding among the monks there, he was struck by a sudden illness and buried in that church. In his place, Kinoc, a priest of the church of Llanbadarn, was promoted to the metropolitan see.

[180] Constantine pursued the two sons of Mordred, and he subjugated the Saxons and recaptured the two cities.[2] Mordred's younger son had taken refuge in the church of St. Amphibalus in Winchester, but Constantine cut him down before the altar. The other son was hidden among the brothers in a monastery in London, but he was discovered and likewise met a cruel death before the altar.[3] For these deeds, Constantine was himself cut down by the judgment of God four years later, and was buried next to Uther Pendragon in the Ring of Giants which had been constructed with great craft near Salisbury and which is now called Stonehenge in the English tongue.

[181] Constantine's nephew Aurelius Conanus, a young man of great prowess, succeeded him.[4] He ruled over the entire island, and would indeed have been worthy of the crown of Britain had he not been such a lover of civil strife. Aurelius Conanus' own uncle, who was supposed

---

poem known as *The Stanzas of the Graves* likewise notes that the site of Arthur's resting-place is unknown. Geoffrey, however, scrupulously avoids mentioning the widespread "Breton hope" that King Arthur would return to liberate Britain from its oppressors. The tantalizing reference to the isle of Avalon here does not mitigate the more important fact of Arthur's death, and the Bern MS states quite plainly that Arthur was "mortally wounded" and wishes that the king's soul "rest in peace."

[1] The Bern MS names this Bishop of Gloucester "N.," later referring to him as Teotius. I have deliberately omitted his first name here.

[2] Geoffrey develops his account of Constantine and of the following kings through Malgo from Gildas' denunciation of five tyrants of his day in *The Ruin of Britain*, though Geoffrey elevates these men to kings of all Britain rather than keeping them the regional monarchs that they are in Gildas.

[3] Constantine in Gildas' *Ruin of Britain* is similarly guilty of slaying "two royal youths" before the altar.

[4] Gildas refers to this figure as Aurelius *Caninus* ("the little dog").

to reign after Constantine, had rebelled, and so Aurelius Conanus secured his reign by throwing his uncle in prison and killing his two sons. He died in the third year of his reign.

[182] After him, Vortipor succeeded to the throne.[1] The Saxons rebelled against him, bringing more of their countrymen to the island by ship. But Vortipor fought a battle against them and triumphed. Gaining the mastery of the realm in this way, he governed the people with peace and love.

[183] After Vortipor came Malgo, the handsomest of all the rulers of Britain. He was a scourge to tyrants, robust in arms, generous to one and all. He would have been famous above all for his greatness had he not given in to the plague of sodomy and thus made himself hateful to the sight of God.[2] He too controlled the entire island, and, after a number of terrible wars, subdued the six outlying islands of the Ocean as well: Ireland, Iceland, Gotland, Orkney, Norway, and Denmark.

[184] He was succeeded by Kareticus, another lover of civil wars. He too was hateful to the sight of God and Britons alike. The Saxons took note of his instability and sent word to Gormund, the king of a group of Africans who had come to Ireland in great ships and had subdued the people of that land.[3] And so this Gormund now sailed with 160,000 Africans to Britain, which was currently being ravaged by the Saxons on the one hand, and the horrible civil wars that the Britons were fighting among themselves on the other. Making a pact with the Saxons, Gormund made war on King Kareticus. After many battles, Gormund was repulsed and fled from city to city until he came to Cirencester, which he besieged. While he was there, Isembard, the nephew of King Louis of the Franks, approached him, offering him a pact of friendship. Isembard abandoned his own Christian faith in entering this friendship, for he was hoping for Gormund's aid in ousting his uncle from the kingdom of Gaul; Isembard claimed that he had been forcibly and unjustly expelled from his rightful kingdom. Joining forces, they captured Cirencester and burnt it to the ground. Then, fighting another battle with Kareticus, they forced him to flee across the Severn and into Wales. Gormund then began laying waste all the farmlands and burn-

---

1   Gildas calls this Vortipor "the tyrant of the Demetians."

2   Geoffrey's charge of sodomy upon Malgo derives from Gildas' comparison of this king (whom he names *Maglocunus*) to "a man drunk on wine pressed from the vine of the Sodomites."

3   The following account reflects Geoffrey's familiarity with *Gormont et Isembard*, a contemporary *chanson de geste*.

ing all the neighboring cities. His fury did not cease until he had ravaged almost the entire surface of the island from sea to sea. All the native settlements were smashed as if with battering rams. All the populace, even the priests of the Church, were overcome by the flashing of swords and the crackling flames of the earth. A remnant of those afflicted with such slaughter managed to flee, but there was little safety to be found anywhere they went.

[185] O you hateful people of Britain, so weighed down by your monstrous crimes: why did you always lust after civil wars, weakening yourselves in domestic strife? Although you had once subdued foreign kingdoms to your own power, now you are like the good vineyard that has gone to seed. Now you are unable to protect your land, your women, or your children from your enemies. Persist, then, in your domestic squabbling, even though you know what the Gospel says on this subject: "Every kingdom divided against itself is doomed, and every house divided against itself will fall." Because your kingdom was so divided against itself, because the flames of domestic strife and the smoke of wrath have clouded your minds, because your pride did not allow you to obey a single king, you shall behold your land laid waste by the most impious pagans. Your houses shall indeed fall, and your descendants shall indeed mourn. They shall see the whelps of the barbarous lioness storm their castles and seize all of their cities and other possessions. Wretchedly bereaved of these things, they will barely ever be able to regain their former state of dignity.[1]

[186] After the nefarious Gormund had ravaged almost the entire island with his innumerable African troops, as described above, he finally ceded the greater part of the island—the area known as Logres—to the Saxons at whose request he had begun his invasion. The remnant of the Britons withdrew to the western parts of the land, particularly to Cornwall and Wales. From there, they made constant forays and deadly raids upon their enemies. At that time, Archbishop Teotius of London and Archbishop Tadocus of York saw all the churches over which they presided razed to the ground. They fled to safety in the forests of Wales, taking with them the priests who had survived such a catastrophe as well as all the relics of the saints. They feared that the relics and holy remains of all the old saints would be lost in the barbarians' plundering if they had stayed behind to suffer a martyr's death. Many of them even

---

[1]   Geoffrey's diction in this paragraph is distinctly reminiscent of Gildas' invectives against his countrymen in *The Ruin of Britain*.

set sail for Armorican Britain since two whole provinces—Logres and Northumbria—had been completely bereft of their monasteries. But I shall discuss these affairs when I translate *The Book of Exile*.[1]

[187] The Britons thus lost the crown of Britain for many years, and they did not even attempt to restore the kingship of the island to its former dignity. Worst of all, in that part of the land where they still remained, they did not follow a single king but instead obeyed three separate warlords who constantly ravaged the land fighting one another. The Saxons did not assume the kingship on their part either; they too followed three separate kings who fought at times amongst themselves and at times against the Britons.

[188] In the meantime, the blessed Pope Gregory sent Augustine to Britain to preach the word of God to the Angles, who, blinded by their heathen superstitions, had wiped out Christianity in every part of the island that they controlled.[2] But Christianity still survived among the Britons, who had accepted it during the time of Pope Eleutherius and had never let it falter. When Augustine arrived, he discovered seven bishoprics and one archbishopric among the Britons, all of which were supplied with priests and with many abbeys where God's flock could keep the strict rule. Among others, there was one particularly splendid abbey in the city of Bangor that had grown so great that it had been split into seven daughter-houses, none of which contained fewer than three hundred monks who lived by the fruit of their own labor. The abbot there was named Dinoot, and he was a man most learned in the liberal arts. When Augustine requested that all the bishops of the Britons submit to him so that they could make common labor of preaching the Gospel to the Saxons, this Dinoot made many subtle arguments to the effect that the British clergy owed Augustine no allegiance and that they would certainly not waste their preaching on their enemies, not so long as they had their own archbishop and the Saxons continued to occupy their homeland. Because of this, they regarded the Saxons with the greatest hatred, cared nothing for the Saxons' faith or religion, and felt they had more in common with dogs than they did with the Angles.

---

[1]   If Geoffrey wrote this book, it has been lost.

[2]   The mission of St. Augustine to Britain is chronicled at length in Bede's *Ecclesiastical History of the English Church and People*. This is also the first time in the history that Geoffrey uses the term *Angles* rather than *Saxons* to refer to the invaders, a fact that coincides with his increased use of Bede as a source and with a somewhat more balanced view of the Germanic immigrants.

[189] When King Ethelbert of Kent saw that the Britons had refused to submit to Augustine and had scoffed at preaching to them, he reacted very gravely. He suggested to Ethelfrid, the king of Northumbria, and to the other Saxon petty-kings that they bring a great army to bear against Abbot Dinoot and the other clerics in the city of Bangor who had consigned them to eternal damnation. All the kings agreed, and they mustered up an enormous host and marched into the areas still under British control. They came to the city of Chester, where Brochmail, the earl there, was awaiting their arrival.[1] There also had arrived at that same city countless monks and hermits from all the provinces of the Britons—and especially from the city of Bangor—who had come to pray for the salvation of their own people. Arranging all the armies, King Ethelfrid of the Northumbrians commenced the battle against Brochmail. Brochmail managed to resist to the last, but his force was much smaller, and he was compelled to abandon the city and take flight, but not before inflicting great slaughter upon the enemy. And so Ethelfrid captured the city. But when he learned of the reason that all the monks had come there, he immediately ordered them to be attacked. Twelve hundred holy men died that day; they were decorated with martyrdom and took their appointed seats in the Kingdom of Heaven.[2]

After that, the abovementioned Saxon tyrant sought to capture the city of Bangor. Hearing of his onslaught, the leaders of the Britons gathered together to intercept him. Duke Bledericus of Cornwall was there, along with King Margadud of the Demetians and King Cadvan of the Venedotians. Together they met Ethelfrid in battle and forced his army to retreat, wounding him in the process and slaying a great many of his men, to the number of 10,066. On the side of the Britons was slain Duke Bledericus of Cornwall, who had commanded the others during these wars.

---

[1] Brochmail ap Eliseg was a historical prince of Powys. Bede describes him as the leader of the Britons at the Battle of Chester in 613 C.E.

[2] Geoffrey draws his account of the Battle of Chester fairly straightforwardly from Bede, 2.2.

BOOK TWELVE

[190] All the princes of the Britons then convened in the city of Chester, and they agreed to make Cadvan their king and to follow him across the Humber in pursuit of Ethelfrid. As soon as Cadvan was invested with the crown of the kingdom, the Britons mustered from all around and crossed the Humber. When Ethelfrid learned of this, he summoned all the kings of the Saxons, and they set out to intercept Cadvan. Once the two armies were finally standing across the battlefield from each other, mutual friends came and arranged a pact between them such that Ethelfrid should rule the land north of the Humber and Cadvan should rule Britain on the southern side of that same river. When they had confirmed this treaty with oaths and the exchange of hostages, such a great friendship sprang up between the two kings that they might as well have ruled all the land in common.

In the meantime, it happened that Ethelfrid had cast aside his legitimate wife and was intending to marry a second. In fact, he held his first wife in such hatred that he had her exiled from the kingdom of Northumbria. Bearing a child in her womb, she came to King Cadvan and begged him to intervene and reunite her with her husband. Although Cadvan was unable to prevail upon Ethelfrid in this matter, the woman remained under Cadvan's roof until the day in which the child that she had conceived was born and delivered to the world. This child was, in fact, born just a short time after the birth of Cadvan's son by his own queen, who had been pregnant at the same time. And so the two boys were raised together as befitted their royal heritage. Cadvan's son was named Cadwallo, and the other's name was Edwin.[1] As the years passed and they grew into young men, their family sent them to King Solomon of the Armorican Britons so that they could learn the arts of war and the manners of the court. Receiving a warm welcome there, they began to grow so close to the king that no one could be more familiar with him nor could anyone speak so jestingly to him as they could. As they grew older, they often fought against their

---

[1] Geoffrey's narrative of the relations between these two kings is based very loosely on the account found in Bede's *Ecclesiastical History*, 2.20, though Bede names the British king Cadwalla. Given his anti-Briton bias, Bede describes Cadwalla as "utterly barbarous in temperament and behaviour," a characterization that Geoffrey deftly avoids.

enemies in battle while Solomon was present, displaying their valor in deeds of great prowess.

[191] With the passing of the years, their parents eventually died and the two youths returned to Britain to take up the governance of the realm, displaying the same friendship that had existed between their fathers. After two more years had gone by, Edwin asked Cadwallo if he could have his own royal diadem so that he could celebrate the ancient customs in Northumbria just as Cadwallo himself was able to celebrate them south of the Humber. While their wiser counselors were commencing negotiations by the River Douglas to figure out how this could best be accomplished, Cadwallo was resting on the other side of the river upon the lap of his nephew Brian.[1] While the legates were conveying various messages back and forth, Brian began weeping, and the tears streamed from his eyes, dampening the king's cheeks and beard. The king, thinking that it had begun to rain, raised his head and saw that the young man was weeping. He asked what was the cause of this sudden sorrow. Brian answered: "I weep ceaselessly for the British people. Though they have been oppressed by barbarian invasions since the days of King Malgo, there has not yet arisen a ruler who can restore Britain to its former dignity. In fact, even the little honor that remains to the Britons is further diminished—and with your consent, no less—now that these foreign-born Saxons, who have so often in the past been our murderers, begin to have their own crowns, sharing the realm with you. With the title of king, they will be made even more famous in the country of their origin, and they will act swiftly and invite even more of their compatriots here, bent on the extermination of our people. Indeed, destroying us has always been their goal, as has driving us out of our homeland. For this reason, I think we ought to be keeping them under our thumb rather than exalting them. When King Vortigern first retained the Saxons, they dwelt here under a guise of peace, apparently willing to fight for our land. However, once they were able to get a sense of our weaknesses, they abandoned Vortigern, giving him one ill turn for another. Then they afflicted the people of our kingdom with hideous violence. They slew Aurelius Ambrosius, and they lethally wounded Arthur in battle after Mordred had dissolved the oath by which they were bound. After that, they abandoned King Kareticus

---

[1]   The name Brian was rare in twelfth-century Britain, and it is quite possible that Geoffrey bestows the name on Cadwallo's heroic nephew in honor of Brian FitzCount (c. 1085–1147), the illegitimate son of Duke Alan IV of Brittany and a strong partisan of the Empress Matilda during the Anarchy.

when they led Gormund of the Africans against him. During that particular invasion, they deprived the Britons of their homeland and most dishonorably drove out our king."

[192] As Brian said these things, Cadwallo began to repent of the pact that was being drawn up, and he sent word to Edwin that he was unable to persuade his counselors to agree to Edwin's petition. They claimed it was against the ancient laws and customs that the island should be under the dominion of two separate crowns. Edwin grew angry. He dismissed the delegation and withdrew into Northumbria, declaring that he would assume a royal crown even without Cadwallo's permission. When news of this came to Cadwallo, he sent messengers with the word that he would cut the head out from under the crown should Edwin presume to crown himself in the island of Britain.

[193] Strife thus arose between them, as each man attempted to defeat the other in many battles. When they finally both met in a battle on the Humber, Cadwallo lost many thousands of men and was forced to flee. He took the road through Alban and went over to Ireland. Edwin, having scored a victory, led his army through the provinces of Britain, burning the cities and afflicting the people with many torments. While Edwin was indulging in such savagery, Cadwallo tried all the while to return by ship to his homeland. But he could not because, in whatever port he tried to land, Edwin was there, blocking his entrance with a great host. This was possible because a certain wise soothsayer from Spain by the name of Pellitus, who could tell the future by the movements of the stars, predicted for Edwin any misfortune that might occur. Forewarned of Cadwallo's attempts to return, Edwin thwarted him at every turn, blockading all the ports and striking at his ships so that all of Cadwallo's comrades were drowned. Cadwallo did not know what to do, and he began to give up hope of ever returning.

Cadwallo then decided to go to King Solomon of the Armorican Britons to ask for counsel and support in returning to his own kingdom. But when he turned his sails toward Armorica, such mighty storms blew up unexpectedly that his men's ships were all scattered in a short space of time, no two remaining together. The helmsman of the king's ship was then seized with such a great fear that he let the rudder go and let Fortune take the ship where it would. In constant peril of death all night long, the ship was tossed back and forth by the oncoming waves. At dawn on the next day, they landed on the island known as Guernsey, and, with great effort, made it ashore. Grief and anger over the loss of his companions constantly afflicted Cadwallo's thoughts, such that for three days and nights he refused to eat and lay ill in bed. Then, at sunrise on the fourth day, a great desire to eat meat came upon him, and he called Brian to him and explained what he desired. So Brian took up his quiver and bow and set off across the island, hoping to catch some kind of wild beast. However, although he traversed the entire island, he was unable to find what he was looking for, and was deeply concerned at not being able to fulfill his lord's desire. Indeed, he feared that the king's illness might lead to death if he were unable to satisfy his appetite. Then he had a new idea: he sliced a piece of flesh from his own thigh, set up a spit, and roasted it, presenting it to the king as venison. Cadwallo, thinking it to be the flesh of a beast, ate it and began to feel better, marveling that he had never before tasted meat of such a sweet flavor. Once his appetite was sated, he became much more merry and cheerful, and within three days his health was completely restored.

[194] When a favorable wind finally arose, they fitted their ship, raised their sails, and set off across the waters, landing in the city of Kidaleta.[1] Then, arriving at the court of King Solomon, they received a warm welcome, as befitted such honorable guests. When Solomon learned the reason for their visit, he promised his aid in this way: "We must mourn, my worthy young men, the fact that the land of your ancestors has been oppressed by this barbarous race and that you have been so ignominiously exiled. Yet it amazes me that, although other men seem to be able to defend their own lands, your people has lost such a fertile island and that it could not fight off the Angles, whom our forefathers esteemed so little. When the people of my Brittany once dwelt in Britain with your forefathers, they dominated all the provincial kingdoms, and there was no race except for the Romans whom they could not subjugate. Even the Romans, though they did manage to subdue Britain for a time, eventually had all of their officials dismissed or slain and they withdrew. However, after the Britons came to this land under the leadership of Maximianus and Conan, those who were left behind in Britain never again had the grace to hold the crown of the kingdom for very long. Though many of the British princes did maintain the ancient dignity of their fathers, they were succeeded by many weaker heirs who could barely hold off the threat of foreign invasions. And so I lament the weakness of your people, since we too are called Britons, sprung from the same

---

[1]   The city of Kidaleta likely represents the ancient Breton town of Aleth (*Kidaleta<Ciwed Aled<Civitas Aleth*). See W. Edwards, "The Settlement of Brittany," *Y Cymmrodor* 11 (1890), 93n.

stock, and yet we are able to defend our own homeland effectively against the incursions of our neighbors."

[195] When he had finished saying these and similar things, Cadwallo was ashamed and answered in this way: "I owe you many thanks, O king from a race of kings, for the aid you will lend me to recover my kingdom. But when you spoke of your wonder that my people did not maintain the dignity of our ancestors after the Britons came to these lands, I am not at all surprised. For the noblest men of the realm followed the two leaders you mentioned, and only the base-born remained behind to care for their homelands. When they in turn began to grow nobler, they became puffed up far more than befitted their condition, and they began to grow haughty in their affluence. They indulged themselves in such fornication as has never been heard of before. As the historian Gildas bears witness, they grew accustomed not only to this vice but to all the other sins that afflict human nature. Most of all, they nourished a hatred of the truth and of tellers of the truth, and a hatred such as this overthrows every other good. They indulged in a love for lying and liars, in undertaking evil deeds rather than good ones, and in cherishing wickedness above goodness. They even accepted Satan rather than the Angel of Light. Their kings were anointed not on account of God but because they were crueler than the others. And not long after that they were murdered by the very men who had set them on the throne, not for any legitimate reason but because even crueler men were found to replace them. If any king seemed to be a bit milder and more dedicated to truth than the rest, everyone's hatred and hostility turned on him, as if he had betrayed Britain itself. At that point, everything that pleased and displeased God hung equally balanced, or perhaps that which displeased God was the heavier. Therefore everyone acted contrary to his own well-being, as if no medicine was offered to him by the True Physician. Not only laymen but even the Lord's flock and its shepherds behaved thoughtlessly. It is no wonder, then, that this degenerate people lost control of its homeland on account of such nefarious crimes, having stained its country in such a manner. God truly wanted to exact vengeance upon them, and he suffered foreign peoples to come and drive the Britons from the lands of their ancestors. However, if God is willing, the time is now ripe for restoring the Britons to their former dignity, lest reproach fall upon us for being weak rulers who did not try to regain our former position while we were able."

"We two even share the same ancestor," Cadwallo continued, "which makes me all the more secure of your assistance. Malgo, the greatest king, who reigned fourth after King Arthur, had two sons: Ennianus and Rhun. Ennianus begat Belin, Belin begat Iago, and Iago begat Cadvan, my own father. Rhun was driven from the kingdom after his father's death by an invasion from the Saxons. He came to this land and gave his daughter to Duke Hoel, son of the great Hoel who helped Arthur subjugate the world. From this daughter was born Alan, from Alan your father Hoel, whom all Gaul feared while he lived and breathed."

[196] While Cadwallo spent the winter under Solomon's roof, they decided that Brian should sail back over to Britain in the meantime and kill King Edwin's wizard in any way he could, lest the wizard should give Edwin warning of Cadwallo's return. And when Brian landed in Southampton, he disguised himself in the garb of a poor beggar and made himself a pointed iron staff with which he could slay the wizard if the opportunity arose. Then he traveled to York, where Edwin was then dwelling. When he entered that city, he joined up with the other beggars who were waiting for alms outside the door of the king's house. As he was pacing there, his sister came out of the king's hall, carrying a basin to bring water to the queen. Edwin had captured the girl from the city of Worcester when he ravaged the lands of the Britons after Cadwallo's retreat. As she passed before Brian, he recognized her right away and began weeping and whispering her name. Hearing his voice, the girl turned her face towards him, though she did not realize who he was at first. But as she drew closer, she did recognize her brother and almost fainted, fearing that some ill chance would lead to his capture by their enemies. So they refrained from exchanging kisses and tender words for the time being, and the girl spoke briefly to her brother as if they were speaking of some other matter, and she told him about the state of the court. Then she pointed out the wizard whom he was seeking, because, by some strange chance, Pellitus happened to be mingling with the beggars while the alms were being distributed. Brian took note of the man, and he ordered his sister to steal out of her chamber the following night and meet him at a certain ancient temple outside the city, where he would wait for her among the crypts there. Then he slipped away into the crowd of beggars and approached the place where Pellitus was conversing with them. As soon as he saw an opportunity to strike, he raised his beggar's staff, which I described above, and pierced the wizard through the chest, killing him with a single blow. Dropping his staff at once, Brian slipped away into the crowd, unsuspected by any of the bystanders, and, by God's grace, made his way to the appointed hiding-place.

As night fell, Brian's sister attempted to slip away from her chamber in many different ways, but she could not because Edwin, who was shaken up by the murder of Pellitus, had posted guards on patrol all around the court, completely blocking all her possible escape routes. When Brian realized this, he left his hiding-place and withdrew to Exeter, where he reported what he had done to the Britons who were mustered there. Sending messengers to Cadwallo, Brian then fortified the city, and suggested that all the British nobility take steps to defend their own cities and fortresses and await the arrival of Cadwallo, who would soon be coming back to command them, accompanied by reinforcements from Solomon. When word of these actions spread throughout the island, King Penda of the Mercians came to Exeter with an enormous force and besieged Brian there.[1]

[197] In the meantime, Cadwallo landed with the ten thousand soldiers pledged to him by King Solomon, and he headed for the siege that Penda was waging. When they were face to face with the enemy, he arranged his troops into four divisions and attacked at once. Almost as soon as the battle had begun, Penda was captured and his army was destroyed. Having no other choice, Penda submitted to Cadwallo and delivered him hostages, promising to fight against the Saxons with him. After this victory, Cadwallo summoned his vassals, who had been scattered for so long, and made for Edwin in Northumbria. He ravaged the countryside as he went. When these events were reported to Edwin, he gathered all the petty-kings of the Angles about him and marched out to meet Cadwallo in the field that is now called Hedfeld, and fought a great battle against the Britons there.[2] The battle did not last long; Edwin was slain, as were almost all the men he led that day, including his son Offrid and Godbold, the king of the Orkneys, who had come to assist him.

[198] With this triumph under his belt, Cadwallo traveled through all the lands of the Angles, and wreaked such havoc among the Saxons that he spared neither women nor children. Hoping to exterminate all the Angles within the borders of Britain, he inflicted dreadful torments upon all whom he encountered. Then he fought a battle against Offric, who had succeeded Edwin, and he killed him and the two nephews who were intending to reign after him. He also slew Cadvan, the king of the Scots, who had come to their aid.

---

[1] Penda, the pagan king of Mercia, appears throughout Bede's *Ecclesiastical History* as a villain.
[2] Bede describes the Battle of Hæthfelth in his *Ecclesiastical History*, 2.20; he dates it to the year 633 C.E.

[199] After the violent deaths of all these men, Oswald succeeded to the kingship of Northumbria. Cadwallo attacked Oswald once he had dealt with the others, and he pursued him all the way to the wall that the Emperor Severus had once built to separate Britain and Scotland. Then he dispatched Penda, King of the Mercians, along with the greater part of his own army, to that place in order to engage Oswald in battle. But one night, while besieged by Penda in a place called Hevenfeld—which means "field of heaven"—Oswald set up a cross of the Lord.[1] He pointed it out to his troops so that, in the deepest part of the night, they all cried out: "Let us all bend our knees, and we shall together implore the one, true, almighty God to defend us from the haughty army of the British king and from its wicked commander, Penda. God knows that we have undertaken this just war for the safety of our people." They all did as Oswald had commanded. They marched against the enemy at daybreak and won the field that day as a reward for their great faith. When this turn of events was reported to Cadwallo, he burned with the bitter flame of wrath. Gathering his forces together, he set off in pursuit of King Oswald. Finally meeting him in battle at a place known as Burne, Penda rushed against Oswald and slew him.[2]

[200] Once Oswald had been killed, along with many of his soldiers, his brother Oswy succeeded him as king of the Northumbrians. This Oswy gave many gifts of gold and silver to Cadwallo, who now controlled all of Britain; in this way, he obtained peace and submitted himself to Cadwallo's authority. As soon as he had done this, his son Alfred and his brother's son Orwald rebelled against him. They were not able to hold out for long, however, and they soon fled to King Penda of the Mercians, begging him to muster an army and cross the Humber to deprive Oswy of his kingdom. Penda, however, fearing to break the peace that Cadwallo had established throughout the kingdom of Britain, refused to initiate an attack without leave unless he could somehow convince Cadwallo himself to march against King Oswy, or until Cadwallo granted him permission to fight Oswy with his own men. Then, on the solemn feast of Pentecost, when King Cadwallo wore the crown of Britain and celebrated the feast in London, attended by all the leaders of the Britons and by all the petty-kings of the Angles except for Oswy, Penda came to the king and asked him why only Oswy was not

---

[1]   Bede describes the Battle of Hefenfelth (634 C.E.) in his *Ecclesiastical History*, 3.2.
[2]   Geoffrey significantly alters Bede's account, wherein Oswald survives the Battle of Hevenfeld and is instead slain six years later—and not by Penda—at the Battle of Maserfelth in 642.

in attendance when all the other Saxon princes were there. When Cadwallo answered that Oswy's absence was due to illness, Penda mentioned that Oswy had sent for more Saxons to come from Germany so that he could wreak vengeance on them both for his brother Oswald's death. Then Penda added that Oswy had personally broken the peace of the realm, attacking his son Alfred and his brother's son Orwald and expelling them from Northumbria. Penda then requested formal permission either to slay Oswy or to drive him from the kingdom.

King Cadwallo gave great thought to this matter, and he summoned his household advisors, commanding them to consider whether to grant Penda's request. Tossing over many ideas, Margadud, the king of the Demetians, said: "My lord, since you have always intended to drive the entire race of the Angles beyond the confines of Britain, why do you now divert from your policy and suffer them to dwell among us in peace? Well now, at least allow them to carry out this internal discord amongst themselves. Perhaps, in destroying each other, they will thus be extirpated from our country. There's no reason to keep faith with one who has always laid snares for the one to whom he should be loyal. Ever since the Saxons first entered our land, they have repeatedly betrayed our people in a most treacherous way. So what faith do we owe them? Grant Penda permission to attack this Oswy at once so that a civil war will arise among the Saxons and, by letting them slay one another, we may be rid of them."

Moved by these words and by many other exhortations, Cadwallo gave Penda permission to fight with Oswy. Penda then organized an enormous army, crossed the Humber, and began to attack Oswy most fiercely, ravaging his lands. But Oswy, driven by the gravest necessity, finally promised Penda countless royal ornaments and so many other gifts that it was difficult to believe, if he would only stop ravaging his domains, lay aside the war he had begun, and go home. Penda did not heed these requests in the least, and so King Oswy then sought God's assistance, for he had by far the smaller army. Then they fought a battle near the banks of the river Wuuned. Penda and thirty of his commanders were slain there, and Oswy won the field.[1] On Penda's death, his son Wulfert succeeded to his kingdom, with the permission of King Cadwallo. He allied himself with Ebba and Edbert, the leaders of the Mercians, and set off to make war against Oswy. However, following Cadwallo's orders, he made peace with him instead.

---

[1]   Bede, 3.24, records Penda's death at the Battle of Winwæd in 655.

[201] After forty-eight years had passed, the most noble Cadwallo, king of the Britons, gave in to illness and old age, and departed from this life on the fifteenth of the month of December.[1] Preserving his body with balsam and fragrant herbs, the Britons placed it within a bronze statue that, by a feat of extraordinary skill, they had cast to his precise measurements. Then they placed this statue, which was strikingly beautiful, atop a bronze horse and set it up above the west gate of London as a sign of Cadwallo's great victory and as a terror to the Saxons.[2] But below the gates they built a church in honor of Saint Martin, where divine masses were sung for Cadwallo and for the others who die in the faith.

[202] Cadwallo's son Cadwallader (whom Bede calls Cadwallo the Younger) then took up the governance of the realm, and at first he reigned both bravely and peacefully. However, twelve years after taking the crown, a great sickness befell him and civil discord arose among the Britons. Cadwallader's mother was, in fact, the sister of King Penda, but her mother had been from a noble family of the Gewissei. The renowned King Cadwallo had wed her after arranging peace with her brother, and he sired Cadwallader upon her.[3]

[203] And so, as I had begun to say, the Britons were afflicted with a lamentable civil discord, and they destroyed the well-being of their country with their terrible divisiveness. Then yet another misfortune struck them: a dire and infamous famine afflicted them so badly that they were deprived of the support of any food at all; their only solace remained in the art of hunting. A deadly plague followed on the heels of this famine, striking down such a multitude of people in so short a space of time that the living were unable to bury the dead.[4] The wretched survivors gathered together in companies and fled from their homeland, seeking out

---

1   Geoffrey has given King Cadwallo an unhistorically long reign, thus extending the tenure of the British kings far into the seventh century. R. William Leckie discusses the significance of Geoffrey's deliberate alterations of the historical record in *The Passage of Dominion: Geoffrey of Monmouth and the Periodization of Insular History in the Twelfth Century* (Toronto: U of Toronto P, 1981).

2   The deposition of Cadwallo's body would seem to fulfill one of Merlin's prophecies in Book Seven: "The man who accomplishes these things will erect a bronze statue of a man, and for many years it will protect the gate of London upon its bronze horse."

3   Cadwallader appears in *The History of the Britons* (early ninth century) as *Catgualart*, a ruler over the Britons who died of the plague during the reign of King Oswy; the *Annales Cambriae* place the date of his death at 682. Cadwallader later appears in the Welsh prophetic tradition as a messiah figure who will extirpate the foreigners (Saxons) from British soil and restore native (Celtic) sovereignty over Britain. The Harleian genealogies record Cadwallader as a king of North Wales.

4   The *Annales Cambriae* place this plague in the year 682.

lands across the seas. Beneath the swollen sails of their ships, they lamented greatly, crying out: "You gave us up, O God, like we were sheep for the slaughter, and dispersed us among the heathens!" Even King Cadwallader himself, taking a wretched ship over to Armorica, added his voice to their lament, saying: "Woe unto us sinners for the many wicked deeds with which we did not hesitate to offend God while we believed we still had time to repent. Now, snatching us out of our native land, the vengeance of His might falls upon us whom neither the Romans nor the Scots nor Picts nor even the treasonous wiles of the Saxons were able to exterminate. In vain, however, have we recovered our homeland from them so many times, since it was not God's will that we would reign here for all time. He is the True Judge, and when He saw that we did not wish to refrain from our wickedness in the least and that no foreign people could dislodge us from our land, He directed his righteous indignation upon us fools, and now we desert our own homeland in droves. Come back, Romans! Come back, Scots and Picts! Come back, Huns and Saxons! Behold! Britain now lies open for you, for the wrath of God has emptied that which you could not empty. Your force has not expelled us, but rather the might of the King of Kings, Whom we have never ceased to offend." [204] When Cadwallader arrived upon the shores of Armorica, lamenting in this way, he made his way with all his host to King Alan, the grandson of King Solomon, who gave him an honorable welcome.

For eleven years, Britain was completely abandoned by all the Britons, except for those few who were spared from death in certain districts of Wales. The land was abhorred by the Britons, and even the Saxons who remained there during this trying period continued to die without any hope of relief. But when this terrible plague finally abated, the Saxons, preserving their ancient custom, sent word to their compatriots back in Germany that the island now was now emptied of its native people and would be easy to subdue if they came to dwell there. When this news was reported to them, that wicked folk gathered together a great host of men and women and landed in the province of Northumbria, and they took up residence in the deserted provinces of Alban and Cornwall. No one was there to prevent their settlement, except for the meager remnant of the Britons who had survived but had now withdrawn to the remote forests of Wales.

From that moment forth the power of the Britons in the isle of Britain came to a close and the Angles then began to rule. [205] After a little time, the Britons began to regain their strength, so Cadwallader turned his attention once more to his kingdom, which had now been cleansed of the plague. He went to Brittany to ask King Alan there for aid in restoring him to his former power. Cadwallader was determined on this course of action, but the voice of an Angel called to him just as the fleet was getting underway. It told him to abandon his plans: God did not want the Britons to reign in Britain any longer, not before the day that Merlin had foretold to Arthur should arrive. The Angel commanded him to go to Pope Sergius in Rome to do penance so that he might be numbered among the blessed. The Angel told him further that the British people would regain the island through their great faith in days to come after the predestined time had passed. And that day, moreover, would not come until the Britons could recover the holy relics that they had lost during the invasions of the pagans.

[206] When that blessed man heard the Angel's message, he went at once to King Alan and explained what had been revealed to him. Then Alan consulted various prophetical tomes concerned with the Eagle of Shaftesbury, as well as books of the verses of the Sibyl and of Merlin, to see whether Cadwallader's vision conformed to one of the recorded prophecies. Since he could discover no discrepancy, he believed Cadwallader's vision to be a divine dispensation. Cadwallader therefore acted on the advice that the Angel had given him and laid Britain aside. He directed his son Yvor and his nephew Yni to rule over the Britons who remained on the island, lest the descendants of that ancient race lose their freedom because of the foreign invasions. Then Cadwallader himself, putting aside the concerns of this world, journeyed to Rome on account of the Lord and the Eternal Kingdom, and he was confirmed in his faith by Pope Sergius.[1] There he was seized by an unexpected illness. On the first day of May in the year of our Lord 689, Cadwallader left behind the weakness of this flesh and entered the great hall of the Kingdom of Heaven.

[207] So Yvor and Yni gathered ships together and, summoning all the men that they could, sailed to the island. For sixty-nine years they fought with great ferocity against the Angles but with little success, for the abovementioned plague and famine, as well as their own penchant for civil war, had caused this once proud people to degenerate to such a degree that they could no longer fend off their enemies. Through their habitual barbarity, they were no longer called Britons but "Welsh,"

---

[1]   Bromwich, *Trioedd*, 299, surmises that Geoffrey has confused (deliberately or not) Cadwallader at this juncture with Cadwalla, a Saxon king of Wessex who died in 689 as a pilgrim in Rome.

a term derived either from their leader Gualo or from Queen Galaes or indeed from their own barbarity.[1] But the Saxons acted more wisely. They established peace and concord among themselves, and they tilled the fields and rebuilt the cities and towns. Casting aside the power of the Britons, they ruled all of Logres under their leader, Athelstan, who was the first to wear the royal crown.[2]

Having degenerated from the nobility they had enjoyed as Britons, the Welsh never again regained the kingship of the island. They instead foolishly persisted in their quarrels with the Saxons or among themselves and were hence constantly engaged in foreign wars and civil unrest.

[208] I leave it to my contemporary Caradoc of Llancarvan to record the kings who continued to rule in Wales, and to William of Malmesbury and Henry of Huntington to discuss the kings of the Saxons.[3] But I insist that they all be silent in regard to the kings of the Britons, since they do not have that book in the British tongue which Walter the Archdeacon of Oxford obtained from Wales. This same book, which deals so truthfully with the honor of the native princes, I have endeavored to translate into Latin as accurately as I possibly could.[4]

---

[1] The Anglo-Saxon word *wealh*, which is the ancestor of the modern term *Welsh*, meant "foreigner" or "slave"; hence Geoffrey's etymology is not far from the mark.

[2] King Athelstan of Wessex (reigned 924–40) was the grandson of King Alfred and was erroneously believed by various medieval writers to have been the first sovereign over all England.

[3] Caradoc of Llancarvan was the author of a twelfth-century life of Gildas. The Welsh *Chronicle of the Princes* (*Brut y Tywysogion*) had long been attributed to him, perhaps on Geoffrey's authority, but modern scholarship has proven that authorship impossible. The famed historian William of Malmesbury (1080–1142) was the author of *The Deeds of the Bishops of England* (*Gesta Pontificum Angliae*) and *The Deeds of the Kings of the English* (*Gesta Regum Angliae*). Henry of Huntington (1084–1155) was composing his own *History of the English* (*Historia Anglorum*) at the same time that Geoffrey was writing *The History of the Kings of Britain*.

[4] The final two paragraphs are present only in the Bern MS. There is no reason not to consider the paragraphs as authorial.

Appendix A: Major Historical Sources

1. From Gildas, *The Ruin of Britain* (*De Excidio Britanniae*)

[*The Ruin of Britain* by Gildas was one of Geoffrey of Monmouth's chief historical sources. From Gildas, Geoffrey culls his description of Britain at the beginning of *The History*, as well as much other material, including his account of the Roman withdrawal from Britain and his portrayal of several of King Arthur's successors. Gildas himself wrote in the first half of the sixth century. His primary goal in this tract is to inveigh against the Britons and their rulers for their habitual sins.]

In this epistle I lament far more than I denounce. But do not blame me if my style is lowly, for my intentions are pure. Let no one think that I scorn all men or esteem myself too highly, but understand that I bewail the loss of the common good and the accumulation of evils through grievous conflicts. I feel my country's hardships and am looking for ways to assuage them....

... The Isle of Britain lies at almost the very brink of the world, toward the west and northwest. When weighed in the divine scales that, we are told, hold the entire earth in balance, it stretches out from the southwest toward the North Pole. It is eight hundred miles long and two hundred miles wide, not counting the great promontories that enclose curving bays of the ocean. As I mentioned, it is protected by a vast and impassable circle of the sea on all sides except the south, where one can travel across the straits to Belgic Gaul. The mouths of the two noble rivers Thames and Severn extend like arms and improve the terrain, as do a number of other rivers, and many luxury items were once conveyed by ship upstream. Twenty-eight cities and numerous fortresses also adorned the island, and they were suitably equipped with walls, gates, houses, and watchtowers whose pointed spires jutted up menacingly from the solid walls. Like a bride bejeweled with various fineries, Britain is ornamented with wide expanses of fields and rolling hills in a lovely landscape that is exceedingly good for the cultivation of crops. Mingled with these are mountain pastures that are perfectly fit for the grazing of livestock. Flowers of many different colors grace the ground wherever one goes, presenting the beholder with lovely vistas. The land is watered by clear springs whose steady waters wash snow-white pebbles into the bright, gently murmuring rivers that meander down with the promise

of delicious rest to those who lie on their banks, and into lakes that over-
flow with the cool torrent of fresh water.

Since the days of its earliest settlement, Britain has been over-proud
in mind and spirit, rebellious against God, against its own citizens, and
even occasionally against kings and peoples from across the sea. What
human deeds, either now or in the future, can be more depraved and
wicked than to deny the proper fear to God or the proper charity to
one's good countrymen? What could be more depraved and wicked
than to deny the obligation one has to those in a higher position,
provided that there is no harm done to the Faith? What could be more
depraved and wicked than to break faith with both God and man, or
to slough one's fear of both heaven and earth and allow oneself to be
ruled by one's personal desires?

I will pass over the ancient errors that were common to all peoples
before they were absolved by the advent of Christ in the flesh, nor shall
I recount the devilish portents infesting the land, whose number almost
surpasses that of the plagues of Egypt, some deformed traces of which
can still be seen unchanged in men's gloomy faces, both within the
abandoned city walls and beyond them. Nor shall I enumerate all the
mountains and hills and rivers, which are now put to such decent use
but which were once so treacherous when blind pagans gathered in
those places to worship. I shall therefore be silent about those monstrous
tyrants of ancient times, whose deeds were so widely sung abroad that
Porphyry—that mad dog of the East and enemy of the Church—
pompously added these words to his ravings: "Britain is a land abun-
dant in tyrants." I shall instead attempt to set down those things that
have occurred in Britain since the days of the Roman emperors,
describing the evils that Britain has inflicted upon others, even those in
far-flung lands. I have had to rely for the most part not on the anti-
quarian writings of native historians, which—if they ever even
existed—have long since been burnt by the flames of foes or carried
off in the ships of exiles, but upon accounts from abroad, though even
these have too many gaps to be useful sources....

... Christ's teachings were received by the native Britons only half-
heartedly at first, though they more or less remained unaltered there until
the nine-year-long persecution under the tyrannical Diocletian.
Churches were then torn down all over the world, and all the Holy
Scriptures were burnt in the town squares whenever they were found,
and the chosen priests of the Lord's flock were slaughtered along with
their innocent sheep so that, if it could be done, no trace of the Christian

religion was left in many provinces. The history of the Church relates what escapes occurred in those days, what executions, what doom for apostates, what crowns of glorious martyrdom, what angry persecutors there were, as well as what patience existed among the saints, who so eagerly and in such numbers turned their backs to the shadows of this world and headed for the wondrous kingdom of Heaven, as if the entire Church were taking its appointed seat.

Wishing that all men be saved, God turned His mercy upon us, for He seeks out the sinful just as much as He summons those who think themselves just. During this same persecution, I believe, God granted us a free gift, lest Britain remain benighted in the thick mist of black night: He lit for us the bright lanterns of the holy martyrs. Their graves and the sites of their martyrdoms would have inspired great love in the hearts of those who visited them, but many of these places have been destroyed by the greedy looting of barbarians and the many wicked acts of the British people. I speak especially of St. Alban of Verulamium, of Aaron and Julius of Caerleon, and of the many others of both sexes who in various places exerted their utmost valor in the army of Christ.

Alban, the foremost of these saints, imitated Christ, Who gave His life for His sheep. Out of pure love, this Alban harbored a certain confessor who had been followed by persecutors and was about to be arrested. First he hid the man in his house and then he exchanged clothes with him, willingly exposing himself to the pursuers while in his spiritual brother's garb. From the moment of his holy confession until the spilling of his blood by the pagans, who displayed the Roman banners most horribly, Alban was pleasing to God, and God adorned his suffering with a miraculous sign. Just as when the Ark of the Israelite Covenant once stood for a while amid the pebbles on a dry path in the middle of the River Jordan, so did Alban's ardent prayers open up a dry road across the bed of the River Thames while one thousand men walked in it, the swelling waters rising like mountains on either side of them. And when his first torturer beheld this miracle, he turned from a wolf into a lamb, causing him too to thirst for and receive the triumphal palm of martyrdom.

The other saints I mentioned were tormented in a variety of other ways, and the trophies of their glorious deaths were soon affixed to the splendid gates of Jerusalem. Those who survived took refuge in the forests and deserts and hidden caves, hoping that God, their just Ruler, would one day mete out severe judgment on their tormentors and provide them with protection in the meantime.

After ten years of such storms, the wicked decrees began to slacken and their perpetrators were overtaken by death, while all of Christ's faithful joyously welcomed the serene light of Heaven's breeze as if after a long and stormy winter night. They rebuilt the churches, which had been destroyed to the very last one; they founded, built, and completed chapels to the holy martyrs, proclaiming them everywhere like the banners of victory. They also celebrated the high feast days, carrying out the holy rites with pure hearts and mouths. All the sons of the Church rejoiced as if they were nestled in their mother's bosom.

This harmony between the head and members of Christ's Church remained until the Arian treachery arrived here from across the sea, spitting venom like a vicious serpent upon us, making our brethren who were living together be lethally separated. Then, as if there were a paved road across the ocean, there came to us every type of deadly beast, their horrible mouths pulsing with pestilent heresies, and their fangs inflicting deadly bites upon a country that always longed to hear something new and that could settle on nothing for long.

Thus it came about that the ever-spreading thickets of tyranny were about to burst forth into an enormous forest, and the island remained Roman in name alone, but not by law or custom. Indeed, it was even then that the land cast out a seedling of its own bitter planting, sending Maximus over to Gaul accompanied by a great cohort of accomplices and bearing the imperial insignia—which he was not worthy to possess, having no legal authority and having been raised to the emperorship by a rebellious military, as befits a tyrant. Relying on clever stratagems rather than valor, Maximus first annexed the nearby towns and provinces to his own criminal kingdom and turned them against Rome through lies and perjuries. Then he spread one wing over Spain and another over Italy and, establishing the capital of his illegitimate empire at Trier, he vented such fury upon his masters—the two legal emperors—that he forced them to flee, one from Rome, the other from a life of great piety. Though emboldened by these beastly deeds, Maximus— he who had overthrown the crowned heads of the entire world—soon had his own wicked head lopped off in the city of Aquileia.

By then, Britain had been stripped of all her armed men, all her military forces, all her illustrious commanders, and all her brave youths, for they had all departed with Maximus, never to return. Now that Britain was completely bereft of any who were skilled in the arts of war, the island suffered and was paralyzed for many years, trodden down violently by two savage peoples from across the sea: the Scots from the northwest and the Picts from the north.

Because of their dire conditions in the face of these attacks, the Britons sent messengers to Rome with letters, requesting military aid in avenging their lamentable situation. They thus reconfirmed their complete subjugation and loyalty to the Roman Empire, as long as it could defend them from their enemies. A legion was quickly dispatched, unmindful of Britain's previous calamities but armed heavily enough. It crossed the ocean by ship to our country and gave battle to those grievous foes, destroying a great host of them and driving the rest beyond our borders. The legion thus saved the citizens of Britain from a brutal invasion and almost certain captivity. The Romans then recommended that the Britons construct a wall stretching from sea to sea across the island which, when fully manned, would frighten away their enemies and protect their people. However, because the wall was erected by an aimless and unreasonable rabble, it was made of sod rather than of stone, and so it proved useless in the end.

As soon as the Roman legion returned home, joyous in their great triumph, their same old enemies, the Ambrones, returned. They were like ravenous wolves, leaping with their dry maws into the sheepfold while the shepherd is away. Thus they returned, conveyed by their oars (which were as fast as wings), by the arms of their oarsmen, and by the wind in their sails. They burst through the frontiers, destroying everything they came across, cutting it down like so much corn in the field.

Once more messengers were dispatched. Just like fearful chicks taking shelter under the wings of their steadfast parents, it is said that it was with torn clothes and dust covering their heads that they pleaded with the Romans for help, lest their wretched homeland be destroyed or the Roman name, which even now echoed through their ears as a mere word, be further reviled by the scorn of an alien people. The Romans were as moved as was humanly possible upon hearing the tale of this great tragedy. Like eagles, they hastened the flight of their cavalry across the land and the course of their navy across the sea, and they buried their fearsome talons—the points of their swords—into their heedless foes, and their enemies fell like the leaves in autumn in this slaughter. The Roman forces were like a tempest-swollen mountain torrent, bursting thunderously from its accustomed course. It foams forth splendidly, with furrowed back and fierce brow, with waves as tall, they say, as the storm clouds that darken one's eyes and dazzle them with lines of shimmering lightning, its surge sweeping aside everything in its path. The battalions of our noble, worthy allies thus almost instantly drove those enemies across the sea, if they were able to escape at all, though year after year they had greedily been shipping their plunder across the waters with no one to stand in their way.

The Romans then announced that they would by no means be troubled any longer with such costly expeditions and that it was beneath them to waste their military forces on land and sea dealing with unruly pirates. Instead, they said, the Britons should get into the habit of relying upon their own forces; they should manfully defend their own lands, riches, women, children, and, above all, their freedom and way of life. Their enemies were no stronger than the Britons themselves, unless they allowed themselves to become idle and sluggish. The Britons should by no means allow themselves to be conquered and cast into chains without a fight. Instead, their hands should be prepared to kill, armed with shields, swords, and spears. Having made these arguments, the Romans hoped to leave behind something that would prove of further use to the people, and so they constructed a wall quite unlike the first one. This new wall was built in the usual Roman manner, drawing upon both public and private funding and the labor of the inhabitants, and it ran from sea to sea, linking together the cities that had been situated there out of fear of the enemy. They then gave the timid Britons some good advice and left plans for implementing their defenses, recommending that the Britons build a series of watchtowers at fixed intervals all along the southern coast of the ocean, for that is where the Britons kept their merchant fleet and therefore where they should most fear an attack from the bestial barbarians. The Romans then bade them farewell, never to return.[1]

As soon as the Romans had sailed home, filthy bands of Scots and Picts, like the black hordes of worms that creep out of the narrow cracks of rocks when the sun is high in the heavens and the air grows warm, emerged from the coracles that had conveyed them across the valley of Tethys.[2] Although different in many of their customs, these two peoples shared a thirst for bloodshed, and they were both more likely to cover their faces with hair than to cover their genitals or nearby regions with clothing. Now, having learned of the departure of our fellow debtors and the unlikelihood of their ever returning, they acted more boldly than usual and captured from the natives the entire northern region of the land down to the wall. A troop of men was garrisoned there to

---

[1]   Many of the lines in this paragraph were reproduced almost verbatim by Geoffrey of Monmouth into Book 6 of *The History*.

[2]   I.e., the sea.

oppose them, but they proved too lazy to fight and unable to flee. With their hearts full of fear, the fools sat there day and night, just withering away at their useless posts. In the meantime, the barbed weapons of their naked foes never ceased to strike, and the wretched Britons were shot from the walls and dashed to pieces one by one. Such an untimely demise actually proved a benefit for those who were slain in that way, for by this speedy death they avoided the terrible pains that awaited their brothers and children.

What more can I say? Once their cities and the high wall were abandoned, all the expected exiles swiftly followed, as did desperate dispersions, and persecution by the enemy, and the cruelest slaughter. The miserable Britons were ripped apart by their foes like sheep by a butcher. And they began to live like beasts of the field, for they took to robbing one another, there being only a scanty amount of food to feed that miserable people. All the onslaughts from these foreigners were multiplied by domestic strife, since, due to these frequent disruptions, all the land lacked any food excepting what comforts the art of the hunt brought.

Once again, the miserable remnant sent a letter, this time to Agitius, a powerful man among the Romans, imploring him thus: "O Agitius, thrice consul, hear the groans of the Britons!" And after saying a few more words, they added: "The sea drives us toward the barbarians and the barbarians drive us into the sea. Two different modes of death await us: we will either be drowned or get our throats cut." But they received no help.

Meanwhile, a dire and notorious plague struck at the feeble and wandering Britons, many of whom, utterly defeated, were now compelled to turn over many things into the hands of their cruel oppressors merely in order to obtain a little bit of food to keep themselves alive. Some of the others fared differently: they kept up the fight, attacking from mountains, caves, meadows and thorny brambles. And then, trusting not in man but in God, they at last slaughtered the men who had been plundering their land for many years. As Philo says: "It is necessary to rely on God when the aid of men fails." Thus the brazenness of our enemies subsided for a brief time, though our own wickedness did not; the enemies retreated from the people, but the people did not retreat from their sins.

It was ever the habit of this people, as it still is today, that they were weak at repelling their armed enemies but strong at waging civil wars and carrying the burden of sins; slow, I say, to follow the banners of peace and truth, but swift to turn to wickedness and falsehood. And so the shameless, lazy Scots might go home, but it was not long before they would return. The Picts also returned to the utmost region of the island for the first time then, and there they remained, though they too still made the occasional plundering raids. The desperate Britons' cruel scars began to heal during this cessation of hostilities, but a new famine—far more deadly than the first—was quietly spreading. Now that the invasions had ceased, the island overflowed with such an abundance of goods that no previous age had ever seen the like, and with these things Luxury increased. Its seed soon spread, so that of those times the saying was aptly applied: "It is actually reported that there is fornication here such as is unknown even among the pagans."[1]

It was not the vice of fornication alone that was spreading, but all the other vices to which human nature is prone, especially the one that proves the overthrow of every good state even today: hatred of the truth and of those who tell the truth, love of falsehoods and of falsifiers, adoration of wickedness instead of goodness, desire for the darkness rather than the sun, and the welcoming of Satan as the angel of light. Kings were anointed not by God but because they were crueler than all the rest. They were, in turn, quickly murdered by their anointers with no consideration for the truth, and crueler men still were chosen in their stead. In fact, if any one of them appeared gentler or more inclined to the truth in any small way, it was as if he were overturning all things in Britain, and everyone heedlessly cast their hatred and weapons at him. And the things that were pleasing and displeasing to God hung evenly in the balance, though perhaps those displeasing to Him fared somewhat better. Thus could the words of the prophet, with which he addresses his own slothful people, be deservingly applied to our land: "O sons who deal corruptly, you have forsaken God and have provoked the Holy One of Israel. Why will you still be smitten that you continue to rebel? The whole head is sick, and the whole heart faint. From the sole of the foot even to the head, there is no soundness in it."[2] And so they acted in all matters in a way that was contrary to their salvation, as though the True Doctor of us all had provided the world with no remedy. And not only laymen but also most of the flock of the Lord and its shepherds, who were supposed to serve as an example to all the people, were lying about in a drunken stupor as if they were sodden with wine. They were so consumed by the kindling of hostility, by the strife of quarrels, by the greedy claws of envy, and by their heedless judgment of good and evil that, as is still true today, they

---

[1] A paraphrase of 1 Cor. 5.1.
[2] A paraphrase of Isaiah 1.4–6.

seemed to hold their princes in contempt, and they were led astray by their follies and wandered in the trackless wild.

In the meantime, God desired to purge His family and to erase the stain of these evils with the mere mention of tribulations. Then the pricked ears of all the folk were filled with the wingèd rumor of the rapid approach of their old enemies, who were now bent, as usual, on the utter devastation and resettlement of the entire island from end to end. But they made nothing of this knowledge and instead, like foolish beasts of burden, they held tight onto the bit of reason with clenched teeth, as the saying goes, forsaking the narrow road to salvation and going headlong down the path that leads through many vices to death.

And so, as Solomon says, "A stubborn servant is not mended by words alone,"[1] and a fool may be flogged and not feel a thing. For then a terrible plague struck brutally at this foolish people. Within a brief time it felled without even a sword such a multitude of people that the living were unable to bury the dead. But even this did not amend them, and the words of the prophet Isaiah were fulfilled yet again: "And God has invoked lamentation and baldness and the donning of the sackcloth. Behold the slaying of the calves and the slaughter of the rams, behold the eating and drinking and the people saying: 'let us eat and drink today, for tomorrow we die.'"[2] Indeed, the time drew near in which all of their iniquities would be complete, as those of the Amorites once were. Then they held a council to decide what would be the best and most helpful way of driving back the cruel and constant invasions and looting by that abovementioned people.

But then all the members of the council, along with their proud tyrant, were blinded: thinking they were devising a means of defense, they instead devised the destruction of the land. Bringing wolves into a sheepfold, they invited to the island those fierce Saxons, whose name should not be said aloud and who were despised by God and man alike, in order to drive away the invaders from the north. Nothing more ruinous or woeful has ever befallen. How deep was the darkness that clouded their senses! How desperate and cruel was the dullness of their minds! For they willingly invited the people whom they feared more than death even when far away to abide under their own roof. Thus, as it is said: "The princes of Zoan are foolish, giving foolish advice to the Pharaoh."[3]

---

1 See Prov. 29.19.
2 See Isaiah 22.12–13.
3 See Isaiah 19.11.

At that point in time a pack of cubs issued forth from the den of the barbarian lioness, arriving in three longships, or *cyulas* as they are called in their tongue. They sailed there on a favorable wind, and favorable too were their omens and augurs, which had clearly foretold that they would occupy the land toward which they pointed their prows for three hundred years, half of which time—that is, one hundred fifty years—they would frequently lay the country waste. At the bidding of that unfortunate tyrant, they first dug their fearsome claws into the eastern part of the island, acting as if they were fighting for our homeland but in reality fighting against it. When their mother country realized that her first brood had prospered, she sent an even greater contingent of guard dogs, which came by ship and immediately joined up with the other false mercenaries. From this the seed of iniquity, the root of bitterness, the pestilent plant that our deeds merited began to sprout ferocious vines and shoots throughout our soil. Once these barbarians had been introduced to the island, they presented themselves, under false pretences, as soldiers who were willing to undergo great tribulation for their hosts, and they asked to be given provisions. Once the supplies were distributed, the dog's maw was shut for a long time, so to speak. Then, embellishing certain specific episodes, they made a new complaint that the remuneration they were given was not enough, and that if they were not granted a greater salary they would break their pact and devastate the entire island. They put their threats into effect without delay.

Because of the Britons' previous sins, the fire of just vengeance swept through the entire island from sea to sea, kindled by those unholy easterners, and it ravaged the cities and the fields and farmlands; once lit, it did not die down until it had burnt almost the entire surface of the island and its terrible red flames licked the western ocean. With this invasion, as with the Assyrian attack against Judea of old, was fulfilled for us what the prophet once said in lamentation: "They have burnt Your sanctuary to the ground, and they have polluted the tabernacle of Your Name," and also "God, a race of gentiles has come into Your inheritance; it has desecrated Your holy temple," and so on.[1] And so all the towns were destroyed by battering rams. All their citizens—the church leaders, priests, and people too—were cut down everywhere by swords and by the crackling flames. And it was a wonder to see in the middle of the town squares the keystones of towers and walls that had been thrown down, alongside the holy altars and fragments of corpses which were

---

[1]   Psalms 73.7; Psalms 78.1.

covered, it seemed, with a purple crust of dried blood—all these things appeared as if they had been mixed together in some horrific wine press. There were no burials either, except beneath caved-in buildings or within the bellies of birds or beasts; the only reverence left was to the souls of the pious, if there were many of those found, who were conveyed by the blessed angels up to high heaven. Then the vineyard that had once been good degenerated into bitterness, and, as the prophet says, there was hardly ever to be seen a cluster of grapes or an ear of corn on the backs of the vintners and reapers.[1]

Some of the wretched survivors were captured up in the hills and slain *en masse*. Many of the others succumbed to their hunger and gave themselves up, offering their hands to their enemies in eternal servitude if they were not slain on the spot, which was, in reality, the greatest of gifts. Others headed across the sea, and, with the wind filling their sails, they sang out great lamentations instead of sea chanties, calling: "You have given us like sheep for the slaughter, and you have scattered us among the nations."[2] Others still anxiously remained in their homeland, dwelling with constant fear in the deep and dangerous fastnesses of the mountains and hills, or in the darkest forests, or by the coasts of the sea.

After a space of time had passed and the cruel marauders had returned home, God granted a new vigor to the survivors. Many miserable people fled to them from all about, as eagerly as honey-bees cluster to the hive when a storm draws near, begging with all their hearts—"burdening heaven with their prayers," as it were—that they not be completely annihilated. Their leader was Ambrosius Aurelius, a gentleman who, perhaps alone of the Roman people, had weathered the onslaught of the recent storms. His family, who had been killed in these troubles, had certainly worn the purple. In our own times, his descendants have greatly degenerated from their ancestor's goodness. Under Ambrosius Aurelius, our people revived its strength and provoked the victors to battle. By the will of the Lord, triumph was theirs.

In those days, the citizens of Britain sometimes emerged victorious, and sometimes their enemies won the day. In this way the Lord tested that people, as is His wont, as if it was a present-day Israel, in order to determine whether it loved Him or not. This state of affairs continued until the year of the siege of Mount Badon, which was the latest (though not the least) of the defeats of those churls. That battle took

---

[1] See Obadiah 5.
[2] Psalms 44.12.

place during the year of my birth, and I reckon that to be forty-four years and one month ago.

But even today the cities of our land are not as populated as they once were but languish in ruin and disorder, because, though foreign invasions have ceased, civil wars have not. Yet the memory of the hopeless downfall of the island and its unexpected revival has lingered in the minds of those who lived to witness both of these miracles. It was for this reason that kings, public and private citizens, priests, and clergy, all clung to their proper positions. But the generation that succeeds them as they die off remembers nothing of that time and has known only the present state of peace, and hence all the guidelines of truth and justice have been shaken off and cast aside so that barely a trace or memory remains among the orders I have mentioned, except among a few—a very few indeed. A great multitude is lost, and people rush headlong into Hell each day. There are so few now remaining that Holy Mother Church hardly notices them, though they lie in Her bosom, the only true sons She has. It is by these men that we are sustained in our infirmity, and it is by their holy prayers (the pillars and posts of salvation) that we are kept from near collapse. Let no man think that I calumniate their noble lives, which are admired by all and beloved by God, if I speak freely and, indeed, mournfully of those who serve their own bellies or even the devil instead of Christ, Who is the Ever-Blessed God, for I am not so much debating as lamenting. Indeed, why should their compatriots conceal what neighboring countries not only already know about but condemn?

[Source: Michael Winterbottom, ed., *The Ruin of Britain and Other Works* (London: Phillimore, 1978), 87–99. Translation by Michael Faletra.]

2. From Pseudo-Nennius, *The History of the Britons* (*Historia Brittonum*)

[The ninth-century *History of the Britons* was long attributed to the Welshman Nennius, though scholars now consider this apocryphal. This pseudo-Nennius seems to have been doing recovery work, wanting to get the facts and stories that he knew on the historical record before his source materials, whether oral or written, were lost forever. The result is a text that lacks the rhetorical polish of many other medieval historians (including Geoffrey) and frequently offers more than one account or version of an event. Pseudo-Nennius should not be derided for this, however, for he has preserved many traditions that would have otherwise been lost and he makes an attempt to organize his disparate sources. Geoffrey of Monmouth relies heavily on *The History of the Britons*, especially when describing the founding of Britain by Brutus and the stories of Vortigern and the prophet Merlin ("Ambrosius" in Nennius), though Geoffrey's general practice is to expand the Nennian material greatly.]

§ *The Founding of Britain*

Should anyone desire to know when this island was first settled after Noah's Flood, I have discovered two conflicting accounts.

This is what is written in the annals of the Romans. After the Trojan War, Aeneas came to Italy with his son Ascanius. Defeating Turnus, he took to wife Lavinia, the daughter of Latinus, son of Faunus, son of Saturn. After the death of Latinus, Aeneas inherited the kingdom of the Romans, or Latins. Aeneas constructed the town of Alba, and, after bringing his wife there, he had with her a son whose name was Silvius. Silvius also took a wife. When she became pregnant, it was reported to Aeneas that his daughter-in-law was pregnant, whereupon he sent word to his son Ascanius to have a wizard examine the woman to ascertain whether the child in her womb was male or female. A wizard then examined her and returned. Because of the prediction that he made, this wizard was killed by Ascanius, for he had declared that the woman carried in her womb a boy-child who would be a child of death, for he would kill his own father and mother and be hateful to all men. And so it came to pass: the woman died in childbirth, and the boy was raised and given the name Britto. After some time had passed, the rest of the wizard's prediction came true: while this Britto was out playing with some friends, he killed his father with an arrow, not intentionally but by accident. And so he was exiled from Italy, and he came to the isles of the Tyrrhenian Sea but was cast out by the Greeks there because of the slaying of Turnus, whom Aeneas had killed. And so Britto came to Gaul, where he founded the city of Tours, naming it after Turnus. Afterwards he came to this island, which is named after him—that is, Britain—and he populated it with his kindred and dwelt there. Thus has Britain been inhabited from that very day until the present....

§ *Late Roman Britain*

... Constantine, the son of Constans the Great, was the fifth Roman emperor in Britain. He died there and his tomb can still be found not far from the city called Caer Segeint, as the letters carved upon the tombstone clearly indicate. He sowed three seeds—of gold, silver, and bronze—into the foundations of the aforementioned city, so that no one would ever be poor there, and the city's other name is Minmanton.

The Emperor Maximus was the sixth to reign in Britain. The consuls came into existence in his day, and the rulers were no longer called Caesars. Saint Martin also flourished at this time in holy deeds and signs, and he conversed with Maximus.

The seventh Emperor to reign in Britain was Maximianus. He led the entire military might of the Britons out of Britain, and he slew Gratianus, the king of the Romans, seizing the imperial power over all of Europe. Not wanting to send the troops that had come with him back to Britain to return to their wives and children and possessions, he granted to them great tracts of land between the lake atop Mount Jove down to the city which is called *Cant Guic* (Quentovic) and all the way over to the Western Hill, that is, *Cruc Ochidient*. It was these Britons who came over the sea on this expedition with Maximianus who are called Armorican Britons, and, not wanting to go home, they razed the western parts of Gaul to the very ground. Giving no quarter to those who piss against the wall, the British soldiers took their wives and daughters in marriage and cut out all the women's tongues so that their offspring would never learn their mother tongue. It is for this reason that we call them *Letewicion*—"the half-dumb"—in our language, for their speech is so befuddled. They are the Armorican Britons, and they never came back here. It is because of this that Britain has been occupied by foreign invaders and its native citizens driven out until God lends His aid.

§ *The Advent of the Saxons*

After the war between the Britons and Romans, in which the leaders on both sides were killed and the tyrant Maximus himself was slain, the power of the Romans passed away, and the Britons lived in fear for forty years. Vortigern was then ruling over Britain, and while he reigned he worried greatly about the Picts and Scots, or about a new invasion by the Romans, not to mention his fear of Ambrosius.[1]

At this very time, three Saxon ships that had been exiled from

---

[1] The figure of Ambrosius is awkward here, for pseudo-Nennius has not mentioned this figure before. A general by the name of Ambrosius Aurelianus was mentioned in passing by Gildas (see above), and it is perhaps he to whom pseudo-Nennius refers.

Germany landed in Britain. In these ships were the two brothers Horsa and Hengist. They were the sons of Wihtgils, son of Witta, son of Wehta, son of Woden, son of Frealaf, son of Fredulf, son of Finn, son of Fodebald, son of Geta, who was, they assert, the son of God; not the son of the God of Gods and Lord of Hosts, amen, but the son of one of the idols they worshipped.[1] Vortigern gave them a warm welcome and placed into their keeping the island known in their tongue as Thanet, but as *Ruoihm* in the British tongue.[2]

Gratianus was reigning as emperor for the second time, with Equitius as his co-emperor, when Vortigern welcomed the Saxons. This was 347 years after the Passion of Christ....

... And so it came to pass, after the Saxons were established on the isle of Thanet, that King Vortigern promised to provide them with a constant supply of food and clothing. The Saxons were pleased by this and promised to fight Vortigern's enemies bravely. However, as the numbers of these barbarians increased, the Britons were unable to keep feeding them. When the Saxons asked for the food and clothing that they had been promised, the Britons answered: "We cannot give you any more food or clothing because your numbers have multiplied too much. You should depart, since we no longer require your aid." On hearing this, the Saxons consulted with their chieftains about whether they should break the peace.

Hengist, however, was an intelligent man, clever and astute. Sizing up Vortigern's weakness and the lack of military experience among the British people, he said to the king: "We are but few; if you wish, we could send word to our homeland and invite warriors from among the many warriors there, so that there will be a greater number of us here to fight for you and your people." King Vortigern agreed that they should do so. The Saxons then sent word, and their messengers sailed across Tethys's vale,[3] and they returned with sixteen ships, each filled with chosen warriors; in one of the ships there also came Hengist's daughter, a lovely girl with a truly beautiful face. After the Saxon ships had arrived, Hengist threw a feast for Vortigern. The king's soldiers were there, along with his interpreter, whose name was Ceretic. Hengist commanded his daughter to serve the wine and spirits, and they all got far too drunk. While they were drinking, Satan entered Vortigern's heart, and he desired

---

[1] Many Anglo-Saxon genealogies traced the royal lineage back to the god Woden.
[2] Thanet is a small island off the southern coast of Britain.
[3] I.e., the sea.

the girl and asked her father for her hand through his interpreter, saying "Ask of me anything you desire, even half of my kingdom." Hengist then took counsel with the elders of his kindred, who had come with him from the isle of Angul, asking them what they should ask from the king in exchange for the girl. They were all of a single mind that they should ask Vortigern for the region that in their tongue is called *Canturguoralen* and in our tongue Kent. And Vortigern gave it to them, despite the fact that Gurangon was then the ruler of Kent; he did not even know that his realm was being handed over to pagans and that he himself would soon fall under their dominion. And so the girl was given to Vortigern, and he slept with her and loved her dearly.

Then Hengist said to Vortigern: "I am your father now and will be your counselor. Do not ever cast my advice away lightly, for you need not now fear being conquered by any man's army, for my people are strong indeed. I shall invite my son and his younger brothers. They are all doughty warriors and will fight against the Scots, and you should give them possessions in the north near the Roman Wall." The king agreed that they be invited, and Octa and Ebissa soon arrived with forty ships. They sailed right past the Picts and laid waste to the Orkneys. Then they headed south and attacked many lands beyond the Frenessican Sea right down to the borders of the country of the Picts. Hengist, in the meantime, continued to invite a few shiploads of Saxons at a time until finally the islands back in Germany from which they originated were left without any inhabitants at all. And while that people increased in both strength and numbers, they settled in the city of Canterbury.

Then, adding to his list of evils, Vortigern took his own daughter to wife and he begat a son upon her. And when this was made known to St. Germanus, he came with all the British clergy to confront Vortigern. While this great synod of clerics and laymen was gathered in single council, the king instructed his daughter to come to the assembly, set the boy upon St. Germanus's lap and then say that he is the child's father. The woman did as she was told. Germanus, however, received the boy warmly and said: "I will be a father to you and I will never dismiss you unless a razor and scissors and comb are given to me and you are able to give them in turn to your father in the flesh." The boy obeyed him, and he went over to Vortigern, his grandfather and father in the flesh, and said: "You are my father. You must shave my head and the hair of my head." Vortigern was silent, and said nothing, and did not wish to respond to the boy. Instead, he grew furious, and fled from the face of St. Germanus, and he was cursed and condemned by the saint and the entire British synod.

After this, King Vortigern summoned his wizards in order to ask them what he should do. They told him: "Go to the farthest reaches of your realm, and seek out a fortified place you can defend, for the people that you invited into your kingdom grow jealous of you and will attempt to slay you through treachery, and will overrun the lands you love and overwhelm all your people after your death." Then the king set out with his wizards to find such a fortress. They journeyed through many lands and many provinces and found nothing at all until they came at last to the country that is called Gwynedd. There, while passing through the vicinity of Mount Eryri, which is called Snowdon in English, he found a place up in the mountains that would be suitable for the building of a fortress. And the wizards told Vortigern: "Build a stronghold in this place, for it will always be safe from barbarous peoples." So Vortigern summoned stonecutters and other artisans, and he procured wood and stone for the construction. Once these building materials were gathered together, however, they all disappeared in the course of a single night. Three times did Vortigern command that these materials be gathered, but the materials were unable to be found anywhere. Then the king summoned his wizards, and he demanded them to explain what was the cause of this evil that was befalling them. They answered: "Unless you find a boy without a father and slay him and sprinkle the fortress with his blood, this fortress will never be built in all eternity."

Vortigern took the advice of his wizards and dispatched messengers all throughout Britain to find a child with no father. Searching through the many regions and provinces of the realm, they eventually came to the Field of Elleti, which is in the region called Glywyssing.[1] There were boys playing ball there. Suddenly two of the boys began to quarrel, and the one taunted the other: "You're no good, you fatherless bastard!" Then the messengers interrogated the boys about this other boy, and they sought out his mother to see whether he had any father. She denied this and told them: "I do not know how I conceived a child in my womb, since I know that I have never been with a single man." Then she swore to them that the boy had no father. They brought the boy with them and presented him to King Vortigern.[2]

---

[1]   This region lies in the southern part of Wales.

[2]   The boy without a father corresponds to the figure of Merlin in later legends. Unlike Geoffrey of Monmouth, pseudo-Nennius does not conflate the boy Ambrosius with the semi-historical sixth-century Welsh bard Myrddin.

On the following day, the king's men gathered together to put the boy to death. And the boy said to the king: "Why have your men brought me to you?" The king replied: "So that you can be killed and your blood sprinkled around this fortress so that its construction can be completed." The boy then said to the king: "Who told you this?" The king answered: "My wizards told me." And the boy said: "Have them brought to me." The wizards were summoned, and the boy said to them: "Who revealed to you that this fortress should be sprinkled with my blood or that it will never be built without my blood being scattered upon it? Who said this thing about me that you think you know so well?" The boy spoke again: "In a moment, O king, I shall elucidate the truth of this entire affair to your satisfaction. But first allow me to question your wizards. What is underneath the foundations of this place? It pleases me to show you what lies beneath." And they replied: "We do not know." And he said: "I will explain: there is a pool beneath the foundation. Dig, and you shall find it." They went and dug and the foundation caved in. Then the boy said to the wizards: "Explain to me what lies within that pool." The wizards were silent and could reveal nothing to him. But the boy declared: "I shall reveal it to you: you will find two vessels within the pool." They looked and saw that it was so. And then the boy said to the wizards: "What do these vessels contain?" The wizards were again silent and could reveal nothing to him. The boy said: "There is a cloth within each of these vessels. Break them open and you will discover that this is so." The king commanded that the vessels be split open, and there were indeed cloths folded within them, just as the boy had predicted. And once more the boy questioned the wizards: "What is enclosed within each cloth? Tell me now." The wizards could explain nothing at all. And the boy proclaimed: "There are two worms within the cloths, a red one and a white one. Unfold the cloths." The cloths were spread out and the two worms were indeed there. And the boy said: "Now wait and see what the worms do." The worms began to push each other away; the one pressed its shoulders against the other until it was confined to one half of the cloth.[1] They did this three times. Each time the red worm seemed weaker and weaker, but the last time it proved stronger than the white worm and pushed it beyond the edge of the cloth; the one chased the other across the pool and the cloth disappeared. Then the boy said to the

---

[1] It is unclear from the original Latin text whether the "worms" described here refer to dragons, as later tradition would have it, or to actual worms, which is problematic because, being invertebrates, worms do not have shoulders.

wizards: "What is the meaning of this wondrous sign revealed within the cloth?" And they said: "We do not know."

Then the boy said: "Yet this mystery is revealed to me, and I will expound it for you. The cloth is a symbol for your kingdom; the two worms are two dragons.[1] The red worm is your dragon and the pool represents the world. But the white worm is the dragon of that people who have overrun the folk and regions of Britain, and they shall possess it from sea to sea, but afterwards our people will rise again and valiantly repel the folk of the Angles across the sea. But you, king, should leave this fortress, for you cannot build it. You should keep traveling through all the lands in search of a safe fortress, and I will remain here."

Then the king asked the youth: "By what name are you called?" He answered: "I am called Ambrosius"; in other words, this boy was shown to be *Emrys Gwledig*.[2] And the king said: "From what kindred are you sprung?" And he responded: "My father is one of the consuls of the Roman people." Then the king gave Ambrosius the fortress, along with all the lands in the western parts of Britain. Vortigern himself went into the north to the region known as Gwynnessi.[3] There he built a city, which was called Caer Vortigern after him.

In the meantime, Vortigern's son Vortimer was strenuously making war upon Hengist and Horsa and their folk, and he made them fall back to the island known as Thanet. Three times he had them entrapped there, and he besieged, attacked, threatened, and terrified them there. The Saxons sent messengers to Germany across the sea, summoning *ceolas* filled with numerous warriors.[4] And these warriors then fought against the kings of our people: at times they were victorious and expanded their territories; at other times they were defeated and pushed back.

§ *Saxon Treachery*

… But the barbarians soon returned in full force, for Vortigern looked kindly upon them on account of his wife. There was no man who was

---

[1]   In Welsh poetry of the earliest period, the word "dragon" was used as a metaphor for "leader, chieftain."

[2]   The Welsh term *Emrys Gwledig* means "Lord Ambrosius." This *Emrys*, one infers, was a popular figure in the Welsh folk traditions on which Pseudo-Nennius draws on, though it is unclear whether he should be identified with the Roman general Ambrosius Aurelianus, who is mentioned by both Gildas and Bede.

[3]   It is not unreasonable to identify this place, as later historians did, with the territory of the Gewissei in the West Country.

[4]   Pseudo-Nennius uses the Anglo-Saxon word *ceolas* ("ships") rather than a Latin term.

bold enough to force them out, for the barbarians were occupying Britain not on their own merits but with the consent of God. Indeed, who can resist the will of God, even if he should try? But the Lord does whatever He wills, and He rules and governs all the nations.

After the death of Vortimer, the son of Vortigern, and the return of Hengist and his hordes, the barbarians hatched a cunning scheme whereby they could destroy Vortigern and his army through treachery. They sent messengers to sue for peace, so that there might be perpetual friendship between their two peoples. Vortigern and his nobles took counsel and considered what they should do. They eventually all agreed that they should make peace, and they sent the messengers back. Then both sides, Britons and Saxons, put their arms aside and met together to begin a solid friendship.

Then Hengist commanded all his retainers to conceal a dagger in their shoes beneath their feet: "And when I cry out to you and say *Eu, nimet saxas!*, pull your knives out of your shoes and rush upon them and attack them boldly.[1] But do not slay their king, but keep him safe on account of my daughter, whom I gave him in marriage. What's more, it would be better for us if we can ransom him." So they came to the meeting. Although the Saxons spoke as if in friendship, they were thinking like wolves, and every man of them sat down next to a Briton as if they were allies. Then Hengist, just as he had planned, cried out, and three hundred of King Vortigern's senior advisors were murdered. Vortigern alone was taken captive and cast in chains. In ransoming his life, the Saxons obtained many possessions, including Essex, Sussex, and Middlesex, as well as several other choice territories.

§ Vortigern's Death

Saint Germanus preached to Vortigern again, urging him to turn back to the Lord and remove himself from his illicit union; but the king fled in all his wretchedness to the region of Vortigernion, which is named after him, and there he took refuge with his wives. Saint Germanus followed him, accompanied by all the British clergy, and they remained there for forty days and forty nights, and the saint himself climbed up on a rock and prayed both day and night. But Vortigern shamefully withdrew once again, this time to the fortress of Vortigern, which is

---

[1]   Hengist's battle-cry seems to be a corrupted or archaic form of the Anglo-Saxon phrase *Nimeth eowre seaxas* ("take out your swords!").

located in the land of the Demetians, by the banks of the Teifi. As usual, Saint Germanus followed him there. Then the saint purposely fasted there with the clerics for three days and three nights. On the fourth night, just around midnight, the fortress was suddenly struck by a fire out of heaven, which burnt it to the ground. Vortigern, along with his wives and everyone else who was with him, was killed. This was Vortigern's end as I found it told in the Book of the Blessed Germanus. Others have told the story differently....

§ *The Campaigns of Arthur*

In those days the Saxons strengthened their numbers and began flourishing in Britain. After Hengist died, his son Octa traveled from the northern regions of Britain to the kingdom of Kent, and from him are descended the kings of Kent. Arthur and the petty-kings of the Britons fought against the Saxons in those days, though he himself was their wartime leader [*dux bellorum*]. The first battle took place at the mouth of the River Glein. The second, third, fourth, and fifth battles were all fought at another river, the Douglas, which is in the vicinity of Lindsey. The sixth battle occurred at the River Bassas. The seventh took place in Celidon Wood, that is, *Coed Celidon*. The eighth battle occurred at the fortress of Guinnion, and it was there that Arthur bore the image of the Blessed Virgin Mary upon his shield, and the pagans fled that day, and they were massacred through the power of the Lord Jesus Christ and his Holy Mother Mary. The ninth battle was fought at the City of the Legions. The tenth battle was fought upon the banks of the River Tribruit. The eleventh battle was fought on Mount Agned. The twelfth battle took place at Mount Badon, where Arthur slew 960 men in a single day. No one felled them but he, and he was the victor in all twelve of these battles. And so the Saxons, defeated at every turn, sought aid from Germany, and they brought back their kings from Germany to reign over them in Britain until the days of King Ida, the son of Eoppa. He was the first king in Bernicia, that is, *Berneich*....

[Source: John Morris, ed., *Nennius: British History and Welsh Annals* (London: Phillimore, 1980), 60–76. Translated by Michael Faletra.]

Appendix B: Merlin

1. *The Apple Trees* (*Afallennau*)

[The direct source of Geoffrey of Monmouth's prophecies of Merlin is unknown. However, it is clear that Geoffrey was aware of the tradition of Merlinic political prophecy flourishing in Wales (and perhaps Cornwall). This Welsh poem, "The Apple Trees," appears in the Black Book of Carmarthen (13th century) but was copied from a version from the late 11th or early 12th century. It is thus representative of the types of Welsh Merlinic prophecy that circulated in Geoffrey's own day.]

I. Sweet apple tree, so sweet its branches,
Bearing the fruit of great deeds, my famous tree:
I foretell before the owner of Machrau
That there will be an English victory
In the valley of Machafwy, blood on a Wednesday,
Bloodstained blades.
O little pig, on a Thursday will you see
A Welsh victory after a mighty battle,
Defending themselves with the swift strikes of swords
And ash spears, battle for the Saxons:
A ball game will be played with their heads.
I foretell the truth without falsity:
A boy will arise in a district of the South.

II. Sweet apple tree, lofty and green its growth,
Fruit-laden its branches, beautiful its trunk:
I foretell a thundering battle,
Men will make merry in Pengwern, mead will be their prize
And everywhere the English, that hateful host,
Will meet their slaughter at the hands of the prince of Snowdon.

III. Sweet apple tree, that golden tree,
Growing on the hilltop, far from the farmlands:
I foretell a battle against the Picts,
Defending their borders with the men of Dublin.
In seven ships will they come across the wide waters,
Seven hundred seamen coming to conquer.

Though many will come, few will be against us
Except the seven dolts after their sore defeat.

IV. Sweet apple tree, growing by the Rhun:
Here at its trunk have I battled to please a girl,
With a shield on my shoulders, a sword at my side.
And I sleep by myself in the forest of Celidon.
O little pig, how can you think of sleeping?
Listen to the birds, their request resounds.
Kings will come on a Monday from across the sea;
My Welshmen will be blessed with their resolve.

V. Sweet apple tree, growing in the glade,
Its power will protect it from the Lord Rhydderch.
People will crowd under its boughs,
Heroes with treasure, rows of soldiers.
I am hateful now to Gwasawg, Rhydderch's protector.
I brought ruin upon his daughter and son.
Death led them all away, and now nobody welcomes me,
No lord honors me now that Gwenddoleu has died.
I have no pleasure in play: my sweetheart visits me not.
In the battle of Arfderydd I bore a gold torque,
But now only the swans pay me any heed.

VI. Sweet apple tree, blooming so tenderly,
Growing secretly within the forest.
Tales were told at the dawn of the day
Of the sulking of Gwasawg, that protector of treasures.
Twice—thrice—nay, four times in a single day,
O Jesus, do I wish my end had come
Before Gwendydd's son was slain by my own hand!

VII. Sweet apple tree, growing by the riverside:
Because of the current no steward can pluck its bright fruit.
I once was thought-laden, sitting by that trunk,
Taking my leisure with that slender, queenly maiden.
For twoscore years and ten have I now dwelt in the wild,
Walking with the madmen and the wood-folk.

VIII. Once I enjoyed the good fortune and pleasant life of poets.
Now only misfortune visits me among the madmen and outlaws.
I no longer sleep, awaiting my leader, my dragon,
My lord Gwenddoleu, the dearest of my kinsmen.
After suffering pain and sorrow in Celidon Wood,
I shall now find favor serving the Lord of Hosts.

IX. Sweet apple tree, blooming so tenderly,
Growing in the wild wood:
I foretell that a pale wanderer will declare
How brave men will brandish their spears
Before the praiseworthy dragons, before the kings.
A leap of destruction will overcome the impious man.
Faced by this daring boy, brilliant as the sunshine,
The Saxons will perish, and the bards will flourish.

X. Sweet apple tree, red its flowers,
Growing in secret within Celidon Wood:
Though seek it one may, hidden shall it remain
Until Cadwallader comes to muster his men
On the banks of the rivers Tywi and Teifi.
He will come to defeat the terrible foes.
He will tame the ragged wild men.

XI. Sweet apple tree, red its flowers,
Growing in secret within Celidon Wood:
Though seek it one may, hidden shall it remain
Until Cadwallader comes to the muster at Rhyd Rheon.
Cynan at his call will rise against the Saxons.
The Welsh will win, splendid their dragon-lord.
All losses will be regained, joyous will be the spirit of the Britons.
The trumpets of joy will ring out a song of sunshine and peace!

[Source: A.O.H. Jarman, ed. *Llyfr Du Caerfyrddin* (Cardiff: U of Wales P, 1982), 26–28. Translated by Michael Faletra.]

2. Geoffrey of Monmouth, *The Life of Merlin* (*Vita Merlini*)

[*The Life of Merlin* was the work of Geoffrey of Monmouth's later years, written around the year 1150. Unlike the "humble" prose style of *The*

History, it was composed in elegant Latin hexameter verse and embellished with considerable descriptive passages, expositions on natural philosophy, and rhetorical flourishes; Geoffrey perhaps thought of it as his tour de force. It narrates the madness of Merlin at the end of his lifetime, having lived many years past the days of Vortigern and Arthur. Inserted within the text are several further prophecies of Merlin, though the poem's closing prophecy is uttered by Merlin's sister Ganieda. The content of these prophecies reveals that Geoffrey had continued to gather information about Merlin and the British past from Welsh sources long after completing *The History*. In fact, the prophecies contained in *The Life of Merlin* correspond far more closely to extant Welsh prophecies than any in *The History* do. The development of the figure of Merlin as a "mad man of the woods" here likewise reveals Geoffrey's deeper knowledge of Welsh traditions. Analogues to the story of Merlin's madness can be found throughout Celtic Britain, as *The Life of St. Kentigern*, the Scots tales of Lailoken, and the Irish stories concerning Suibne Geilt (Yeats's "mad Sweeney") suggest. Written shortly before Geoffrey's elevation to the bishopric of St. Asaph's at the end of his life, *The Life of Merlin* might best be seen as the capstone of Geoffrey's career, an opportunity both to capitalize on the continuing popularity of Merlinic prophecy and to display his own erudition and poetic ability.]

[1–18] I intend to sing a pleasing tale about the madness of the prophetic bard Merlin. Robert, glory among bishops, may you guide my pen, for we all acknowledge that Philosophy has endowed you with her divine nectar and has made you learned in all matters so that you will show yourself to be the foremost teacher in the world.[1] Grant your favor, therefore, upon my endeavor, and may you prove a more auspicious patron than the man you have now so deservedly succeeded. Your morality obtained that honor for you, as did your righteous lifestyle, your family origins, and your capacity for the office, and both the clergy and the laity supported you. And so happy Lincoln is now in the seventh heaven. I wish indeed that I were worthy of composing a poem fine enough to do you justice. But I am not so worthy, not even if Orpheus and Camerinus and Macer and Marius and Rabirius of the mighty voice were all to sing through my words or if the Muses themselves served as my accompanists. However, Sisters, since you are accustomed to singing with me, let us now recite the poem before us. Strike the *cithara*![2]

---

[1]   Geoffrey of Monmouth's dedicatee is Robert de Chesney, the bishop of Lincoln from 1148–66.

[2]   The medieval *cithara*, of ancient origin, was similar to the lyre.

[19–37] As the years passed by, many kings came and went, and Merlin was still renowned throughout the world. He was both a king and a prophet, administering the laws to the fierce men of South Wales and telling the future to their chieftains. And so it happened that strife arose between some of the different leaders of the realm, and they despoiled the innocent people in all the cities of the land. Peredur, the Lord of the North Welsh, was busy waging a war against Gwenddolau, who reigned over the kingdom of Scotland, and the day they had agreed upon for battle had arrived.[1] Their generals oversaw the battlefield and their soldiers had entered into the fray: men on either side fell in that terrible massacre. Merlin had accompanied Peredur to that battle, as had Rhydderch, the king of the Cumbrians, and they were both fearsome warriors.[2] They slew whoever stood in their path with their dreaded swords. Peredur's three brothers, who had followed him to this war, were also there in the press, slaying their foes and breaking the lines of battle. Yet they fought their way with such reckless abandon through the thick enemy ranks that they were quickly cut down and slain.

[38–53] How you grieved at that sight, Merlin! Your bellowing voice carried this piteous lament throughout the battalions: "What ill chance could have been so harmful as to snatch from me such dear companions, who were until just now feared by so many kings and in so many far-off lands? Alas for the doubtful fate of mortal men, for death is ever near, ready to strike them with its sudden sting and force the wretched life from their bodies. Alas, for these splendid youths! Who will now be my companions-in-arms, helping me to drive away the lords who come to harm? Who will repel the enemy hosts rushing at me? Boldest of men, it was your very courage that stole from you many sweet years of tender youth. A mere moment ago you were racing through the enemy lines, but now you are beating the ground, reddening the soil with your lifeblood."

[54–62] Thus, with the tears rolling down his cheeks, did Merlin bewail his companions amid the tumult. Yet that terrible battle did not cease: the lines of men clashed against each other and foe fell to foe. Blood

---

[1] A semi-historical Peredur is preserved in Welsh tradition. He was a member of the Coeling dynasty of pre-Saxon northern Britain and presumably lived in the fifth century. Gwenddolau was another northern British chieftain (not a Scot, as here). The Welsh Annals record his death at the Battle of Arfderydd in 573 AD, and it is not unreasonable to identify this battle with the battle described in the poem, especially because the Annals also tell us that Merlin went mad at that same time.

[2] Rhydderch Hael (Rhydderch the Generous) appears in the Old Welsh genealogies as a northern British prince. There is no evidence linking him to the Battle of Arfderydd, however.

was spilled all around, and men perished on both sides. But the Britons finally assembled their men into formation once more. Now mustered together, they rushed down in a fully-armed attack upon the Scots, cutting them down and inflicting many wounds. They did not cease until the enemy troops turned tail and retreated along seldom-trod paths.

[63–80] Merlin then summoned his remaining comrades from the battle and had them bury the brothers in a finely adorned chapel. Then, weeping for them, he poured out constant laments, scattering dust on his hair and tearing his clothes to shreds. Then he cast himself upon the earth and rolled back and forth. Peredur began to comfort him, as did the other nobles and chieftains, but Merlin had no wish to be consoled or to hear their words of comfort. For three entire days he grieved in this way, and his sorrow was so keen that he refused even to eat. Finally, having already filled the air with so many mournful cries, a new fury took hold of him, and he stole secretly away, not wishing to be seen as he fled into the forest. Upon entering the forest, he was quite happy to remain hidden beneath the ash trees and observe the beasts grazing in the woodlands. At times he would chase them, and at other times he simply ran right past them and fed upon roots and grasses and herbs and upon fruit from the trees and upon the mulberries that lay in the thickets. He became a wild man of the woods, a devotee of the forest itself.

[81–112] Not a soul came across Merlin that entire summer. Heedless of his kinsmen and of his very self, he lurked among the trees and concealed himself like a wild animal. However, the approach of winter took away all the fruits from the trees, leaving him nothing to feed upon. He then unleashed this piteous lament: "O Christ, God of Heaven, what shall I do and where shall I dwell? I cannot remain in these parts with nothing to eat. I see neither the grass of the earth nor the acorns of the trees here. Nineteen apple trees laden with apples once stood here.[1] Now they are standing no more. Who has taken them away from me? Where have they disappeared to so unexpectedly? Now I see them, now I do not: the fates act both for me and against me, since they both provide the apple trees and then do not allow me to see them. Now I have neither apples nor anything else. The forest stands without fruit or leaf, and I mourn doubly because I cannot now cover myself with leaves or eat any fruit. The winter has taken these things away, as has the South Wind with its falling rains. Whenever I happen

---

[1]   Merlin's reference to apple trees here suggests Geoffrey's familiarity with Welsh prophecies similar to *The Apple Trees* (see above, Appendix B1).

to find any turnips deep in the ground, hungry pigs and gluttonous boars rush in and snatch them from me even as I dig them up. And you, my dear friend the wolf, who have been meandering the lonely paths of the woods along with me: now you can scarcely make it across the very fields; harsh hunger has made us both weak. You have dwelt in these woods longer than I, yet age has made your hairs white before mine, and you have nothing to put in your mouth either, nor do you know where to get anything. I am amazed at this, for the forest is teeming with wild goats and other beasts that you could catch. Perhaps hateful old age has snatched away your vigor and denied you the ability to run and hunt. You have only one thing left: to fill the breezes with your howling and stretch out your weary limbs upon the ground." Thus did Merlin complain amid the thickets and the hazel copses.

[113–137] A passerby happened to hear the sound of these laments, and he made his way down towards where he heard Merlin's voice upon the breeze. When he reached that place, he discovered the speaker there. As soon as Merlin espied him he ran away. The passerby followed him but could not keep up with the fleeing man, so he resumed his journey and got back to his own affairs, though the encounter had filled him with pity. Eventually this traveler met a man on the road who had come from the hall of Rhydderch, the king of the Cumbrians, who had married Ganieda and was quite happy to have such a beautiful wife. This Ganieda was Merlin's own sister, and she regretted her brother's misfortune and had sent her servants into the distant woods and fields to bring him back.[1] It was one of these very servants whom the traveler met, and they greeted each other and exchanged a few words. Ganieda's servant asked if the traveler had seen Merlin in the forests or the fields. The traveler confessed that he had seen the very man amid the dense thickets of the Forest of Celidon, but that when he had attempted to sit down and speak with him, the man had quickly fled among the oaks. When the traveler had related these things, the servant departed and made his way to the forest. He scoured the deepest vales, traversed the high hills, and sought out the most remote places in search of his man.

[138–164] There was a spring on the summit of a certain hill, surrounded on all sides by hazel trees and thick patches of briars. It was here that Merlin had established himself, and from this place he roamed

---

[1] Ganieda corresponds to Gwendydd, the bard Myrddin's sister in the Welsh traditions, where she appears in three prophetic poems, *The Apple Trees, The Ohs of Myrddin,* and *The Dialogue Between Myrddin and His Sister Gwendydd.* In the Welsh poems, the sister is not married to Rhydderch and is markedly hostile toward her prophetic brother.

throughout the forest, watching the running and playing of the woodland beasts. The messenger crept silently up to that high place, seeking the man. When he beheld the spring, there was Merlin sitting upon the grass next to it and making a lament in these words: "O You Who rule over all things! Why is it that the seasons, which are already distinguished by being four in number, are all so different? Spring, following her own law, ushers in flowers and leaves. Summer delivers the crop, while autumn brings ripe apples. Icy winter follows them all, and it devours and ravages them as it carries in snows and rains. Winter drives the other seasons away, destroying them with its storms. It will not allow the soil to bring forth its many flowers, or the oak its acorns, or the apple trees their deep-red fruit. O, if only there were no winter or hoary frost! I wish that it were spring or summer and the singing cuckoo had returned, or else the nightingale, who softens mournful hearts with her kindly song, or the turtle-dove, who keeps her chaste vows. I wish that all the other birds were also warbling harmoniously amid the newly-leafed boughs, providing delightful music for me while the new soil breathed forth the scent of the fresh flowers amid the green grass and the sweetly babbling fountains trickled beside the dove upon the bough, who would spill forth her soothing laments and lull us to sleep."

[165–197] The messenger heard the prophet and he interspersed Merlin's laments with chords from the *cithara* he had brought with him, hoping to allure and pacify the madman. Picking out notes and orderly scales with his fingers, he remained hidden behind Merlin and sang in a quiet voice: "O, for the terrible groans of Gwendolena in mourning! O, for the wretched tears of the bleary-eyed Gwendolena! I bewail the miserable, dying Gwendolena! There was in all Wales no woman more beautiful than she, whose loveliness surpassed that of the goddesses and the petals of the privet and the roses in bloom and the lilies of the field. The glory of springtime glowed within her, and the radiance of the stars once gleamed in her eyes. Her gorgeous hair shone with the luster of gold. But all this had now perished. All her beauty has passed away: her complexion and her snow-white visage and the splendor of her flesh. She is not what she once was, having mourned overmuch. She knows not where her lord is gone, or whether he is alive or dead. And so she languishes most wretchedly, wasting away in protracted grief. Ganieda is her companion in mourning, grieving inconsolably for her lost brother. The one woman weeps for her brother and the other for her husband; they both lead lives of weeping and mourning. Such is the grief that oppresses them both that food does not nourish them, nor does sleep find them as they wander by night beneath the greenwood. In this same way did Sidonian Dido weep when Aeneas' fleet had weighed anchor and was ready to depart.[1] Thus also did wretched Phyllis weep and wail when Demophon did not return in the appointed hour.[2] And thus did Briseis weep when her Achilles had gone away.[3] Sister and wife thus mourn together, and they constantly burn within because of their grief."

[198–214] Thus went the messenger's sad song. His music calmed the prophet's ears, and he grew milder and even began to take pleasure in the singing. The prophet stood up at last and spoke pleasantly to the young man, requesting him to pluck out the notes with his fingers and sing that mournful tune once again. The messenger then moved his fingers across the strings and sang again as requested. His music forced Merlin's madness to recede little by little, so captivated was he by the sweetness of the instrument. Then Merlin's memory started to return, and he recalled what he used to be, and he was startled at his madness and began to hate it. He returned to his right mind and came back to his senses; sane once again and now moved by pity, he groaned to hear mention of his sister and wife. Having returned to his right mind, he asked to be led to the court of King Rhydderch. The messenger obeyed him, and they soon left the forest behind them and arrived joyously at the city of the king.

[215–237] Queen Ganieda rejoiced at having her brother back, and his wife Gwendolena was also gladdened by the return of her husband. They competed in showering him with kisses, and they threw their arms about his neck, so greatly were they moved by their love for this man. The king also welcomed him with due honor, as did the noblemen of the city, who thronged merrily about the king's house. But when Merlin cast his eyes upon all the people who were crowded there, he was unable to tolerate them. His madness returned, and he was filled with fury anew. He longed to go back to the forest and attempted to slip away quietly. But Rhydderch had him restrained, posted a guard about him, and attempted to assuage Merlin's madness with the music of the *cithara*. Saddened, Rhydderch implored Merlin to exercise his reason and remain there instead of returning to the woods to live like a beast and dwell beneath the trees. Merlin, he insisted, could be wielding a royal scepter and ruling over his fierce people. Then Rhydderch promised to give him many gifts, and he ordered clothing to be brought forth, as well as hawks

---

[1]   Ovid, *Heroides*, Letter 7; and Virgil, *Aeneid*, Book V.
[2]   Ovid, *Heroides*, Letter 2.
[3]   Ovid, *Heroides*, Letter 3.

and hounds and swift horses and gold and sparkling gemstones and chalices that had been fashioned by Wayland in the city of Segontium.[1] Rhydderch offered every single one of these things to the prophet, urging him to remain with him and forsake the woods.

[238–253] The prophet refused the gifts, claiming "Let noblemen who are bothered by their seeming poverty take these gifts, for they are never happy with moderation but snatch up as much as they can get. I far prefer the wide forest of Celidon with its oak trees and lofty mountains with green meadows at their feet. Such things are far more pleasing to me than any gift, King Rhydderch; you can take these things away with you. The Forest of Celidon, so abundant in nuts, shall have me, and I choose it over all else." Therefore, since the king could not retain the sorrowful Merlin through the offering of gifts, he had him bound with a heavy chain so that he could not escape to the solitary forest. When the prophet felt the fetters upon him and realized he was not free to return to the Forest of Celidon, he began to sulk and became gloomy and silent. All joy was wiped from his face to the extent that he did not utter a word or even smile.

[254–279] In the meantime, the queen was wandering through the court in search of the king. The king greeted her as she entered, as was befitting, and he took her by the hand and asked her to sit down. He then embraced her and pressed a kiss upon her lips. Turning his face toward her, he noticed a single leaf dangling from her hair, which he took in his fingers and pulled out. Tossing it on the ground, he joked about it with his true love. The prophet Merlin cast his glance their way and began to laugh, which made the men who were there stare at him, for he was not in the habit of laughing. The king marveled at this and asked the madman what had suddenly made him laugh. He entreated him with many gifts. But Merlin was silent and refused to explain his laughter. Rhydderch kept trying to persuade the prophet more and more with pleas and bribes until at last Merlin said: "A miser loves a gift and a greedy man is always trying to procure one. The greedy would change their minds about anything at all, being so corrupted by the thought of gifts. They are not happy with what they already have, but I am: the acorns of Celidon and its bright streams that flow through fragrant meadows are all I need. Gifts do not entice me. Let the miser

---

[1] *Wayland* (or *Weland*) was a legendary smith in English folklore, connected no doubt to the Scandinavian Volund and probably originally an ancient pagan Germanic divinity. *Segontium* was a Roman fortress in North Wales near Caernarvon. It lay in ruins in Geoffrey's day.

take them, for unless I am given the freedom to return to the green-wood glens, I shall not explain my laughter."

[280–293] As soon as Rhydderch realized that he would not be able to entice the prophet with gifts to explain why he was laughing, he ordered that his chains be taken off and gave him leave to return to the solitary woodlands. In releasing him, Rhydderch hoped that Merlin would explain his laughter. Rejoicing at being able to go, Merlin then said: "Here is why I laughed, Rhydderch: you have done a deed that is worthy of both praise and blame at the same time. When you pulled out that leaf which the queen did not realize she had in her hair, you behaved more faithfully than she did to you when she went into the thicket to meet her lover and lie with him. While she was lying there, that leaf which you unwittingly removed got stuck in her outspread hair."

[294–322] Rhydderch grew very solemn upon hearing of such an offense, and he at once turned away from her and cursèd the day he married her. But Ganieda was not upset at all, and she concealed her shame with laughter and spoke to husband in this way: "Why, my love, would you be so sad, and why so angry at me, who have been unfairly accused? Why do you believe this madman, who lacks all reason and confuses the truth with lies? The man who believes this fool is far more foolish indeed! Now then, if I am not mistaken, I will prove to you that he is quite mad and has not spoken true." This clever woman then caught sight of one of the many boys who were attending court, and she quickly thought of a plan by which she could prove her brother a liar. So she had the boy come forward, and she asked her brother to predict how the boy would die. Her brother replied: "O, dearest sister, when this boy has become a man, he will perish by falling off a high rock." She smiled at his words and ordered the boy to go away and to take off the clothes he had on and then to put on different clothes and crop his long hair. Once he had done these things, she ordered him to come back, looking completely different. The boy obeyed, for when he returned his garb was completely changed. As soon as the queen saw him, she asked her brother once more, "Now tell your beloved sister what this other boy's death will be like." Merlin replied: "When this boy comes of age he will let his mind wander and meet with a violent death in a tree."

[323–346] The queen later explained what Merlin had said to her husband: "To think that this false prophet could have ever made you think that I had committed such a crime! You should know what nonsense he has just declared regarding this boy so that you will indeed believe that he fabricated those things about me so he could go back to the forest. I would never do anything of the sort. I will keep our marriage-bed chaste, and I will remain chaste as long as there is breath left in me. I proved Merlin to have spoken false regarding the boy's death, and now I shall do it once more. Watch and decide for yourself." Having said this, she very quietly told the boy to leave and then come back in dressed as a girl. The boy stepped away and did as he had been commanded, for when he returned he was wearing feminine attire as if he were a girl. He stood before the prophet, to whom the queen then said, as if in jest: "So, brother, tell me all about the death of this maiden." "Maiden or no maiden," Merlin replied, "she shall die in a river." Merlin's reasoning moved King Rhydderch to laughter, for he had claimed that the same boy would die in three different ways. The king therefore concluded that Merlin had spoken incorrectly about his wife, and he no longer believed him but instead regretted the fact that he had trusted him to the point of condemning his beloved. Perceiving the king's thoughts, the queen pardoned him with kisses and embraces, making him happy once again.

[347–367] Merlin, in the meantime, had decided to return to the forest, and he left his abode and commanded the gates to be opened for him. His sister, however, tried to prevent him, begging him most tearfully to remain with her for the time being and to forget his madness. But Merlin was determined and, having no desire to give up his plans, kept trying to force his way outdoors. He struggled and yelled and fought until his uproar forced the servants to open the gates. Then, since there was no one else who was able to hold him back, the queen asked Gwendolena, who had not been present for these events, to try to detain him. She came and, on bended knees, implored her husband to stay; but he rejected her pleas and would not remain, nor would he even look upon the woman whom he had once beheld so lovingly. She grieved and shed many tears and tore her hair and rent her face with her nails and rolled on the ground as if in death-throes. At this, the queen said to Merlin: "Here is your Gwendolena, who is dying for you. What shall she do? Should she be given to another man or should she live as a widow? Or should she go wherever you are going? She would indeed go with you and dwell in the wild and the woodland groves and the green meadows so long as she can have your love."

[368–386] The prophet responded to her words thus: "Sister, I have no desire for a cow that sprinkles water upon the broad surface of a fountain like the virgin's urn in the summertime.[1] Nor shall I alter my

---

[1]   This expression is quite impenetrable, and the Latin text may in fact be corrupt here.

care as Orpheus did when Eurydice placed her baskets into the keep-
ing of boys before she swam back across the Styx.[1] Freed from you
both, I shall be clear of the stain of love. She should therefore be given
a fair opportunity to remarry, and let her have any man she deems fit.
But the man who marries her would do well not to cross my path or
come anywhere near me. He should keep away, for if I meet him he
may well feel my flashing blade. However, when the day of their solemn
nuptials arrives, and the various meats are being spread out for the
banquet, I shall be there in person with generous gifts and shall endow
Gwendolena most profusely when she is wed." Having spoken, Merlin
then bade farewell to them both and headed for his beloved woodlands
with no one now to stand in his way.

[387–415] Gwendolena and the queen stood sorrowfully in the door-
way, moved by the strange misfortunes of their dear Merlin. They were
amazed that a man so mad had known about so many secret things and
especially that he had known about his sister's love affair. But they still
thought he was wrong about the death of the boy, for he had predicted
three separate deaths when there should have been only one. For this
reason his words seemed vain for many a long year until that boy grew
up, when everything Merlin had said was suddenly made clear. For one
day while the man was out hunting with his dogs, he spied a stag hidden
within a cluster of trees. He let loose his hounds, who, as soon as they
caught sight of the stag, ran along untrodden paths and filled the air
with their baying. He spurred his horse on in pursuit and guided his
huntsmen with many a call from his horn or throat, urging them to
hurry. There was a high mountain in that place, encompassed all about
with rocks and a stream that flowed along the plain at its base. The stag
fled that way until it came to the river, where it looked for a place to
hide, as creatures of its kind will. The young man pushed onward, right
over the mountain, in search of the stag among the rocks that were
there. Then it happened: in his zeal for the chase, his horse slipped off
one of the steep banks and the man fell off a cliff and into the river.
One of his feet got caught in a tree in the fall, while the rest of his body
was submerged in the waters. And thus he fell, and was drowned, and
was hanged in a tree, and this threefold death proved the prophet true.[2]

---

[1] This detail of the classical myth of Orpheus and Eurydice is otherwise unattested.

[2] The motif of the threefold death occurs in several texts that are closely affiliated with
The Life of Merlin, including the tales of the wild man Lailoken and Jocelyn's *Life of
St. Kentigern*.

[416–423] In the meantime, Merlin himself had gone off to the forest and led the life of a wild beast, feeding off of the frost-hardened mosses, always out in the snow and rain and the terrible blasts of the wind. This pleased him far better than enforcing the laws or governing fierce subjects. And while Merlin let the years slip by as he ran with the sylvan flocks, his wife Gwendolena, with her husband's consent, was given in marriage to another man.

[424–463] One night, when the bright horned moon was glowing and all the stars were shining from the vault of the heavens, the night air was much clearer than usual because the cold and bitter North Wind had chased away all the clouds, making the heavens serene and drying up the mist with the dryness of his breath. The prophet, standing atop a lofty mountain, was inspecting the wheelings of the stars, and he spoke quietly to himself out there in the night air: "What could this beam from Mars signify in its redness except that the king has just died and that a new one will arise? That is precisely what I see, for Constantine has perished and his nephew Conanus, assisted by an evil chance and the murder of his uncle, has seized the crown and become the king.[1] And you, lofty Venus, sliding there along your established course through the Zodiac with your companion the Sun, what is it about this double beam shining from you and slicing through the very air? Might this splitting not portend the splitting from my love? A beam such as that indeed means that love is now divided. Gwendolena, perhaps, has abandoned me because I have been away, and she now cleaves to another man and finds joy in a new husband's embraces. Thus am I defeated and another man occupies her. My legal rights have been snatched from me while I have tarried here, for a slothful lover is often supplanted by one who is not slothful and who is near at hand. But I am not jealous. Let her marry now while the omens are favorable, and let her take on a new husband with my permission. When the morning sun rises, I shall go and bring the gift that I promised to her when I left." He finished speaking and set out walking all about the woods and fields, and he gathered together an entire herd of stags—along with does and she-goats as well—into an orderly array. He mounted one of the stags, and when the next day dawned he drove that herd before him, hastening toward the place where Gwendolena would be married. Upon arriving there, he made the stags stand patiently in a row outside the gates while he called out: "Gwendolena, Gwendolena! Come out! Your wedding presents are waiting for you!" Gwendolena

---

[1]   See above, *The History of the Kings of Britain*, Book Eleven.

came out at once with a smile upon her face, and she was amazed that Merlin was riding a stag. She marveled as well that he was able to make so many wild beasts obey him and that he had been able on his own to gather so many animals together as easily as a shepherd is able to lead his flock to pasture.

[464–480] The bridegroom was observing this scene from a high window, marveling at this rider upon his steed, and he laughed out loud. But Merlin, catching sight of him, grew furious when he realized who he was. He ripped the antlers from the head of the stag he was riding, whirled them around, and cast them up at the groom. They crushed his head completely, knocking the life out of him and causing his spirit to slip away into the breeze. Then, with a swift shake of his heels, he caused the stag to turn and flee and he made his way back toward the forest. Hearing the commotion, the servants hurried out from all directions and set off after him, pursuing him at great speed through the countryside. Merlin was so swift that he would have made it unscathed back to the forest if a river had not been in his path: as the stag leapt over it, Merlin slipped off its back and into the rushing currents. The servants surrounded him on the riverbanks and caught him as he swam. Escorting him home, they presented him in fetters to his sister.

[481–500] The prophet grew sad in captivity and desired to return to the woods once more. He struggled to break his chains and refused to laugh or eat or drink. His sorrow made his sister gloomy as well. Finally, Rhydderch, noticing that Merlin was driving all happiness away and that he did not wish to partake in any of the fine meals that were laid before him, took pity on him and ordered him to be led out into town. There he would be able to walk through the marketplace and see the people and the many types of merchandise that were being sold there. As he was leaving the king's hall, he espied just by the gates a man of shabby appearance who served as the gatekeeper and who was tremulously begging passersby for some money to have his clothing mended. As soon as he beheld this pauper, the prophet stopped in his tracks and burst out laughing. Then, as he walked a bit further, he saw a young man carrying new shoes and in the process of buying some leather patches for them. He laughed out loud once more and refused to go any further through the market because the people he was watching were staring at him. Instead, he longed for the forest, gazing back at it and trying to direct his path there, though it was forbidden to him.

[501–532] Upon their return home, the servants related how Merlin had been moved to laughter twice and how he had tried to go back to the forest. Rhydderch desired to learn at once what he had meant by this laughter, and so he ordered that Merlin's bonds be loosened and granted him leave to return to his woodland haunts if he would only explain his laughter. Much gladdened by this, the prophet responded: "That porter was sitting just outside the gates wearing very ragged clothing, and he was asking for money to get his clothes mended from the people going by as if he were a beggar. All the while, unbeknownst to all, he was a rich man, for there is a hoard of coins buried right beneath him. That is why I laughed. Go ahead and turn up the earth beneath him and you will discover coins that have been preserved there for a long time. After that, as I was led further out beyond the gates, I saw a man buying shoes along with some leather strips so that when the shoes wore out and had holes he would be able to patch them up and make them as good as new. Well, I laughed that time," Merlin added, "because that poor wretch will get no use from either the shoes or those patches, for he has already drowned in the waves and is floating toward the shore. Go there and you will find him." Wishing to confirm the prophet's words, Rhydderch ordered his servants to hasten down along the riverbank so that they would be able to bring him swift tidings if they should find such a man upon the shore. Obeying their lord's orders, they hurried down along the river and indeed found a drowned man lying upon a patch of rough sand. Once they had found him they returned home immediately and reported it to the king. But the king, in the meantime, had dismissed the gatekeeper, overturned the earth, and discovered the treasure lying there. He gave the prophet hearty praise.

[533–564] After these events had occurred, the prophet made ready to go back to the forest that was so familiar to him, for he detested the people in the city. The queen enjoined him to remain with her and postpone his return to his beloved forest until the chills of white winter, which were just setting in, had passed and summer had returned with the tender fruits to live upon while the weather grew warm in the sun. Determined to leave despite the weather, he refused her with these words: "Dearest sister, why do you seek to detain me? The winter with its storms does not frighten me, nor does the cold North Wind when he rages with his awful blowing and pelts the flocks of sheep with his sudden hail. Neither does the South Wind bother me with the driving waters that fall from his rain-clouds. Why should I not seek out the solitary groves and green meadows? Content with only the bare minimum, I shall be able to endure the frost. There, under the leaves of the trees, among the fragrant flowers, I will enjoy myself in the summer. However, lest food does prove scarce in the winter, build me a house in the forest and send servants there to attend me and prepare food for me when the earth will not yield grain or the tree fruit. Before all other buildings, build me a house in a remote locale with seventy doors and seventy windows through which I may watch flaming Phoebus and Venus and behold the stars gliding through the heavens all night long: these things will inform me what will happen to the people of the realm.[1] There should also be seventy scribes there, learned enough to write down what I say and eager to record my prophecies in their tablets. You, my dear sister, should come there often as well, and you will be able to relieve my hunger with food and drink." This he said, and then hurried back into the forest.

[565–604] His sister obeyed his wishes and built a great hall and the other edifices and things he had demanded. But as long as the apples remained on the boughs and Phoebus still climbed through the Zodiac, Merlin was quite happy to remain beneath the trees, wandering the woodland groves amid the gentle breezes. Then winter arrived: the winds were bitter and frost-laden, snatching away all the fruit from the trees and meadows. Because the rains were at hand, Merlin had no food, and so he came, sad and hungry, to the hall. The queen frequented that place as well, and she gladly brought food and drink to her brother. After he had taken his fill of the various foods, Merlin rose at once and praised his sister; then he wandered throughout the abode, examining the stars and prophesying things that would come to pass: "O madness of the Britons, whose abundance of riches makes them feel more exalted than they should! They do not wish to enjoy the fruits of peace and are instead stirred up by the Fury's goad. They are involved in wars with their own relatives and countrymen, and they suffer the churches of the Lord to fall into decay, driving the holy bishops into far-off exile. The nephews of the Boar of Cornwall are wreaking chaos, setting traps for each other and slaying each other with their evil swords.[2] They refuse to wait to obtain the kingdom lawfully but attempt to seize the crown. The fourth king to come after them will be even crueler and more terrible. He it is whom the Sea Wolf shall overcome in battle, and he shall flee in his defeat across the Severn through the lands of the barbarians. The Sea Wolf shall then surround Kaer Ceri with a siege and with sparrows, and he shall cast its walls and houses down to their

---

[1] Merlin's reliance upon astronomy to predict the future is at odds with Geoffrey's depiction of the prophet's powers in *The History*, where they appear more supernatural. This departure may reflect Geoffrey's own interest in astrology.

[2] See *The History of the Kings of Britain*, Book Seven, prophecies 2–3.

very foundations. Then he shall hunt down the Gauls in his ship, but he will succumb to the weapon of a king. Rhydderch shall die, and after that discord will long hold sway over the Scots and Cumbrians until Cumbria itself gets allotted to a growing tooth. The Welsh will make war first on the Gewissei and later on the Cornish, and there will be no law to hold them back. Wales will rejoice in the spilling of blood. O you people who are always hostile toward God, why do you take joy in bloodshed? Wales forces brothers to fight against their own families, damning them to a wicked death.

[605–621] "Bands of Scots will often cross over the Humber and, setting aside all feelings of mercy, will slay any man who stands in their way. They shall not do this with impunity, however, for their leader will be killed. He will have the name of a horse, which is why he will prove so fierce. His heir shall be repelled and will depart from our lands. Scots, put away your swords, which you have unsheathed far too hastily; your strength will not be up to dealing with our fierce people. The city of Alclud shall fall, and no king shall reign there for an age, not until the Scot is subdued in war. Carlisle, robbed of its shepherd, shall lie empty until the scepter of the Lion restores its pastoral staff. Segontium with its towers and splendid palaces shall sit weeping in ruins until the Welsh return to their ancient lands. Porchester will behold its walls in ruin in its own harbor until a rich man with a fox's tooth rebuilds it. The city of Richborough will lie splayed out upon the shore; a Fleming in a crested ship will restore it.

[622–653] "The fifth from him will repair the walls of St. David's. Through him the pall lost from that city for years will also be restored. Into your bosom, Severn, shall fall the city of Caerleon, and it shall lose its inhabitants for a long time.[1] The Bear within the Lamb shall bring them back when he arrives. Exiling the citizenry, Saxon kings will then control the cities, countryside, and homesteads for a long space of time. From that people three dragons shall don the crown thrice. Two hundred monks shall perish in the city of Leir, and the Saxon will drive out the city's ruler and unman her battlements.[2] The Englishman who first wears the crown of Brutus shall restore the city that had been emptied by slaughter. A cruel people shall then prohibit the Holy Chrism throughout the land, and they will set up false idols in the houses of God.

---

[1] Geoffrey surely would have known that the city of Caerleon was situated on the Usk, not the Severn.

[2] A reference to the Battle of Chester, 613 C.E. See *The History of the Kings of Britain*, Book Eleven.

Rome will afterwards restore God by means of a monk, and a holy priest will sprinkle the houses with holy water, and he will restore them once more and place shepherds within them. Many of them shall continue to preserve the commandments of the divine Law, and they shall rightfully enjoy Heaven. Another impious people full of poison shall then attack that place anew, and they will violently confuse right and wrong. That people will sell their sons and other relations across the sea, incurring the wrath of the Thunderer. How terrible a crime that men, whom God bestowed with free will, deeming them worthy of the honor of Heaven, should be sold like oxen and hauled away in chains! Even you, wretched man, who even once turned traitor to your lord when you first came to the throne, shall yield before God. The Danes in their fleet will overwhelm you and, having subjugated the people, will rule for a brief space until they suffer a defeat and withdraw. Two shall give them their laws, but the serpent, heedless of his treaties, shall strike them not with the garland of his scepter but with the sting of his tail.

[654–671] "After that, the Normans will sail over the waves in their wooden ships, their faces looking both forward and backward. In their iron tunics and bearing sharp swords, they shall grievously attack the English and crush them and enjoy the field of victory. Many realms shall they subjugate and many foreign peoples shall they rule for a while, until the Fury, flying all about, pours her poison upon them. At that time, all peace, faith, and honor shall be no more, and people will fight wars all across their homeland.[1] Men will betray their fellows, and friends will not be found. Husbands will scorn their wives and take up with whores, while wives, scorning their husbands, will marry whomever they desire. There will be no honor left to the Church either, and all order shall pass away. Bishops will take up arms and set up military camps.[2] They shall construct towers and fortifications upon holy ground, and they shall give to the soldiers what belongs to the poor. Obsessed with riches, they shall run along the path of worldly things, and they shall snatch away from God that which the holy office forbids.

[672–680] "Three shall wear the crown, and after them shall arise the favor of the new men. The fourth will wield the scepter; an unpropitious piety will harm him until he dresses as his father did. Only then,

---

[1] This prophecy is a none-too-veiled reference to the civil anarchy of Stephen's reign, 1135–54.

[2] One criticism of the English clergy during the civil unrest of Stephen's reign—including Geoffrey's former patron, Bishop Alexander of Lincoln—was that they too often maintained fortresses and armies as if they were secular lords.

girded with the boar's teeth, will he cross the shadow of the helmeted man. Four will be anointed, each seeking the highest things, and two shall succeed, wearing the crown in turn so as to provoke the Gauls to make war on them. The sixth shall overthrow the Irish and their walls. Wise and pious, he shall restore the people and the cities.

[681–688] "All these things have I already sung to Vortigern in explicating for him the riddle of the two warring dragons when we sat together by the sides of the drained pool. Now, my dear sister, go home to see the king, who is now dying, and command Taliesin to come, for I wish to discuss many things with him.[1] He has just returned from Brittany, where he has gleaned sweet teachings from the wise Gildas."

[689–731] Ganieda returned home to find Taliesin just arrived, the king dead, and the servants in mourning. She collapsed in tears, weeping amidst her friends and tearing her hair. She cried out: "Weep with me, women, weep for the death of Rhydderch, a man the likes of whom this age of the world has never seen. He was a lover of peace, enforcing the laws upon a fierce people so that violence was never perpetrated upon anyone. He treated holy priests with the proper respect and ensured that both the mighty and the humble alike were governed by the law. He was magnanimous, giving generously and keeping hardly anything at all for himself. He was all things to all men, doing whatever was proper in a given situation. He was the flower of knights, splendid among kings, a true pillar of the realm. Woe is me! You once were living, but now you are suddenly food for worms, and your body rots in the urn. Can this now be your bed, after sleeping in fine silks? Can it be true that your fair flesh and royal limbs will be hidden by a cold stone, and that you will be nothing but bones and ashes? Indeed, it is true. Thus has been the wretched doom of men for all time: that they may never get back to their former state. The glory of this transient world is therefore worthless, for it comes and goes, deceiving and harming those who wield power. The bee moistens with its honey that which it later stings. The glory of this world likewise caresses as it fades away, deceiving and striking us with its ungrateful sting. What is best in this world is far too brief, and nothing the world offers can endure. Anything that is helpful passes away like so much running water. What

---

[1]   Like the figure of Myrddin, Taliesin was a Welsh bard who lived during the sixth century. He was associated with the court of Urien Rheged, and several genuine poems of his still survive, although, as with Merlin, much extraneous material (some of it prophetic) was later attributed to him. He and Myrddin both feature in a Welsh prophecy of c. 1100 entitled *The Discourse of Myrddin and Taliesin (Ymddiddan Myrddin a Thaliesin)*.

does it matter if the rose is red, if the white lily blooms, if a man or a horse or anything else at all is comely? These belong to the world's Creator, not to the world itself. Happy instead are they who nurture a pious heart, who serve God and renounce the world. Unto them Christ, Who rules eternally and Who created the world, grants honor forever. Therefore, I shall now renounce you all—my retainers, lofty walls, household gods, sweet children, and all other earthly things.[1] I shall dwell in the forest with my brother, and there, cloaked in black, shall I worship God with a joyous heart." These things Ganieda said, and she paid all her husband's debts and inscribed the following verse on his tomb: *Rhydderch the Generous: there was none in the world more generous than he. A great man sleeps in this little urn.*

[732–763] In the meantime, Taliesin had come to visit the prophet Merlin, who had sent for him in order to discover what the wind was and what rainstorms were, for both types of weather were heading toward him and the clouds were approaching. Taliesin propounded this explanation, taking his cue from his friend Minerva:[2] "The Creator of the world brought forth the four elements *ex nihilo* to be a first cause for things as well as to provide the material for all other bodies when yoked together in harmonious proportions: first the Heaven itself, which he adorned with stars and which stretches above us and encloses everything else like a shell encloses a nut. Then he created the Air, which is useful for making sounds, and in which the Day and Night manifest the stars. He also created the Sea, which surrounds all the lands in a series of four circles; with its mighty tides, the Sea also strikes the Air so as to engender the winds, which are held to be four in number. He then established the Earth, which stands of its own power and is not easily moved. It is divided into five sections, the midmost of which is uninhabitable due to the heat, and the two outer regions are avoided because of the cold. He allowed the remaining two regions to enjoy a moderate climate: men dwell in those regions, as do flocks of birds and herds of wild beasts. God then added clouds to the sky in order to provide occasional rainstorms by whose mild showers the fruits of the

---

[1] Ganieda's mention of "household gods" should not undercut the generally Christian tone of her lament and should be regarded merely as a bit of classically-inspired rhetorical flourish on Geoffrey's part.

[2] The majority of Taliesin's discourse is drawn from *The Etymologies* of Isidore of Seville (c. 560–636), an encyclopedic Latin compendium of science and lore on natural philosophy. Two Welsh poems touching on natural philosophy, the *Canu y Byd Mawr* and the *Canu y Byd Bychan*, were also attributed to Taliesin.

trees and soil could grow. With the sun's aid, the clouds—in accordance with some mysterious law—are replenished like waterskins in a river. Then, climbing up through the air propelled by the winds, they pour out the waters they have gathered. Thence comes rain and snow and the round hailstones, which fall when a cold moist wind penetrates a cloud just as it was about to let its showers fall. Each of the winds assumes a nature of its own, similar to that of the region where it arises.

[764–778] "Above the firmament in which He fixed the stars, God established Ethereal Heaven, assigning it as a home for the legions of angels, whom worthy contemplation and the extraordinary sweetness of God refresh forever and ever. This place he has adorned with stars and with the radiant sun and has set the laws whereby each star moves only along the particular path through the heavens to which it is appointed. Below this He fixed the Airy Heaven, which is aglow with the body of the moon and which is filled with hosts of spirits who take pity upon us or else rejoice with us when matters go well. Their custom is to carry the prayers of men through the air and ask God if these prayers can be granted; they return bearing God's will, either by word or in a dream or through some other sign by which men may be enlightened.

[779–787] "The sublunar regions are rank with horrible demons who are skilled in deceit and who seek to trick us and tempt us. They often will take on a corporeal form made of air and appear to us, and many things often befall as a consequence. They may even have intercourse with women and impregnate them, thus begetting offspring in a profane way. God has thus created the heavens to be populated with this threefold order of spirits so that each order has its place and the world itself may be renewed from this ever-new seed of things.

[788–819] "God divided the Sea as well into various sections so that it would be able to reproduce the forms of things out of itself forever. One region of the Sea boils and another region freezes over, while the third part receives a moderate temperature from the other two and thus attends to our needs. The region of the Sea that boils flows around a great gulf and a vicious people; as its diverse currents flow back, they separate the orb of the Earth from Hell; in doing so, the Sea increases its own heat from the infernal fires. Those who put aside God and transgress the law go to that place. Their twisted will leads them where it wants, and they proceed, eager to corrupt that which has been forbidden to them. The grim judge is standing there, weighing his balanced scales and meting out to everyone his merits and just deserts. The second area of the Sea, which freezes over, laps narrow beaches of sand, which it first produces from the nearby vapor when it is mixed with the rays of Venus. The Arabs claim that this star also gives birth to sparkling gems when it passes through Pisces and its waters look back through the flames. These gemstones benefit those who carry them, healing many people and maintaining their health. The Maker also distinguished the various types of gems so that we can discern from their shape and color what kind of powers they possess. The third region of the Sea is the one that encircles the lands we live in, and by its proximity to us it serves us in many beneficial ways. It nourishes the fish and produces salt in abundance and bears upon it the vessels that carry all of our commerce back and forth, so that even the poor man may become suddenly wealthy. The Sea also makes the land near it fertile, and it provides food for the birds, who, it is said, arose from the Sea just as the fish did; although they are like the fish in this respect, they are governed by a very different rule of Nature. The Sea is, in fact, dominated more by the birds than by the fish, for they soar easily up from it through empty space to the lofty regions above.

[820–854] "The moisture of the Sea, however, affects the fish and keeps them beneath the waves, and it does not let them live when they are exposed to the dry light of day. The Creator also divided the fish into a variety of species, giving distinct characteristics to each so that they would forever be marvelous and healthful to the ailing. Indeed, they say that the *mullet* mitigates the heat of desire but that it also blinds the eyes of those who eat it too often. The *thymallus*, which derives its name from the thyme plant, has an odor that it passes to other fish that eat of it too often until all the fish in the river smell like itself. Contrary to all the laws of Nature, they say that all *morays* are of the feminine sex, but that they copulate and reproduce and multiply their brood from the seed of other species. Snakes often happen to come along the shore making sweet hissing sounds that attract the morays, and they couple with them according to their custom. It is also to be wondered at that the *remora*, which is only half a foot long, clings so tightly to a ship that it is as if it is aground; it thus detains the vessel and will not allow it to cast off to sea, and its power should rightly be feared. There is a certain fish they call the *swordfish* because it attacks with its sharp snout. People often fear to approach even in a ship when a swordfish is swimming nearby, for, if caught, it swiftly makes a hole in the vessel, chops it to pieces and then sinks it down a sudden whirlpool. Ships also fear the *sawfish* because of its crest, for it pierces them from below and slices them to bits, throwing the pieces into the water, where it should be feared as if it were indeed a sword. The *sea-dragon*, which men claim has poison under its wings, should also be feared by those who capture one, for when it stings it also injures with its venom. The *stingray*, they say, has a quite different mode of attack. If someone should touch a live stingray, his arms and feet and other members will immediately turn numb and are stripped of their powers as if dead, so noxious is the aura from its body.

[855–874] "God granted the sea unto these and many other types of fish, but He also adorned it with many islands in bloom. Men dwell in these lands, which are famous for the fertility that the Earth brings forth from their soil. The foremost and greatest of these islands is said to be *Britain*, which produces every sort of thing in its abundance. Indeed, it bears crops every year that render the noble gift of fragrance for human enjoyment. There are also forests, fields redolent with honey, lofty mountains, broad meadows all abloom, springs and rivers, fish and cattle, wild beasts, fruit trees, gemstones, precious metals, and whatever else abundant Nature can provide. In addition, it possesses springs that can heal the sick with their hot waters and provide delightful baths. These baths send people home swiftly cured of their illnesses. King Bladud established these baths when he held the scepter of the kingdom, giving them the name of his wife Alaron.[1] They are useful to so many sick people because of their medicinal properties, but especially to women, as the waters have often proven.

[875–892] "Not far from Britain lies the island of *Thanet*, which is abundant in many things but which has no venomous snakes; if soil from Thanet is mixed with wine, it is a remedy for poison. The sea also separates the *Orkneys* from mainland Britain. These thirty-three islands rest together in the ocean. Twenty of them are uncultivated, but the remaining ones are cultivated. The island of *Thule* is called 'Furthest Thule' because the summer sun makes its solstice there but then turns its rays the other way and proceeds no further; the sun instead takes away the day, so that the night air in that place is ever disturbed with shadows and the sea freezes over from the terrible chill, thus preventing the concourse of ships. The most impressive island besides our own is said to be Ireland, with its delightful fertility. It is quite large and has few bees or birds and does not allow serpents to breed in it at all. Hence it is that if soil or a stone is brought out of Ireland, it repels snakes and bees.

[893–907] "The *Isle of Gades* is located near the Gates of Hercules. A tree grows there with gum dripping from its bark; gemstones are produced when pieces of glass are smeared with this gum. The island is said to harbor

---

[1] See *The History*, Book Two.

a guardian dragon, who, they say, keeps vigil beneath the boughs of the trees that bear the Golden Apples. Women with goats' bodies dwell in the *Gorgades Islands*, and they are said to be able to run faster than hares. The islands of *Argyre* and *Chryse* are said to abound in gold and silver as much as Corinth abounds in ordinary stones. The *Isle of Ceylon* flourishes delightfully because of its fertile soil. It brings forth crops twice in a single year; it has two summers and two springs, and twice a year grapes and other fruits are harvested, and it is also most pleasant because of its sparkling gemstones. The *Island of Tiles*, which enjoys eternal spring, produces flowers and fruits which bloom the whole year long.

[908–940] "The *Isle of Apples*,[1] which is also called the Fortunate Isle, derives its name from the fact that it produces everything for itself: there is no need for farmers to till the fields there, and there is no agriculture at all beyond what Nature herself provides. It produces ample grain and grapes, and apple trees grow amid the close-clipped meadows in its forests. Instead of mere grass, the soil there produces an abundance of all sorts of things. The inhabitants live to be a hundred years or more. Nine sisters govern that place, administering a very pleasant law code over those people who come to them from our lands. The foremost among these sisters is most learned in the art of healing, and she surpasses them all in beauty. Her name is Morgen, and she has learned the helpful properties of all the various herbs in order to cure the bodies of the sick.[2] She also possesses the great skill of being able to transform her appearance and to sail through the air with new feathers, just as Daedalus did. She can be at Brest or Chartres or Pavia whenever she desires. And she can also glide down to your shores at will. It is said that she taught mathematics to her sisters, whose names are Moronoe, Mazoe, Gliten, Glitonea, Gliton, Tyronoe, and Thiten, who is best known for her *cithara*.[3] We carried the wounded Arthur to the Isle of Apples after the battle of Camlann, guided by Barinthus, who

---

[1] I.e., Avalon. Compare the following description to Geoffrey's cryptic reference to Avalon in Book Eleven of *The History of the Kings of Britain*. The word *Avalon* bears a relationship (perhaps only a coincidental one) to the Welsh word *afal* meaning "apple."

[2] The figure of Morgen here corresponds to the Morgan le Fay of the later Arthurian romances. Scholars have variously traced her origins to a Breton water fairy, to *the Morrigain*, a pagan Irish war goddess, and to the ancient Celtic goddess *Matrona*. Although Geoffrey probably was not the first to associate this character with the Arthurian cycle, *The Life of Merlin* is the earliest surviving text in which her name occurs.

[3] Basil Clarke admits that the names of Morgen's sisters, which sound vaguely classical and vaguely Irish, are difficult, if not impossible, to trace. Geoffrey has omitted the name of one of Morgen's sisters.

knows all the seas and all the stars of heaven.[1] With Barinthus at the helm, we arrived there with the prince, where Morgen gave us an honorable welcome. She had the king lain upon a golden bed in her chambers, where she inspected his honorable wound with her very own hands. She gazed at it for a long while and finally said that he could return to health if he stayed there with her for a long time and reaped the benefits of her knowledge of healing. We joyously committed the king to her care and sailed back upon the first favorable winds."

[941–952] Then Merlin replied: "My dear friend, how the kingdom has suffered since the peace was broken! What once was no longer exists, for the nobles through an evil twist of fate have turned against one another and have disrupted things to the point that troves of wealth have left the country and all goodness has fled. The desperate citizens will soon abandon their walls. The Saxon people, fierce in warfare, shall overtake them, and shall once again cruelly overcome us and destroy our cities and defile God's law and His churches. Indeed, because of our crimes, God will suffer this devastation upon us in order to correct the foolish."

[953–976] Merlin had not quite finished speaking when Taliesin declared, "Then it is now necessary for the people to send for their leader to return in a swift vessel, if he has healed by now, so that he may drive out the enemies as he used to and restore to the people the peace they once enjoyed." "No," Merlin answered, "the Saxon people shall not leave in that way, now that they have dug their claws into our lands. At first they shall subjugate the kingdom and the people and the cities, and they shall rule the land by force for many years. Three among us, however, shall resist them courageously and slay many of them, and finally conquer them in the end. But their efforts will not endure, for it is the intention of the Highest Judge that the Britons in their weakness shall lose the kingdom for many an age, until Conan comes over from Brittany in his chariot and Cadwallader, the honored leader of the Welsh, unites the Welsh, Scots, Cornish, and Armoricans in a firm pact, returning the lost crown to its people. Then, with their enemies repulsed and the Age of Brutus restored, they will govern their cities according to the holy laws.[2] The kings will once more begin to conquer far-off peoples and subjugate their realms in mighty wars."

---

[1]   Geoffrey probably drew this helmsman's name from one of the companions of St. Brendan in his legendary voyages across the ocean.

[2]   Compare the preceding sentences with Merlin's prophecy 20 in *The History of the Kings of Britain*, Book Seven, where the coming of Conan and Cadwallader is given a some-what different emphasis.

[977–1016] Taliesin then said: "No one now living will be alive to see those days. And I do not believe that anyone has seen so many wars between fellow citizens as you have." "No, indeed," Merlin replied, "for I have lived a long time and have seen many wars, both amongst ourselves and against barbarian peoples who overturn all order. The most heinous crime I remember was when Constans was betrayed and his young brothers, Uther and Ambrosius, fled across the sea.[1] The realm, having no leader, was immediately plunged into war. Then Vortigern, the consul of the Gewissei, led his armies against all the other tribes in order to be the leader of all of them, and he savagely massacred the innocent peasants. He seized the crown unexpectedly, having executed many of the nobility, and he subjugated the entire kingdom to his power. But those who had been allied to the dispossessed brothers by blood took this ill and began to put all the cities of this ill-fated prince to the flame, despoiling his realm with their cruel armies. They would not allow him to rule it in peace. Unable to subdue these rebellious people, Vortigern decided to invite men from abroad to help him fight his enemies in this war. Almost immediately, bands of warriors arrived from diverse parts of the world, and they were all given an honorable welcome. The helmed force of the Saxon people, who had come in their horn-prowed vessels, entered into his service then. They were led by two daring brothers, Hengist and Horsa, who later inflicted great harm upon the people and cities with their wicked treachery. Having served the king diligently for a time, they were able to sway him to themselves, for they saw that the people were distracted by a civil dispute, and they easily overcame Vortigern. They then turned their fierce weapons against the Britons. They broke their faith and, in a cunning plot, slew the British princes, who were sitting together with them in order to draw up a new peace treaty. Vortigern himself they drove away across the snowy mountaintops. These are the things I told him would happen to the kingdom. The Saxons then began roving around setting homesteads to the torch, and they sought to subdue the entire realm to themselves.

[1017–1042] "But when Vortimer perceived what dire straits the kingdom was in and the fact that his father had been exiled from the hall of Brutus, he took the crown himself with the consent of the people. Then he attacked the cruel folk who were destroying the

---

[1] The remainder of Merlin's speech recapitulates the major events of *The History*, Books Six to Eleven, though there are many significant changes in emphasis and detail.

Britons, and after many battles he forced them to retreat to Thanet where the fleet that had brought them here was waiting. The warlike Horsa and many others fell as they fled, slain by our men. King Vortimer pursued them to Thanet and besieged them there by land and by sea. But he did not prevail, for the Saxons suddenly took to their ships and broke the blockade with great force, hurrying home to their own country. Having triumphed over his enemies in many victorious battles, Vortimer became a ruler who was much-respected across the world, and he governed with just measure. Hengist's sister Renwein, however, was incensed at his success.[1] Masked by deceit, she became a wicked stepmother on her brother's account: she mixed poison for Vortimer and gave it to him to drink. It killed him. She sent at once across the sea for her brother to return with enough men to be able to conquer the warlike people of Britain. This he did, arriving with so great a host that he was able to plunder until quite sated, and he put all the homesteads throughout the land to the torch.

[1043–1058] "While these events were unfolding, Uther and Ambrosius were in Brittany with King Budicius. They were already girded with swords and had been proven in war, but they now allied themselves with soldiers from many different lands so that they could seek out their native soil and drive out the people who were even now laying waste to their patrimony. Therefore they set their vessels upon the wind and sea and soon came ashore to protect their countrymen. Vortigern they pursued all the way through the kingdom of Wales until he was shut up in a tower; they burned the tower down, and him with it. Next they turned their swords toward the Angles, defeating them in many battles, though they were sometimes defeated in turn. With great effort, our men finally attacked the Angles in hand-to-hand combat and wounded them grievously. They slew Hengist, and, by the will of Christ, they were victorious.

[1059–1106] "After these things were finished, the realm and the royal crown were given to Ambrosius by the will of both the clergy and the general populace, and he proved a just ruler in all affairs. However, after four years had passed, he was betrayed by his physician and died drinking poison. His younger brother Uther succeeded him, but he proved unable at first to keep the peace, for the treacherous Saxons returned again and laid everything waste, as was their army's habit. Uther met them in fierce battles and drove them back across the ocean in their oared ships. With this conflict concluded, Uther soon restored peace, and he sired a

---

[1]   In *The History of the Kings of Britain*, Renwein is Hengist's daughter, not his sister.

child who was in later days such an outstanding man that no one could match him in virtue. His name was Arthur, and he held the kingdom for many years after his father Uther's death. This he accomplished only through great pains and labors and the slaying of many men in battle. For while Uther was lying ill, that faithless people came again from the Angle, and they subdued all his lands and regions north of the Humber with their swords. Arthur was but a boy then, and was not able to repel them on account of his age. He therefore followed the advice of the clergy and laity and sent for help from Hoel, the King of Armorica, sending a swift fleet to request his aid. They were, after all, united by love and common blood, and felt bound to relieve one another at need. So Hoel summoned fierce men from all around and brought soldiers to us by the thousands. Allying his forces with Arthur's, he drove away the enemies with frequent attacks and bitter slaughter. With Hoel's aid, Arthur was strong and secure in his forces when he moved against the enemy, whom he at last defeated and forced to withdraw from Britain. Then, applying the moderation of the law, Arthur restored order to his kingdom. Not long after this, he waged fierce wars upon the Scots and Irish, subduing them and their lands with the armies he led. Next he subjugated the far-off Norse across the broad sea, as well as the Danes, attacking them with his dreaded fleet. He conquered the folk of Gaul after slaying their leader Frollo, to whom the Romans had entrusted their power there. The Romans themselves, who sought to wage war against his kingdoms, Arthur also fought and defeated, killing the Procurator Lucius Hiberius, the colleague of Emperor Leo, who had come at the Senate's command to drive Arthur from the territory of Gaul.

[1107–1135] "In the meantime, Mordred, that disloyal and foolish regent, began to subdue Britain for himself, and he engaged in an illicit affair with the king's wife. It is said that the king, desiring to attack his enemies, had entrusted both the queen and the realm to him. However, when news of such evils reached his ears, he put aside the waging of his war and returned to Britain, coming ashore with a force of thousands. Arthur then fought with his nephew and forced him to retreat across the sea. There that traitor mustered the Saxons and commenced another war against his lord. Mordred fell in battle, however, betrayed by the same godless folk whom he had trusted in his undertakings. Oh, how great was the slaughter of the men and the grief of the mothers whose sons fell in that fray! After the battle, the king, who was mortally wounded, deserted his realm and traveled across the waves with you, as you mentioned earlier, coming to the hall of the nymphs. Then Mordred's two sons, each desiring to control the kingdom, began to wage war against each other, and they subsequently slew many of their close relations. Then King Arthur's nephew Duke Constantine rose up against them and cruelly ravaged the people and the cities. When he had put both of the brothers to a terrible death, he took the crown of the realm and ruled the people. But that peace did not last because his kinsman Conanus commenced a fierce war against him and laid everything waste, killing the king and snatching up for himself those lands that he now governs without stability or reason."

[1136–1178] While Merlin was saying these things, the servants rushed in and announced that a new spring had arisen at the foot of the mountains and was pouring forth clean waters which even now were spreading all through the valley and splashing through the meadows as it skipped along. Both Merlin and Taliesin arose at once to see this new spring. Once they had inspected it, Merlin sat down upon the grass and praised the locale and the rushing stream, and he marveled at how it had burst forth out of the earth. He soon became thirsty and bent his head into the river, drinking at his pleasure, and the water passed through his stomach and internal organs. The moisture of that draught coursed through him and its humors settled within his body. At once he regained his mind and recognized himself. His madness fell away, and the feelings that had for so long been dormant within him returned. He became as sane and whole as he had ever been, his reason now restored. Then, exalting God, he raised his face to the heavens and uttered these words of holy praise: "O King through whom the wheeling of the starry heavens exists, through whom the ocean and the earth with its lovely grasses flourish and feed their own and, in their profuse fertility, offer constant aid to the human race! O King through whom my sense has returned and the wandering of my mind has ceased! I was outside of myself, and I knew of the deeds of people past and I predicted the future as if I were a spirit. I understood the secrets of nature and the flights of birds and the wanderings of the stars and the gliding of fish, but the unswerving laws of these things also haunted me, denying me the peace that is natural to the human mind. I have now come back to myself. And now I appear to be moved with the same power by which my soul used to animate my body. Therefore, exalted Father, I must now obey you, uttering worthy praise from my worthy breast. Joyous forever more, I shall make joyous offerings to you. In giving me this new spring out of the green earth, Your generous Hand has helped me twofold, for I possess both the water which I needed, and I have also healed my mind by drinking of it. But where, my dear Taliesin, does this power come from? How does a new spring erupt in this way, and how does it make me who I was again, when I had been until now quite insane?"

[1179–1238] Taliesin answered: "The wondrous Creator of all things distinguished flowing waters into different types, giving each its own special power to offer constant aid to the sick. There are springs, rivers, and lakes in the world; by their power they frequently heal many people.[1] In Rome there flows the swift *Tiber*, whose salubrious waters are said to cure wounds through their proven medicinal properties. There is also a spring in Italy called *Cicero's Fountain*. It cures every kind of ailment of the eyes. It is said that the Ethiopians have a pool that makes a face cleansed in it glow as if washed with oil. Africa possesses a spring that the people there call the *Zema*. Its virtues give the drinker a beautifully sonorous voice. *Lake Dictonus* in Italy gives one a distaste for wine, while people who drink the water of the spring at *Chios* are said to become sluggish. They say that the land of Boeotia has two fountains. One of them causes the drinkers to forget things, while the other restores their memory. Boeotia also contains a lake, so noxious because of its awful pestilence, which induces an excess of aggression and sexual desire. The spring of *Cyzicus*, on the other hand, extinguishes love and erotic desire. A stream flows in the country of Campania whose waters, they say, make sterile people fertile and also cure men of insanity. The land of Ethiopia has a spring with red waters: he who drinks of it goes home raving mad. The spring of *Leinus* always prevents miscarriages. There are two springs in Sicily, one of which makes girls barren while the other makes them fertile according to its kind law. There are two rivers of great power in Thessaly. The sheep that drinks from the one will turn black, while the other will turn it white. Drinking from both produces dappled fleece. *Lake Clitumnus* in Umbria is said to bring forth large oxen from time to time; the hooves of horses will become hardened as soon as they step upon the sands of the *Reatine Marshes*. Bodies can never sink in the *Asphalt Lake* of Judea as long as life remains in them. On the other hand, there is a pool called *Syden* in India where nothing can float but just sinks right to the bottom. There is a lake called *Aloe* in which nothing can sink but even pieces of lead will float. Then there is the *Spring of Marsidia*, where stones can float. The *River Styx* flows out of a rock, and it kills those who drink from it. The land of Achaia bears witness to these slayings. It is said that the unusual law that governs the *Idumean Spring*

---

[1]   Here again Taliesin's discourse is largely derived from Isidore's *Etymologies*.

causes it to change color four times throughout a period of time. First it becomes turbid, then it turns green; then its order shifts and it turns red, until finally it turns to clear water in a lovely stream. Each of these colors is said to last for three months throughout the course of the year. Likewise, the waters of *Lake Trogodytis* flow out bitter three times a day and then sweet three times with a pleasing taste. Torches, they say, are lit from the spring at *Epirus*, and they relight themselves if they are put out. Rumor has it that the spring of *Garamantes* is so cold during the day and so hot at night that one cannot come near it because of the cold and the heat. There are elsewhere waters so hot that they are dangerous, and they become so hot because they flow through alum or sulfur, both of which possess the virtue of fire, which is useful for healing.

[1239–1253] "God endowed flowing water with these and other powers in order to provide helpful remedies for the ailing and to make it known how much the Creator presides over things as they are happening through Him. I judge these waters to be curative in the highest degree, and I believe that they can confer rapid healing. Until now their currents have flowed through dark subterranean caverns like the many others that are said to be coursing there as well, ready to burst forth at any time. Perhaps their sudden breaking out is due to some kind of obstacle—the falling of a stone or the settling of the ground. I suppose that some underground current, making its way back toward the surface, has finally broken through the earth here and given us this new spring. You can see many streams of this sort that burst out and then run back underground to their caverns."

[1254–1291] While they were discussing these matters, the word began spreading that this new spring had arisen in the Forest of Celidon and that a man who had drunk from it had been cured of a madness that had long afflicted him, for he had dwelt in the wilderness and lived like a beast. Soon all the lords and chieftains were coming to visit the spot and to congratulate the prophet who had been healed by the spring. After reporting to Merlin about the state of his land, the nobles asked him to take up his scepter again and lead a normal life among his people. Merlin answered: "Young ones, my age prevents me. I am slipping into old age and my limbs are so weak now that I am hardly able to walk through the fields. I have lived a long time, and that is enough, taking joy in the happy days when an abundance of great riches smiled boundlessly upon me. In yonder wood stands an oak tree still hale in its strength, but old age, which devours everything, has assailed it to the point where it has no sap left and is rotting within. I myself witnessed this very tree first grow; in fact, I saw the falling of the acorn from which it sprang, while a woodpecker stood over it and watched the branch. Here have I watched it grow as it would, and I have noted everything about it. I held a deep reverence for it there in the meadow, and I memorized the precise spot where it stood. So I have lived for a long time indeed. My old age weighs me down, and I refuse to rule again. Dwelling here beneath the green boughs, I take more pleasure in the riches of Celidon than in the gems of India or the gold that is said to lie on the banks of the Tagus, more than in the wheat fields of Sicily or the grapes of sweet Methys, and more than in lofty towers or wall-girded cities or clothing scented with Tyrian perfumes. Nothing pleases me enough to tear me away from my Celidon Forest, which I deem eternally lovely. I shall stay here for as long as I live, quite content with only apples and herbs, and I shall cleanse my flesh with holy fasting so that I may be worthy enough to enjoy eternal life."

[1292–1386] While he was saying these things, the noblemen spotted long rows of cranes in the sky, flying in a circle pattern and forming distinct letters in the air. The flock seemed well-ordered indeed up there in the bright sky. Gazing upon them, the nobles asked Merlin to explain why it was that they were flying in such a formation. Merlin soon replied: "The Creator of the World endowed all things according to their particular nature.[1] This I have learned from living so many days in the wilderness. It is the nature of *cranes* that, if there are many together flying aloft, we often see them take on some formation or another in their flight. One of the cranes will call out and warn them to maintain that formation while they fly so that they do not break their ranks and depart from their normal order. And if that one crane becomes hoarse, another will take its place. They also post a watch throughout the night, and the sentry grasps a small stone in his claws when he wishes to awaken the others; when the cranes see anyone at all they burst out with a sudden squawking. Their feathers grow black as they age. The *eagle*, on the other hand, whose name derives from the acuity of its eyesight, is said to have such powerful vision that it can gaze upon the sun without flinching. Eagles hang their chicks in the sun in order to know if there are any weaklings among them by seeing whether the chick avoids the sun's rays. They soar high as a mountaintop above the water and yet are able to discern their prey far beneath the waves. Then they plunge down through the air and snatch up the swimming fish, as Nature demands.

---

[1]   Merlin's exposition on birds also relies heavily on Isidore's *Etymologies*.

The *vulture*, having set aside interest in sexual intercourse, often conceives and bears offspring without a mate, strange though that is to say. Soaring aloft like the eagle, the vulture, with her widened nostrils, can catch the scent of a corpse from far across the water. She has no distaste for flying down—albeit slowly—to dead bodies in order to glut herself on her desired prey. The vulture remains alive and robust for one hundred years. With its raucous voice, the *stork* is the harbinger of spring. It is famous for nourishing its young so devotedly that it plucks out its own feathers and leaves its breast exposed. People say that the stork avoids the winter storms and heads instead for the coastlands of Asia, following the crow. When it grows old, its own young feed it because it fed them in the days when it owed them such care. A bird most beloved by sailors, the *swan* surpasses all the other birds with the sweetness of its song when it is dying. It is said that up in the land of Hyperborea it is possible to attract a swan with the music of a lyre played loudly upon the shore. The *ostrich* deserts her own eggs, burying them in the sand so that they might be cared for when she herself forgets to tend them. Hence these birds enter the world hatched not by their mother but by the sunshine. The *heron*, fearing the rain and storms, flies ahead of the clouds in order to avoid these perils. That is why sailors say that the heron portends sudden storms whenever they espy one high in the air. The *phoenix* will always be unique because of its divine gift. It rises with a renewed body in the land of the Arabs, and when it grows old it goes to a place that is quite hot from the sun's warmth. There it gathers together an enormous mound of spices and builds itself a funeral pyre. Lighting this mound with the swift beating of its wings, it then sets itself upon it and is completely immolated. The ashes of its body give rise to a new bird, and by this law is the phoenix reborn over and over again forever. The *cinnamolgus* fetches cinnamon when it desires to nest, building its home in a tall oak. For this reason, men are accustomed to driving it away with arrows and then taking away the stockpile of spice to sell. The *halcyon* is a bird that frequents saltwater marshes, and it builds its nests in the winter. When it lies at rest, the seas are calm for seven days, and the winds die down and storms grow calm and recede, ushering in peace and quiet. Then there is the *parrot*, who is supposed to talk in human speech as if it were its inborn call, so long as no one happens to be looking at it. It mingles *ave* and *chere* with jesting words.[1] The *pelican* habitually kills its

---

[1]   *Ave* is Latin for "hail," and is used primarily in religious formulae, especially the Hail Mary (*Ave Maria*) prayer; *chère* is French for "dear, darling, beloved."

young and then mourns for three days, mad with grief. It rends its flesh with its own beak and, cutting the veins, it spills its own blood, which it then sprinkles over the chicks and restores them to life. Whenever the *diomedae* birds burst out in a woeful voice or sudden cry, it is said to portend either the death of kings or great peril to the realm. And when they catch sight of anyone, they know immediately whether he is a Greek or a barbarian, for they approach a Greek joyously, with the flapping of wings and caresses. With barbarians, however, they circle hostilely and treat them like enemies, approaching with a terrible sound. The *memnonides*, they say, go on a long flight every fifth year to the tomb of Memnon, lamenting that prince who was slain in the Trojan War. The splendid *hercynia* possesses a wondrous feather that shines through the dark night like a burning lamp, and it lights a traveler's way if he holds it out before him. When the *woodpecker* makes its nest, it pulls nails and wedges out of the tree that no one else can pull out. The surrounding area echoes with its hammering."

[1387–1422] When Merlin had finished speaking, a certain madman happened upon them, or perhaps fate had led him there. He filled the woods and the air with a terrible noise, and he foamed at the mouth like a wild boar and threatened to attack them. They captured the man quickly and forced him to sit with them so that he might move them to merry laughter with his speech. As the prophet Merlin looked at the man more carefully, he recognized who he was, and a groan arose from deep within his breast. He said: "This was not how he looked back when our youth was in full bloom. He was a handsome and powerful knight in his day, a noble scion of the blood royal. He was among the many whom I had with me when I was wealthy, and I deemed myself fortunate to have so many fine companions, and fortunate I was indeed. And so it happened one time that we were hunting up in the mountains of Arwystli when we came upon an oak whose spreading branches stretched high into the air. A spring was flowing there, surrounded by a green lawn, and its waters seemed fit to drink. Since we were all thirsty, we sat down there and drank greedily from the clear stream. Then we espied some fragrant apples lying upon the tender grass on our side of the stream. The man who first glimpsed them picked them up and gave them to me, laughing about this unusual gift. I then passed the apples out among my companions, though I did not keep one for myself because there was not enough to go around. The others with whom I had shared the apples laughed and called me generous, and with hearty appetites they gobbled them up and complained that there were no more. Then at once a wretched madness seized this man and the others. They quickly lost all reason and began biting and tearing at each other like dogs, foaming at the mouth and rolling insanely upon the ground. They finally ran off like wolves, filling the empty breezes with their miserable howls.

[1423–1441] "I believe that these apples were in fact intended not for them but for me, for I afterwards learned that there was a woman who dwelt in those parts who had once been in love with me. She had for many years satisfied her desire with me, but after I spurned her and refused to sleep with her, she was seized by a fierce longing to injure me. When she could discover no other way to get close to me, she left these gifts coated with poison by that spring where she knew I would return; she hoped to harm me with that trick if I partook of those apples lying in the grass. However, good fortune saved me from them, as I have just explained. But now let me ask you to have this man drink the healthy waters of this new fountain so that, if he is able by any chance to regain his sanity, he might come back to his senses. Together, we will labor in these meadows in the Lord's name for the rest of our lives." The noblemen did what he said and the man, who had arrived there raving mad, drank the water and returned to himself. Upon his recovery, he recognized his friends immediately.

[1442–1451] Then Merlin said: "You must now faithfully enter the service of God, Who restored you to the self that you only now behold, that for so many years has lived like a beast in the wilderness, prowling about with no sense of shame. But now that you have regained your senses, do not leave behind the fruit groves and the green meadows that you frequented while insane. Instead, stay here with me so that, in the service of the Lord, you might strive to restore those days that your awful madness snatched away from you. And we shall hold all things in common as long as we both shall live."

[1452–1463] Maeldin, for that was the man's name, responded thus: "Venerable father, how could I refuse to do this? I shall be glad to dwell here in the forest with you and worship God with all my heart, so long as my spirits, for whose restoration I thank your care, still guide my trembling limbs." "I too shall spurn the things of the world," said Taliesin, "and we shall be three together. I haved lived long enough in vanity, and the time is now come to restore me to myself under your guidance, Merlin. But you, my lords, leave now and defend your cities. It would not be right for you to disturb our tranquility beyond all measure with your chatter. You have congratulated my friend quite enough."

[1464–1483] The noblemen then left. There remained only the three men, and the prophet's sister Ganieda made four. She had at last started to live a chaste life after the death of the king. Although she had ruled all the people in accordance with the laws, she now found no life sweeter than living in the forest with her brother. At times, the spirit so moved her that even she uttered prophecies regarding the future of the realm. And so it happened that on a certain day, when she was standing in her brother's hall watching the windows gleam in the sun, she spoke out these doubtful words from her doubtful breast: "I behold the city of Oxford filled with helmeted men and the holy men and holy bishops bound up in chains upon the recommendation of a youth. The Shepherd of the lofty tower shall be admired, and he shall needlessly be forced to unlock it, to his own injury. I behold Lincoln walled in by a ferocious army, and I behold two men penned in there, one of whom will escape and will return to the walls with a bestial people and their leader. He will conquer that cruel army once he has captured its commander.

[1484–1495] "What a crime it is that the stars, without using force or waging war, should capture the sun, below which they are supposed to sink! I see two moons in the sky near Winchester and two Lions behaving with excessive ferocity, and one man is gazing at two men, and another man is doing the same, and they are preparing for battle and facing each other at close quarters. The others rise up and bitterly attack the fourth, but none of them can prevail: the fourth stands his ground and maneuvers his shield and fights back with his weapons and, victorious, swiftly overcomes his three enemies. Two of them he drives across the frozen realms of the north; he pardons the third, who has begged for mercy. The stars therefore retreat through all the parts of the field.

[1496–1504] "The Armorican Boar, under the protection of an ancient oak, kidnaps the moon, waving its swords behind her back. Two stars I see fighting a battle against wild beasts beneath the hill of Urianus where the Deirans and the Gewissei once met during the reign of the great King Coel.[1] O how the men drip with sweat and the ground drips with blood when the wounds are meted out to foreign peoples! A star falls together with another star into the darkness, and it conceals its light from the renewed light.

[1505–1517] "Alas! Such dire famine shall arise that it will clutch at the people's bellies and drain the vigor from their limbs. It starts with

---

[1] Mount Urianus appears in Merlin's prophecy 47 in Book Seven of *The History*, though Geoffrey omits all mention of it in his account of King Coel in Book Five.

the Welsh and then spreads through all the corners of the kingdom, forcing the miserable folk to cross the sea. The calves that are used to living off the milk of the Scottish cows, who are dying of this wicked plague, shall flee. Leave, Normans, and stop your wanton armies from bearing their weapons through our homeland. There is nothing left now worth feeding your greed, for you have gobbled up everything that Mother Nature has long produced here in her marvelous fertility. Christ, aidYour people! Hold the Lions back. Restore the realm's tranquility and freedom from wars."

[1518–1524] Ganieda did not fall silent even here, and her companions marveled at her. Her brother Merlin went up to her at once and congratulated her with these friendly words: "Sister, does the spirit, having silenced my tongue and shut my book, wish you to predict the future now? This labor is now given to you. Take joy in it, and speak out everything with true devotion.You have my blessing."

[1525–1529] I have now brought my song to an end. Therefore, Britons, give the laurel wreath to Geoffrey of Monmouth. He is yours indeed, for he has sung of your battles and of your leaders, and he wrote a book that is now called *The Deeds of the Britons* and is famous throughout the world.

[Source: Basil Clarke, ed., *The Life of Merlin: Geoffrey of Monmouth's Vita Merlini* (Cardiff: U of Wales P, 1973), 52–134. Translated by Michael Faletra.]

3. From Gerald of Wales, *The Journey Through Wales (Itinerarium Kambriae)*, II.8

[The many works of the half-Norman, half-Welsh writer Gerald of Wales (1147–1223) testify to the pervasive influence of *The History of the Kings of Britain*. In this passage, Gerald voices some of the contemporary fascination with the figure of Merlin, and he attempts to reconcile Geoffrey of Monmouth's account of the prophet with that of certain other traditions.]

Not far from the source of the River Conway at the top of Mount Snowdon, which extends north from here, lies *Dinas Emreis*, that is, the hill-fort of Ambrosius, where Merlin once sat upon the edge of the pool and declared his prophecies toVortigern. There were actually two Merlins. This one was also called Ambrosius, and thus had two names, and he prophesied when Vortigern was king. He was sired by an incubus and was discovered at Carmarthen, which, in fact, means "Merlin's town," deriving its name from the fact that he was discovered there. The other Merlin hailed from Scotland and is surnamed Celidonius because he made his prophecies in the Forest of Celidon. He is also called Merlin Silvester because he once looked up into the air in the middle of a battle and beheld a horrible monster there. This drove him mad and he fled to the forest, passing the rest of his life as a wild man of the woods. This second Merlin was alive during the days of King Arthur and it is said that he made far clearer and more numerous prophecies than the other Merlin.

[Source: James F. Dimock, ed. *Giraldi Cambrensis Opera, Vol. VI: Itinerarium Kambriae et Descriptio Kambriae* (London: Longmans, Green, Reader, and Dyer, 1868), 133. Translated by Michael Faletra.]

Appendix C: King Arthur, From Myth to Man

1. From Aneirin, *The Gododdin*

[*The Gododdin* is a series of elegies attributed to the seventh-century Welsh poet Aneirin that commemorates the Britons who fell at the Battle of Catterick (c. 600 AD). One of the elegies contains the first extant reference to the figure of Arthur. Although Gwarddur in this elegy is compared to Arthur, it is impossible to tell here whether the poet understood this Arthur as an historical personage or was simply referencing him as a legendary renowned warrior.]

Over three hundred of the best men were slain.
Gwarddur pierced them in the center and on either side.
He stood out among that noble host,
In the winters he gave out horses from his herds.
Gwarddur summoned the black crows down before the fortress walls,
Though he was no Arthur.
Amongst his doughty men in battle,
The bulwark of the front lines was that Gwarddur.

[Source: A.O.H. Jarman, ed., *Y Gododdin: Britain's Oldest Heroic Poem* (Llandysul, Wales: Gomer, 1988), 65. Translated by Michael Faletra.]

2. From *What Man is the Gatekeeper? (Pa gur yw y porthor?)*

[Several early Welsh poems narrate the exploits of Arthur and his retinue of famous and powerful companions. In "What Man is the Gatekeeper?" the poet presents Arthur and his band as the vanquishers of a variety of supernatural monsters. One can already see in this early poem, which appears only in the thirteenth-century Black Book of Carmarthen but which has been dated to the tenth century, the association of the figures of Kay and Bedivere with Arthur.]

"What man is the Gatekeeper?"
"Glewlwyd Strong Grasp."
"What man is asking this?"
"Arthur and Kei the fair."

"Who are those accompanying you?"
"The best men in the world ..."

... Although Arthur may have been laughing,
Blood did he spill
In the hall of Afarnach
Battling with a hag.
He cleaved Penpalach's skull
Within the houses of Dissethach.
Up upon Mount Eidin
He fought against men with dogs' heads,
He felled them by the hundreds
With the accomplished Bedwyr by his side ...

[Source: A.O.H. Jarman, ed. *Llyfr Du Caerfyrddin* (Cardiff: U of Wales P, 1982), 66–67. Translated by Michael Faletra.]

3. From *The Stanzas of the Graves*

[Another early poem that appears in the thirteenth-century Black Book of Carmarthen, "The Stanzas of the Graves," sings of the resting places of a multitude of legendary Welsh heroes. Arthur stands out among the rest for having an indeterminate resting place, a fact that might reflect the early development of legends of Arthur's return and that anticipates Geoffrey of Monmouth's handling of Arthur's unusual departure.]

There is the grave of March and the grave of Gwythur,
And the grave of Gwgawn Red-Sword,
But the world's marvel indeed is the grave of Arthur.

[Source: A.O.H. Jarman, ed. *Llyfr Du Caerfyrddin* (Cardiff: U of Wales P, 1982), 41. Translated by Michael Faletra.]

4. From *Trioedd Ynys Prydein: The Welsh Triads*

[In Welsh bardic tradition, a triad is a terse grouping of three related terms, usually relating to legendary heroes of the British past. Likely used as mnemonics by bards in the oral composition of poetry, many of them bear witness to a Welsh historical and legendary corpus that antecedes Geoffrey of Monmouth.]

The Three Tribal Thrones of the Isle of Britain: Arthur as the High Prince in Menevia and Dewi as the High Bishop and Maelgwn Gwynedd as the High Elder; Arthur as the High Prince in Celliwig in Cornwall and Bedwin as the High Bishop and Caradoc Breichbras as the High Elder; Arthur as the High Prince in Pen Rhionydd in the North and Gerthmwl Wledig as the High Elder and Cyndeyrn Garthwys as High Bishop.

The Three Rash Assaults of the Isle of Britain: The first of them was when Medrawd came to the court of Arthur at Celliwig in Cornwall; he left behind no food or drink that he did not consume, and he cast Gwenhwyfar from her royal throne and dealt her a blow. The second Rash Assault was when Arthur arrived at Medrawd's court. He left no food or drink in the court. The third Rash Assault was when Aeddan Vradawc came to the court of Rhydderch Hael at Alclud, and he left no food nor drink, nor any beast alive.

The Three Futile Battles of the Isle of Britain: The first of these was the Battle of Goddeu ... The second was the Battle of Arfderydd ... And the third was the worst, namely the Battle of Camlann, which came to pass because of an argument between Gwenhwyfar and Gwenhwyfach. The reason these battles were called futile is because they were all brought about by so pointless a cause.

[Source: Rachel Bromwich, ed., *Trioedd Ynys Prydein: The Triads of the Island of Britain*, 3rd ed. (Cardiff: U of Wales P, 2006), 1, 153, 217. Translated by Michael Faletra.]

5. From *The Legend of St. Goeznovius (Legenda Sancti Goeznovii)*

[The anonymous *Legend of St. Goeznovius*, which may date from the year 1019, provides a rare glimpse of Arthur as a historical figure in the period before Geoffrey's work.]

... Vortigern eventually usurped the throne. Ruling the greater part of a kingdom he had so unjustly seized, he invited warlike men from Saxony and allied them to himself for protection. Because these Saxons were pagans and given over to great devilry, they adorned themselves with the human blood they spilled and visited much wickedness upon the Britons. Their pride was later checked for a time by the great Arthur, king of the Britons. He drove them from the island, for the most part, and imposed servitude upon them. But when Arthur, having achieved many impressive victories throughout Britain and Gaul, was summoned from this life, the way was again clear for the Saxons to return to the island, and the Britons were then greatly oppressed and their churches cast down and their saints persecuted....

[Source: E.K. Chambers, *Arthur of Britain* (London: Sedgwick & Jackson, 1927), pp. 241–42. Translated by Michael Faletra.]

6. From William of Malmesbury, *The Deeds of the Kings of the English* (*Gesta Regum Anglorum*)

[Geoffrey's somewhat older contemporary, William of Malmesbury (1080–1142), completed his *Deeds of the Kings of the English* in 1125. He is the first English historian to mention Arthur, whom he posits as a mere military leader rather than a figure of legend, though even William credits Arthur with incredible feats on the battlefield.]

After Vortimer died, the power of the Britons waned; with their hopes broken, they fled. Soon they would have perished completely if Ambrosius, the sole survivor of the Romans, who became monarch after Vortigern, had not quelled the rebellious barbarians with the powerful aid of warlike Arthur. This is the same Arthur of whom the Britons even today spout such nonsense: a man worthy to be celebrated not by false fables but in authentic history. Indeed, for a great time he upheld his tottering homeland and roused the hearts of the people to war. At last, at the siege of Mount Badon, bearing the image of the Mother of Our Lord, he fought nine hundred of the enemy single-handed; and he dispersed them with great slaughter.

[Source: R.A.B. Mynors, R.M. Thomson, and M. Winterbottom, eds., *Gesta Regum Anglorum: The History of the English Kings*, Vol. 1 (Oxford: Clarendon, 1998), p. 26. Translated by Michael Faletra.]

7. From Caradoc of Llancarvan, *The Life of Gildas* (*Vita Gildae*)

[In the final lines of his *History*, Geoffrey of Monmouth refers favorably to Caradoc of Llancarvan, whom he identifies as a contemporary historian. Although no true historical material by this Caradoc survives, we do have his *Life of Gildas*, which reveals access to historical traditions that do not appear in Geoffrey's work. It was written in the early- to mid-twelfth century.]

The holy Gildas lived at the same time as Arthur, the king of all of Britain, and he loved the king dearly, striving always to obey him. His twenty-three brothers, however, were continually rebellious toward Arthur and refused to acknowledge him as their overlord. They repeatedly defeated him, driving him out of the woodlands and the fields of battle alike. The eldest of these brothers, Hueil, was a vigorous man in battle and a renowned warrior, and he submitted to no one, let alone King Arthur. He in particular would antagonize the king, stirring up a great anger between them. This Hueil often made forays down out of Scotland, pillaging the countryside and putting it to the torch, achieving victories and great acclaim. When the king of Britain learned that this boisterous young man was committing such acts, he struck back and pursued that most successful youth, whom the people at one time claimed and believed would be king. After a bitter pursuit and a war-council on the island of Menau, Arthur finally slew that young brigand. Victorious, Arthur went home after this murder jubilant at having defeated the bravest of his enemies. Gildas, the historian of the Britons, happened to be in the city of Armagh in Ireland, teaching and preaching, when he heard that his brother has been killed by King Arthur. Upon hearing this news, he was sorely grieved and wept in great lamentation, as beloved brothers should. While he prayed daily for his brother Hueil's soul, he also prayed for Arthur, his own brother's enemy and murderer, in fulfillment of the commandment of the Apostle, which says "Love those who persecute you and do good to those who hate you."

[Source: Hugh Williams, ed., *Two Lives of Gildas* (Felinfach, Wales: Llanerch, 1990), 90–92. Translated by Michael Faletra.]

8. From Gerald of Wales, *The Description of Wales* (*Descriptio Kambriae*), II.2

[The Cambro-Norman writer Gerald of Wales (1147–1223) bears witness to the continuing fascination with the issue of Arthur's historicity in the wake of Geoffrey's account. Gerald here speculates as to why no author before Geoffrey of Monmouth provides a reliable historical narrative of the king.]

The Britons insist that Gildas upbraided his own people so bitterly because King Arthur had killed his brother, who was a leader among the Scots. Upon learning of his brother's death, they claim, Gildas took all the books that he had written in praise of the Britons or of the deeds of Arthur and cast them into the sea. And that is why you will discover no book that provides an accurate account of that mighty king.

[Source: James F. Dimock, ed. *Giraldi Cambrensis Opera, Vol. VI: Itinerarium Kambriae et Descriptio Kambriae* (London: Longmans, Green, Reader, and Dyer, 1868), 209. Translated by Michael Faletra.]

9. From Gerald of Wales, *The Education of Princes (De Principis Instructione Liber)*, 1.20

[In this selection, Gerald of Wales (see above) describes the discovery of King Arthur's tomb in Glastonbury sometime during the 1180s. Gerald's Arthur is unquestionably historical and unquestionably dead.]

In our own times,[1] the body of Arthur was discovered at Glastonbury, even though tales would have us believe that there was some kind of mystery regarding his end and that the king had somehow evaded death and was carried off to some remote locale. The corpse at Glastonbury was found deep underground beneath a hollowed-out oak between two monuments of stone that had long ago been erected in the churchyard. The corpse had been endowed with tokens that were fabulous, indeed almost miraculous. The monks carried the body into the church and gave it a respectable burial within a marble tomb. Beneath the king's body there was a slab of stone; it was not placed on top as is the custom in the present. Underneath this slab there was attached a leaden crucifix. I have personally inspected this crucifix and have traced the letters that had been etched into the side that faced the slab rather than on the other side, which would make them more visible. The epitaph read as follows: *Here in the Isle of Avalon lies buried the famous King Arthur and Guinevere, his second wife.*

We can make several observations regarding this discovery. Arthur, it seems, had two wives, the second being buried with him. Her bones were found along with but separate from her husband's. The upper two thirds of the coffin held Arthur's remains, while the lower third, at the

---

[1]   Gerald is writing around the year 1190.

king's feet, contained his wife's. A golden tress of woman's hair, still preserving its golden luster, was also discovered within the coffin. However, as one of the monks tried to pick it up, it fell away into dust.

There had been a few indications within the abbatial records that the king's body would be discovered at this location. The inscriptions on the two monuments offered yet another clue, but they had almost completely worn away from the passage of time. The holy monks and other clerics had also had visions and revelations in this regard. However, it was King Henry II of England who, having heard a story from an old British singer of tales, informed the monks that Arthur's body could be found buried at least sixteen feet underground, and not in a stone sarcophagus but in a hollowed-out oak at that. It was, in fact, buried just that deep and had been very skillfully hidden so that the Saxons would not find it, for Arthur had ceaselessly fought them for his entire life and, though he did manage to eradicate them, they still occupied the island after his demise. That is why the epitaph that announced the truth was cut into the inner side of the crucifix, facing the slab. This inscription kept the secret of that burial-place for many long years until, when the time was propitious, those letters at last revealed the secrets they had concealed for so long.

In ancient times, the place now known as Glastonbury was called the Isle of Avalon. Since it is surrounded on all sides by marshes, it is practically an island. The Welsh name it *Ynys Avallon*, which means "The Island of Apples." *Aval* happens to be the Welsh word for apple, and that fruit once grew there bountifully. After the Battle of Camlann, a noble lady by the name of Morgan, who was the ruler and benefactress in that area and was also a close kinswoman to Arthur, conveyed the king to that island that is now known as Glastonbury in order to tend to his wounds.[1] Long ago, that place had also been called *Ynys Gutrin* in Welsh—namely, the Island of Glass. From this locution the Saxons later devised the name *Glastingeburh* for that place. In the Saxon language, the word *glass* corresponds to *vitrum* in Latin, while *burh* corresponds to the Latin *castrum* or *civitas*.

Let it be known that when Arthur's bones were discovered in that place, they were found to be so large that the verse of the poet seemed to have come true: *All men will marvel at the size of the bones that have been exhumed.* The abbot himself showed one of the shin-bones to me. When he set it up against the foot of the tallest man around, it still

---

[1] Gerald's discussion here suggests his familiarity with Geoffrey's *Life of Merlin* (See Appendix B2 above).

extended at least three inches above that man's knee. And the skull was so impressively large that it truly seemed a natural wonder: the area between the brow-ridge and the eye-sockets was the same width as a grown man's hand. At least ten wounds could be discerned, though all but one of them had been healed. This last one was far greater than the others and had left an enormous impression. It was doubtless this very injury that had caused Arthur's death.

[Source: James F. Dimock, ed. *Giraldi Cambrensis Opera, Vol. VIII: De Principis Instructione Liber* (London: Eyre & Spottiswoode, 1891), 127–29. Translated by Michael Faletra.]

10. From William Caxton's Preface to Sir Thomas Malory's *Le Morte Darthur*

[The renowned early printer William Caxton (c. 1422–91) set up the first printing press in England in 1474 and published the compendious *Morte Darthur* by Thomas Malory (d. 1471) in 1485. His preface to Malory's work insists on King Arthur as a legitimate historical figure.]

... many men hold the opinion that there was no such Arthur and that all the books that have been written about him have been fictions and fables, holding that some chronicles make no mention of him and say nothing about him or his knights.

Some men—and one person in particular—answered that great folly and blindness might well be imputed to anyone who said or thought that there was never a king called Arthur, for he said that there is much evidence to the contrary. First, you may see Arthur's tomb in the monastery of Glastonbury. Also, *The Polychronicon*, in Book V, chapter 6, and in Book VII, chapter 23, states that his body was buried and afterwards discovered and transferred into that monastery. You shall see also in Boccaccio's book *De Casu Principum* the history of part of his noble deeds and his fall. Geoffrey [of Monmouth] in his British book recounts Arthur's life as well. And in various places in England there are still many remembrances of Arthur and his knights and there shall be forever more. First, in Westminster Abbey in the shrine of St. Edward there remains the imprint of his seal in red wax encased in beryl, upon which is written: *Patricius Arthurus Britannie Gallie Germanie Dacie Imperator.*[1]

---

[1] The noble Arthur, Emperor of Britain, Gaul, Germany, and Denmark.

And in the Castle of Dover you may see Gawain's skull and Caradoc's mantle, while at Winchester you may see the Round Table, and in other places Lancelot's sword and many other things.

So, all things considered, no man can reasonably deny that there was a king of this land named Arthur. For in all places Christian and heathen he is reputed and held to be one of the Nine Worthies, and the foremost of the three Christians. Also, he is even more spoken of beyond the sea than in England and more books are made about him there in Dutch, Italian, Spanish, and Greek as well as French. And in the city of Camelot in Wales, the great stones and marvelous works still remain as a record of witness to him, as do the works of iron lying underground and various royal vaults, which many now living have seen. Therefore it is a marvel that he is not more renowned in his own country, except that it accords with the word of God, which says that no man is taken for a prophet in his own country.

[Source: Thomas Malory, *Works*, ed. Eugene Vinaver, 2nd ed. (New York: Oxford UP, 1971), xiii–xiv. Translated by Michael Faletra.]

Appendix D: Early Responses to Geoffrey of Monmouth

1. From Henry of Huntington, *Epistle to Warin the Briton*

[The English historian Henry of Huntington (c. 1085–1155) is the first person to give a written account of Geoffrey of Monmouth's *History*. Little did Henry know that Geoffrey had gently disparaged his own life's work, *The History of the English* (Historia Anglorum) in the conclusion to *The History of the Kings of Britain*. In this letter to an associate named Warin the Briton, Henry describes his discovery of Geoffrey's book in a Norman monastery in 1139, a mere year or so after its completion.]

Warin the Briton, you are a refined and pleasant man. You have asked why, in my narration of the history of our country, I have begun in the time of Julius Caesar but have neglected to describe the flowering of the kings who ruled from Brutus to Caesar. I will answer that, though I have often made verbal and written inquiries regarding the history of this period, I never turned anything up. Dark are the clouds that jealous Time casts over the glorious deeds of mortal men, if they are not lost altogether. However, this very year,[1] while accompanying Archbishop Theobald of Canterbury to Rome, I discovered to my great surprise at the monastery of Bec a book that fleshed out these very periods of history. I also met a monk there by the name of Robert of Torigny, a man devoted to researching and collecting writings on subjects both secular and religious. After interviewing me regarding the continuous history of the kings of England that I had published, and listening intently to my discourses on the subject, he presented for my perusal a book that discussed the kings of the ancient Britons, who had occupied our island before the English. I send excerpts from this book to you, my dear friend, in as short a form as the brevity of this letter will allow…. if you should desire even more on this subject, ask to see the great book by Geoffrey Arthur[2] at Bec, wherein you will find these matters discussed diligently and at great length.

---

[1] I.e., 1139.

[2] Geoffrey of Monmouth often witnessed charters as "Geoffrey Arthur," Arthur presumably being his father's name, and many twelfth-century writers referred to him thus.

[Source: Robert of Torigny, *Chronica*, ed. R. Howlett, repr. in *Arthur of Britain*, E.K. Chambers (London: Sedgwick & Jackson, 1927), 249–50. Translated by Michael Faletra.]

2. From Gerald of Wales, *The Journey Through Wales* (*Itinerarium Kambriae*), I.5

[In this passage from his *Journey Through Wales* (1188), Gerald of Wales (see Appendices B and C) relates a tale that sheds much light on later twelfth-century reactions towards Geoffrey's *History*.]

May it be noted that in our own times there was a certain Welshman who dwelt here in the vicinity of Caerleon by the name of Meilyr, and he was most knowledgeable about the future and the occult, which gave him insight on events to come … Whenever any falsehood was uttered in his presence, Meilyr could detect it immediately: for he saw a demon jumping up and down and laughing upon the liar's tongue. Upon inspecting a mendacious book, he could tell whether it was completely untruthful or even whether it contained any falsehood at all; in fact, he was immediately able to place his finger upon the lie, even though he was almost completely illiterate. If asked how he perceived such a thing, he explained that the demon indicated the lying passage first with its own finger. Likewise, when entering the dormitory of a monastery, Meilyr was able to point out the bed of any false monk whose religion was for show and not from the heart. He said that demons of gluttony and greed were beyond sordid, but that demons of libidinousness and lust, though more beautiful to behold, were even more revolting.

Whenever it happened that he could not withstand the insults of these unclean spirits, the Gospel of St. John was placed on his lap and the spirits vanished at once, fluttering away like birds. If afterwards, however, Geoffrey Arthur's *History of the Kings of Britain* were placed on his lap instead, the demons would land in greater numbers not only all over his own body but all over the book as well, settling in for longer than usual and being even more annoying.

[Source: James F. Dimock, ed. *Giraldi Cambrensis Opera, Vol. VI: Itinerarium Kambriae et Descriptio Kambriae* (London: Longmans, Green, Reader, and Dyer, 1868), 57–58. Translated by Michael Faletra.]

3. From William of Newburgh, *The History of the Deeds of the English (Historia Rerum Anglicarum)*

[The Augustinian canon William of Newburgh (c. 1135–98) spent most of his life in his Yorkshire priory composing a history of Norman England. In the preface to his *History of the Deeds of the English* (1198), which was generally written with a scrupulous eye toward historical evidence, William disparages Geoffrey of Monmouth's work. His critique formed the basis for many subsequent criticisms, culminating in the discrediting of Geoffrey's *History* in the sixteenth and seventeenth centuries.]

It was Bede, that venerable priest and monk, who first wrote down the history of our people, the English. In order to approach his chosen subject more authoritatively, he commenced his history with the ancient Britons, who are known to have been the original inhabitants of our island, briefly touching upon the more celebrated of their deeds. Before our Bede, the British people had Gildas as their historian, some of whose words Bede inserts into his own text: this I discovered years after first reading Bede when I happened to read Gildas' book. Since his locution was rather rough and unpolished, very few people have transcribed or possessed his book, and it is indeed hard to find. His integrity, however, can hardly be disputed, for he does not spare even his own people in promoting the truth, and, though he does say some good things about them, he laments their many bad qualities. We should not think that the truth has been silenced when a Briton writes about his fellow Britons that they were neither powerful in war nor constant in peace.

However, in order to expiate the Britons of their sins, a writer has emerged in our own times who has woven the most fantastic lies regarding them and has with shameless boasting elevated their virtues far beyond those of the Macedonians and Romans. This man is called Geoffrey, and he is surnamed Arthur due to the fact that he put the fabulous deeds of Arthur into Latin, drawing from the old yarns of the Britons and from his own imagination and cloaking them with the name of actual history. He has also brazenly published the most fallacious prophecies of Merlin, to which he has certainly added much of his own invention while translating them into Latin; and he has presented them as though they were genuine prophecies that reflected the unchanging truth. He also relates that this Merlin was the son of a woman and an incubus, and that it is his paternal heritage that provides his deep and extensive knowledge of future events. Yet we are correctly taught both by reason and by Holy Scripture that demons, who are shut out from the light of God, cannot ascertain the future through contemplation. They instead infer certain future events by interpreting the signs, of which they are far more knowledgeable than we; they thus conjecture rather than actually foresee. However subtle their predictions may be, they often fool themselves as well as others. But they are still able to impose these delusional predictions upon the unwise and assume for themselves a prescience that they do not possess in the least. There are in fact clear errors in those prophecies of Merlin that are known to refer to the kingdom of the English after the death of this Geoffrey, who translated this doggerel from the British tongue, adding much to it from his own imagination. Then he tailored these fictitious prophecies of his to fit events that occurred either before or during his own lifetime, as he might quite easily do, in order that they receive a fitting interpretation. Furthermore, only someone who knows nothing about ancient history could ever doubt when he comes across that book, which is called *The History of the Britons*, that it is anything but wanton and shameless lies.

[Source: Hans Claude Hamilton, ed., *Historia Rerum Anglicarum Willelmi Parvi*, Vol. 1 (London: English Historical Society, 1861), 3–5. Translated by Michael Faletra.]

4. From Ranulf Higden, *Polychronicon*, V

[The Benedictine monk Ranulf Higden of Chester (d. 1364) composed his *Polychronicon*, a massive Latin compendium of world history, in the first half of the fourteenth century. Although he follows Geoffrey's narrative in the main for his account of pre-Saxon Britain, he here evinces a reasonable skepticism regarding the historicity of King Arthur.]

Men may indeed wonder how the things that have been said about this Arthur, whom Geoffrey praises more than any other, could be true, since Geoffrey relates how he conquered thirty different realms. If he did indeed defeat the king of France and slay Lucius Hiberius, the Procurator of Rome in Italy, it is peculiar that the chronicles of Rome, France, or the Saxons never mention such a noble ruler in their accounts, even though they do make note of many men of humbler position. Geoffrey states that Arthur defeated Frollo, the king of France, yet there is no evidence of anyone of that name in France. He also claims that Arthur slew Lucius Hiberius, the Procurator of Rome during the reign of Emperor Leo. However, according to all the histories of Rome, there was no Lucius Hiberius governing Rome at that time. Arthur too was not even born then, but lived in the time of Justinian, the fifth emperor after Leo. Geoffrey tells us that he has wondered at the fact that neither Bede nor Gildas mention Arthur in their narratives, but I must wonder why Geoffrey gives so much praise to a man upon whom the old authorities, those renowned writers of histories, never touch.

[Source: Joseph Rawson Lumby, ed., *Polychronicon Ranulphi Higden Monachi Cestrensis*, Vol. 5 (London: Longman, 1874), 332–36. Translated by Michael Faletra.]

Works Cited and Recommended Reading

Works of Geoffrey of Monmouth

Clarke, Basil, ed. *The Life of Merlin: Geoffrey of Monmouth's Vita Merlini.* Cardiff: U of Wales P, 1973.

Evans, Sebastian, trans. *Histories of the Kings of Britain by Geoffrey of Monmouth.* London: Temple Classics, 1896.

Faral, Edmond, ed. *La légende arthurienne: études et documents.* Vol. 3. Paris: Champion, 1929.

Griscom, Acton, and R.E. Jones, eds. *The Historia Regum Britanniae of Geoffrey of Monmouth with Contributions to the Study of Its Place In Early British History Together with a Literal Translation of the Welsh Manuscript No. LXI of Jesus College, Oxford.* London: Longmans & Green, 1929.

Hammer, Jacob, ed. *Geoffrey of Monmouth: Historia Regum Britanniae. A Variant Version Edited From Manuscripts.* Cambridge, MA: Medieval Academy of America, 1951.

Lewis, Henry, ed. *Brut Dingestow.* Cardiff: U of Wales P, 1974.

Parry, John J., ed. and trans. *The Vita Merlini.* University of Illinois Studies in Language and Literature 10.3. Urbana: U of Illinois P, 1925.

Roberts, Brynley F., ed. *Brut y Brenhinedd: Llanstephan MS. 1 Version.* Dublin: Institute For Advanced Studies, 1984.

Thorpe, Lewis, trans. *The History of the Kings of Britain.* Harmondsworth, Middlesex, England: Penguin, 1966.

Wright, Neil, ed. *The Historia Regum Britannie of Geoffrey of Monmouth, I: A Single-Manuscript Edition from Bern, Burgerbibliothek, MS 568.* Cambridge: D.S. Brewer, 1984.

——, ed. *The Historia Regum Britannie of Geoffrey of Monmouth, II: The First Variant Version, A Critical Edition.* Cambridge: D.S. Brewer, 1988.

Other Primary Sources

Aneirin. *Y Gododdin: Britain's Oldest Heroic Poem.* Ed. A.O.H. Jarman. Llandysul, Wales: Gomer, 1988.

Bartrum, P.C. *Early Welsh Genealogical Tracts.* Cardiff: U of Wales P, 1966.

Bede. *Bede's Ecclesiastical History of the English People.* Eds. Bertram Colgrave and R.A.B. Mynors. Oxford: Clarendon, 1969.

Bromwich, Rachel, ed. *Trioedd Ynys Prydein: The Triads of the Island of Britain.* 3rd ed. Cardiff: U of Wales P, 2006.

Bromwich, Rachel, and Simon D. Evans. *Culhwch and Olwen: An Edition and Study of the Oldest Arthurian Tale*. Cardiff: U of Wales P, 1992.

Caradoc of Llancarvan. *The Life of Gildas*. In *Two Lives of Gildas*. Ed. Hugh Williams. Felinfach, Wales: Llanerch, 1990.

Dimock James F., ed. *Giraldi Cambrensis Opera, Vol. VIII: De Principis Instructione Liber* (London: Eyre & Spottiswoode, 1891), 127–29. Trans. Michael Faletra.

Ford, Patrick, trans. *The Mabinogi, and Other Medieval Welsh Tales*. Berkeley: U of California P, 1977.

Gerald of Wales. *Giraldi Cambrensis Opera, Vol. VI: Itinerarium Kambriae et Descriptio Kambriae*. Ed. James F. Dimock. London: Longmans, Green, Reader, and Dyer, 1868.

Gildas. *The Ruin of Britain and Other Documents*. Ed. & trans. Michael Winterbottom. Arthurian Period Sources Vol. 7. London: Phillimore, 1978.

Henry of Huntington. *Historia Anglorum (History of the English People)*. Ed. & trans. Diana Greenway. Oxford Medieval Texts. Oxford: Oxford UP, 1996.

Higden, Ranulf. *Polychronicon Ranulphi Higden Monachi Cestrenis.* Vol. 5. Ed. Joseph Rawson Lumby. London: Longman, 1874.

Howlett, Richard. *Chronicles of the Reigns of Stephen, Henry II, and Richard I*. Rolls Series 82. 4 vols. London: Tubner, 1884–89.

Jarman, A.O.H., ed. *Llyfr Du Caerfyrddin*. Cardiff: U of Wales P, 1982.

Juvenal. *A. Persi Flacci et D. Iuni Iuuenalis Saturae*. Ed. W.V. Clausen. Oxford: Oxford UP, 1992.

Livy. *Ab Urbe Condita, Volume I: Books I-V*. Ed. Robert Maxwell Ogilvie. 2nd ed. Oxford: Oxford UP, 1974.

Lucan. *Pharsalia*. Cambridge, MA: Harvard UP, 1928.

Malory, Thomas. *Works*. Ed. Eugene Vinaver. 2nd ed. New York: Oxford UP, 1971.

Morris, John, ed. *Nennius: British History and the Welsh Annals*. Arthurian Period Sources Vol. 8. London: Phillimore, 1980.

Orosius, Paulus. *Historiarum Adversum Paganos Libri VII*. Ed. C. Zangemeister. Leipzig: Teubner, 1889.

Roberts, Brynley F., ed. *Breudwyt Maxen Wledic*. Dublin: Institute for Advanced Studies, 2005.

——, ed. *Cyfranc Llud a Llefelys*. Dublin: Institute for Advanced Studies, 1975.

Vergil, Polydore. *Polydore Vergil's History, Vol. 1*. Ed. Sir Henry Ellis. London: Camden Society, 1846.

Virgil. *Opera*. Ed. Roger A.B. Mynors. Oxford: Oxford UP, 1969.

Wace. *Roman de Brut: A History of the British*. Trans. Judith Weiss. Exeter: U of Exeter P, 1999.

William of Malmesbury. *Gesta Regum Anglorum: The History of the English Kings*. 2 vols. Eds. R.A.B., Mynors, Rodney M. Thomson, and Michael Winterbottom. Oxford: Clarendon, 1989–99.

———. *The Deeds of the Bishops of England [Gesta Pontificum Anglorum]*. Trans. David Preest. Cambridge: Boydell, 2002.

William of Newburgh. *Historia Rerum Anglicarum Willelmi Parvi*. Vol. 1. Ed. Hans Claude Hamilton. London: English Historical Society, 1861.

Williams, Ifor, ed. *Armes Prydein*. Trans. Rachel Bromwich. Dublin: Institute for Advanced Studies, 1982.

———, ed. *Pedeir Keinc y Mabinogi*. Cardiff: U of Wales P, 1951.

———, ed. *The Poems of Taliesin*. Trans. J.E. Caerwyn Williams. Dublin: Institute for Advanced Studies, 1987.

Secondary Works

Ashe, Geoffrey. "'A Certain Very Ancient Book': Traces of an Arthurian Source in Geoffrey of Monmouth's *History*." *Speculum* 56 (1981): 301–23.

Bartrum, Peter. "Was There A British Book of Conquests?" *Bulletin of the Board of Celtic Studies* 23 (1968): 1–6.

Bell, Kimberly. "Merlin as Historian in *Historia Regum Britanniae*." *Arthuriana* 10 (2000): 14–26.

Blacker, Jean. "Where Wace Feared to Tread: Latin Commentaries on Merlin's Prophecies in the Reign of Henry II." *Arthuriana* 6 (1996): 36–52.

Brooke, Christopher. "The Archbishops of St. David's, Llandaff, and Caerleon-on-Usk." *Studies in the Early British Church*. Ed. Nora K. Chadwick. Cambridge: Cambridge UP, 1958: 201–42.

Brooke, C.N.L. "Geoffrey of Monmouth as a Historian." *Church and Government in the Middle Ages*. Eds. C.N.L. Brooke et al. Cambridge: Cambridge UP, 1976: 77–91.

Chambers, E.K. *Arthur of Britain*. London: Sedgwick & Jackson, 1927.

Cohen, Jeffrey Jerome. "The Flow of Blood in Medieval Norwich." *Speculum* 79 (2004): 26–65.

———. *Of Giants: Sex, Monsters, and the Middle Ages*. Minneapolis: U of Minnesota P, 1999.

Crawford, T.D. "On the Linguistic Competence of Geoffrey of Monmouth." *Medium Aevum* 51 (1982): 152–62.

Crick, Julia. "Geoffrey of Monmouth: Prophecy and History." *Journal of Medieval History* 18 (1992): 357–71.

———. *The Historia Regum Britannie of Geoffrey of Monmouth, IV: Dissemination and Reception in the Later Middle Ages.* Cambridge: D.S. Brewer, 1991.

———. *A Summary Catalogue of the Manuscripts of Geoffrey of Monmouth's Historia Regum Britannie.* Cambridge: D.S. Brewer, 1988.

Curley, Michael J. *Geoffrey of Monmouth.* New York: Twayne, 1994.

Ditmas, E.M.R. "Geoffrey of Monmouth and the Breton Families in Cornwall." *Welsh History Review* 6 (1973): 452–61.

Donohue, Dennis P. "The Darkly-Chronicled King: An Interpretation of the Negative Side of Arthur in Lawman's *Brut* and Geoffrey of Monmouth's *Historia Regum Britannie.*" *Arthuriana* 8 (1998): 135–47.

Dumville, David N. "An Early Text of Geoffrey of Monmouth's *Historia Regum Britanniae* and the Circulation of Some Latin Histories in Twelfth-Century Normandy." *Arthurian Literature* 4 (1984): 1–33.

Echard, Siân. *Arthurian Narrative in the Latin Tradition.* Cambridge: Cambridge UP, 1998.

Edwards, W. "The Settlement of Brittany." *Y Cymmrodor* 11 (1890): 61–101.

Faletra, Michael A. "Narrating the Matter of Britain: Geoffrey of Monmouth and the Norman Colonization of Wales." *The Chaucer Review* 35 (2000): 60–85.

Finke, Laurie A., and Martin Shichtman. *King Arthur and the Myth of History.* Gainesville: UP of Florida, 2004.

Fletcher, Robert Huntington. *The Arthurian Material in the Chronicles.* Boston: Harvard UP, 1906.

Fleuriot, Lucien. "Old Breton Genealogies and Early British Traditions." *Bulletin of the Board of Celtic Studies* 26 (1974): 1–6.

Flint, Valerie J. "The *Historia Regum Britanniae* of Geoffrey of Monmouth: Parody and Its Purpose. A Suggestion." *Speculum* 54 (1979): 447–68.

Gillingham, John. "The Context and Purposes of Geoffrey of Monmouth's *History of the Kings of Britain.*" *Anglo-Norman Studies* 13 (1990): 99–118.

Golding, Brian. *Conquest and Colonization: The Normans in Britain, 1066–1100.* London: St. Martin's, 1994.

Gransden, Antonia. *Historical Writing in England from Gildas to Geoffrey of Monmouth.* Vol. 1. Ithaca: Cornell UP, 1974.

Hanning, Robert. *The Vision of History in Early Britain.* New York: Columbia UP, 1966.

Higham, N.J. *King Arthur: Myth-Making and History.* London: Routledge, 2002.

Ingham, Patricia Clare. *Sovereign Fantasies: Arthurian Romance and the Making of Britain.* Philadelphia: U of Pennsylvania P, 2001.

Ingledew, Francis. "The Book of Troy and the Genealogical Construction of History: The Case of Geoffrey of Monmouth's *Historia Regum Britanniae.*" *Speculum* 69 (1994): 665–704.

Jarman, A.O.H. "The Merlin Legend and the Welsh Tradition of Prophecy." In *The Arthur of the Welsh.* Ed. Rachel Bromwich et al. Cardiff: U of Wales P, 1991.

Jones, Timothy. "Geoffrey of Monmouth, *Fouke le Fitz Waryn*, and National Mythology." *Studies in Philology* 91 (1994): 233–49.

Keeler, Laura. *Geoffrey of Monmouth and the Late Latin Chroniclers, 1300–1500.* Berkeley: U of California P, 1946.

Knight, Stephen. *Arthurian Literature and Society.* London: St. Martin's, 1983.

Leckie, R. William. *The Passage of Dominion: Geoffrey of Monmouth and the Periodization of Insular History in the Twelfth Century.* Toronto: U of Toronto P, 1981.

Lloyd, John E. "Geoffrey of Monmouth." *English Historical Review* 57 (1942): 460–68.

Loomis, Laura H. "Geoffrey of Monmouth and Stonehenge." *PMLA* 45 (1930): 400–15.

Otter, Monika. *Inventiones: Fiction and Referentiality in Twelfth-Century English Historical Writing.* Chapel Hill: U of North Carolina P, 1996.

Padel, Oliver. "Geoffrey of Monmouth and Cornwall." *Cambridge Mediaeval Celtic Studies* 8 (1984): 1–27.

Parry, John Jay, and Robert A. Caldwell. "Geoffrey of Monmouth." In *Arthurian Literature in the Middle Ages.* Ed. Roger Sherman Loomis. Oxford: Clarendon, 1959.

Partner, Nancy F. *Serious Entertainments: The Writing of History in Twelfth-Century England.* Chicago: U of Chicago P, 1977.

Patterson, Lee. *Negotiating the Past: The Historical Understanding of Medieval Literature.* Madison: U of Wisconsin P, 1987.

Reeve, Michael. "The Transmission of the *Historia Regum Britanniae.*" *Journal of Medieval Latin* 1 (1991): 73–117.

Roberts, Brynley F. "Geoffrey of Monmouth and the Welsh Historical Tradition." *Nottingham Medieval Studies* 20 (1976): 29–40.

———. "The Treatment of Welsh Personal Names in the Early Welsh Versions of the *Historia Regum Britanniae.*" *Bulletin of the Board of Celtic Studies* 25 (1973): 274–98.

Robertson, Kellie. "Geoffrey of Monmouth and the Translation of Insular Historiography." *Arthuriana* 8 (1998): 42–57.

Shichtman, Martin, and Laurie Finke. "Profiting from the Past: History as Symbolic Capital in the *Historia Regum Britanniae.*" *Arthurian Literature* 12 (1993): 1–35.

Short, Ian. "Gaimar's Epilogue and Geoffrey of Monmouth's *Liber Vetustissimus.*" *Speculum* 69 (1994): 323–43.

Shwartz, S.M. "The Founding and Self-Betrayal of Britain: An Augustinian Approach to Geoffrey of Monmouth's *Historia Regum Britanniae.*" *Medievalia et Humanistica* 10 (1981): 33–58.

Southern, R.W. "Aspects of the European Tradition of Historical Writing: 1. The Classical Tradition from Einhard to Geoffrey of Monmouth." *Transactions of the Royal Historical Society*, 5th series, 20 (1970): 173–96.

Stein, Robert M. *Reality Fictions: Romance, History, and Governmental Authority, 1025–1180.* Notre Dame, Indiana: U of Notre Dame P, 2006.

Tatlock, J.S.P. *The Legendary History of Britain: Geoffrey of Monmouth's Historia Regum Britanniae and Its Early Vernacular Versions.* Berkeley: U of California P, 1950.

——. "The Origin of Geoffrey of Monmouth's Estrildis." *Speculum* 11 (1936): 121–23.

Taylor, Rupert. *The Political Prophecy in England.* New York: Columbia UP, 1911.

Warren, Michelle R. *History on the Edge: Excalibur and the Borders of Britain, 1100–1300.* Minneapolis: U of Minnesota P, 2000.

Waswo, Richard. "Our Ancestors, the Trojans: Inventing Cultural Identity in the Middle Ages." *Exemparia* 7 (1995): 269–90.

Wright, Neil. "Geoffrey of Monmouth and Bede." *Arthurian Literature* 6 (1986): 27–59.

——. "Geoffrey of Monmouth and Gildas." *Arthurian Literature* 2 (1982): 1–40.

Index of Proper Names

Eldad, Bishop of Gloucester, 126, 148–49
Eldad, son of Ebraucus, 62
Eldol, Earl of Gloucester, 126–27, 144,
  146–48
Eldol, King of Britain, 82
Eledem, 177
Eleutherius, Pope, 96, 203
Eli, 58
Elidur the Faithful, King of Britain, 80–82
Elijah, 63
Eliud, King of Britain, 82
Elsing, King of Norway, 71
England, 94
English language, 200
Ennianus, 210
Enniaunus, King of Britain, 82
Eosa, 148–49, 156–57, 160–61
Epistrophus, 182
Eppingford, 124
Er son of Hider, 189
Erging, 144
Eristenus, 61
Eryri, Mount, 127
Estrildis, 59
Ethelbert, 204
Ethelfrid, 204–05
Europe, 95, 171
Evander, 182, 188–89
Exeter, 93, 211

Fagan, 96
Ferreux, King of Britain, 68–69
Flanders, 196
France, 43
Franks, 65, 75, 108, 201
Frea, 120
Frollo, 172–73
Fulgenius, King of Britain, 82

Gabius, 76–77
Gad, 62
Gael, 62
Gaius Metellus Cocta, 182, 192
Gaius Quintillianus, 186
Galaes, 62
Galaes, Queen, 217
Galabes, 137–38, 150
Galabroc, 101
Galluc, 174
Gallus, Luvius, 100–01
Gascony, 173

Gaul, son of Ebraucus, 62
Gaul, 51, 54, 62, 65, 68, 74–75, 84, 92,
  108–09, 131, 133, 135, 137, 145, 154,
  172–74, 177, 179–80, 183, 186, 197, 201,
  210
Gauls, 55–56, 62, 74, 76, 86–88, 109, 116,
  173, 191
Gawain, 170–71, 186–87, 190, 194–95, 197
Genoreu, 144
Genvissa, Queen, 94–94
Geoffrey of Monmouth, 41, 130, 197
Geraint, King of Britain, 82
Gerin, 175, 180, 186, 190, 193
Germanus, St., 123–24
Germans (see also Saxons), 153, 180
Germany, 59, 62, 76, 109–10, 120–21,
  125–26, 132, 153, 156, 160, 163–65, 197,
  213, 215
Gero, 51
Geta, King of Britain, 99
Gewissei, 103, 116, 139, 150, 214
Gildas, 41, 58, 70, 73, 97, 122, 209
Gillabor, 199
Gillafer, 199
Gillomanius, 151–53, 155
Gillamorius, 169–71, 175
Gillapatric, 199
Gillarum, 199
Gladys, 62
Glamorgan, 97
Glamorganshire, 174
Gloigin, 62
Gloio, Duke, 94
Gloucester, 94–95, 98, 126, 139, 141, 144,
  146, 148, 174, 200
Godbold, 211
Goffar the Pict, 52–54
Gogmagog, 57
Gogmagog's Leap, 57
Golden Death, Julius Caesar's sword, 86
Goneril, 64–66
Gorangon, 123
Gorboduc, King of Britain, 68
Gorbonian map Sgoit, 175
Gorbonianus, 80–82
Gorgon, 62
Gorlois, 148, 156–60
Gormund, 201–02, 207
Gotland, 171, 175, 180, 201
Gratianus the freedman, King of Britain,
  111–12

The interior of this book is printed on 100% recycled paper.